Graham Dunstan Martin

LANGUAGE
TRUTH AND
POETRY

οὔτοι ἀπ' ἀρχῆς πάντα θεοὶ θνητοῖσ' ὑπέδειξαν,
ἀλλὰ χρόνῳ ζητοῦντες ἐφευρίσκουσιν ἄμεινον.
καὶ τὸ μὲν οὖν σαφὲς οὔτις ἀνὴρ γένετ' οὐδέ τις ἔσται
εἰδὼς ἀμφὶ θεῶν τε καὶ ἅσσα λέγω περί πάντων.
εἰ γὰρ καὶ τὰ μάλιστα τύχοι τετελεσμένον εἰπών,
αὐτὸς ὅμως οὐκ οἶδε . δόκος δ' ἐπὶ πᾶσι τέτυκται.

The gods did not reveal, from the beginning,
All things to us; but in the course of time
Through seeking we may learn, and know things better.

But as for certain truth, no man has known it,
Nor will he know it; neither of the gods,
Nor yet of all the things of which I speak.
And even if by chance he were to utter
The final truth, he would himself not know it;
For all is but a woven web of guesses.

(Xenophanes, 6th century BC,
translation by Karl Popper 1969, 26)

*

To Anne,
without whom
this book would never
have become a line at all —
let alone any sort of
diagonal

GRAHAM DUNSTAN MARTIN

LANGUAGE
TRUTH AND
POETRY

*Notes towards a Philosophy
of Literature*

*

AT THE UNIVERSITY PRESS
EDINBURGH

Preface

AN EARLIER VERSION OF this book was read by Professor R. W. Hepburn, Mr Norman Macleod and Professor A. J. Steele, and parts of it by Mr Peter Jones, Professor John Lyons and Dr Peter Sharratt. I want to express my considerable gratitude to them for their patient perusal of the manuscript and for the generous and invaluable suggestions and advice they gave me. Naturally they are not responsible for the opinions and prejudices here advanced, nor for any errors and lapses which, despite all their good offices, I have at times obstinately persisted in.

G. D. M.

✳

Contents

Introduction

IN A FAMOUS PASSAGE of his *Language, Truth and Logic*, A.J. Ayer attacks one of his favourite *bêtes noires*: 'So far from producing propositions which are empirically verifiable, [he] is unable to produce any intelligible propositions at all. And therefore we say that his intuition has not revealed to him any facts. It is no use his saying that he has apprehended facts but is unable to express them. For we know that if he really had acquired any information, he would be able to express it. He would be able to indicate in some way how the genuineness of his discovery might be empirically determined.'[1] Now the empirical approach is invaluable; and we should all have the greatest respect for facts. But what 'are' facts? Reading this, one perceives that an extremely narrow definition has been put upon them. And what of the verb 'express'? Not merely does Ayer seem to have a touching faith in the omniscience of language, in its inbuilt capacity to weigh moonshine and hot air upon the scale of truth— and come out with a zero reading; not merely does he evidently reject all modes of expression save the verbal and the mathematical —he also confines language itself within the logician's cramped bounds: 'express' means simply 'express in such a way that a scientific experiment could verify the expression'. 'Intelligible' is equally restricted in meaning. Yet the modern physicist (as we shall see) has no difficulty in 'understanding' such impossibilities as a square circle.[2]

It is true that Ayer was talking here of mystical experience, not of art. But in *Language, Truth and Logic* his attitude to both is similar: art becomes merely the expression of subjective emotion: it is meat for the psychologist or sociologist; aesthetic judgments have no 'objective validity'[3]; knowledge and truth are terms reserved for science. The gulf between 'Two Cultures' could not be more brutally asserted.

The statements of science are, of course, more certain than the suggestions of poetry. But art has the curious faculty of seeking truth without at the same time pretending to certainty. We could perhaps, on the analogy of Heisenberg's principle, enunciate a Law of the Uncertainty of Human Knowledge, according to which the more certain a fact is the less one can know of it, and the more one knows of it the less certain it can be.[4] Thus, a formula describing the behaviour of waves in a liquid medium may no doubt be highly certain; but it contains less of any possible human experience than Melville's lines: *And heaved and heaved, still unrestingly heaved the black sea, as if its vast tides were a conscience.*

Not that I wish to assert any mystical truths, or claim in fine French nineteenth-century style that the poet is a mage, a seer, an initiate of the occult. If there is anything especially valuable about poetry, it is a value that belongs to the real world and is expressed in the speech of the unregenerate human animal: poetry's means are linguistic and semantic, and its subject-matter is experience.

This book may be greeted with cries of protest by scholars in other disciplines than my own, complaining that I have trespassed on their fields and clumsily trodden their data and their principles into an unrecognizable (though doubtless poetic) mishmash. I am unrepentant. If the practice of literature can be valorized, it is necessary to make claims for it which will bear some tentative comparison with those made for such studies as philosophy, linguistics and (above all) science. However, it might well be that 'what little I have to say is valuable only in so far as it enables others to contradict it'.[5] In other words, this book might at least serve as fodder for discussion of a more rational and less acerbic kind than greeted the controversy over the 'Two Cultures' a number of years ago. There are indeed two cultures —or three or four—and none of them are all-embracing, and none of them can claim to monopolize that Protean lady, Truth.

For Truth, like Einstein's universe, looks different according to where one is standing. This means that science does not confute literature, or even clash with it. The two are simply different ways of viewing the world. If any clash does occur, it is between philosophers and logicians on the one hand, and science and art on the other; and I suspect that the deductive world of the former looks like flat-earthism beside the more complex, ambiguous and bewildering worlds of the latter. 'Science comforts, art disturbs,' said Braque. But no: both science and art are, in their utterly different ways, assaults on prejudice, complacency and *partis pris.*

This book does not proceed smoothly forward in a horizontal direction like Tristram Shandy's unattainable ideal straight line, nor (I hope) plummet downwards like his line of gravitation; nor will it be thought (I trust) that it wanders circuitously about like the complex squiggle poor Tristram actually achieved, but (I should like to think) in a sort of diagonal, appropriating and aggrandizing various territories of language, linguistics, science and philosophy. For poetry deals in language, but so does linguistics; and in experience, but so does science; and all these matters are unmanageable, and hence the concern of philosophy.

Part One is the most technical section, for here I shall be forced to use other people's jargon and my own. It is concerned with those linguistic features which allow poetry to exist at all, though I do not discuss these from the point of view of any contemporary linguistic wisdom, since I have not found one which seems adequate (as yet) to cope with the complexities of literary meaning. I have chosen therefore to be both more traditional and less cautious than the linguist. For, though I make absolutely no claim for rigour or completeness here,[6] ultimately one would wish for a theory of life which could account for both amoeba and man, a theory of language which could account for both proper name and Shakespearian play. No theory of this kind can be adequate if it denies complexity to the mental processes of language. And even philosophy, despite all its discussion this century of problems of meaning, might perhaps profit from some aspects of the analysis suggested here.

Part Two is mainly concerned with the language of literature, and contains chapters on metaphor and on the methods used by poets to jolt our attention and refresh our awareness. A new solution is offered to the age-old problem *by what precise mental process* poetry may sometimes seem to give us so concrete an impression of reality. This is the centre of the book, but again I do not pretend to completeness. The question of structure, for instance, is barely touched upon; for my basic topic is the 'logic' of poetic discourse. One fundamental problem, no doubt, is how we apprehend reality and how we talk about it. Science, I shall claim, justifies the practice of the arts. It is neither the idol of absolute truth that the average unscientific man so uncritically adores, nor the heartless mechanical monster of literary legend. We need also to refute the commonly-held superstition that art is merely irrational, emotive and entertaining. I shall attempt to define the differences between various modes of discourse, the common, the scientific, the logical and the poetic.

The book might perhaps have stopped there. It moves off, however, at a Shandean tangent. Art and science, I shall claim, both appertain to a single frame of mind, one that admits complexity and uncertainty, a certain ultimate vagueness in things, and is healthily suspicious of claims to absolute truth, whatever their origin. Some things, no doubt, are more certain than others; but the only thing that is totally certain is that one may be mistaken. The only valid ideology is an anti-ideology.

But here two, or even three, cheers are in order: for this means that there will always be new worlds to conquer.

Part One

THOUGHTS ON
MEANING

*

How to Avoid Defining a Concept

Some members of some human communities have been observed to interact by means of vocal noises.   (An American Behaviourist)

Timidity in dealing with ideas is contrary to the spirit of the scientific method, and the thinker who is afraid of looking like a fool has tied one hand behind his back before entering the ring.

(Donald Hebb 1964–5, 382–3)

We must do away with explanations, and description alone must take their place.   (Wittgenstein 1968, 47e)

Description is the first stage in constructing explanations.

(Jerrold Katz 1972a, 184)

WE NEED A THEORY of meaning. We need it because current theories may be adequate to describe some aspects of some kinds of language, but they cannot explain enough aspects of enough kinds of language, and in particular cannot cope with the language of books. And it is in books that we find the most significant uses of language, for it is here above all that words can make us feel something unexpected or think something previously unthought. I shall not of course offer a complete or definitive theory. No theory *is* definitive anyway. But I shall attempt to fill in certain gaps by concentrating on aspects of meaning which tend to be missing from the theories of linguists and philosophers; they do not usually concern themselves with the language of literature, and hence have been able to overlook some of the essential characteristics of words.

In some ways the fragmentary theory I shall sketch out here is not so far removed from other literary critics' theories. It will use such familiar concepts as 'connotation' and 'ambiguity', and will lean heavily on what others have said of metaphor. And if this were not so, one might well be rather suspicious. For it would be distinctly odd if I were to contradict all my predecessors. But I should certainly like to take the whole question further than they. And I should like to assert more strongly than they have done, that the general principles of the literary critic's approach to language, as we have seen it in this century, are correct—and that they are correct not merely because they are useful to us critics, fiddling away on the verges of some trivial phenomenon called art, but because they have vitally important things to tell us about the workings of normal language too.

Clearly such considerations will for a while lead us away from literature, and into deep and controversial waters. But if the practice of literary criticism is to be justified, it must be shown that the terms in which critics think of language are reasonable ones. And received ideas must continually be tempered by speculation if any progress is ever to be made. I shall seek therefore in this first part of the book to sketch out some fragments of a theory of meaning, and to show that it is relevant to a number of linguistic problems (linguistic in the broad sense). After that, we shall be able to settle down more comfortably to consider the relationship of literary discourse to reality and to other forms of discourse.

First we must consider the knotty question of 'meaning'. What is it? Or perhaps, how does it function? Or at least, what definition of it do I propose to adopt?

According to J. L. Austin, such questions are profitless: ' "the meaning of a word" ', he says, 'is a spurious phrase.' Yet he himself claims to be able to define the square root of a number 'such that, for any given number x, "the square root of x" is a definite description of another number y.'[1] Similarly it is possible to define meaning as has been done so many times before, as the *formula of a relationship*.

The relationship in question is classic. Perhaps its most famous enunciation was by Ogden and Richards in *The Meaning of Meaning*. They express meaning *via* the so-called Semiotic Triangle, which normally looks something like figure 1.[2] This corresponds to

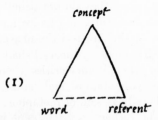

(1)

our normal intuitions about the working of language. If I hear the word 'tree' pronounced for instance, I may know that a neighbouring tree is being referred to; and I 'know' this (as indeed the verb indicates) through some inner mental process of my own. Word refers to Referent *via* a mental process which I am calling Concept. To give a slightly more precise (but still rough) account of this, the word 'tree' is the word as spoken or heard (its acoustic pattern). The concept 'tree' is the idea we have of trees and/or the tree in question (or the mental process that goes on when we refer to a tree or hear it referred to). The referent tree is the actual object in the outside world to which we are referring.[3] (Let us ignore, though just for the moment, the many questions begged by such words as 'concept' or 'actual object'. We shall return to them.)

The unbroken lines between word and concept indicate there is a direct relationship: we use a particular word to signify a particular concept. The relationship between concept and referent is again direct: our concept is 'of' a particular object. The relationship between word and referent is however indirect, as is indicated by the dotted line. The Schoolmen were right in their dictum 'Vox significat mediantibus conceptibus', for words of course are not directly related to things, as is shown by the old story of the English nobleman who claimed that the English were the most logical race; for, he said, 'the French call fish *poisson*, and the Spanish call it *pescado*; but *we* call it *fish*, which is obviously what it is.'

A supposedly scientific distaste for thoughts, feelings and what used, alas so loosely, to be termed 'the contents of the mind', has in recent years inhibited discussion of this formula of meaning. It is true that it is easy enough to find the diagram in the textbooks. But it is also true that modern linguists on the whole make little use of it. I propose therefore to see whether the formula can be resuscitated, whether it can be employed usefully, and whether the concept of 'concept' can be made to operate in a plausible and revealing way.

Before setting about this task, I had originally thought of mounting an onslaught on the tenets of behaviourism—behaviourism, that is, of the classic variety, which considered that until we have definite knowledge of the workings of mind or brain, it is pointless to theorize about such things. Its influence *via* the school of Leonard Bloomfield for a long time discouraged twentieth-century linguists from tackling the problems of linguistic meaning.[4] They learnt to shudder at the words 'mind' and 'concept', and utter the word 'mentalist' with all the vehemence of a medieval pope pronouncing the anathema. I am assured, however, that the behaviourist horse is dead, that it is a waste of time to flog it, and that those Bill Brewers and Jan Stewers of contemporary linguistics who are still haunted by it, are lost on a lonely moorland, where they can safely be left. It is true that the last few years have seen an extraordinary revolution in the attitude of linguists to meaning. This is due to the salutary influence of Chomsky. And a great deal of work is now concerned with semantics, as can be seen by opening the pages of any contemporary linguistic journal.

Nonetheless, it is probably best to say a few words in defence of my approach. To do this, I shall point out (1) that mere description of the surface data of language will not suffice to explain how it works; (2) that we need therefore to posit concealed and partly unconscious processes that go on in the brain when we speak; and (3) that it is not properly scientific to confine oneself to mere description of phenomena: the scientific spirit requires us to form hypotheses about hidden mechanisms. If it is asked on what objective basis we can talk about such unobservables as concepts, I shall reply (4) that science spends a considerable amount of its time talking about unobservables—which are of course always deduced from the observable—and that in doing so science always appeals to the ultimate consensus of other scientists, of other human beings. And in making these claims, I shall have at least to touch on the directly opposite counter-claims of classic behaviourism.

Behaviourist theories of linguistics are usually traced back to the teaching of Bloomfield. He offers a Jack-in-the-Box theory of meaning. Just as the Pavlovian dog is stimulated into slavering by hearing a bell, so the Bloomfieldian man is stimulated into opening a door by hearing someone say: 'Open the door!' In other words, person A provides person B with a stimulus in the form of a sentence, and person B reacts with other words, or with actions. A stimulus produces a response. But what happens between stimulus and response is left hidden in darkest night. One of Bloomfield's apologists, Charles C. Fries, proposes the following diagram of what goes on when one person talks to another. It is based on Bloomfield himself:

Individual A		Individual B	
S	r . . . . . s		R
Effective field of the stimulus	Sounds as produced	Sounds as heard	The practical response

The particular speech act which becomes an effective stimulus for B through language.

Fries goes on: 'In general, for linguists, the "meanings" of an utterance consist of the correlating, regularly recurrent sames of the stimulus-situation features, and the regularly elicited recurring sames of response features. These meanings are tied to patterns of recurring sames of vocal sounds.'[5] We might paraphrase this hide-ously expressed statement by saying that people in similar situations tend to make the same remarks, which other people then hear and respond to in similar ways. But *why* do they so respond? We know that when we open the lid of a Jack-in-the-Box, the doll pops up, not because it pops up, but because it is set on a spring. But what sort of spring is concealed within the human organism? What sort of connexion is there between stimulus and response in Fries's diagram? How do we bridge this gap?

Bloomfield himself seems to think that no answer is necessary: language itself is all that we need to explain the process: 'It is [my] belief that the scientific description of the universe . . . requires none of the mentalistic terms, because the gaps which these terms are intended to bridge exist only so long as language is left out of account.'[6] But this will not do at all. If we refer again to Fries's diagram, we see that language is defined *as* the stimulus heard by individual B. How then can it explain what happens within that individual *between* the stimulus and his response? Only if an individual were as simple and uncomplicated an object as a castle of cards, which *responds* by collapsing when it receives the *stimulus* of a breath of wind, would we be able to dismiss this question easily. As it is, Bloomfield has committed the howler of identifying thought with language.

Thought is not identical with language, as Chomsky has pointed out; for otherwise we could not know that a sentence like the war-time headline 'Monty flies back to front' can be interpreted in two ways. The same is true of all ambiguous sentences, such as the familiar linguists' examples, 'The shooting of the hunters was fright-ful' and 'They are flying planes'. Surface identification of thought with language will not do in cases like the following either: 'John is easy to leave'/'John is eager to leave' and 'The sugar is easy to dissolve'/'The sugar is slow to dissolve'. Although the structure of these two pairs looks at first sight identical, the structure of their meanings is clearly not, since the third sentence (for instance) means 'It is easy for one to dissolve the sugar' and the fourth does *not* mean 'It is slow for one to dissolve the sugar'. In other words, as the modern linguist puts it, they have different deep structures.[7] That is, the underlying structure of these sentences is different, despite their superficial resemblance.

The case with 'The shooting of the hunters was frightful' and 'They are flying planes' is even clearer. In different contexts, these sentences will require different responses such as 'No, they're

climbing trees', or 'No, you've got spots before your eyes'. The only
reasonable explanation is that the mind is capable of putting different
interpretations on the same statement, and that an inner process of
some kind therefore occurs . . . as indeed we knew all along.

Skinner (who is certainly still eminent and influential enough to
be tilted at) attempts to evade this conclusion by claiming that it is
different aspects of the stimulus (here the ambiguous sentence) that
produce a different reaction from us, and not our own ability to
interpret it in different ways. But no theory can be called scientific
unless we are able to test it: it must have predictive power, and we
must be able to decide if its predictions are right or wrong. Skinner's
theory of language is on this score *not even scientific*: for it cannot
predict how the hearer will respond. And some would say that, if
the truth or falsity of a theory cannot be tested, it is meaningless.
Thus, in criticizing Skinner's views, Chomsky writes:

> A typical example of *stimulus control* for Skinner would be the
> response to a piece of music with the utterance *Mozart* or to a
> painting with the response *Dutch*. These responses are asserted
> to be 'under the control of extremely subtle properties' of the
> physical object or event.[8] Suppose instead of saying *Dutch* we
> had said *Clashes with the wallpaper, I thought you liked abstract
> work, Never saw it before, Tilted, Hanging too low, Beautiful,
> Hideous, Remember our camping trip last summer?* or whatever
> else might come into our minds . . . Skinner could only say
> that each of these responses is under the control of some other
> stimulus property of the physical object . . .

But in these circumstances, we cannot identify the stimulus before
we hear the response:

> We cannot predict verbal behaviour in terms of the stimuli in
> the speaker's environment, since we do not know what the
> current stimuli are until he responds.[9]

Bloomfield does not go so far as to deny the speaker all participa-
tion in the situation, as in this case Skinner seems to do. But
Chomsky's objection effectively crushes both of them. Neither
Skinner's version of behaviourism nor Bloomfield's can give us any
hint as to what a speaker will reply *until* he replies. Behaviourist
theory is thus void of predictive power, and one might as well revert
to 'mentalist' procedures, and go about asking people why they res-
ponded in such and such a way, and what they meant by it when
they did so. This in fact is what is normally done in practice, even by
Bloomfield and his followers. All discussion of meaning in language
presupposes an appeal to other people for agreement and ultimately

for some kind of consensus. This is no more subjective than Osgood, Suci and Tannenbaum's experiments where they asked people how clean, happy, thick, cold and sharp they thought words like 'mother', 'sin' and 'America' were.

Fries seems to think that it is a sufficient defence of Bloomfield to say that he sought to exclude psychology from the scientific discussion of linguistic matters. This means, he says, that Bloomfield did not interpret language 'in terms of a behaviouristic psychology'.[10] But of course to exclude psychology is precisely what behaviourism consists in: it regards the brain as an embarrassing and obscene organ whose workings (if any) should have a discreet veil of reticence drawn across them. Behaviourism could be accurately and briefly described as a psychology which leaves out psychology.

That the mind cannot be left out is sufficiently proven by the following observations of Vendler: for there are clearly numerous cases where there is *no observable response whatever*, and yet we would still have to say that the listener had understood.

> Wittgenstein asks us to imagine a language 'consisting of the words "block", "pillar", "slab", "beam". A calls them out; B brings the stone which he has learnt to bring at such-and-such a call. . . .' Suppose A calls out to B (*To* B, say, by turning his face towards B) 'Slab'. C, an onlooker, hears this. What is he to do? Are we to assume that everybody within earshot is supposed to grab the nearest slab? Were C to do such a thing it would show that he did not understand what A said. If, on the other hand, he does not do [anything] what does his understanding consist of? Shall we say, then, that he did not understand what A said? But he is supposed to know the language . . .[11]

This surely clinches the case against those who insist on talking only about 'observables'.

Skinner's definition of meaning shows to an even higher degree the behaviourist tendency to abolish anything internal to the speaker. Indeed, though Skinner's style is such a fog of abstractions that he is extremely hard to follow, he appears to be identifying meaning and reference when he defines meaning thus: 'the probability that the speaker will emit a response of a given form in the presence of a stimulus having specified properties under certain broad conditions of deprivation or aversive stimulation. *So far as the speaker is con-concerned*, this *is* the relation of reference or meaning.'[12] Now we have just seen that the properties of the 'stimulus' cannot be thus specified: we have to wait for the speaker to speak before we know what they are. We have also seen that to identify meaning and reference is a fundamental howler. But 'probability' too deserves a word of comment. Chomsky points out that the reactions Skinner regards as most probable, namely 'Mozart' or 'Dutch', are perhaps not so probable as he thinks. What, however, is quite clear is that the more interesting the guest's comment on the record or painting, the more unexpected, that is, improbable, his words are likely to be. The principle is enunciated by Lyons: the less predictable an utterance is, the more meaning it has.[13] More meaning in what sense? Simply in the sense of its being unpredictable? No,[14] for then we would be left with a worse paradox, that one might say or write down *anything*, provided it was unexpected.

If this is accepted, namely that the more probable an utterance, the less meaning it has, then Skinner's definition of meaning falls to the ground. For he ties meaning to the predictable response to a specified stimulus. But, as common sense would say, such a response is mechanical. It is lack of predictability which characterizes human speech, at least when it is meaningful. Thus, the less a response corresponds to Skinner's definition of meaning, the more meaningful it is.

A similar paradox confronts all those who, like the earlier Lyons, hope to be able to define meanings solely on the basis of the physical and verbal contexts of a word's use.[15] For how can it be asserted that (1) this is the only scientific means that we have of establishing meanings, and yet that (2) a word has more meaning the less often it is used in the same context? For then, the more meaning a word had, the less we should ever be able to tell what that meaning was!

Behaviourists would say that if we are faced on the one hand with accepting an account of meaning which leaves out any mental processes, and on the other with the traditional account of the mind, with its implications for free will and other 'unscientific' notions, how can we, as good scientists, fail to reject the latter and embrace the former? The answer to this dilemma is plain: it is a false one. It is sheer misrepresentation to imply that these are the only two possible views of the matter; and it is perfectly reasonable to take up a position midway between these two extremes, and define meaning as a process occurring in the brain. Haas's description of the traditional theory of meaning runs as follows: 'As, in a human person, a soul or mind is supposed to accompany the body and its overt behaviour, so, in a linguistic sign, a meaning is supposed to accompany the form in its various occurrences. The linguistic sign is supposed to emerge from a correspondence, a kind of psychophysical parallelism, between a form and a meaning.'[16] I *may*, of course, believe that concepts accompany language in the same way as an immortal soul accompanies a body. I *might* go further and, with Plato, posit the existence of eternal 'forms' or 'ideas'. But I am not committed to any such beliefs. I am merely making the minimum assumption that, when we speak or think, certain cerebral mechanisms are at work. This is Chomsky's position, and he terms it 'mentalism';[17] in his terms it is perfectly possible to be a mechanist and a mentalist at the same time, and hold for instance that meaning is a function of electrical and or chemical processes in the brain. And when I use the term 'concept' in this book, I am not necessarily assuming any more than this.

Behaviourism, then, of that extreme form which refuses to speculate about any inner mechanism whatever, is mistaken. Although its failure was predictable, no doubt it was right to try whether language could be described and explained by the stimulus-response model. Its value to us now, however, is that it *has* failed, and in so doing has shown us clearly that hidden mental processes are at work. And this, any modern behavioural theorist (such as Quine, for instance) would, I trust, be willing to grant.

Operational and distributional definitions of meaning are open to similar objections. After all, their purpose is much the same: somehow to talk meaningfully of meaning without implying the existence of mind. Wittgenstein's famous slogan 'Don't look for the meaning of a word, look for its use,' deserves our utmost respect. For it points directly to the essential fact that words are used in many different ways: they do not have 'a' meaning, they have different 'uses'. Thus, 'I can hit a bull's-eye' may mean, depending on the context, 'Look! I've just hit a bull's-eye,' that is, 'I was able to hit a bull's-eye this once,' or 'I can regularly hit a bull's-eye,' or 'I might if I tried hit a bull's-eye,' and so on.

So far so good. But Wittgenstein's intention was to define meaning *as* use.[18] A number of philosophers have followed him in this. For instance Ryle writes: 'to know what an expression means is to know how it may and may not be employed'.[19] And Strawson writes: 'To give the meaning of an expression . . . is to give *general directions* for its use to refer to or mention particular objects or persons; to give the meaning of a sentence is to give *general directions* for its use in making true or false assertions.'[20]

This will not do in any unusual context, especially in any context where the word or expression is heard or read for the first or only time. What, for example, of Shakespeare's 'dark backward and abysm of time'? The criterion of 'use' will tell us that the phrase is a synonym for the past. It will also tell us no doubt that it produces a certain emotional effect seen or suspected in the audience. Is it being used then (1) as a synonym for 'the past', and (2) to produce emotion in the audience? Does that sum up its meaning? Why would a different set of words, e.g. 'the past', not produce that emotional effect? We cannot explain Prospero's use of the phrase, that is its effect *upon* the audience, unless we can suggest what it means *to* them. The fact that 'the dark backward and abysm of time' and 'the past' have ostensibly the same referent (that is, the past) indicates quite clearly that, if the audience's reaction to the two phrases is different, this difference must be due, not to their reference, but to some other factor. To sweep this aside as 'emotional' or 'aesthetic' is to evade the issue. One can only suppose that 'the past' is given a special emotional flavour by describing it in Prospero's terms: that the words make the audience see it in a new light; that the more normal meanings of those words are present to the audience's mind, and temporarily colour their awareness of 'the past'.

If the notion of 'use' were expanded in this fashion, there would be little objection to it. This would, however, entail our supposing that uses of words have some stability in our minds, that we are often aware of other contexts in which they are used, and that they carry with them special overtones of emotion or of meaning. But since philosophers who have discussed 'use' have in general done so with the clear intention of avoiding such 'conceptual and mentalistic' language, we can look for no help from them.[21]

There is nothing unscientific in the positing of mechanisms (that is explanations and theories) for the working of processes. Or if there is, then science itself is unscientific. Romano Harré relates the following instructive anecdote:

> I once met an elderly philosopher of great fame. The great man was maintaining that induction was an unsolved problem. There was, he maintained, no more reason for supposing that the clock on the mantelpiece would go on keeping time than that the next person passing the window would be wearing a blue jacket, as the last person had. Our mutual host then silently rose and turned round the clock, which was revealed as one with glass sides and back, through which one could see the beautiful mechanism that ensured its regularity. He then remarked: 'There is no Air-Force station nearby, so I can see no reason why we should expect a flush of blue jackets.' On hearing this, the great man changed the subject.[22]

The point that Harré is making is this: our ability to make reasonable predictions about events depends on our understanding the causes of them.[23] When we see five red cars in a row we do not assume that the next five cars we see will also be red unless we have reason to suspect something might cause this to be so, such as our being just outside a factory where cars are being painted red. The solitary airman passing the window was a coincidence, as common sense would say: there was no system behind his appearance.[24] Whereas the clock's accurate time-keeping depended on a well-understood causal mechanism. In short, for our philosopher to claim that chance sightings of airmen are as probable as the smooth running of meticulously constructed clocks, is to wilfully overlook the difference between coincidence and cause. Science is not interested in meaningless concatenations of data, but in the mechanisms responsible for events. A scientific hypothesis is not normally of the form 'Green cockatoos have green cockatoo chicks', but of the form 'Green cockatoos have green cockatoo chicks *because . . .*'

Now these mechanisms, in the case of any really profound scientific insight, such as the theory of gravitation, or of evolution, or quantum mechanics, or Bohr's planetary model for the atomic nucleus, are hypothetical: they are not directly observable, any more than the workings of the mind are. In short, to ascribe a mode of operation to the mind (or, for materialists, to the brain) is no more intrinsically 'mentalist' than to ascribe a mode of operation to the solar system.

So when W. V. Quine writes: 'I think the behaviourists are right in holding that talk of ideas is bad business even for psychology. The evil of the idea idea is that its use . . . engenders an illusion of having explained something,'[25] we may properly retort that the danger of the no-idea idea is that its use engenders a distrust of ever explaining anything. Skinner is (at any rate at times) consistent: he seems implicitly to reject the whole idea of 'explanation' as unscientific and improper![26]

Less honest, in a sense, are those writers who claim to be giving explanations when in fact they are providing nothing. The early Gilbert Ryle in *The Concept of Mind* is an example of this, *passim*:

> We know quite well what caused the farmer to return from the market with his pigs unsold. He found that the prices were lower than he had expected. We know quite well why John Doe scowled and slammed the door. He had been insulted . . . The cyclist knows what makes the back wheel of his cycle go

round, namely, pressure on the pedals communicated by the tension of the chain. The questions (1) 'What makes the pressure on the pedals make the chain taut?' and (2) 'What makes the tautening of the chain make the back wheel go round?' would strike him as unreal questions. So would the question (3) 'What makes him try to make the back wheel go round by pressing on the pedals?'[27]

Ryle's questions are all precisely the sort of thing that scientists ask. In the case of questions 1 and 2 they have explanations to give. In the case of question 3, some scientists are currently working upon the problem.[28] One can only comment that if the cyclist is uninterested in these questions, the more fool he!

This passage from Ryle indicates in fact just how pointless such talk is: it is a refusal, a refusal to pose and hazard an answer to questions. Its common sense is the common sense of the ostrich. It takes the words we use as narrowly and literally as it accuses mentalists of taking words about 'mind'. It assumes that all there is to be said, for instance about learning something, is that we *say* that it is learned: 'We could paraphrase this by saying that he was for three weeks forming the abstract idea of contour. But it would be safer and more natural to say that it took him three weeks to learn how contour lines are read and used and how the word "contour" is used.'[29] Should we be grateful for such enlightenment as this?

In fairness to Ryle—and not without providing myself with further ammunition—I must add that at the very end of his book he agrees that the Cartesian picture of the mind has been more fruitful than the mechanistic one.

Not to accept some such schema as the semiotic triangle involves us, I think, in inextricable difficulties. As an instance let us take Charles W. Morris, trying on the one hand to scotch the absurd idea that abstractions can be observed—and on the other hand to evade the evident fact that they 'happen' in some sense in the mind. I shall paraphrase his argument, for he uses a different terminology from mine, and his exposé is hard to follow. He begins:[30] 'A sign (e.g. a word) must have a designatum' (by which he means a referent); 'yet obviously every sign does not, in fact, refer to an actual existent object.' (Note the prejudice that the world consists exclusively of 'objects'.) 'The difficulties which these statements may occasion are only apparent difficulties and need no introduction of a metaphysical realm of "subsistence" for their solution.' (This of course is an unexceptionable statement: we cannot admit that words constitute a realm of perfect essences floating in a transcendental void.) Morris

goes on to point out that some referents ('designata', in his terminology) do not physically exist as such. 'No contradiction arises,' he
continues, 'in saying that every sign has a designatum but not every
sign refers to an actual existent. Where what is referred to actually
exists as referred to,[31] the object of reference is a *denotatum*. It thus
becomes clear that, while every sign has a designatum, not every
sign has a denotatum. A designatum is not a thing, but a kind of
object or class of objects—and a class may have many members, or
one member, or no members. The denotata are the members of the
class.' This sounds like the White King asking whether Nobody had
passed Haigha and Hatta on the road, and, if so, why hadn't he got
there first. If Morris's statement means anything, it must mean that
his class of objects which don't exist are 'concepts'; and to admit as
much outright would clear up the whole muddle.

The truth is of course that considerable progress can be made
with the so-called 'mysteries' of meaning if we allow ourselves as
much freedom to indulge in hypothesis as the practitioners of
natural science customarily do. For it is no good behaviourists,
operationalists and the like telling us that concepts are imaginary.
There is nothing to prevent me hypothesizing the existence of many
different types of subatomic particles to explain the observed facts
of traces on photographic plates, etc. As I write this paragraph news
comes of the possible discovery of a new massive nuclear particle by
some researchers at Leeds University. The original evidence for this
particle's existence was, of course, a kink on a graph.[32] In both
linguistics and science we must find explanations, and these explanations must be sufficient for our knowledge of the facts. The
question is not whether our theories are indubitably true, but rather
whether they will adequately explain the facts as we know them,
and whether they are currently the best theories available. If we
are to explain meaning, we need some sort of hypothesis: we need at
least to speculate about what goes on inside our organisms when we
think and speak. And in fact we are in a *firmer* position than the
atomic physicist to assert the reality of some such hidden process: for,
unlike the scientist, we obtain double corroboration from the evidence of introspection. And if we are told that the observing consciousness is notoriously liable to error, of course we should agree,
but point out that the subjective element in the observing scientist
is these days more and more emphatically confessed by scientists
themselves. The presence of the scientist as observer, we are told,
affects his very data.[33]

What too of those branches of science where people are positively

encouraged to introspect? I will cite for example medicine 'Tell me
where it hurts?' or Richard Gregory's experiments with optical
illusions 'Tell me what you see?' or certain branches of linguistics
itself 'Tell me what word you associate with this?' What too of
philosophy 'Tell me what you think'? Enough has been said to
indicate that (1) there is no rational reason for refusing to discuss
concepts; (2) *a fortiori*, discuss them we must, for otherwise literature, politics, philosophy, history, economics and the science of
linguistics itself would be so much hot air—hot air which would be
meaningless and could therefore be interchanged at will, with no
noticeable difference in effect.

Let us with a clear conscience, then, see what can be done with
'concept'. I gave a rough definition of the term above as 'the mental
process that goes on when we refer to (say) a tree or hear it referred
to'. No doubt the question will be asked, 'What *is* this mental process? What mental events may be assumed to occur?' But in fact no-
one could give a full answer to such a question, and much that
could be said is not relevant to my concerns in this book. I shall confine myself at this point to listing only a few of the characteristics
that such mental events need to have. What I shall say here will
form a basis for the discussion and expansion of the concept of
'concept' in the next few chapters.

(1) I can see no objection to identifying 'concept' with what the
linguist would call 'the semantic element of a lexeme, or lexical
item,' where this term means 'an entry in the dictionary of the
mind'. If I prefer the word 'concept', this is merely because of the
neatness of the term. As I have suggested already, I intend by it no
irrelevant overtones of its being a psychic or immaterial entity.

(2) I do not assume a mental 'image' of the referent, at least in
any literal sense of the word 'image'.[34] I shall be using 'image'
frequently throughout this book, both in its literary sense and in
various other senses. I want to issue a clear warning here and now
that in all these senses it is intended metaphorically: it is unlikely
that I shall speak of 'our image of beauty', but if I were to do so I
should not be implying that this was some sort of visual image. I do
not assume that every time we say 'dog' a mental picture of a dog
passes across the mind's eye (though this sort of thing certainly does
sometimes happen, at least with many people). I assume merely that
corresponding to actual dogs there is a mental content 'dog', whether
this be apprehended pictorially, schematically, abstractly or whatever.

(3) We do not need to know exactly *how* the word is connected to

the concept, whether this link is associative or causal, or anything else. It is sufficient for my purposes that there is such a link, and I shall leave it to others to discuss what its nature may be.

(4) We saw on p. 16 that a certain stability in the use of words must be assumed. We know very well that the way we use 'dog', 'mother', 'green', 'stupid' and 'excruciating' this year usually differs little from the way we used them last year; and no continuity of thought or language would be possible without such relative stability. Nonetheless, I do not of course assume total stability of meanings. It seems reasonable to assert that one's concept of 'radio set' altered, however slightly, when minute transistor sets first came to one's notice. Similarly 'boat', until the advent of iron ships, entailed for most people a wooden construction; and until the advent of funnels it entailed oars or sails. Masses of evidence for this kind of thing can be found in such works as Gustaf Stern's *Meaning and Change of Meaning*. A concept is thus only relatively stable. It may change; and we shall see later that its boundaries are hard to define.

(5) I do not assume that each individual element within a sentence is separately 'pictured',[35] so that 'The cat sat on the mat' breaks up neatly into six concepts corresponding to its six words. It is rather that words in combination produce an overall 'picture'. In a rather similar way, we do not hear all the notes of a harmonized melody separately, but rather as a single developing whole. 'It has a dying fall,' we say, referring to the total effect of a musical phrase. Nonetheless, this does not prevent most of the words in a sentence from referring to particular elements in the concrete situation being described. The point can be easily proved, since the reference of the sentence becomes quite different the moment one alters any element of it. 'The cat sat *by* the mat' shows us that 'on' has in context a distinct reference and a distinct conceptual content. On the other hand, as is usually rightly said, words like 'a' or 'the' contribute to the meaning of other elements in the sentence, rather than being definable as concepts in themselves. But there is no need for us, at every point of speaking and listening, to be conscious of every separate detail of an utterance. We need only be conscious of the utterance as a whole, and of what changes are brought about in its meaning if some element of it is changed.

William Alston is thus right when he asks one to take a sentence at random, for example:

'When in the course of human events, it becomes necessary for one people to . . .' and utter it with your mind on what you are saying; then, ask yourself whether there was a distinguishable idea in your mind corresponding to each of the meaningful linguistic units of the sentence. Can you discern an idea of 'when', 'in', 'course', 'becomes', etc., swimming into your ken as each word is pronounced? In the unlikely event that you can, can you recognize the idea that accompanies 'when' as the same idea that puts in an appearance whenever you utter 'when' in that sense? Do you have a firm enough grip on the idea to call it up, or at least know what it would be like to call it up, without the word being present? In other words, is it something that is identifiable and producible apart from the word? Do you ever catch the idea of 'when' appearing when you utter other words—'until', 'rheostat' or 'epigraphy'?[36]

Alston concludes that, since such clear and definite observables cannot be observed, the theory of concepts is nonsense. But to insist that we must only talk about observables is itself nonsense. Katz points out that a good deal of what goes on when we speak is tacit, half-conscious and subconscious; and this indeed is the clear implication of the Chomskyan brand of modern linguistic theory. 'Deep structure' is certainly not consciously present to the mind when we speak. Yet how else can we account for syntactic ambiguities such as those mentioned on p. 11 above, unless we posit some such tacit or unconscious process?[37] There is of course no point in positing unobservables where these are merely a fruitless luxury. But this is not the case here; such unobservables are necessary since only they will explain the data.

By a curious irony I should like to agree both with Alston and with Katz. In normal discourse a very large amount of the implied content of what we say or hear is certainly not noticed or felt. This is not to say, however, that it is not there, or that it cannot to some degree be brought to consciousness. It will be a part of this book's thesis that literary language brings to our notice, raises into consciousness, more of the content of the language we speak than does ordinary discourse, that when reading poetry we become more aware of implications and meanings that usually escape us. Let us be grateful to Alston for showing us just how slippery and elusive our language normally is, and just how unconscious we normally are of its potential content.

(6) We require to draw a distinction between all the different uses to which a word may be put, and each particular use to which it is put. Clearly there is a sense in which my concept of 'dog' is not the same when I am talking of a dog standing up and of a dog lying down, or when I am talking of a beagle, or of a collie. We can even

go further and ask how the concept 'dog' can be the same when we call a man a 'dog', or when we speak of 'a dog's life'.

We can avoid this objection by drawing a distinction between 'concepts' and 'conceptual events'. We may regard the concept as the (relatively) stable structure as a whole. It covers a large area of possible meanings, including all dogs we have heard of and seen, and has the potential to include of course all dogs we are ever likely to speak or hear of. Except when we say 'all dogs', however, we do not in any particular use of the word 'dog' cover this entire area. In short, in any one 'conceptual event' a particular sense of 'dog' is given, and this particular sense illuminates (as it were) only a small area of the concept's potential 'surface'. I shall return to this point in chapter 4, but it is worth saying here and now that it would be more accurate to amend the semiotic triangle as follows, so as to show that, in any particular instance of the use of a word, it is only *a sense* (s) of the total concept that is evoked (figure 2). Here, s is a particular sense, a point or area within the concept's total potential space.[38]

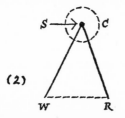

(2)

(7) I do not propose here or elsewhere to answer the question 'What is a concept?' where that question means 'Is it fish, flesh, fowl, electricity or immaterial spirit?' As Katz points out, such questions frequently halt all progress. Men did not need to ask what numbers were before starting to establish a theory of arithmetic, or what planets were before describing their movements.[39] Similarly, it is quite reasonable of us to describe how concepts can be assumed to operate even if we have no idea if they are neurological, electro-chemical or even ghosts in a machine.

To sum up the argument of this chapter: it is an unscientific superstition to suppose that we may not posit theories involving un-observables, such as the force of gravitation, the gene, the nuclear particle or the presence of conceptual apparatus in the brain. More-over, in this last case we are in the happy situation of being able to introspect, even though much of what we see is through a glass darkly. We may however appeal to the experience of others to confirm our own, as is properly done in such scientific fields as the investigation of perception or the study of animal behaviour. Working on these principles, it is clear that the concept of concept is in some form or other both reasonable and necessary. If concepts had not been given to man to introspect, he would have had to invent them.

The Semiotic Rectangle

ULLMANN, BEING A SEMANTICIST, naturally accepts the necessity for the concept. Ironically, however, he rejects the referent, as being 'outside the linguist's province'.[1] That a relationship is assumed by speakers to exist between what they say and the outside world is itself a very interesting linguistic phenomenon and deserves our attention. Besides, there are a number of problems that arise from our apparently referring to abstractions, like 'beauty' or 'simplicity', or referring to things metaphorically, as when we say 'outside' or 'linguist's province', in which case many interesting things can be said. And when we are discussing literature, there is the particular difficulty of the relationship (if any) of imaginary constructs like 'Mr Pickwick', 'Moby Dick' or 'Albertine' to reality. In short, the referent may or may not be outside language; but the presumed relationship of concept and word *to* it is very definitely our concern.[2]

Let us therefore accept the elements word, concept and referent, and take a closer look at our semiotic triangle. The first thing to note is that it is not an adequate diagram for the total language situation. For one thing, 'word' can and should in principle be subdivided. For the actual sound of a word as heard and its image in the hearer's mind are presumably not identical. There is a great deal of variation between different pronunciations of the same word by different English speakers, and indeed by the same speaker, but we think of them all as 'the same word'. Thus Yorkshire 'bootte(r)' and Scottish 'bu'er' are both interpreted as English 'butte(r)'. Even in the 'Received Pronunciation' of English, there are countless such phenomena, like the use, in rapid speech, of a glottal stop for the first 't' in the word 'fortnight'.[3] Roger Brown puts this point succinctly when he writes:

> Variations in pronunciation are . . . certainly ubiquitous, but our early extensive training in disregarding the dimensions of speech that are not significant for distinguishing English words causes us to overlook them. So long as phonetic essentials are preserved we identify utterances as the same, although they change greatly in loudness, pitch, quaver, breathiness and the like. From acoustic studies we know that even one speaker 'repeating' the same vowel does not produce identical sounds.[4]

We must therefore distinguish between word-form (the word as we hear it pronounced in any particular instance) and word-image (our mental apprehension of it, and assimilation of it to other similar sounds all interpreted as 'the same sound'. (I invent these terms to avoid the rather cumbersome linguistic terminology of 'phonetic' and 'phonological representation'. These correspond, however, to word-form and word-image respectively.)

The distinctness of these two elements of what we loosely call the 'word' is interestingly demonstrated by one of the disabilities that may result from a certain type of brain injury. According to Goldstein, 'if a heard sound does not awaken the idea of a known word, it will not be understood. The word-sound will seem strange, like words of a foreign tongue . . . The patient, moreover, will not be able to direct the motor act in attempting to speak such a word. Therefore, he will not utter it because it will seem strange and wrong . . . [In therapy] we must first acquaint the patient with words *and show him that variations in pronunciation do not change the meaning of the word.*'[5] That it is structurally correct to distinguish word-form (W-F) from word-image (W-I) will be sufficiently evident from this.

It would therefore seem to be truer to the facts of the linguistic situation to give our formula of meaning a rectangular shape (figure 3). Here again direct relationships are indicated by unbroken lines,

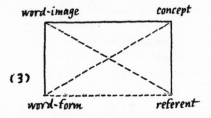

(3)

indirect ones by broken lines. This diagram more or less reproduces the ancient Indian conception of the speech situation.[6] In Bartṛhari's analysis of this, we have (1) 'the actual sounds of the words uttered . . .' (my word-form). (2) These sounds reveal the *prākṛta-dhvani*, which is described as either the permanent word as it figures in the language[7] or else 'the linguistically normal form devoid of irrelevant personal variations'.[8] (The latter resembles my word-image.)

There is a striking symmetry about this rectangular model. For word-form and referent are apprehended as physical events or objects in the outer world; word-image and concept are both mental.

Whereas word-image and word-form are verbal, and concept and referent concern the world and our experience of it. We might therefore divide the diagram as in figure 4. More interesting than this

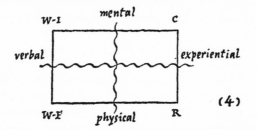

rather artificial symmetry, is the fact that W-I stands in much the same relationship to W-F as C does to R. For W-I can be viewed as a generalization from W-F: we interpret different instances, different pronunciations of the same word as being 'the same word'. Similarly the concept can be seen as a generalization from different instances, that is, from different referents: we interpret different corgies, borzois and Dobermann pinschers all as 'dogs'.

Why am I proposing this model of the speech-situation?—for which, by the way, I am going to claim usefulness but not completeness. Well, it illuminates the relationship we call 'meaning'— or some parts or all of which we call 'meaning'. The term 'meaning' as used in this book can be defined as (1) the total relationship shown in this diagram, or (2) any of the constituent relationships shown there. For instance, suppose a visiting American is puzzled by the Yorkshire pronunciation of 'butter'; he asks a friend what the Yorkshireman means; the friend replies, 'He means "butter" '. In this little exchange the meaning of 'meaning' is the relationship W F-W I. If I do not know the meaning of the French word 'imbrication', a friend may explain to me, 'It means "overlap".' The relationships involved here are W F-W I-C. 'That's my car,' observes an acquaintance. 'Which one do you mean?' I ask. 'That one,' he replies, pointing. The relationships involved here are W F-W I-C-R. It is however true that in all the above cases our attention is mainly on one particular element of the speech-situation: in the first case, it is on the word-image; in the second on the concept; and in the third, on the referent. This is why we tend to identify meaning with one or other of these elements. On the other hand, it is also the case that the other relationships are always potentially present: our American friend, told that the Yorkshireman means 'butter', will doubtless find the concept of butter called to mind, and will then know (if he is in a grocer's shop) that a particular pat of butter is being referred to. Other relationships may be implied too. In the case of the identification of the car, for instance, there are the indirect relationships WI-R and WF-R. Which is why we often say a *word* 'means' an object. And I assume (although we do not, I think, call this 'meaning') that when, as we say, an object or an idea flashes across one's attention or into one's mind at the start of the process of talking about it, the relationship involved is C-R.

However, for most of this book I shall not be concerned with the relationship WF-WI. It will be more convenient, and will enable me to be more concise, if I collapse the rectangle back into the triangle, and speak of word, concept and referent.

Proper Names and Common Nouns

> . . . Any theory of natural languages which does not take metaphor into
> account will be inadequate to explain how such languages function.
>
> (Bickerton 1969, 51)

WHAT IS THE SIMPLEST form of our formula of meaning? It is
when someone says '. . . Jonathan . . .', thus signifying his concept of Jonathan, and referring to him. Now it has been held that
there is something mysteriously 'other' about proper names: that
they have no 'meaning' for instance. And indeed, in normal usage,
when we ask the meaning of a name, we usually want its derivation
(as when we learn to our surprise that Cuthbert means 'a well-
known splendour'). On the other hand we also often say 'Who do
you mean?', expecting the person in question to be pointed out, or
wanting a description of him. I am not defining meaning in this
book, however, according to the sundry usages of normal English.[1]
And it will be evident that, *according to our definition of meaning,
proper names do mean*, that is all terms of the relationship W-C-R
hold good. For, as I said in the last chapter, I am using 'meaning' in
the sense of all or any of the relationships involved between word,
concept and referent. When philosophers have said that proper
names have no meaning, this is because they have had definitions of
meaning different from mine: they have claimed for instance that
they have no meaning because they have no connotations, or no
sense, or are not general terms for classifying things. I propose to
give a further illustration of how the formula of meaning works by
briefly discussing these questions, which can be clarified, I shall
claim, by introducing the term 'generalizing function'. Apart from
familiarizing themselves with this term, it may well be that those
who are not interested in such arid questions as whether proper
names have meaning, could profitably skip most of this chapter.

The definition given so far does not distinguish in any way between
proper names and common nouns: 'Jonathan' (W) refers to a particular 'Jonathan' (R) by way of 'Jonathan' (C). 'Tree' (W) may also
refer to a particular 'tree' (R) by way of 'tree' (C). But there is of
course an additional factor: when we call a tree a tree, we assimilate
it (if only by implication) to other trees. We classify it. What
mainly distinguishes proper names from common nouns is that the

concepts of the latter involve a *generalizing function*. Behind the concept of this particular tree stand the vague shadows of all other trees we have known.

'The fundamental intellectual process,' says Price, 'seems to be the experience of *recognition*.'[2] I should assent to this. It is inconceivable that we should be able to either think or act if we could not classify objects and experiences as being 'the same', 'similar', 'rather different', 'quite different' and so on; if we could not place them, that is, upon a scale ranging from identity through similarity to difference. This can be most clearly shown if we take an instance from the animal kingdom: the rabbit must, for the sake of its own survival, on the one hand be able to 'recognize' different foxes as being foxes, and on the other hand to distinguish between the fox and other rabbits, for instance. It must, at the very least, be able to interpret certain signs, smells and so on, as signifying danger. Whether this is a conscious or automatic reaction is beside the point, for even in the second case this would mean that the rabbit's reflexes would have been conditioned to react as if they perceived certain similarities and differences.

Besides, we may appeal to the findings of the father of behaviourism in this matter.

One of Pavlov's important discoveries is the way in which animals show *generalization*. Let us suppose that a dog's first conditioned reflex has been established, the conditioning stimulus being a tone of 500 cycles per second. Now a new stimulus is presented, a tone of 600 c.p.s. The dog secretes saliva. Why since he hears this now for the first time? The answer is that dogs, like people, generalize: having learned to make a response in one situation they will make the same response in other more or less similar situations. The dog does not confuse 600 c.p.s. with 500 c.p.s., but can distinguish such tones perfectly well, as Pavlov also showed. By continuing to feed the dog following 500 c.p.s., but never feeding following 600 c.p.s., 400 c.p.s., and so on, he could readily get a dog to a stage at which the Conditioned Response was always elicited by the 500 c.p.s. tone and not by any others.[3]

I think we may take it that the ability to perceive similarities and differences, the ability (that is) both to particularize and to generalize, is fundamental.

Is there anything in the 'nature' of proper names to prevent their use as generalizing terms? Clearly not. There is often a period in a baby's learning to talk when it extends 'dada' to all the men it sees.[4]

As adults we do the same when we call someone 'the Mozart of cricket'[5] or, taking the process a stage further, say 'He's a Mozart'. We reach yet another stage when someone's proper name becomes an accepted term for, say, meanness or pessimism: 'He's a Scrooge, a Jeremiah, a Cassandra!' And the final stage comes when the word's status as a proper name is totally forgotten: 'Reynard the Fox' becomes the normal word for a fox in French: 'renard'. This infinite series of grades between 'proper nameness' and 'common nounness' is further evidence of my point,[6] since it is hard to see where a line could be drawn between the two; and the moment someone says (of David, perhaps), 'Why, he's just like Jonathan,' the generalizing function is foreshadowed. For it depends upon an apprehension of *similarity*.

The hypothesis of a 'generalizing function', as I have called it here, gains additional support from the observations of Goldstein in his treatment of cases of brain injury. Some of his patients suffered from an inability to call a table a table, that is to assimilate it to the category 'table'. This he calls the 'impairment of the abstract attitude'. Such patients had no difficulty in giving the name of individuals, that is with proper names: their difficulty was confined to the category of common nouns.[7]

Jakobson's more recent accounts of work on aphasia do nothing to refute this interpretation.[8] Throughout his writings on aphasia he makes, among other distinctions, a dichotomy between speech disorders which are due to (1) loss of perception of likeness, and (2) loss of grasp of contiguity. There seems to be no objection to identifying 'perception of sameness or likeness' with a 'generalizing function'.[9]

The importance of 'generalizing function' as a concept will gradually become apparent in what follows. First, however, we need to define 'connotation'. Let us look at the question like this. A tree has branches, a trunk, leaves, a certain size, and so forth, and it is by virtue of these features that we recognize it. Similarly, it is on the basis of his characteristics that I recognize my friend Alexander. In other words it is by a referent's attributes that we recognize it, and having recognized it can apply the word 'tree' or 'Alexander' to it. One crucial term in this statement is the word 'recognize'. For our recognition of a tree or a friend is a mental process, and it is the features *we see* in our trees or our friends which enable us to recognize them: connotations, in short, are those features *as seen, perceived or assumed by ourselves*. Thus, the referent possesses features, attributes, characteristics or 'properties'; our concept of the referent has connotations, which I shall define as 'those properties we *attribute* to referents, which we use in determining the application of a word, or which are called to mind by its application'.

It has been claimed that one difference between proper names and common nouns is that the former 'have no connotations'. Clearly, this depends on how one defines connotations. Ogden and Richards for example define them as 'the properties (1) used in determining the application of a [word] and (2) in virtue of which anything is a member of the set which is the denotation.'[10] It would seem at first sight that it is not *properties* that determine our application of the name 'Alexander' to Alexander, but somebody's decision to name him thus. This is true if we are speaking of the original giving of the name 'Alexander' (though there are certainly vaguer and more emotional criteria involved in the giving of names, as we shall see later). In what way, however, does this differ from the original giving of the name 'tree' to a tree? It is not the *properties* of trees that are the cause of their being called 'trees', but the accident that that is their name in English. We never know what to apply any word to, whether it be a proper name or a common noun, until we are shown how to use it in the first place.

Moreover, how are proper names and common nouns differentiated once we know their use? Once we have learnt to use 'Alexander' of one particular individual, is it not in virtue of certain attributes that we recognize him and can use his name correctly? Of course it is. I recognize my friend Alexander by his characteristics: he is six-foot tall, has curly red hair and a broken nose, and often wears a kilt. I can recognize him as an individual for the same reasons as I can recognize a tree as a member of a category, on the basis of his and its attributes.

On the score of properties, therefore, names and nouns cannot be distinguished.[11] There is a difference, certainly, but it is the difference between individuals and classes, not the difference between attributes and a supposed lack of them. Proper names apply to different instances *of the same individual*, common nouns apply to different instances of different individuals *of the same kind*. They attach different individuals to a common classification, different towns to the category 'town', different trees to the category 'tree', and so on. In short, with common nouns the generalizing function comes into play, with proper names it does not.

It will be observed that the Ogden and Richards definition given above subsumes under one heading ('connotations') *both* the properties we attribute to referents *and* the generalizing function. These are quite separate factors, and it is surely preferable to give them different names and distinguish them clearly from each other. For otherwise proper names are going to be strangely bereft of properties, and we shall be unable to see how it is that we can tell one proper name from another. I shall say, therefore, that both proper names and common nouns have connotations, but only the latter are generalized to different individuals.

The second alleged deficiency of proper names is that they can have no meaning because the name 'Fred' for instance, can be applied to anything: to a man or a dog, or perhaps even a girl, or a picture on the wall. This again is true. But again we must remember the distinction made above between first uses of a word, and subsequent uses. I should argue that, *once a name is given* to an individual, it means that individual. It is merely because we do not apply the generalizing function to it that we have to learn, each time it is given for the first time to a different individual, to *what* individual, and even to what sort of individual it is applied. In short, the argument I am refuting overlooks the vital presence or absence of the generalizing function.

A third alleged deficiency of proper names is connected with the last one: it is that I can get no inkling from my first hearing of a name what sort of person or object it applies to. Not all red-haired Scotsmen with broken noses are called 'Alexander'; nor is Alexander addressed as 'Jimmy' when he isn't wearing a kilt. But this phenomenon has already been explained: it is because we do not generalize the characteristics of one Alexander to all other Alexanders that this is true. The absence of the generalizing function is again the key.

As Peter Geach writes:

> It has often been argued that it cannot be part of the meaning of a proper name that its bearer should be a man, because we cannot tell this just by hearing the name, and because there is nothing to stop us from giving the same name to a dog or a mountain. You might as well argue that it cannot be part of the meaning of 'beetle' that what it is applied to must be an insect, because we cannot learn this meaning just from the sound of the word, and because 'beetle' is also used for a sort of mallet. *In a given context*, the sense of 'beetle' does include: being an insect, and the sense of 'Churchill' does include: being a man.[12]

'Churchill' in one context is a twentieth-century statesman; in another, a place. Reading the two different contexts, we know this: that is, we attribute different connotations to the name, and it is these connotations which distinguish its different uses.

In this particular instance, the connotations are not carried over from one use of the name to another. But in certain cases, they may be. Why, for instance, should I call my dog (supposing I had one) 'Alexander'? Why is the name 'Thomas' often used in an obscene sense? (One thinks of the early version of *Lady Chatterley's Lover* which is called *John Thomas and Lady Jane*.) The fact of the matter is that these extensions of the names are made *precisely because* to extend them to dogs and penises is to attribute (a) humanity to the former and (b) as it were an independent will and human importance to the latter. Of course in such a case, some of the normal connotations of humanity are suppressed: nobody wishes to imply that a dog called Alexander has fingers and hands or can talk, or that a sexual organ called Thomas has two legs. But far from these names being applied because they have no connotations, the very reverse is true: it is because they do have them that they are so applied; and we cannot in fact explain such usages except on the basis of the names possessing connotations.

Lastly, it has been claimed that proper names cannot have meanings because even when the attributes of an object or person have changed, we continue to call them by the same name. John Stuart Mill writes:

> A town may have been named Dartmouth, because it is situated at the mouth of the Dart. But it is no part of the signification . . . of the word Dartmouth, to be situated at the mouth of the Dart. If sand should choke up the mouth of the river, or an earthquake change its course, and remove it to a distance from the town, the name of the town would not necessarily be changed. That fact, therefore, can form no part of the signification of the word . . . Proper names are attached to the objects themselves, and are not dependent on the continuance of any attributes of the object.[13]

Now this is manifestly true. If we nickname someone 'Curly', he will doubtless continue to be called 'Curly' long after he has gone completely bald. And I daresay the nickname would then become more popular still! A proper name will continue to refer to the same referent, even when that referent has changed in some respect.

This argument will not hold water either, for precisely the same thing happens with common nouns. Even when the well-known musical instrument ceased to be made of horn, it was still called one.[14] Or take the word 'volume'. It comes from the Latin 'volumen' meaning 'a roll', for indeed volumes were originally rolls of parchment. But when books ceased to be rolls, and became packets of sheets, the word 'volume' did not for that reason cease to be applied to them, any more than we stop calling Curly 'Curly' when he loses his hair. What happens in the two cases is evidently exactly the same: Curly and the volume are so named because of one outstanding feature of their appearance (curly hair, the rolled form). Once they are so named, however, the name is applied to them as complete wholes, and not merely to that single aspect of them. They each have many other features, and since it is by virtue of these too that we recognize them, and since it is these too that may be called to mind by any mention of their names, it is easy enough for the initial connotation (curly hair, the rolled form) to be submerged or even forgotten. Both 'Curly' and 'volume' are then felt to denote the person or object as a whole, *and also* to connote any other features that we happen to see in them.

We see, then, that the absence or presence of the generalizing function is the only thing that distinguishes proper names and common nouns. The other alleged differences are false or misleading, or are merely matters of definition. But of course we must not take the generalizing function to be an absolute. We are at liberty, if we wish, to treat a proper name as if it were a common noun. When we identify trees as 'trees' by virtue of our seeing them to be similar to the trees we already know, we are extending our use of the word in precisely the same way as we extend 'Jeremiah' to other prophets of despair.

The process of extension is the generalizing function at work. It can already be seen in children first learning to talk. C. W. Valentine notes that his boy B at 1 year and 5 months pointed to a print of a clean-shaven man and said 'Dada'. He goes on: '1; 6. Calls pictures of women as well as men "Dada": even pictures of statuary: of course recognition (implicit) of similarity does not mean that differences are not also recognized, and as clearly. 1; 7. Pictures of bearded men and one of a woman in evening dress elicited the cry of "Dada".' In another case, B had learned to call birds 'Kukuk'. At 1; 6 he called a pinafore with birds on it 'Ku-kuk'; and later a pinafore *without* birds. At 1; 7, having learnt to call his grandfather 'Ga-ga', he called his grandfather's photograph 'Ga-ga', and later his father's photograph, and pictures of men generally.[15] As another commentator on Valentine's remarks neatly puts it:

> If we were to enter in a lexicon the child B's word ku-kuk, we might write:
>
> Ku-kuk. Origin probably Cuckoo, the call of the bird Cuculus Canorus, Linn. Hence

1. By extension, Any bird.
2. Trop. Any representation of a bird, and particularly any pinafore containing a representation of a bird.
3. By extension, Any pinafore.

This is typical of an entry in any lexicon of a word in any language. In the light of a common apparent character two classes of objects are classed together, and the meaning of the name of one of them is extended to the other and becomes a symbol for the enlarged class, and can thence be extended to other objects classed with the latter.[16]

In practice (and with hindsight) one might regard such extensions of the word by a child as serving an exploratory function: it discovers by trial and error what is the normal range of the word.[17] From this point of view the normal range of a proper name is 1; and in this respect it is similar to words like 'Dada'. But clearly nothing prevents a proper name's extension if the circumstances are right. Just as we employ the term 'tree' for a plant that possesses the right features, so if Neville Chamberlain in 1938 calls Winston Churchill a 'Jeremiah', it is in virtue of characteristics thought to be descried in common between him and the original Jeremiah, which we might neatly wrap up together as prophecies of impending doom expressed in sonorous biblical style. In other words, the extension of a proper name is in virtue of the connotations possessed by a particular use of it; and without such connotations its extension would be totally inexplicable.

I said above that the generalizing function is the 'only thing' that distinguishes proper names from common nouns. But in fact, as Jespersen says, 'proper names (as actually used) "connote" the greatest number of attributes,'[18] a greater number, that is, than common nouns do. For once we have identified Alexander (this of course is an important qualification), our criteria for recognizing him are more numerous than our criteria for recognizing just any man or person. For he possesses all the criterial attributes of humanity, and in addition those other criterial attributes which distinguish him as an individual from all other men.

It should also be noted that, even before we know their precise application, many proper names do often convey as much information to us as a common noun would. This is at least true of proper names of a familiar sort, such as 'Alexander', 'Mary', 'Thomas' or 'Jane', for we know that they normally belong to men or women. Ullmann writes that 'a proper name like *Thomas* or *Alexander* will convey no information beyond the bare fact that it denotes a person'.[19] But this is no argument, for the word 'man' or 'person' itself conveys no more!

There is, then, despite my remarks on page 33 above, a class of proper names which does normally connote humanity (and either one sex or the other[20]). Now it is perhaps not a condition of the use of 'Thomas' or 'Jane' that it *has* to connote a human being. But it is equally not an absolute condition of the use of 'tree' or 'leg' that it *has* to imply all the criterial connotations of trees or legs. 'Tree' or 'leg' can be extended metaphorically, on the basis of *some* of their connotations.[21] Similarly, 'Thomas' or 'Jane' can be applied to creatures and objects which are not human, though I do not think that we would necessarily call these uses metaphoric. And, as we saw on page 36 above, there is normally a reason for such odd applications of a name. Thus the claim that proper names can be arbitrarily applied to anything you like, is at best a half-truth. Proper names (of the familiar sort) do have a normal range; and when they are used outside that range, this is never arbitrary: there is always a reason for an unusual use.

This is clearly shown by the fact that there are few parents who call their sons 'Belinda' or 'Fido' or 'Empire State Building'; and that there are special reasons why in China some should name their children 'Seven-Year Plan' or 'Electrification Scheme'. Nor is our choice of names for our children arbitrary in the sense that we indifferently choose *any* ordinarily acceptable name for them. If 'Ezekiel' summons up a picture of an old man with a white beard and a finger raised in imprecation; if 'Jemimah' suggests a puddle-duck rather than a person; if one is acquainted with the story of Delilah or Jezebel; then these names will not be given. These are extreme examples of course; but they illustrate the sort of reasons why we avoid certain names and favour certain others. Thus, during the War, a small rash of Winstons appeared upon the ledgers of Somerset House; and for a much longer period a much larger rash of Marlenes. And the noble family that always calls its eldest son Gervase St John de Lacy does so because of the feudal overtones of those resounding names. There are even criteria, then, for the *giving* of names—though these may be largely emotional.

It is time to sum up. This chapter has enabled us to add an important element to our definition of meaning, namely the generalizing function. We have seen that the distinction between proper names and common nouns can be explained by means of it; and that proper names are deficient in meaning only in this one respect. My definition of meaning can thus resolve the disagreement between

Mill, Ullmann, Geach and Jespersen. Their discord is merely a discord between definitions; and to analyze meaning in terms of the semiotic triangle plus the generalizing function, resolves the problem.

On the Structure of Meaning

> The most interesting features of the world, for instance Colour, Sound, Pain, Heat and Cold, Taste and Smell, etc., are not features of the world at all, but features of the interpretative mechanisms of the brain. (Sir David Eccles.)

WE SHOULD NOW BE able to make some further attempt to define denotation and connotation. It is often said that most definitions of these terms are too vague to be of any use.[1] Ogden and Richards define denotation as the members of the set of things to which a word can be correctly applied; and we have already seen their definition of connotation. They dislike the whole notion of the denotation/connotation distinction however, apparently for positivist reasons, for they object that connotations are 'a selection of properties or adjectives; but properties are not to be found by themselves anywhere . . . '[2] However, some of these allegedly intangible properties are of the kind 'having four legs' (dogs, cats and horses) or 'having a blue bottom' (baboons), which seem concrete enough. When we say that baboons' bottoms are blue, we do not mean to imply that they possess a transcendental quality of blueness subsisting in some Platonic heaven: we just mean they look blue. In short, I think it is not too difficult a matter to redefine the notions denotation and connotation in terms not of properties or qualities, but in terms of the various characteristics we perceive in, or attribute to, the referent, and the various suppositions we have about it. Distinguishing characteristics of trees and dogs are in a sense elements of the referent. But it is of course *we* who distinguish them (as I pointed out in chapter 3 above). And what we are concerned with here is the mental content of the concept: connotations I shall say are identical with the word's 'intension': they are the conceptual elements into which the concept as a whole can be divided.

May we call connotations 'linguistic'? They are not necessarily so, though we can often define them in words. We can say for instance that horses 'have four legs', that they 'neigh' and 'gallop'. But we certainly often recognize horses first and foremost by their shape, and this is clearly a primary criterion of our applying the term 'horse'. We could hardly say that the horse's shape is apprehended verbally: nor would we in practice find it easier to describe that shape in

words than to describe a bicycle to Julius Caesar. (Cf. p. 163 below.)
Nor can the sense impressions of 'redness', or a scent of poppies, or
the sound of trumpets, be described as such, though they are certainly our prime means of recognizing such items—and though we
may certainly use verbal associations to evoke them. I shall say
therefore (with all due caution) that though some connotations may
be verbal, all are most certainly not. The connotations of our concepts are in touch with our mental models of the world, with the
internal 'encyclopaedia' that we all carry around in our heads. They
are in touch with all that we remember.

This has important consequences for the imagery of poetry, for it
has often been claimed that poetry strongly evokes imagined sensations: *ut pictura poesis*. If, as I shall claim, poetry works first and
foremost by evoking connotations in the reader's mind, by making
such connotations more conscious than they normally are, and if
some at least of these connotations are not verbal, and if some again
are irreducible images of sensations, then this may explain poetry's
ability to make us 'see' or 'feel' reality more clearly.

Let us now turn to 'denotation'. This is normally used by philosophers and logicians as a synonym for 'referent'. I propose however to
define it as literary critics usually do (for 'referent' is already a perfectly satisfactory term).

I shall say then that denotation is the basic 'shell' of the concept,
the concept reduced to its utmost possible simplicity, the concept as it
refers to the object as a whole and without accretions. The object has
parts, and the denotation implies those parts of course, but does not
refer to them as such. The tree consists of leaves, branches, a trunk,
etc., but it is only the tree as a whole that is referred to by the denotation. The tree has a context too, but the denotation refers only to
the tree, and not to its surrounding fields, bluebells, woodpeckers or
squirrels.

The denotation is a unity, but the connotations are many. From a
strictly logical point of view, we might hope to establish a certain
minimum number of connotations which are the criteria or conditions for calling a tree a tree. Just what this absolute minimum
would be is rarely if ever clear. My copy of the *Encyclopaedia
Britannica* for instance does not mention 'branches' as a criterion of
trees—which is accurate enough if we wish to include for example
palm-trees in our extension of 'tree'. However the ground for extending 'tree' to cover 'family-trees' is the *branching* element in both.
This perhaps demonstrates no more than that branches are normally
thought of as a basic connotation. More seriously, it is impossible to

define the exact height at which we start calling a shrub a tree, as the puzzled *Encyclopaedia* only too clearly shows.[3] Mill himself admitted these fringes of uncertainty.

We should not be too alarmed by such doubts, however: that judgments are always approximate is a basic condition of thought. Wherever we are to draw the line between criterial and non-criterial attributes, it is clear that there might in principle be such a line. We might also make further distinctions; secondly, those non-criterial attributes, such as branches, which one thinks of as being 'normal', or those characteristics, such as deciduousness, which are certainly not true of all trees. All these (along with nuts, flowers, bark, etc.) are characteristics *of* trees, and we might call them 'inner connotations'. But there is also the immediate environment of the tree, the wood it grows in, the birds that nest in it, the air, sky and sunlight it grows towards, the earth its roots are embedded in. These constitute the tree's immediate environment, and are likely enough to be called to mind by it. Besides, they are all either conditions of the tree's existence, or of our experience of seeing trees, or depend *upon* the tree in their turn (like the birds, for instance). 'Tree' is thus enmeshed in a web of connotations whose relationships to it are of many different kinds: causal or contingent. There are however also connotations which depend upon our human attitudes to, and uses for, trees. We assault them with saws and axes, we hammer nails into their timbers, we burn them on fires and so know them to be combustible. We may also use trees for shade or shelter from the rain: we may associate them with particular landscapes—perhaps those that we particularly prefer, or with 'home' for instance. Thus, the great French chansonnier Georges Brassens indites a charming song to 'Mon Arbre': 'Auprès de mon arbre je vivais heureux . . .' The tree is associated in this song with security, home, companionship and strength. Some of these we might term 'outer connotations', since they relate to the tree's normal environment and surroundings, as also to its normal function in our lives. Equally, other connotations seem chiefly emotional, though even here the causal basis of the emotion is usually quite evident.

We might call these emotional connotations 'overtones' or 'harmonics' so as to avoid confusion. We have arrived thus at the following schema for the internal and external structure of the concept: a simple denotation, which is, so to speak, a mere hollow shell, within which are inner connotations; outside it are outer connotations; and 'outside' this again are our human emotional overtones (figure 5).

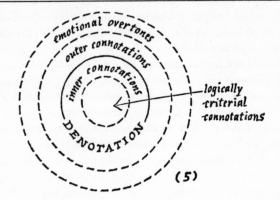

(5)

This is a way of visualizing the structure of what Charles Bally[4] calls the associative field:

> Le champ associatif est un halo qui entoure le signe et dont les franges extérieures se confondent avec leur ambiance... Le mot 'bœuf' fait penser: (1) à 'vache, taureau, veau, cornes, ruminer, beugler,' etc.,; (2) à 'labour, charrue, joug', etc; enfin (3) il peut dégager, et dégage en français, des idées de force, d'endurance, de travail patient, mais aussi de lenteur, de lourdeur, de passivité. Le langage figuré (comparaisons, métaphores, proverbes, tours stéréotypés) intervient comme réactif; comparez (1) 'un vent à décorner les bœufs', 'ruminer une idée', (2) 'mettre la charrue devant les bœufs', 'la pièce de bœuf' (la chose essentielle), (3) 'fort comme un bœuf', 'c'est un bœuf pour le travail', 'un gros bœuf', etc., etc. [The associative field forms a halo round the sign, whose outer fringes merge into their surroundings... The word 'ox' makes one think of: (1) 'cow, bull, calf, horns, chewing the cud, lowing,' etc.; (2) 'plowing, plow, yoke,' etc; and finally it can evoke, and does evoke in French, ideas of strength, endurance and patient toil, but also of slowness, heaviness and passivity. Figurative language (similes, metaphors, proverbs, locutions) interacts with this system; compare (1) 'a wind fit to blow the horns off an ox', 'chewing over an idea', (2) 'putting the [cart before the horse]', 'the [essential thing]', (3) 'strong as an ox', 'he's a [glutton] for work', 'a clumsy ox', etc.]

This quotation is enough to show that the boundaries between the various types of connotation I have defined are in fact very hard to draw. It is useful no doubt to draw them so as to give ourselves a structure to think with—and as scientists do when they arbitrarily draw a boundary between 'red' and 'orange' on the spectrum. But we must not suppose that there is a clear and absolute break between for instance factual connotations and emotional overtones. The notions of passivity, endurance, slowness and so forth, mentioned above by Bally, are also factual elements of our experience of oxen, despite their being relative to our *own* apprehensions. Facts are always the causes of emotions. And even something so factual and visual as the trunk of an oak-tree may be sufficient to give us the notion of strength. Experience of the referent is what is mainly responsible for giving us the concept's connotations and overtones.

It follows as a consequence of this that we may have highly personal and subjective overtones for certain concepts. Thus the sound of bells, for the narrator of *A la recherche*, had highly tragic personal overtones relating to the impermanence of love. Someone who as a child saw something nasty in the woodshed no doubt feels differently about woodsheds from the way I do. And so on. Now a large number of authorities, faced with these facts, seem to suffer a sort of linguistic vertigo: 'No, no,' they cry, raising their hands in horror and backing away from such a messy tangle of conflicting subjectivities, 'that can't be so! Words after all do have meanings! How could we understand each other if we didn't mean the same thing?'

The answer of course is, as everyone knows perfectly well, that we frequently don't. But such writers evidently suffer from a profound yearning for absolute certainty. The French philosopher Brice Parain writes: 'Si nous croyons que les mots n'ont d'autre sens réel que celui que chacun leur donne, il n'y a pas de communication possible, sauf par des approximations, par des malentendus, qui se paient ensuite en actes de violence, lesquels sont de nouveau interprétés, donc altérés, par ce qu'on dit. Penser dialectiquement ne fait qu'aggraver cette folie.'[5] [If we believe that words have no real meaning apart from that which people attribute to them, then no communication is possible, save at the cost of approximations and misunderstandings, which are atoned for eventually by acts of violence, themselves in turn reinterpreted and hence altered by what is said about them. Dialectical thinking only makes this madness worse.'] But precisely! Parain is blissfully unaware that he has defined exactly those dangers that follow from his own too confident reliance on the universality of meanings.

On the other hand, to the extent that our experiences with the same words are similar, then we do indeed understand each other. Fortunately, with simpler and more concrete examples like 'tree', 'horse', 'after' and 'red', there will be considerable agreement. With more complex and abstract concepts like 'religion', 'justice' or 'democracy', considerable disagreement habitually occurs, and our personal world-views are inextricably involved. Like everything else, understanding each other is a matter of degree. A well-known writer on metaphor complains, for instance, that Paulhan claims a word never has the same sense for two different people.[6] This Konrad says, must be false because it is always the same object that is being referred to (*sic*). But this is simply to confuse concept with referent. It is also to disregard overtones. And it is no good claiming, as she does, that the word symbolizes a 'structure', and that the structure itself remains unchanged, where the structure is always in part a subjective structure imposed by us upon the object: it is what we as human beings *suppose* the structure to be; and when our understanding of the necessary conditions for calling someone a 'father' alters, our concept of 'father' necessarily changes too.[7] Such absolutist positions are, in fact, quite untenable, and are due to an over-rigid analysis of meaning, and to yearnings for mathematical and conceptual certainty. The only consolation we can offer such people is to point out that, in general, within the same linguistic community, and when referring to widely shared experience, our concepts coincide well enough for ordinary purposes. But of course everyone knows that in some (comparatively rare) communicative situations we have to take a great deal of care in spelling out the connotations we intend.[8]

Some authorities have complained that the distinction between emotive and cognitive connotations is not clear.[9] However, I am afraid very few distinctions ever *are* clear. The scientist's decision to call one side of a hypothetical line upon the spectrum 'orange' and the other side 'red' is equally arbitrary. It is also equally useful, so long as we do not take it to be ordained in the nature of things.[10]

For consider Robbe-Grillet's famous statements on objectivity in the novel. Robbe-Grillet, at one stage at least of his career as a novelist, was insistent that objects were merely objects, that meanings of a human kind were improperly attached to them, and that the objects he described in his novels had no symbolic sense whatever.

> L'homme regarde le monde, et le monde ne lui rend pas son regard . . . Il ne refuse pas pour cela tout contact avec le monde; il accepte au contraire de l'utiliser pour des fins matérielles: un ustensile, en tant qu'ustensile, n'a jamais de profondeur; un ustensile est entièrement forme et matière—et destination. L'homme saisit son marteau (ou une pierre qu'il a choisie) et il frappe sur un pieu qu'il veut enfoncer. Pendant qu'il l'utilise ainsi, le marteau n'est que forme et matière: son poids, sa surface de frappe, son autre extrémité qui permet de la saisir.

L'homme, ensuite, repose l'outil devant soi; s'il n'en a plus
besoin, le marteau n'est qu'une chose parmi les choses: hors de
son usage, il n'a pas de signification.[11] [Man gazes at the world,
and the world does not return his gaze . . . Nonetheless he does
not refuse all contact with the world; he consents to use it for
material ends: a utensil, insofar as it is a utensil, never has hidden depths; a utensil is entirely form and matter—and function. Man takes up his hammer (or a stone he has selected) and
knocks a post into the ground. While he is using it thus, the
hammer is merely form and matter: its weight, its striking surface, the end which allows him to grip it. Man then sets down
the tool in front of him; if he no longer needs it, the hammer is
now no more than an object among objects: outside of its use,
it has no meaning.]

One might immediately observe that to say that the hammer has no
meaning 'outside of its use' is already a most important concession.

But as Hagopian in a clear-sighted article[12] has pointed out, none
of those qualities which Robbe-Grillet ascribes to the hammer, in
fact inhere in the hammer itself, but only in the hammer as
perceived by man. And he quotes Sir Russell Brain to the effect that
pure objectivity of perception does not and cannot occur;[13] for 'the
sensory qualities of normal perception, such as colours, sounds,
smells, touches, are generated by the brain;' and we have no reason
either to suppose that they are 'like' the external events to which we
attribute them, or to know what such a 'resemblance' would signify.
Our perception of the world is inevitably charged with subjectivity,
therefore. And twist and turn as he might, Robbe-Grillet's own
images, to which he himself seeks to attribute 'objectivity', have
definite emotional meaning.

Take, for instance, the image of the chairs on the verandah, in his
novel *La Jalousie*. These insensate objects are charged with human
meaning for the narrator. At first there are four of them, for
Franck, Christiane, the narrator and the narrator's wife, A . . . Two
of them are particularly close together, namely the chairs of Franck
and A . . . But Christiane never comes, and so in the first scene her
chair is empty,[14] and on our next return to the verandah it has been
removed altogether.[15] The three chairs, like the three places set for
dinner (of which one is removed when it becomes clear that Christiane will not turn up),[16] clearly indicate to the narrator the presence
of another man with his wife: they constitute an image for the
'eternal triangle'. The closeness of two of them arouses a suspicion
of guilty intimacy. The removal of Christiane's chair feeds the

narrator's suspicion that the foursome has become a threesome, where he himself is now superfluous. In fact these three chairs are very interesting; for they are from one point of view factual evidence for the well-foundedness of the narrator's jealousy; but this evidence itself is thereby charged with emotion.[17]

What, moreover, does Robbe-Grillet think he is doing in a passage like the following: 'Il lui reste encore deux petits millimètres dont il n'a rien fait. Deux derniers petits millimètres. Deux millimètres carrés de rêve . . . Ce n'est pas beaucoup. L'eau glauque des canaux monte et déborde, franchit les quais de granit, envahit les rues, répand sur toute la ville ses monstres et ses boues . . . '[18] [He still has two little millimetres left that he hasn't done anything with. Two last little millimetres. Two square millimetres of dream . . . It's not much. The grey-green canal water rises and spills over, laps across the granite quays, invades the streets, spreads through the whole town its monsters and its mud . . .] The mathematical obsession is typical of Robbe-Grillet. Here it stands for some tiny detail that won't fit in a detective's reconstruction of a crime . . . and this minute discrepancy is enough to let in a whole flood of fears and obsessions, symbolized by the dirty water of the canal. No clearer instance could be found in any novelist's work, let alone Robbe-Grillet's own, of the inseparability of human emotion and concrete image.[19]

It might be thought, then, that it would be better to abandon the whole distinction between emotive and cognitive connotations. But the fact that a coin has two sides and yet is indivisibly the same coin, being valueless if one side is split from the other, does not lead us to deny a difference between those two sides. The very fact that we could distinguish, above, between the *evidence* of the three chairs and their *emotional meaning*, shows that however indivisible in practice these may be, the distinction in theory and thought can be a useful one.[20]

As for the outer boundaries of the associative field, these again cannot be drawn except by an arbitrary act of definition. For where do the outer connotations cease? Oxen recalls yoke, yoke recalls servitude, servitude involves slaves, slaves recall slave-markets or Barbary pirates or the cotton-fields of Louisiana. This is what Valéry means when he says 'the bottom of the mind is paved with cross-roads'. Note that this all forms a very complicated internal and external structure: for each connotation (whether 'inside' the denotation or 'outside' it) is itself a denotation, which again calls up its own connotations.

It is here that the phenomenon of metonymy belongs. The tongue is the principal agent of speech: consequently we call languages 'tongues'. (Or is it the other way round? But this approximation will do for the moment). In other words, where we have two words that are associated by their closeness in our experience, we may in certain circumstances use one for the other. (Another example is 'yoke' for 'slavery'). Here we have not so much uncertainty in the boundary (where it is to be drawn) as the wholesale shifting of a word across that boundary. Here too belongs synecdoche: when we speak of 'forty sail', meaning 'forty sailing ships', we are using, as we say, the part for the whole, that as an inner connotation stands for the whole denotation.

There is, however, a further important connexion between concept and concept to be considered. This is the relationship of analogy, and upon it depends the figure of speech that is often said to be basic to poetry, namely *metaphor*. There are for instance, 'some factors in common between the human neck, the narrow part of a bottle, a narrow outlet for road traffic, and certain obstacles and constrictions hampering the smooth working of administrative or business machinery'. The resultant semantic change is the metaphor 'bottleneck'.[21] It is amusing that there were complaints in the French press a few years ago that people were using the term 'embouteillage' to mean 'traffic jam', and that this 'was not the proper meaning of the word'. This merely shows the irremediably literal frame of mind of the complainants. Changes of meaning of this kind are not only colourful, but useful, and not only useful but necessary. For how else are we to treat a new phenomenon? By inventing some cumbrous latinism?

But upon what does the process of analogy depend? Upon the perception of similarities. We are here again, in fact, in presence of what I have called the generalizing function. For it is by overlooking their differences that an English oak, a prehistoric tree-fern and a baobab are all called 'trees'. By a further perception of similarities—or suppression of differences—we conventionally call the Cross (as part of a dead tree) 'The Tree'. Taking the branching form of the tree for our basis, we arrive at 'family trees'. And sometimes it is even impossible to say whether the term we are using is a metaphor or not. 'When we call a table-leg a *leg* (as we always do of course) are we using the word literally or metaphorically?' Or, to phrase the question generally: 'What are the "proper" extensions of meaning of a word; where does it cease to be literal and become metaphoric?' I. A. Richards' discussion of this is calculated to properly confuse us and to rightly humble those who write to French newspapers complaining that not everything is always literal. 'We notice that (with the word "leg") the boundary between literal and metaphoric uses is not quite fixed or constant. To what do we apply it literally? A horse has legs literally, so has a spider, but how about a chimpanzee? Has it two legs or four? And how about a starfish? Has it arms or legs or neither? And, when a man has a wooden leg, is it a metaphoric or a literal leg? The answer to this last is that it is both.'[22]

Thus, we have extensions of meaning via (1) association (or contiguity)—and (2) extensions via perceived similarities (or suppression of perceived differences). There are connexions of *contiguity* and connexions of *similarity*.[23] And in neither case are the boundaries between one concept and the next always easy or even possible to draw. The concept, one might say, is an *area* capable of analysis into smaller areas: thus, one dimension along which 'tree' can be divided, is (1) the dimension of its connotations (or its 'intension', as this is often called): here it divides into branches, twigs, leaves, etc. The other dimension along which it can be split up is (2) its 'extension',[24] that is its application to all the trees it can stand for literally, and to all the objects which it can stand for by metaphor or analogy.[25] I propose to call each individual use of a word, that is each individual application of a word to a *particular* tree or a particular *kind* of tree, or a particular *metaphorical* tree, a Sense.[26]

No two-dimensional diagram on the page will do to depict this complicated situation. Here then, to supplement the diagram of denotation and connotation already given, is a diagram of the concept's 'extension' (figure 6). We may visualize the particular senses

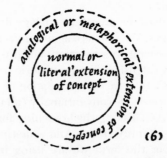

(6)

in which the word is used as being spots or points within these two broad areas, namely (1) the intension and (2) the extension of the concept. And we might speak of a word's intensional sense, and of its extensional sense. As for the boundaries of a word's extension, these as I have pointed out above are shifting and uncertain. This is true not only of the 'literal' senses of the concept, but also of its metaphorical extensions. And some poets have even gone so far as to suggest that anything can be compared to anything.[27]

What is it that controls the sense? What is it that allows us to determine which tree is being referred to (extensional sense) or what sort of tree it is (intensional sense)? Clearly, more than one factor is present here. The word's morphology is important. If it is singular or plural, for example, this helps to define the scope of its extension; if it is possessive, this helps to define its relationship to other elements of the sentence; and so on. The syntax also helps to determine the word's sense. These elements are all 'given' in the utterance (except in the case of ambiguous form or syntax).

The immediate context is 'given' too, and helps to impose an interpretation. Our understanding of the first two words in 'Christ hung upon a Tree' allows us to deduce that here 'Tree' = 'Cross'. This in turn selects the appropriate connotations of the word 'tree' in its context, for example, its woodenness, the fact that the cross is made of parts of a tree, that it stands up like a tree, that its base is embedded in the earth, that it branches something like a tree, and so forth. Equally interesting is the fact that certain of a tree's characteristic features are missing in the cross (as of course is always the case with metaphoric extension), and that in this case we may see the absence of these features as highly significant. The clash between vehicle and tenor, between the connotations of tree and cross, draws our attention to the cross as an instrument of torture and death. For this 'tree' is dead and cut down, has no leaves, and is nailed together; and these facts remind us of its sinister function, remind us too that the victim is nailed to it.

Similarly, the context determines, in the following lines from *A Midsummer Night's Dream*, that the wall holds at first pleasant connotations for Pyramus—then, abruptly and comically, his feelings about it change. Pyramus in this passage makes these overtones explicit:

Pyramus: Thou *wall*, O *wall*, O sweet and lovely *wall*,
  Show me thy chink, to blink through with mine eye.
  Thanks, courteous *wall*. Jove shield thee well for this . . .
  O wicked *wall*, through whom I see no bliss;
  Cursed be thy stones for thus deceiving me!
Theseus: The *wall*, methinks, being sensible, should curse again.

(Act V, scene I)

We may visualize the process of understanding a passage of writing or speech something as follows: The word is like a torch-beam scanning the area of the concept, and seeking to come to rest on the appropriate spot. The context of the word's use is so to speak the hand that directs the torch-beam at a particular point. The area illuminated by the beam may be larger or smaller as the case may be. In 'all trees' the area may coincide with the whole area covered by 'tree', in 'that tree there' it is reduced to a particular tree, in 'tree of knowledge' it is (or rather was originally) extended outside its normal range. Different aspects of the concept may be illuminated too. 'Tree of knowledge' is a case not only of unusual extension but also of an unusual content of 'tree'; 'He chopped down the tree' implies that it was standing; 'In the shade of the old apple-tree' implies leaves on the tree; whereas 'You get a good view through the trees in winter' implies that they are leafless and deciduous. As we saw above, sense may vary in two ways, (1) according to the range and number of cases covered (extension) and (2) according to what is being said or implied of the object in question (intension).

In the light of these examples, readers may be wondering whether anything distinguishes my sense of 'connotation' from other writers' 'presupposition', 'implication', 'entailment', or even 'semantic marker'. And indeed the answer is: 'very little'. I am using 'connotation' in this book in a particularly wide sense, to cover any element of meaning that is not explicit in, but is implied by, a particular use of words. And I shall banish further discussion of this point to the more discreet tedium of a note.[28]

When we speak of context controlling the sense of an utterance, we cannot limit ourselves merely to the immediate verbal context or (come to that) to the immediate social or physical context. It is not of course just the immediate surroundings of 'Christ hung upon a Tree' which allow us to interpret 'Tree' correctly; for anyone with a fairly small knowledge of Christianity—and even if he had never heard 'Tree' used in this sense before—would be likely to make the right deduction about its meaning. Often whole areas of our experience of life may be called upon. The sense of words is controlled by their form, by their syntax, by their immediate context, and by the wider context of our experience as a whole.

Thus, to speak simply of the context 'imposing' an interpretation on the words, is misleading. For it certainly does not impose an interpretation on them in the same unambiguous and explicit way as a morphological feature (as when a final -s tells us a word is plural, or a final -ess that it is feminine). In a sense, nothing is imposed by the context at all: the listener is obliged to seek his own interpretation *for the sake of understanding the utterance*. Let us be clear about this: the *effort* to understand language is a necessary condition for actually understanding it. Hearing 'You get a good view through the trees in winter', our listener knows that if the trees are conifers the sentence cannot be true. He knows that if the view is taken from between the tree-trunks, there would be no point in saying 'in winter'. He casts about for an interpretation which would (as we say) 'make sense'. We understand language, in short, because we tend to regard everything we hear as 'meaningful, if only it is interpreted in the right way'. We do not give up at the first interpretation that springs to mind, and say, 'That's nonsense, you can't see through trees.' We seek about for conditions under which the sentence *would* be meaningful, and interpret it that way.[29] We make sense of it by eliminating possibilities that do not fit, just as we pick our way through a maze by taking the only route which contains no dead ends. We make sense of it by seeking to make sense of it.[30]

And in so understanding language we often have to exercise a great deal of ingenuity, and draw upon a considerable amount of our experience of the world. An amusing example is Antony Kenny's anecdote about walking down the Canongate in Edinburgh and seeing on the façade of a shop the words 'Thistle Freezers'. 'Goodness,' he thought to himself, 'whoever would want to freeze thistles?' Then he made a rapid mental adjustment: 'Of course: this is Scotland: the thistle is the national emblem: it must be a brand name.'[31]

This instance involves being able to parse 'thistle freezer' in two different ways: (1) as something that freezes thistles, (2) as something that freezes things, and is called a thistle. We might compare this with Landesman's example, 'The shooting of the hunters was quite distressing'. He writes:

> What is ambiguous about the sentence is that the phrase 'the shooting of the hunters' may be interpreted as exemplifying either of two distinct grammatical constructions. One is an action-object construction derived from 'The hunters were shot', and the other is an agent-action construction derived from 'The hunters were shooting'. [The listener] is not in doubt about some global features of the sentence, such as its meaning, but about some special feature, namely the grammatical structure of a phrase.[32]

Common sense would reply that grasping the phrase's two grammatical structures is the means by which we understand its two meanings. But there is nothing in the grammar to tell us *which* of the two to select. Only the sort of meaning that is required by the context can tell us that. The words 'shooting of the hunters' do not come ready labelled 'Action/Object/Agent' like the numbered fragments of a marquetry set. Understanding language is more like composing a jigsaw puzzle: the individual parts may fit equally well into a number of different places. Which we choose for them depends on the requirements of the picture we are putting together.

In instances like this, therefore, it is not the case that you have to know what the grammar is before you can tell what the meaning is; on the contrary, you must know what the meaning is before you can decide between the two possible parsings. Kenny's example is even more interesting. It suggests that in some cases the meaning may even *suggest* an alternative grammar to us. To begin with he did not even realize that there *were* two alternative interpretations. He was puzzled, not because the phrase 'thistle freezer' seemed ambiguous, but because it seemed absurd. For there are two possible alternative processes: (1) that he then tried parsing 'thistle' as a name used adjectivally, and saw that this fitted the context; or (2) that he thought how else 'thistle' could be interpreted (that is, as an emblem), and then saw that this would fit grammatically. Which of these happened, it is not for me to say. But surely either is conceivable.

Apparently one way of avoiding the conclusion that meaning may either (1) adjudicate between different grammars, or (2) actually suggest different grammars, would be to assert that interpreting 'thistle freezer' as 'something for freezing thistles' is forbidden by the laws of English grammar. This in effect is to widen the concept of grammar by including in it what is normally called meaning.

The reasons why linguists have sought to do this are doubtless praiseworthy. For on the one hand, grammar does to some extent carry meaning, as when an apostrophe *'s* indicates possession, or when the suffix *-ing* tells us that an action is going on. And on the other hand, the attempt to 'include' meaning in grammar is part of a worthy attempt by many modern linguists to get to grips once again with the problems of semantics. A serious difficulty arises, however. For just how much of human experience would have to be included under the heading of 'grammar', for us to be able to explain our understanding of language? I would suggest that we should have to include *the whole of a man's knowledge*. If this is so, to extend the term 'grammar' to cover all of this, would make it so vague as to abolish its usefulness.

'Thistle freezer' is a case in point. It is perfectly comprehensible interpreted in the unlikely way: it is not nonsense, it just seems absurd. Now under what circumstances might it cease to seem absurd, and become perfectly acceptable? If scientists were to discover, say, that keeping thistles in deep freeze for five years broke down their chemical structure in such a way that a valuable new drug could be extracted from them. 'Thistle freezer' would then become a perfectly 'grammatical' phrase to those who knew this fact, but not to those who didn't. Thus, the 'grammar' of thistles depends on one's knowledge of thistles. The cause of such 'grammatical rules' is our knowledge of the world, and there is no evading this point. Consider too for a moment just how much knowledge Kenny has to call upon before he can interpret 'thistle freezer' correctly. He has to know that a thistle can be an emblem; that it is not frozen; and that it is not even plausible that it should be. I would suggest that a lot of information has to be available to him.

As Terry Winograd writes:

> When we see the sentence 'He gave the boy plants to water', we don't get tangled up in an interpretation which would be parallel to 'He gave the house plants to charity'. The phrase 'boy plants' doesn't make sense like 'house plants' or 'boy scouts', so we reject any parsing which would use it. The ability to integrate semantics with syntax is particularly important in handling discourse . . . [33]

Hence, in his rather impressive attempts to get a computer to 'understand' normal human language, he explains:

> As a concrete example, we might have the sentence 'I rode down the street in a car'. At a certain point in the parsing the (computer) program may come up with the constituent 'the street in a car'. Before going on, the semantic analyser will reject the phrase 'in a car' as a possible modifier of 'street' . . . Since the semantic programs are part of a general deductive system with a definite world-model, the semantic evaluation which guides parsing can include both general knowledge (cars don't contain streets) and specific knowledge (for example, Melvin owns a red car). Humans take advantage of this sort of knowledge in their understanding of language, and it has been pointed out by a number of linguists and computer scientists that good computer handling of language will not be possible unless computers can do so as well.[34]

Language cannot be understood without a detailed background of human experience. The difference in implication between 'He threw another log on the fire' and 'He threw a bucket of water on the fire' depends on our knowing certain simple facts about fire and water.

The structure of linguistic meaning necessarily corresponds to the structure of human experience: when I learn what the French term 'Grande Ecole' means, I fit it into what I already know of French educational structure, and indeed of education in general; when I learn the term 'carcinogenic' it takes on immediate emotional tone from the area into which my mind 'slots' it. This of course is why the attempt to build translation machines was given up: the structure of meaning is so complex that it coincides with the structure of human thought and experience, and a proper metaphor for its working would be an encyclopaedia rather than a dictionary.[35]

There is moreover no *regular* system or structure of connotations: this can be seen by contrasting 'stallion' with 'bull elephant', and with 'male horse'. 'Stallion' carries with it implications of sexual aggression and potency that are lacking in both the other terms; 'bull' carries with it notions of strength and tanklike unstoppability, that have to do with the particular qualities of bulls in conjunction with those of elephants. The terms have connotations *of their own*, which they obtain from our experience of the differences between stallions and bull elephants, and which consequently cannot be reduced to a neat and symmetrical system. There is not *a* structure of meaning which can be extrapolated to all similar meanings: 'bull elephants' are not just 'elephants + male', but have connotations additional to both 'elephants' and 'males'. Each denotation contains its own particular structure, which depends in part on factors inside language, in part on factors outside it.

Whether the structure of denotation and connotation that I have suggested above corresponds to anything in the structure of the brain is doubtless a further fascinating question. Equally certainly it is not one that anyone can answer at the moment. I believe in fact that the spatial metaphors I have been using (*areas* of meaning, *boundaries* between inner and outer connotations, and so forth), though convenient, are objectively incorrect, and that what we should find in the language-manipulating part of the brain would be (not merely a web of interconnecting neurons, of course—we know that—but) a web of associated linguistic processes which might well be described more accurately *as* a web or net. Researchers into word associations already publish charts of this sort, but they are very rudimentary.

A further question would be whether the connexions between these linguistic processes are *qualitatively* differentiated from each other or not. It is certainly possible to think of them in a qualitatively different way: for instance, the difference between the relationship 'tree-axe' and the relationship 'tree-boat' is clearly considerable, even though they would probably both come under the same rough heading in Bally's scheme (his heading (2); see p. 42 above). And even 'tree-axe' and 'tree-saw' are clearly entirely different in relationship.

The brain is reported to contain about ten thousand million units, each of which may communicate with ten thousand others. Is our sense of qualitative distinctions a *function* of such vast quantities? Might we one day describe semantic structure in terms purely of the *number* of connexions established between word and word (or process and process), and the direction in which such connexions go? But I mention all this only to underline more clearly the hopelessness of the idea that one might arrive at a consistent, neat picture of the structure of (even a single word's) meaning.

The structure of the concept, then, is both fluid and complex. It is fluid, because it is capable of extension on the basis of analogy, of 'stretching' (as indeed we often say) to cover non-literal referents. It is fluid also, because we can never be certain exactly where the boundary between literal and metaphoric comes. It is complex because it contains within it so many connotations, other connotations flock round it, and because it is thus connected indirectly with a potential infinity of other concepts. It is not surprising that St Augustine should have complained: 'Quid est ergo *tempus*? Si nemo ex me quaerat, scio, si quaerenti explicare velim, nescio.'[36] Valéry makes a similar observation: 'le fond de la pensée est pavé de carrefours.' (The bottom of the mind is paved with crossroads.)[37] And Wittgenstein wrote: 'Words are like the film upon deep water.'[38]

Are Meanings Atomic?

A dictionary is a frozen pantomime.   (Bolinger 1969, 567)

What [Darwin] upset was the Linnaean *Scala Naturae*, the ladder of
nature, whose great keystone, as essential to it as the divinity of Christ
to theology, was *nulla species nova*: a new species cannot enter the
world. This principle explains the Linnaean obsession with classifying
and naming, with fossilizing the existent. We can see it now as a foredoomed attempt to stabilize and fix what is in reality a continuous
flux, and it seems highly appropriate that Linnaeus himself finally
went mad; he knew he was in a labyrinth, but not that it was one
whose walls and passages were eternally changing. (Fowles 1969, 53)

With good fortune psychology may hope eventually to achieve that
degree of implausibility—and fertility—that now characterizes the
longer established sciences.   (Donald Hebb 1972, 290)

BUT HOW DEEP IS the water? Could we ever reach the bottom of it?
In other words, could we analyze a meaning into *atoms* which would
then be incapable of being further analyzed? And should the fate of
the physicists' old atomic theory, the fact that it was discovered that
atoms were *not* the ultimate constituents of matter, be a warning to
those who seek such solutions? I think it should, at least if by 'atom'
is meant something clear, distinct and determinate, with no hazy
edges.
   The first thing to note is that no one has ever (as far as I know) set
out to prove that *emotional* meaning is even in principle analyzable
into ultimate elements. So that poetry at all events might be held to
be immune to such heartless surgery. But various attempts have
been made to do something of the kind with 'denotational meaning'
or the 'logical elements of meaning'. The likelihood is however that
they were failures.
   First, we consider Russell's attempt to lay down the principles of 'logical atomism'.[1] He did this under the influence of
Wittgenstein; but his attempt is a failure from the very first pages.
For instead of facing the problem fairly and squarely by asking
whether it is plausible that meanings can be reduced to indivisible
elements, he goes about it as follows: 'suppose—as one always has to
do—that "red" stands for a particular shade of colour. You will
pardon that assumption, but one can never get on otherwise.'[2] Well,

I am afraid that I shall not pardon that assumption, and furthermore I have no desire for Russell's argument to get on. 'Red' cannot be supposed to be a 'simple symbol', for the simple reason that it stands for a number of different shades and intensities. Moreover even ordinary language so organizes it (crimson, scarlet, carmine, puce, vermilion, etc.). Red, scientifically speaking, is an arbitrary name attached to a certain part of the spectrum, and may be defined as the wave-lengths between x and y. But each wave-length is different within this scale. If Russell wishes us to accept his basic assumption, he would have to make it at least *seem* more plausible. One does not hope to show that hot cross buns cannot be divided, by pointing to Christmas cakes, *which can.*

Wittgenstein's attempt to do something rather similar is presented to us in the *Tractatus.* Elegant and exciting though this great work is, it does not prove this point. I quote from a recent critic of Wittgenstein: 'Wittgenstein did not claim to be able to produce any examples of complete analyses which might reinforce [the conclusion that there *are* ultimate elementary propositions], or even illustrate it. He merely specified elementary propositions as a class of logically independent factual propositions, and he left the precise nature of their elements, which he called "names", shrouded in mystery.'[3] Pears then asks if these elements are supposed to be sense-data or particles. From the point of view of science perhaps it doesn't matter too much which they are: in either case, any proposition about seeing something red, for instance, could be reduced to a proposition about the movements of photons, electrons, neutrons, etc. Moreover it is clear that any experience can in principle (and in *physical* terms) be reduced to such a statement. But we know from the Heisenberg uncertainty principle that our knowledge of the exact state of, say, the electrons in a cloud of red gas is *and must in the nature of things remain* vague. It seems therefore that there must be a limit to the analysis of experience, and that this limit is laid down by the laws of the physical world itself: at the level of microphysics, indeterminacy creeps in. This indeterminacy is fatal to Wittgenstein's argument; for it demonstrates that the most basic factual propositions *are inherently vague*: an electron can be asserted either to be at point p or to be travelling with momentum m; but both assertions can never be made at the same time.[4] Under certain circumstances, separate electrons cannot be viewed as having separate identity.[5] And so forth. But these facts are in clear contradiction to Wittgenstein's proposition 2.031: 'In a state of affairs, objects stand in a determinate relation to one another' (*Tractatus*).

It is only fair to point out at this juncture that the later Wittgenstein (a quite different philosopher from his former self) makes the point in *Philosophical Investigations* that some factual propositions are inherently vague, and raises the question whether logic idealizes the structure of language, that is, distorts it. About this, he is clearly right, and perhaps we may take Wittgenstein's change of mind as corroborative evidence for my thesis here. Nor have most modern philosophers been impressed by doctrines of logical atomism.

Apart, then, from the capacity of language (even of the language of mathematics) to analyze the world into distinct atomic parts, it will be clear that quantum mechanics asserts that the ultimate nature of the world itself resists any such analysis. The worldstuff is ultimately hazy. Physicists are fond of describing an experiment in which electrons are fired through a hole in one screen to form a pattern of strikes on a second screen placed behind the first. The mark left by each electron can be detected, just as if it were a particle. If now a second hole is opened in the screen, we do not get two patterns of strikes each resembling the first one, but a single pattern similar to that of a wave interference pattern. Do the electrons interact with one another? But if one fires single electrons at the two holes, with long intervals between each shot, so that individual electrons could not be influencing each other, the wave pattern still emerges. It is as if each electron knew there was a second hole, and was influenced in its behaviour by this knowledge—or as if each particle went through both holes at once! And if the scientist then sets out to determine through which hole each electron goes, he may do so; but in thus interfering with the electrons' behaviour, he destroys the wave pattern.[6]

Quantum physicists have found it impossible to cope with this and other paradoxes in the behaviour of elementary particles except by assuming that such a particle is rather a packet of potentialities than a distinct object in the normal sense of that word. Though statistical calculations about the behaviour of large numbers of such particles can be made with satisfactory accuracy, the behaviour of any one particle cannot be predicted beyond a certain level of precision. The language of modern quantum mechanics thus refers to 'objects' which are indeterminate, and to possibilities, not facts. 'Atoms are not *things*,' writes Heisenberg. 'The electrons which form an atom's shells are no longer things in the sense of classical physics, things which could be unambiguously described by concepts like location, velocity, energy, size. When we get down to the atomic level, the objective world in space and time no longer exists, and the mathematical symbols of theoretical physics refer merely to possibilities, not to facts.'[7] And Bohm writes: 'as we try to improve the level of accuracy of description' (at the subatomic level) 'the classical program of analysis into parts eventually becomes infeasible.'[8] . . . 'The entire universe must, on a very accurate level, be regarded as a single and indivisible unit in which separate parts appear as idealizations permissible only on a classical level of accuracy of description.'[9]

Russell and Wittgenstein's early dream of a logical atomism can thus obtain no support from modern physics. But a further point should be made here: it would not even be *useful* to arrive at a fully determined, fully 'logical' language: it would indeed be downright detrimental not only to the ordinary business of life, but to the practice of science itself. Consider the following statements by B. F. Skinner about an 'ideal language'[10] (I shall comment in the course of the quotation): 'Under the conditions of an ideal language' (he means a *logically* ideal language) 'the word for *house*, for example, would be composed of elements referring to colour, style, material, size, position, and so on. Only in that way could similar houses be referred to by similar means. The words for two houses alike except for colour would be alike except for the element referring to colour. . . . Every word in such a language would be a proper noun, referring to a single thing or event.' (We see here the characteristic prejudice of Western mechanistic thinking, that the world is made up exclusively of *objects*: a mental attitude of a curious static rigidity seems to result.)[11] 'Anyone who spoke the language could immediately invent the word for a new situation by putting together the basic responses separately related to its elements . . . Abstract responses would simply be incomplete responses.' (Thus, in such a state of affairs, until we knew everything about the mind and its workings, we could never make any statements about our feelings or ideas: we should in fact be reduced to the state of rats in a behaviourist cage.) 'Such a language is manifestly impossible.' And Skinner goes on to explain that language could not contain the amount of detail *plus* the amount of correspondence to fact necessary for his 'ideal'. It is clear that such a language would (in any rational and non-logical account of things) be far from ideal.[12] If the vocabulary for colour confined itself to the seven colours of the Western spectrum, for instance, since direct factual correspondence would have to exist between each word and each colour, then how could one ever speak of intermediate shades? Speech would become impossible.

But it is not perhaps generally realized that thought would become impossible too. R. B. Braithwaite, writing on *Scientific Explanation*,[13] is very clear about this:

It is only in theories which are not intended to have any function except that of systematizing empirical generalizations
already known that the theoretical terms can harmlessly be
explicitly defined. A theory which it is hoped may be expanded
in the future to explain more generalizations than it was
originally designed to explain must allow more freedom to its
theoretical terms than would be given them were they to be
logical constructions out of observable entities.[14]

And Hermann Bondi writes:

. . . take Newton's second law of dynamics—that the rate of
change of a body equals the force applied. It is a perfectly precise statement, but it leaves it entirely open to you to put in
under the heading of 'force' any force so far discovered. And if
you find some new kind of force there is no reason why you
should not put that in . . . More than that, I regard it as an
essential of any scientific theory to have room for putting in
what one does not know yet . . . *It is an essential part of science
that you should be able to describe matters in a way where you
can say something without knowing everything.*

And he adds that, according to a well-known story, opponents of Newton
complained that it was ridiculous to propose a theory of gravitation
when next to nothing was known about the interior of the Earth.[15]

The moral is clear: if we had to wait until we knew everything
about a topic before we could make any statements about it, then we
should never be able to say—or think—anything at all! And as for
the Behaviourist school of thought, it is clear that if writers like
Carnap and Skinner regard their hypothetical logical languages as
reflecting a scientific ideal, this simply proves that their view of
science is mistaken.

In an interesting extended parallel he draws between thought and
quantum processes, David Bohm suggests that the two are alike 'in
that they cannot be analyzed too much in terms of distinct elements,
because the 'intrinsic' nature of each element is not a property arising
separately from and independently of other elements, but is, instead, a property that arises partially from its relation with other
elements.'[16] This is exactly like language.

Bohm goes on to distinguish two kinds of thought process, the
'general' or more usual kind, and the logical process. In classical
physics, separable and determinate elements are defined; similarly
with logic. This capacity for close definition and for separability is of
course invaluable for certain thought processes. However, in the
more usual type of thought, 'the component ideas are not separate,

but flow steadily and indivisibly. An attempt to analyse them into separate parts destroys or changes their meanings.'

Bohm then compares new ideas, like Archimedes' famous discovery in the bath, to a quantum jump, and speculates, with Bohr and Bondi, whether the brain may not, at certain key points, function at the quantum level, that is at a level where the laws of classical causality break down. He thinks the parallel between quantum systems and thought processes is at any rate too close and too striking for this possibility to be rejected out of hand.[17] Could further intuitive evidence not be found for this? Bohm suggests that when we try to visualize a moving object, our 'picture'[18] of it is hazy, like that of a motion photograph of a racing car, its edges blurred, so that an impression of movement is given. If we try to visualize the boundaries of the car distinctly, we can do so; but at the cost of visualizing it statically, and being unable to 'grasp' its motion. This, he suggests, is exactly like the situation in quantum mechanics, where an exact position and an exact momentum cannot be simultaneously determined. Does the mind grasp at least some phenomena in a quantum-physical way? It is perhaps upon this characteristic of perception that our assent to Zeno's paradox of the arrow rests. It will be recalled that Zeno questioned the reality of the arrow's motion on the following grounds: that at any point on the arrow's trajectory, the arrow itself has a determinate position. How then does it get from one determinate position to the next? This puzzle would indeed not be a puzzle at all, if it were not that the mind finds it difficult to imagine both a determinate position and movement at the same time. I am inclined to agree with Bohm about this. The only way of confirming it, of course, is to ask for each individual's subjective impression. But it is at least a very pretty piece of speculation.[19]

As for the brain perhaps functioning at key points according to quantum principles, it is clear that vision may be triggered by two or three quanta, as when we watch a distant star. And Firsoff argues that 'the forces, waves or particles that trigger off nerve synapses in the brain are of the right order of magnitude for quantum mechanics to apply, and so the result is unpredictable within the limits of Heisenberg's principle'.[20]

The consequences of these speculations are startling: they suggest that the basic indeterminacy of the subatomic universe (what Reichenbach neatly calls *interphenomena*) is reflected in the mind, as and of its very nature. And if there is no good reason for attributing sharply outlined, geometrical or blocklike qualities to thought, there can be no good reason for attributing them to language either.

Thus, insofar as language is a materialization, ordering and reproduction of thought, it will be inappropriate to attribute absolute determinacy to language. Determinate languages can be invented, and are so invented by logicians. But natural language is determinate only to some extent, and indeterminate to some extent. This ought to be so, if it is to represent either thought or the ultimate constituents of matter accurately. Indeed, this is language's great strength: if Archimedes' lever, with which he proposed to move the world, were not to *give* a little, it would *snap*.[21]

One good thing might however be said about Skinner's ideal language: such a language might (if we could understand it—which clearly we could not) impress us by its precision about a *particular* house, a *particular* experience. For it would contain an amazing amount of factual detail, and would 'evoke' the house with singular clarity! If by 'ideal language' we mean the language that comes closest to, and most accurately depicts, experience, then Skinner's language, frozen into the rigidity of absolute logical correspondence, is not our ideal language. I hope, in good time, to show that the language of poetry is our ideal language.

At least one of the reasons why this is all worth saying, is that there is currently a movement in linguistics which seeks to analyze the meanings of words into elements. Thus *boy* will be analyzed into 'animate-human-male-not adult'; *woman* into 'animate-human-female-adult' and so forth. There is nothing wrong with this; and indeed it would be strange of me to object, for these elements of the meaning of *boy* and *woman* are clearly (in my terms) criterial connotations of the concepts in question. Moreover some of the conclusions we might draw from such analysis of our concepts may well turn out to be very interesting. Manfred Bierwisch gives the example of looking at expressions such as 'the price is high', for the light they might cast on human perception and psychology.[22] And in conversation with me, Paul van Buren gave the instance of his explaining 'blunt' to his small son as meaning 'not sharp'. He then thought to himself: 'But that's odd: I wouldn't have explained "sharp" as meaning "not blunt".' And he drew the very fair deduction that it is the nature of our perceptions that control our attitude to, and our conception of, such terms.

A word of caution is, however, in order here. Some at least of these writers seem to be in danger of making claims for componential analysis[23] that resemble those of Wittgenstein. I want firmly to contradict the suggestion that all meanings could ultimately be reduced to a clearly determined and finite set of factors.

If *woman* for instance is defined as 'animate-human-female-adult', then these components are certainly not themselves atomic. For there are in turn criteria for being 'female', and these criteria are the possession of whatever sexual characteristics happen to be primary in the case of the animal in question. These vary of course between animals: fish have ovaries, mammals have ovaries *and* wombs, and so on. The criteria vary as between one group of animals and another. The connotation 'female' is therefore not itself atomic, for it can be analyzed, and moreover it has a different content in different cases.[24] But we cannot stop even here: there are in turn criteria for applying 'womb' or 'ovary', and in turn criteria for applying those criteria, and so on. We seem to be involved in an infinite regress, and it is difficult to see how 'atoms' of meaning could ever be arrived at. We should at the very least ask componential analysts to produce some plausible answer to this point before assenting to their theory.

Could this conclusion be avoided if we eliminate the different contents of 'female' in different cases, by defining it in as general a way as possible? We could for instance say that the criteria of being female are 'to belong to the offspring-bearing sex', as one of my dictionaries puts it. Very well. But we then require criteria for 'offspring', criteria for 'bearing', criteria for 'sex', and criteria in turn for these criteria. I do not think the difficulty can be avoided in this way.

A further problem is that some of the criteria are themselves distinctly fuzzy at the edges. The criteria of 'human' for instance, include 'having two arms', 'having two legs' and 'having a certain shape'. But what exactly is this shape? It is incapable of precise definition, as Mill himself asserted: '. . . it is clear that the word man, besides animal life and rationality, connotes also a certain external form; but it would be impossible to say precisely what form; that is, to decide how great a deviation from the form ordinarily found in the beings whom we are accustomed to call men, would suffice in a newly-discovered race to make us refuse them the name of man.'[25] And Leech writes: 'Perhaps a picture of the animal [wolf] would come closest to the spirit of representing the single atomic feature "species".'[26] Certainly. But what is atomic about a picture? The example only proves the vagueness and multifariousness of the criteria involved in judging an animal's shape, and the impracticability of reducing it to words.

While talking of multifariousness, an explanation of meanings based on a finite number of atomic components would no doubt be powerless to explain our immediate understanding and rejection of phrases like: 'The elephants have eighty legs'; 'Elephants have horns'; 'Some elephants talk sensibly'. Leech discusses these phrases, and comes to the conclusion that to analyze the meaning of *elephant* fully would involve us in listing an indefinite (I should say 'perhaps infinite') number of connotations. This he naturally rejects as impracticable and points again to the direct connexion between our understanding of meanings and our encyclopaedic knowledge of the world.[27] Similarly Bolinger notes the same problem, *via* these examples: '*He walked right through the bachelor* is anomalous because a bachelor is (Solid). *He broke the bachelor in two* is anomalous because a bachelor is (Pliable). *He welded the bachelor* is anomalous because a bachelor is (Organic) . . . If we are to account for the fluent speaker's ability to recognize an anomaly . . ., then the number [of connotations] is indeed legion . . .' And he proposes that a natural language is not so much like a dictionary as a thesaurus, where each semantic marker (or connotation, in my terms) would appear only once, and each sense of a lexical item would appear as a particular path linking marker to marker.[28]

We see then that a finite number of atomic elements of meaning cannot be arrived at. For (1) each atom can be further analyzed, and each analysis analyzed in its turn; (2) some of the atoms are themselves capable of only vague definition; (3) even if one managed to restrict the number of criterial connotations, one would need to give a vast list of non-criterial connotations, whose number would be equal to our knowledge of the world.[29]

This conclusion agrees rather well with that of Cohen and Margalit, who look at componential analysis in the light of metaphor, and argue that language has an infinite potential for new metaphor, just as it has an infinite potential for new sentences. Their argument runs something like this. Assume that we can describe the connotations of the words of a sentence, and on this basis predict the meaning of the sentence as a whole. Then, if metaphorical meanings occur in a sentence, these must have already been described among the connotations. But it is a truism that the most striking metaphors have never been used before, and produce an entirely new effect. Prediction of such meanings is therefore impossible, and componential analysis is powerless to explain metaphor.[30]

As Beardsley wrote some years ago, 'suppose we take the modifier from the metaphor 'rubber questions' (E. E. Cummings) and combine it with a variety of nouns: 'rubber cube roots', 'rubber melody', 'rubber joy', 'rubber garden', 'rubber cliffs', 'rubber hopes'. Some of these are certainly nonsense; in others, the combination yields a strange new meaning because the subject singles out for attention a hitherto unnoticed connotation of the modifier.'[31] In this context let us recall the splendid title of a Beatles record 'Rubber Soul'. It is true that we can assist the comprehension of 'rubber hopes' for instance by explaining that rubber is elastic, that it bounces back, and that it does so immediately, and by adding that it has also a certain softness. We might say, then, that rubber hopes are hopes that cannot be damped down, but which have no hardness or violence about them, none of the tenseness of a desperate hope. But is this more than a pointer to what the phrase's meaning might be, is it more than a signpost assisting our understanding, but not taking us the whole way? Certainly the linkage of 'rubber' with 'hopes' is new, and the combination may well be felt to have a certain quality of its own, which paraphrase cannot exhaust. We meet a fundamental haziness, linked paradoxically to a feeling that these hopes have been described with unusual precision. I wonder if we may not see this effect as language's capacity to reflect reality, to evoke for us that fundamental haziness of the worldstuff which I mentioned above.

It might be said that though we may not be able to define *the* effect of a poetic metaphor, the *sort* of effect it has might be predicted. The explanation of 'rubber hopes' depends on the interlocking of certain fairly obvious features of both rubber and hopes. Cohen and Margalit's case is supported, however, by the many extraordinary metaphors we continually find in language. We do not even have to comb literature for such metaphors; their case is made even more convincing by the fact that ordinary discourse is full of such metaphors, whose meaning could surely never have been predicted in advance. Take Dwight Bolinger's analysis of the meanings of 'soup' for instance. Who could have predicted from the basic senses of 'soup' that 'in the soup' could (on the analogy of a missionary in a cannibal's cooking-pot) have come to mean 'in a hopeless predicament'?[32] Any language contains a mass of idioms ('over the moon', 'dog's-leg', 'apple-pie order', 'raise the roof', 'ride the tiger', 'cry wolf', 'pull rank') of which it might convincingly be asked: 'In what possible dictionary of connotations could their meanings possibly have been foreseen?' Cohen and Margalit are almost certainly right.

But even in cases where prediction might seem possible in broad terms, any exactness of prediction is often quite out of the question, and we are taken beyond verbal analysis to the point where we have to match our experiences of the world against each other. Take for instance the Robert Lowell phrase 'yellow dinosaur steamshovels'. We can fairly readily see that dinosaurs and steamshovels have in common a set of large teeth, a long 'neck', a particular motion of the neck as it snatches at objects on the ground, a gnashing motion of the teeth, and so on. But all this is simply too abstract and general. We have to bear both dinosaurs and steamshovels in mind, superimposed as it were upon each other, to be able to see exactly what the comparison consists of. And then the motion of the dinosaur's neck and of the steamshovel's shafts give a precision to each other which is quite beyond verbal description. We are in fact not drawing on verbal data, but upon elements of our experience, when we interpret this metaphor—elements of our experience such as our having seen a picture of *tyrannosaurus rex*, for instance, in a book on prehistory. As Cohen and Margalit say, 'When a child learns the meanings of sentences in his native language, or a linguist those of sentences in a foreign language, he acquires an ability that no mere paraphrase-machine ever possesses—viz an ability to match sentences with appropriate circumstances.'[33] And in doing so he draws upon elements from his total experience of the world.

With a metaphor like this, then, the elements of meaning do not reduce to interchangeable components ('long', 'neck', 'teeth'), but are rather used in combination to evoke irreducible fragments of experience, which cannot be substituted for each other like counters in a game of ludo. If writers wish to call these irreducible fragments 'atoms', well and good. But it must then be accepted that there are as many such 'atoms' as there are 'atoms of experience'[34] in the human brain; and it must also be accepted that the 'atoms' themselves are incapable of clear definition.

Componential analysts may well have foreseen some of these objections: Fodor and Katz's intention to decompose meaning is carefully confined to single senses of single words; and Edward H. Bendix accepts that semantic indeterminacy is widespread.[35] And those philosophers who follow the later Wittgenstein admit an inherent vagueness in language. We should welcome this. It is vital that a word should, on occasion, be able to conjure up, like a rabbit out of a hat, an entirely unforeseen sense. For just as Chomsky reminds us that we can understand sentences we have never heard before, so sentences we have never heard before may make us understand something we have never understood before.

In this chapter, then, we have seen that (1) the worldstuff is ultimately hazy. It cannot be totally analyzed beyond a certain point, and deterministic accounts of it are inexact. (2) Scientific thought has to be flexible and leave room for the unknown and the un-expected. If the content of a scientific concept were totally deter-mined, we should on the one hand have to know everything about that concept's application before we invented it—which is im-possible—and on the other hand this would leave no room for the concept's extension to other cases. (3) Thought processes themselves appear to share the haziness and unanalyzability of quantum pheno-mena; and we cannot rule out of court the possibility that this may be because they *are*, in part, quantum phenomena. (4) Language shares this haziness. But, in any case, if it is to do its job properly it must be able to reflect the haziness that mind and matter both possess as of their very nature. (5) Room must be left for the unexpected to be thought or said—just as room is left for the unpredictable quantum jump in atomic physics.

Therefore, simple solutions of the problem of meaning will not do. The structure of every concept is different from that of every other: its content varies from person to person; its extension and intension are both indeterminate; and indeterminacy is a necessary feature of language, to be welcomed moreover because it reflects both the outer world of facts and the inner world of thoughts. Any philosophical or linguistic doctrine which tends to conceal these facts is grossly misleading, and betrays truth in the name of that delusive idol, certainty. As a recent writer puts it:

'If the world in which we live were characterized only by a finite number of features, and these together with all the modes in which they could combine were known to us, then provision could be made in advance for every possibility. We could make rules, the application of which to particular cases never called for a further choice. Everything could be known, and for every-thing, since it could be known, something could be done and specified in advance by rule. This would be a world fit for "mechanical" jurisprudence.' It would also be a world fit for mechanical linguistics. But 'plainly, this world is not our world.'[36]

Plainly, also, such a language is not our language. It is for this reason that we should insist again that the attention of philosophers should be levelled on literary language, where simple answers and rigid formulae can rapidly be seen to be delusions. For there we may see how writers set about saying what had never hitherto been said: we may see how room is made for the unexpected.

The Status of the Referent

It is the capacity of making mistakes which is the mark of the higher stages of intelligence.   (Price, 87)

Sign-cognition is cognition of the absent.   (Price, 95)

LET US NOW TURN to the referent. This, says Gustaf Stern,[1] 'may be concrete or abstract, actually existing or imaginary; in short, anything that is capable of being made the topic of . . . thought and speech.' In a way, this formulation may seem surprising. For, though it is crystal clear that when we say, 'Give me half a pound of butter, please,' there is a referent 'butter', that is an actual existent pat of butter in the outside world, it is perhaps not immediately obvious that a referent is involved at all in sentences like, 'He was talking about beauty.' For 'beauty' (*pace* Plato) exists nowhere in heaven or earth, although the word exists in dictionaries, and the concept exists (in shockingly vague fashion) inside our heads. Why do we need more, then, than an amputated diagram to represent the meaning of such terms (figure 7)? However, when one speaks of relativity,

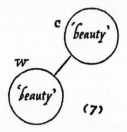

(7)

for instance, 'the concept "relativity" is the speaker's subjective apprehension of relativity; and it is clear that such apprehension will vary widely for different individuals, as well as for the same individual on different occasions. But the trans-subjective concept of relativity remains untouched by these variations.'[2] Thus, my own apprehension of 'relativity' is extremely general, partial and sketchy, though perhaps accurate in its broad lines (for I do not possess the necessary mathematical knowledge, etc.); thus also a student of the subject gradually comes to a better understanding of it: his concept of relativity comes to approximate more and more to Einstein's original definition of it.

But Stern's 'trans-subjective concept' is confusing. It suggests a kind of highest common factor between the concepts of different individuals. But this, whatever might be said about words like 'beauty', is not helpful in the case of 'Einsteinian relativity', about which it may plausibly be said that Professor Bondi, say, knows more than I do. Besides, the highest common factor of a number of different people's concepts would remain merely conceptual. I think, in fact, Stern has got it wrong. The question we need to ask is the apparently unphilosophical one, 'What "is" relativity?'

What indeed? Can it be said to 'exist'? And indeed it does not exist in the sense that cats, dogs, hula hoops and the moon exist, though perhaps it may be said to 'happen', and we could identify it with a relationship: it is a relationship seen or rather deduced between certain facts in the outside world. It thus relates to reality (though not simply or directly), as indeed do other abstractions like 'purchasing power', 'gravity', 'misapprehension', etc. We could schematize this indirect relationship as follows (figure 8).

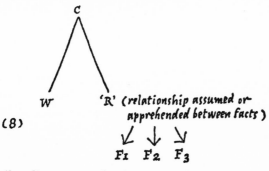

A similar diagram results from considering more concrete cases, such as 'redness' or 'hardness'. 'Redness' we often describe as a 'quality': it is a distinguishable aspect of many different objects, those objects to which we apply the adjective 'red'. When we talk of 'redness' we are in effect referring to one aspect of a number of things, that is, to the colour of a number of objects. We have therefore the following very similar schema (figure 9). For the actual objects of reference are the same with a phrase like 'the redness of apples' as with 'all red apples'. 'Redness' is an abstract noun; 'red' is an adjective; but these categories are purely verbal and conceptual; they are merely different ways that language has of representing an identical reality.

People have been confused about abstract nouns ever since they were first discussed by the Greeks. And indeed it must be admitted that they are confusing. Looked at naïvely, the structure of language seems to suggest that nouns stand for objects, adjectives for qualities, verbs for actions, adverbs for ways of acting, and so on. It is however philosophers who have been confused, and not linguists, who are aware that abstract nouns are treated by language in a different way from concrete nouns. 'I saw beauty' is not a normal sentence; in 'I saw the beauty' the referent is interpreted as an actual woman, not as a Platonic form floating down the road; and 'I met murder on my way, He had a mask like Castlereagh' is well understood to involve a figurative use of 'murder'.

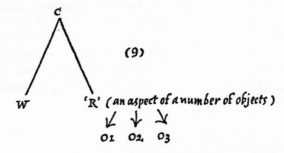

Abstract nouns, however, are very useful to us: their existence contributes greatly to the flexibility of the language. They enable us to talk of 'the beauty of the town', not just of 'the town being beautiful'; to be able to nominalize it no doubt allows us to put it in many more relationships to other parts of speech. How useful it would be in real life if we could attach a wall to a colour, and not just a colour to a wall! This is an instance of a fairly general rule: that many of our referents can be talked about in a number of different ways. For example, 'motion' can be treated substantivally or verbally: 'The *motion* of the car was rapid' or 'The car *moved* rapidly'. The event being referred to is one and the same; it is merely the linguistic treatment (and perhaps the conceptual content) that is different. The relationship we call 'distance' can be treated adjectivally, substantivally, adverbially and prepositionally: 'The *distance* from Dover to Calais' (substantival), 'Calais is not far *distant* from Dover' (adjectival), 'From Dover, Calais can be seen *in the distance*' (adverbial), 'I travelled *from* Dover *to* Calais' (prepositional). But in all these cases, the italicized words refer to the same referent, that is, to the same arrangement of objects.

It will be seen from this that the definition of referent I am using here is wider than usual. I mean by it 'any referred-to object, arrangement of objects, event, or aspect of an object or an event'.

Referent and predicate are frequently distinguished: the referent is 'What one is talking about'; the predicate is 'What one is saying about it/him/her'. Thus, in 'The boy is running', 'The boy' would be the referent, and 'is running' the predicate. But in my terms, the whole sentence has reference to a given situation in the outer world, and this situation can be divided into two referents: (A) 'The boy' and (B) 'is running'. When I use this sentence, I am referring to both A and B, but also of course ascribing B to A. I am not of course denying the usefulness of the term 'predicate'; I merely need a single term (referent) to stand for all those objects and events in the external world that are being referred to, no matter what the grammatical form of that reference may be.

As for the reality of referents like my dog (supposing I have one) or the steak I am going to eat for dinner tonight (supposing it is not a kipper) it might be thought there was no problem. They exist and there's an end of it! But of course this is a philosophers' favourite stamping-ground; and indeed I think the philosophers are right to concern themselves. When Morris talks, for instance, of the existence of the referent 'as referred to', what on earth does he mean? (see ch. 1, p. 19 above) Can one establish how it is being referred to and whether it exists in just that way? It is not at all certain that the referent exists 'as referred to' by the concept; for the concept is just our picture[3] of the referent. And does our picture of the referent ever reproduce the referent *exactly*? Take, for example, Wittgenstein's famous puzzle as to whether the fact of the cat sitting on the mat is represented identically by the two statements 'The cat is on the mat' and (in a hypothetical language) 'Catamat'.[4]

It is perhaps better to take an actual example from two actual languages, and for this purpose let me quote John Lyons considering the deliberately banal example of 'The cat sat on the mat' and its French equivalent.

> There is a problem straightaway with *sat*. Is the sentence being used to express the fact that the cat was in a certain position (*être assis*) or that it took up a certain position (*s'asseoir*)? Here, as elsewhere, French grammaticalizes a distinction that English does not . . . But these differences between the two languages are matters of grammar rather than vocabulary. How do we translate *the cat*? As *le chat*, knowing that the animal being referred to was male or being ignorant of or unconcerned with its sex? Or as *la chatte* knowing that it was female? The fact that French will use *chatte* in reference to a female cat, known to be female, whereas English will not necessarily use a

phrase like *tabby cat* in the same circumstances means that the distinction between *cat, tom cat* and *tabby cat* does not match the distinction drawn between *chat* and *chatte* in French.[5]

The same cat is thus conceived of differently by the speakers of the two languages. More is left out of the English utterance. And we may use this example to show that when we refer, *our reference is always incomplete*. 'But wait a minute,' you will say: 'you haven't shown that at all: you've merely shown that in this instance the English reference is incomplete compared with the French.' True. But consider the implications. Suppose that the cat is in fact female. 'Cat' in English leaves out the cat's sex. Its reference is therefore incomplete. But 'chatte' in French, though more complete in this respect, equally leaves out other aspects of the cat, such as its colour. And if we could have a language that built into its grammar a description of the cat's colour, then shades of that colour would be indeterminate, and other aspects of the cat would still be missing. For there is no end, as we shall see Waismann asserting in chapter 11, to the possibilities of further describing an empirical object. Moreover, we can never *know* everything about a referent: we have always the possibility of learning more about it, just as we have always the possibility of saying more about it. We may therefore enunciate the law: 'Our concept of the referent, our reference to the referent, is always incomplete.'

Here we have a paradox: we may also say: 'Our concept of the referent, our reference to it, is always *complete*.' For when we talk of the cat sitting on the mat, we are always merely referring to it *as* we are referring to it. It is only those aspects of the referent that we are referring to that constitute the referent in any given case. When I say simply 'The cat sat on the mat', I am not referring to the cat as being male or female, black or tabby; these things are irrelevant to my concerns.

Even if this is not granted, even if it is claimed that when I say 'cat', all the other things I might say or think about it are implied, it still remains the case that these are merely what *I* (or another human being) might say or think. My conceptions of the world are limited in principle by my human nature, and in practice by what I know and believe about the world at any given time. As Russell lucidly puts it:

When I say that something is 'undeniable', I mean that it is not the sort of thing that anybody is going to deny; it does not follow from that that it is true, though it does follow that we shall all think it true—and that is as near the truth as we seem able to get . . . You are [never] concerned simply with the question what is true of the world, but 'What can I know of the world?'[6]

It would seem that only some form of the coherence theory of truth is viable. We may think our conceptions correspond to the real facts, but we can never be certain because the latter are, as far as we are concerned, merely our conception of those facts. The best we can do is to establish as much coherence as we can between data and data, and between data and theory.

Grave dangers undeniably ensue. We are all acquainted with people who have an extremely dogmatic view of life, even with scientists who have an extremely dogmatic view of science. These people have achieved the most absolute coherence between their theories and their conception of the facts. But they do so by defining all facts in precisely the way *they* wish them to be defined, and in no other way. For the behaviourist, a thought, or the appearance of a thought, is always to be explained away, because it does not fit with principle. For the Calvinist Wringhim, even the clear evidence that Gil-Martin is diabolic can be explained in some other way, because to think that his wishes and those of the devil might coincide would contradict his picture of himself and the world. But this in itself suggests a way out of the vicious circle: for we may say of such people that they are extraordinarily good at overlooking incoherences in their world-picture. 'If I can't fit it in, I won't accept it; if it doesn't suit me, it isn't there.'

Let us therefore resolve the problem of whether we can know truth through the *correspondence* of what we think to the world, or by the *coherence* of what we think, as follows. We are indeed caught in a hall of mirrors: facts to us are always, and will always remain, nothing but what we *know* of these facts. We shall never escape into the sunlit fairground of reality, and even if we did, how should we know it? For we should then have to know that we were right, whereas it is human only to know when we are wrong. The best we can do is to seek correspondence whilst only achieving coherence. All is still well however if our coherence remains incomplete. For then we shall not be deluded into thinking that we know . . . and we shall have continually to amend our views. In science itself the situation is identical:

> Scientific discovery is like the fitting together of the pieces of a great jigsaw puzzle; a revolution of science does not mean that the pieces already arranged and interlocked have to be dispersed; it means that in fitting on fresh pieces we have had to

revise our impression of what the puzzle-picture is going to be like. One day you ask the scientist how he is getting on; he replies, 'Finely. I have very nearly finished this piece of blue sky.' Another day you ask how the sky is progressing and are told, 'I have added a lot more, but it was sea, not sky; there's a boat floating on top of it.' Perhaps next time it will have turned out to be a parasol upside down; but our friend is still enthusiastically delighted with the progress he is making . . . These revolutions of thought as to the final picture do not cause the scientist to lose faith in his handiwork, for he is aware that the completed portion is growing steadily.[7]

We proceed therefore by building on the ruins of our old coherences. Or, to improve the metaphor, the boat of knowledge is a leaky old tub—fortunately so, for the water that seeps into it is the seawater of reality—or so it is healthy to assume—till there comes a point when we cease to bail and patch, decide the leaks are incurable, and redesign our boat.

It is not surprising then that there are some who say that a referent is always a hypothesis.[8] But you do not even have to agree with me about this. All that is necessary is that you should admit, with J. L. Austin, that a certain *roughness* customarily enters into our concepts. Take for instance his favourite examples of our galaxy being shaped like a fried egg, or France being shaped like a hexagon. '. . . Is it true or false? Well, if you like, up to a point . . . It is good enough for a top-ranking general, perhaps, but not for a geographer.' And he adds that if someone insists on asking 'Is it true or is it false?' the only right and final answer is that 'It is just rough.'[9]

What I have been saying corresponds instructively to the two wings of my paradox. Though our concepts refer only to what we intend them to refer to, it is reality that we normally aim at describing. We thus only refer to certain presumed elements of that reality, but we ought always to be aware that there is more to a fact than what we have just presumed of it. And it can be a function of language to refer, precisely, to elements of reality which are not normally mentioned or even envisaged. We can stretch language to make it perform this task for us; and in saying this I am both underlining one of the conclusions of the last chapter and looking forward to the conclusions of later chapters.

As for determining the real existence of our referents, whatever its ease or its difficulties, this is a question that can only be answered by searching outside language itself. And of course some of our referents cannot be found in the actual world at all. If someone uses the sentence 'The King of France is bald', when in fact there is no King of France, could his statement be called meaningful? What happens to the formula of meaning when the referent does not in fact exist? Negative sentences can give us a clue here. 'There is at present no King of France, bald-headed or otherwise' is a true statement, but equally certainly it points to the same non-existent referent, 'the King of France'. Yet no one has ever tried to say that such a sentence is meaningless. (The reason is that people have usually tied reference to a truth/falsity value. But it may be illuminating to tackle the question another way.)

It is not therefore the *non-existence* of the referent *as such* which destroys meaning in a sentence. Also, it would seem odd to claim that 'The King of France is bald' is meaningless, when we can perfectly well understand it, know what it implies, and determine for ourselves whether there is such a king or not. This is exactly the same situation as an eighteenth century chemist talking about phlogiston. The 'existence' of phlogiston was a hypothesis (albeit a false one) founded on logical relationships. Everyone knew to what the chemist was alluding: they knew in what direction to look for the proof or disproof of the hypothesis. This clearly shows what the formula of meaning achieves with respect to referents: it 'points' to them, and does so clearly enough, even if, after considerable straining of the eyes, we fail to see anything in that direction. The linguistic situation is thus as follows (figure 10). That is, the relation-

(10)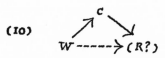

ship C–R is an element in meaning even if R itself does not exist. Or, to phrase it differently, the function of a statement is to make us look in the required direction. Importantly enough, we always know in such cases what would be the case *were* there an existent referent. Just as one can point with one's finger without there being anything in that direction, so one can use language to point in the direction of something non-existent. Similarly, one can take a taxi to the station and find the train has gone. And by the way, does the absence of the train mean that there was no taxi either? Of course not. Therefore, making a statement about something that doesn't (as a matter of fact) exist, is not meaningless, at least in the terms by which I define meaning: for all the relationships of the formula of meaning are fulfilled. Only the extra-linguistic criterion of verifiable truth is not.

I may seem here to have been toiling portentously over the most self-evident of commonplaces. As a matter of fact, this question or something like it has been similarly toiled over by numerous philosophers.[10] But that is hardly the point. My excuses for raising it are two: (1) It is necessary to clearly establish that language points to a referent even when that referent does not in fact exist. (2) There is at least one interesting fact to be elicited from this discussion: that our estimate of the truth or otherwise of the referent affects our understanding of it: in other words, it affects the connotations and sense of our concept of that referent. Let me now demonstrate this.

In practice, when we hear the sentence 'The King of France is bald', how do we deal with it? We interpret it. Since the phrase cannot be taken as both literal and true, we would not in practice, in any *actual* linguistic context, simply dismiss it as 'nonsense'. We should attempt to see what the speaker means by it. (And it is clear that he must normally mean something by it, even if he is himself using it to say 'Nonsense!' If I said for instance, 'Hitler was a Jew,' and if he replied, 'Yes, and the King of France is bald,' then he would evidently be saying to me: 'You're talking nonsense.')[11]

Different contexts would suggest different interpretations: (1) If the speaker is a royalist, we can assume that he is referring to the current pretender to the French throne. (2) If we may assume that by 'King of France', the speaker means the President of that country, then he is using a metaphor (as *Le Canard Enchaîné* did of de Gaulle) which may perhaps imply his belief that the President behaves like an absolute monarch. (3) If the speaker is for instance a child mistakenly identifying the bald man he sees in procession down the Champs-Elysées as the King instead of the President, then we may suppose that he attributes the same functions to this bald pate as he does to a crowned head. (4) If the sentence 'The King of France is bald' is part of a fiction, then sentence and fiction relate to reality in various indirect ways which will be briefly suggested in my next chapter.

It will however be apparent that in all these cases the relationship between word, concept and referent is complete. In each case the connotations, and therefore the particular sense, of 'The King of France' is different. Meaning in ordinary speech is thus not dependent merely on the 'truth' of a statement (interpreted in the flattest and most unimaginative way). The moment we see that a referent does not in fact exist quite as its literal interpretation would demand, then we try out different interpretations on it. Thus, the meaning of a sentence is never destroyed by the non-existence or absurdity of the references it contains: that meaning is not *erased*, it is *altered*. And this is in fact the means by which meanings which are more than ordinarily detailed or subtle can be presented to us: by preventing us from interpreting a phrase in the usual way, our interlocutor forces us to seek out an unusual interpretation. It is, in short, when the link between concept and referent is broken, that we are forced to re-establish it in different terms. The failure of the literal installs not less understanding, but more. For any of the above interpretations are more enlightening about our interlocutor's thoughts and attitudes than any purely ordinary statement of his would have been.

Even if the only interpretation that can be put upon a sentence is that 'It's sheer hair-brained fantasy,' this may still be useful to our imaginations, may still 'exercise' our minds, as we so aptly say. One may even ask: 'If one were incapable of understanding a fiction, how could one understand *anything*?' As Chomsky rightly (and so often) remarks, one of the most remarkable features of language is our ability to understand sentences we have never met before.[12] This ability must be intimately connected with our ability to visualize hitherto unknown objects. For it must be possible (as it in fact was) for a traveller from Australia to return with the bizarre news that he had seen *black swans*. His hearers' reaction to this might have been: 'Nonsense, there's no such thing!' but they must at least have been able to understand his statement, which involved the putting together (in a relation that might just as well, for all they knew to the contrary, have been *fictional*) of features which are not normally associated. This shows that it is an essential part of the linguistic process for us to be able to separate our concepts, and put them together in new combinations—or, if you like, imagine new objects, new experiences, new situations.

Yet of course these new objects may turn out to be fictions; and many of them (in fiction itself, for example) are patently and admittedly fictions. Indeed, how much of our normal picture of the world is fictional, rough, corresponding only more or less to the facts? What, for instance, is the status of the theory of the Expanding Universe? What is that of the Steady State Universe? To be able to comprehend science, we have to be capable of imagination. And to be capable of imagination, we have to be capable of fiction.

Fiction is not the same as nonsense. It is customary for philosophers to distinguish between verbal combinations which are unthinkable, because self-contradictory and hence nonsensical, and those which could occur, but simply (as far as our own experience goes) do not. This point can perhaps be established even more strongly by referring to the thought of a very different civilization from our own—the ancient Indians, who also differentiated 'between inconceivable combinations like "the circular square"and the conceivable combinations which are against our experience such as "the rabbit's horn". Kumārilabhaṭṭa says that incompatibility with the actual facts does not prevent verbal comprehension, but only the validity of the knowledge.'[13]

And—this cannot be underlined too heavily—it is the symbol in all its shapes and forms (and principally language, of course) that allows us to think—because we can manipulate symbols when the objects for which they stand are still absent, and so cannot themselves be manipulated—or are yet to be invented—or may never turn out to be feasible at all.

Speaking of those basic symbols of the absent or imagined which are pictures, Richard Gregory writes:

> No eyes before man's were confronted by pictures. Previously, all objects *in themselves* were important or could be safely ignored. But pictures, though trivial in themselves, mere patterns of marks, are important in showing *absent* things. Biologically this is most odd. For millions of years animals had been able to respond only to present situations and the immediate future. Pictures, and other symbols, allow responses to be directed to situations quite different from the present; and may give perceptions perhaps not even possible for the world of objects. Apart from pictures and other symbols, the senses direct and control behaviour according to the physical properties of surrounding objects—not to some other, real or imaginary, state of affairs. Perhaps man's ability to respond to absent imaginary situations in pictures represents an essential step towards the development of abstract thought. Pictures are perhaps the first step away from immediate reality; and, without this, reality cannot be deeply understood.[14]

I have no personal experience of seeing a basilisk or a roc. Nor have I any personal experience of seeing a dodo or an aye-aye. The process whereby I imagine the one, however, is exactly the same as that whereby I imagine the other. The conclusion is clear: without being able to understand the fictional and imaginary, we could never understand anything, except what was immediately present.

I say it is 'exactly the same'. In fact, the essential difference is not in our imagining these creatures, but in the different degrees of likelihood we attribute to their existence. When we imagine an aye-aye, we attribute truth-value to it; when we imagine a basilisk, we attribute falsity-value to it: rather as we can attribute a plus or a minus sign to a number, or as we can visualize the word 'man' and the same word crossed out.

Between these two extremes, of presumed truth on the one hand and presumed falsity on the other, there lie any number of degrees of 'may' and 'might be'. There are many different views for instance of the status of 'King Arthur', as a fiction, or as a more or less likely historical figure. The past is a huge patchwork of near-certitude, guesswork and doubt. The future is one vast domain of possibility and probability, not of fact or certainty. *Terra firma* is rather a small islet. To be able to cope with experience at all, we have to be capable of imagining a series of different possibilities; and the better we are at imagining them, the better (no doubt) we shall be at coping with any that come up.

This multiplicity of possible states-of-affairs is studied by the modern modal logician under the title of 'possible worlds'. Possible Worlds Logic allows for different people to view truth and possibility in different ways; for them to be able (though not always) to visualize each other's different worlds with varying degrees of accuracy; for them to know what different states-of-affairs would be like with varying degrees of clarity; for them to be able to visualize worlds containing the same objects as the real world, but standing in different relations; or with new and strange objects as well; or without some of the objects that inhabit our world. It will be clear that they are building towards an account of the way in which we view all the alternatives that surround us and the host of possibilities we can imagine.[15]

Just how basic is an account of our thinking in terms of Possible Worlds, can be guessed from the banality and everydayness of some of the examples given by contemporary linguists. They talk of such instances as 'John wants to catch a fish and [wants to] eat it,' which seems perfectly grammatical, and 'John wants to catch a fish and he'll eat it', which (they say) does not.[16] For 'will eat it' falls within a world of quasi-certainty, but the fish that John *wants* to catch belongs to a different world: one of intention and wishful thinking. The words that give us entry to possible worlds are countless: 'to dream' (as in McCawley's 'I dreamed that I poured my mother into an inkwell'), 'to think' (as in the same author's 'Harry thinks that his toothbrush is trying to kill him')[17]—or simply the ubiquitous little particle 'if' (as in 'If wishes were horses, beggars would ride'). Clearly, if such everyday terms as these are involved, possible worlds are fundamental to our thinking.

In view of what I said above about the roughness of our references to the actual world, and *a fortiori* if my other remarks about the uncertainty of their correspondence to it are accepted, it would seem best to view reference as *the intention to refer*.[18] Even when a speaker is 'certain' about the real existence of a referent, his reference to it tends to be approximate. We should think of all the possible states-of-affairs we can imagine, from nightmare and the wildest fantasy right down through our alternative futures to the actual world that now surrounds us, as being all equally a set of possible worlds, to each of which we attribute a different degree of likelihood. For, as I said above, the way in which we imagine these different possibilities (or indeed impossibilities) is in all cases much the same. I am intrigued by the suggestion of some writers that what we need is 'une sémantique sans vérité . . . Par exemple, faire comprendre quelque chose consisterait à faire croire, à faire tout en sorte qu'une situation décrite soit plausible, sans qu'elle soit nécessairement vraie.'[19] [A semantics without truth . . . For instance, to inform someone of something would amount to making him believe, doing one's best to ensure that the situation being described is plausible, without being necessarily true.]

Clearly, the more things I can 'imagine', the more connexions and consequences I am capable of having in my mind. I would say, therefore, that the ability to 'imagine' what cannot possibly be true is a *condition of our intelligence*. Were Man not capable of writing fiction, he would not be capable of understanding fact.

It is true that this capacity lays us open to the dangers of meaningless metaphysics, jejune dogma, religious and political fanaticism; but our incorrect beliefs are the price we have to pay for our correct ones. In short, the great positivist hope (Ayer's for instance) of branding all religions, philosophies, arts, moral standpoints and subjectively felt emotions as 'meaningless metaphysics' is not merely absurd: it would actually be damaging: the cure would be worse than the disease. Not that the disease is not very grave, and one which may indeed yet prove to be fatal. But the only safeguard here is in fact not to direct our minds narrowly upon a single track of truth— for who can be sure *exactly* where that is?—but to seek the greatest possible flexibility of the imagination. Fiction, drama and poetry are in short a training for the mind, an invaluable exercise in flexibility, a priming for the intelligence.

Their justification is not so much that they 'show us truth'; for truth depends not upon the word or the concept but on external fact. It is rather that they allow our minds to contemplate a mass of different possibilities, a mass of might-have-beens and very-nearly-weres. Such flexibility of mind is evidently of practical utility to us, since it allows us to speculate about alternative possibilities. Fiction *allows our minds to play*.

And there is, as with children, a distinction between useful and useless play. (Under the former heading come all games or reading or amusement where the child explores his environment and develops his mental and physical capacities.) It is, as with children, a question of exercising the mind, developing it, flexing its muscles.

But further, it is the positive *advantage* of literature that, within it, experience is removed from the realm of fact and dealt with in the realm of imagination. I do not mean this simply in the banal sense that we cannot all, nor would we wish to, go through the experiences of Phaedra or Hamlet or Dmitry Karamazov. I mean that the whole knotty and unsatisfactory question of truth is sidetracked and averted. Of a novel, we no longer ask: 'Did this actually happen like this?' For we know perfectly well that it didn't. We ask instead: 'Can we imagine it happening like this?' It is removed from the realm of corroborative evidence and placed in that of inner self-consistency.

We have at least two methods that we normally use to ascertain the truth of an event: in the first place we may depend on the reliability of the evidence and of the witnesses. This is corroboration. In the second place we may ask ourselves if the reported event is in itself plausible, if it is for example consistent with itself and with the framework of fact in which we live. This is consistency. A good instance of a clash between the two is given by the modern research on extra-sensory perception, for which, in numerous university departments throughout the world, a great deal of apparently sound statistical evidence has built up over the years. Yet the majority of scientists still refuse to accept ESP as proven. The reason is that it conflicts too radically with the known framework of the universe. We may say therefore that the evidence is good, but that the phenomenon does not fit into the scientific framework that it is expected to do—that is, at least in the eyes of conventional scientists. It is clear however that if the evidence did become good enough, even the sceptics might eventually begin to relent.[20]

In the case of novels, there is no evidence to be sought. They ask their readers not to discover the real facts about the experience they report, but to assent to the inner consistency of those events. Because of this, we can dissent from a newspaper report, but not from a great novel. For if we are presented with an experience that has been recreated imaginatively, and that rings consistently true, this may not (literally) be a fact—but it is always (psychologically) an *instance* of fact. This is the meaning of 'might have been'. The fictionality of novels is thus their great virtue: they remove one of the two tests of truth, and depend purely upon persuasion. They may thus be less easily rejected as pictures of truth than either history or journalism can.

A further advantage of art—its utility as *mental training*—could be the way it organizes *emotion* rather than (no—not knowledge, for it is also knowledge) rather than intellectual statement. Donald Hebb[21] insists that emotion is closely linked to intelligence: the higher the animal, the more emotional it is, and what would leave a spider unmoved may upset a dog, and so on up the evolutionary scale. Human beings are the most emotional of all; and adult human beings are more emotional than children. Emotional arousal is linked to the degree of attention we direct on things; and of course if the arousal gets too great the individual reaches a state of emotional disturbance. We human beings are more liable to such emotional disturbance than are chimpanzees, and they in turn than monkeys, and so on. At first sight, this seems unlikely: we mentally compare the small child's tantrum with the behaviour of the adult human being, and react with 'nonsense'. As Hebb points out, however, it is by dint of our carefully organized social systems that we control and repress the emotions that might otherwise tear us apart. Society has devised elaborate checks and balances to moderate (when at peace) the violent effects of emotion; and art, sport, thrillers, circuses (as in Ancient Rome) and so on, are the safety valves that, in a civilized society, operate to keep us from murdering one another. Indeed our civilized societies may be more civilized mainly *because* we have such sophisticated, numerous and generally available ways of amusing ourselves, catharizing our dangerous emotions.

As for actual positive evidence of the greater emotionality of the adult human being, Hebb points to the dangerous emotions of racial hatred and religious intolerance, and to the unparalleled violence of human war.[22] Unparalleled, I mean, in that the animal kingdom has no analogy for it: dog does not eat dog, as the saying goes, and apparently this is factually true: nature is red in tooth and claw only so far as the members of other species go: the defeated wolf rolls over and presents his belly to the victor . . . who then desists. Man is distinguished from animals in many ways, but also in this: that he alone destroys his own kind.

It might be argued that I am talking here of emotionality rather than emotion. But the point is that it is evidently profitable for us to learn to organize and control our emotions. There is an important consequence for art, if Hebb's picture of the interplay of intellect and emotion is correct, that is, that increased intellectual attention is associated with increased emotion, and that there is an optimum level of this increased emotion, beyond which emotional disturbance sets in. This would suggest that practice in organizing the emotions might help us to prevent them *dis*organizing the mind. In short, Hebb's remarks have a direct bearing on the validity of I. A. Richards' view, half a century ago, that poetry has a *psychological* effect, that it is of value to mental processes.[23]

I do not wish to go too far: we commonly describe as *bookish* those obsessive readers who have no experience of life, and whose living is like the French spoken by those who have never visited France: stammering, over-grammatical, and prone to the uncolloquial *faux pas*. And . . . (or rather But . . .) bookish people frequently do not understand books: I will not say that one has to commit adultery to be able to understand *Madame Bovary*, but clearly to have experienced sex as a romantic fog on the one hand and as a physical reality on the other, helps. There has to be an *interaction* between life and art (and life is the more important). And with this (actually rather small) proviso, let us leave this topic to the reader's further speculation.

Does Literature Refer?

LET US NOW TURN to yet another aspect of the referent: its relevance to literature. Here I shall make a first brief excursion into poetry. For it has sometimes been asserted that 'poetry does not refer'.

A classic statement of this point of view is Frege's:

> In hearing an epic poem, for instance, apart from the euphony of the language we are interested only in the *sense* of the sentences and the images and feelings thereby aroused. The question of truth would cause us to abandon aesthetic delight for an attitude of scientific investigation. Hence it is a matter of no concern to us whether the name 'Odysseus', for instance, has *reference*, so long as we accept the poem as a work of art.[1]

Frege's *sense* is the nearest term he uses to my 'concept', and in this context we may take it to be roughly equivalent.

Clearly the 'sense' of a work of art is important: that is, its conceptual effect. But, although it is a matter of indifference to me whether Odysseus was a historical figure or not, the poem is usually said to contain 'truths' of some kind or other. And equally clearly, this is not a matter of indifference: far from it. For if poetry is supposed to be a form of discourse which does not, *in any way*, *even indirectly*, refer to the world, what interest would there be in it? One cannot allow Frege's comment to pass, therefore, without careful investigation.

For this investigation, let us turn to the best-known recent expression of this point of view: that of Ogden and Richards. These writers make a broad distinction between what they call 'symbolic language' and 'emotive language'. For 'symbol' is defined by them, not in the usual literary or psychological way, but as a word or sign only in so far as it refers to a real existing referent. 'Symbolic language' thus refers to actual scientifically definable objects in the phenomenal world. 'The symbolic use of words is *statement*, the recording, the support, the organization and the communication of references. The emotive use of words is a more simple matter, it is the use of words to express or excite feelings and attitudes.'[2]

Thus the term 'truth' is to be kept for scientific utterances only: 'The best test of whether our use of words is essentially symbolic or emotive is the question—"Is this true or false in the ordinary strict scientific sense?" If this question is relevant then the use is symbolic; if it is clearly irrelevant then we have an emotive utterance.'[3] 'Emotive utterances' are not true or false in the ordinary scientific way; they are 'true' (in inverted commas) in a different way, that is, 'convincing, sincere, beautiful', etc. We may compare Austin[4] (This is the earlier Austin, taking a more positivistic stance than the later one): 'Words as discussed by philologists, or by lexicographers, grammarians, linguists, phoneticians, printers, critics (stylistic or textual) and so on, are not true or false: they are wrongly formed, or ambiguous or defective or untranslatable or unpronounceable or misspelled or archaistic or corrupt or what-not.'

Later we shall see that the term 'Truth' has a particular and limited sense in scientific discourse, that science cannot pretend to a monopoly of the field of truth, that statements of any kind (even scientific ones) are subject to uncertainty, and so on. However, it is true that if the language of poetry or literature in general were amputated from its referent—or rather had no referent—then its irrelevance to truth in any normal sense of human experience would be proved. Is this however the case? In actual fact, Ogden and Richards do not assert this roundly: they admit that 'some element of reference probably enters—into almost all use of words'. (p. 150) And obviously such a statement as 'All men must die', made with tedious regularity over the centuries by almost every poet one can think of, not only entails reference to fact, but is also true.

It is true of course that some poems are hardly paraphraseable into statements at all. Such a poem is Dylan Thomas's 'After the Funeral':

> After the funeral, mule praises, brays,
> Windshake of sailshaped ears, muffle-toed tap
> Tap happily of one peg in the thick
> Grave's foot, blinds down the lids, the teeth in black,
> The spittled eyes, the salt ponds in the sleeves,
> Morning smack of the spade that wakes up sleep,
> Shakes a desolate boy who slits his throat
> In the dark of the coffin and sheds dry leaves,
> That breaks one bone to light with a judgment clout,
> After the feast of tear-stuffed time and thistles
> In a room with a stuffed fox and a stale fern,
> I stand, for this memorial's sake, alone
> In the snivelling hours with dead, humped Ann
> Whose hooded, fountain heart once fell in puddles
> Round the parched worlds of Wales and drowned each sun . . .

Here, there is perhaps little in the way of statement except 'She is dead and I am grief-stricken'. (One notes as usual the absurdity of any paraphrase.) But clearly there is *reference*: reference not merely to the hideous paraphernalia of death, but to a whole world of experience. To the question 'But does the poem refer?' one can only reply 'Of course it refers: to death, to graves, to a lost friendship, to pity, to life, to a complete and drastic loss which *is* the experience in question.' The fact that it also does so by way of metaphor and rhetoric does not entail loss of reference: it entails in fact *increase* of reference. For if we use merely the single word 'death', we refer merely to death. There is no need for us to notice the details of it.

But the details built up in the first few lines of 'After the Funeral' all *converge* on the concept of 'Death': all in one way or another connote it. For instance, the 'muffle-toed tap tap' recalls a muffled drum, as in a funeral march, suggests a sinister one-legged figure, who might be death himself; one-leggedness is hinted at by the 'one peg in the thick / Grave's foot' of the next line, for we speak of a 'peg-leg'; the spade digging the grave is of course 'one-legged'; a coffin only has 'one leg'; not only is the sound of drum or spade suggested, but 'tap tap' is even more appropriate of the sound of nails going into a coffin; and so on. The skeleton of the denotation 'death' is thus dressed out in certain of its connotations: the empty shell is filled with substance. The poem thus presents us with a more than ordinary plenitude, not of logical statement, but of meaning. And this is how it seeks to recreate experience.

Later in Richards' *Principles of Literary Criticism*, he gives two special ways in which poetry may be 'true'. These are still not the scientific way—but we need not quarrel with him there: the scientific way of truth is clearly different: it is a matter of statements *about* particular causal relationships, and has nothing directly to do with emotion or with the way in which experiences occur to us. Richards gives two senses of truth in literature: acceptability and sincerity. 'The "truth" of *Robinson Crusoe*,' he tells us, 'is the acceptability of the things we are told, their acceptability in the interests of the effects of the narrative, not their correspondence with any actual facts involving Alexander Selkirk or another.'[5] This is a wholly unexceptionable statement. And the particular sense of 'truth' that he is putting forward here is a necessary condition, certainly, for our accepting a work of art as meaningful. However, he has chosen to mention only *one* of the two possible ways in which literature may correspond with outer reality, namely, that of *literal* correspondence of the characters in a novel with real live people outside it whose history it might be supposed to relate. He is not of course guilty of the fallacy of those who seek the origins of Proust characters in the details of the author's life, and then think they have explained the novel by finding them. And he is right to reject this fallacy. But in rejecting it he goes too far in the opposite direction, by leaving us with the impression that direct reference to real-life historical characters is the only form that reference can take. But because there was presumably no real King Lear, are we therefore to conclude that Shakespeare's play has nothing to say to us about reality? I. A. Richards is in fact far from believing this, of course, though unfortunately he omits to say so. He has perhaps been misled by the over-simplicity of his model of reference.

His second condition for literary truth is a necessary one too: sincerity.[6] However, this is equally internal to the work of art. And if 'truth' in a work of art is to be purely internal, this would cut it off from all relevance to the external world of fact. Such views have sometimes been put forward, most recently by the avant-garde French group *Tel Quel*. They however had a special motive for doing so. Being Marxists, yet wishing to avoid Stalinist criticisms of their art as being avant-garde and hence 'bourgeois' and politically reactionary, they seek to assert that on the contrary it has nothing to say about life or society; on the other hand, its *form*, they point out, is revolutionary and this is a kind of analogy for world revolution, particularly the continuing revolution favoured at the time by Maoists.[7]

But are *Tel Quel* right? Surely not. For what of fictitious characters like Robinson Crusoe, Satan, Moby Dick or Faust? Don't they rather resemble some abstract referents in that we can talk about them but not point them out, and I may have a different idea of Pickwick from yours?

Yet there is a 'truth' about Pickwick to know (that is, the 'facts of his life' as recounted by Dickens, and what we are to make of them). And in a way I can even be more certain of the 'facts' about Pickwick than I can ever be of the facts about Napoleon. This sounds paradoxical; yet a moment's reflection will show it to be true: many of the historical facts about Napoleon are controversial, uncertain or unknowable. But in the case of Pickwick, no 'facts' can be uncertain: they are all in Dickens' novel; and there are no other facts about him to be known. Or if this is putting it too strongly, we know all the evidence there is to know in Pickwick's case; we can never know it all in Napoleon's. Thus, just as we may talk about a referent 'relativity' (of which we may have different notions), so we can talk about a referent 'Pickwick'.

And, just like abstractions, fictions like Pickwick may themselves be taken to refer. Faust, as literary critics never tire of repeating, is Goethe's image of Man. The referent 'Faust' has of course no status in the real world: science declares him 'untrue'—'never to have existed'. But as metaphor, symbol or allegory, his story relates to certain essential and tragic elements of human experience.

There are two alternative ways of schematizing this sort of meaning. We may visualize it as in figure. 11 Here (and anticipating my remarks on metaphor in chapter 16) we see a fictional character func-

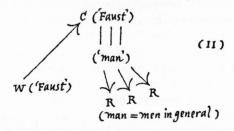

tioning rather as metaphor functions, the concept 'Faust' being superimposed on that of 'man', so that we see both in double focus: man in the guise of Faust. Certainly this seems to be the process when I am present, say, at a stage rendering of James Hogg's *Confessions of a Justified Sinner*, and am constantly aware that the bigoted Wringhim and his gay aristocratic brother are an allegory for the divided Calvinist soul; when, that is, I am constantly generalizing from the fictional hero and anti-hero to a number of real-life human beings.

But there is another way we may visualize a fictional referent (figure 12). Here, Faust is an instance of man, just as Napoleon or

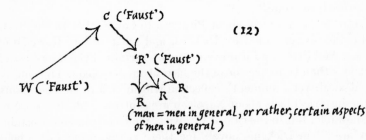

Julius Caesar can be used as instances of conquerors, or Alexander Selkirk as an instance of a castaway. But no: not quite. We might either read the true story of Alexander Selkirk as simply the true story of that individual; or we might read it for what it has to tell us of human nature; or both. But in the case of Faust, we know perfectly well there was no such person, and we may therefore be led to understand him primarily as an instance of human nature. For we are concerned, as I said in the last chapter, with the credibility and consistency (within its own often fantastic limits) of a work of fiction. If we say of it (as we often do) that it is credible, that it seems as if some almost realistic life has been recreated by the author, then it is clear that a comparative process has been at work, however dimly: that we have been checking the fictional illusion against our own factual experience, and that we can perceive a convincing degree of correspondence between them.

Of what does this correspondence consist? We are led to compare Faust's 'life' with what we know of life in general: his 'life' refers us to life. He acts as the *focus* for a number of selected details of human experience—those particular details which Goethe has chosen for us. Faust is an amalgam of those details. In this he is not very different from Alexander Selkirk, *if* we read about him for what he has to tell us of human nature. Defoe's way of *compelling* us to do so, was to turn Selkirk into a fictional character, Crusoe. For it is a sentimental error to which some readers are prone, to take *Crusoe* to be merely the exciting story of one individual, to read it merely for its excitement, and thereby (perhaps deliberately) blind themselves to any further reference the story may have to experience in general. Readers who do this are in fact *confining* the reference of Crusoe to one man and one man only, and we may say that this particular form of sentimentalism and the total rejection of reference by such thinkers as the theorists of *Tel Quel*, are both ways of confining the reference of a work of fiction, and so discounting it. Both views are a form of escapism, a way of rejecting the relevance of literature to experience.

Faust, then, is a focus for, an amalgam of, certain features of human experience. We might term him a 'constructed referent'.[8] And in this respect he is not perhaps very different from any scientific theory such as relativity, which abstracts certain features from the world of facts, and sets them in a new relationship to one another. Such terms as 'gravitation', 'relativity', 'quantum mechanics', etc., are themselves constructed referents. As we saw in the last chapter, our references point, more or less accurately, in the general direction of the intended referent. They imply that there is something around in that area that is *rather like* them, and not necessarily *absolutely like* them. We may point, but we can never be sure our aim is perfect; we may get near the bull's-eye, but the umpire is God, who will certainly not tell us our score in this world.

So let us not be too distressed by the fictionality of Faust, Crusoe and Wringhim. Their difference from the constructed referents of science (namely, that they are admittedly inventions) is not so striking as their resemblance to them (namely, that both are *rather like* the true facts). The absolute identity of the theory of relativity with truth is uncertain, though we may for the time being proceed on that assumption. But where do scientific theories go when they die? To the land of approximate truths. Every reference we use contains and will contain for ever the implicit proviso: *something like*.

At this point let me recall another conclusion of chapter 6, that it is one of literature's advantages that it removes the question of truth from the realm of correspondence to fact, and places it in that of inner self-consistency. This is certainly one sense of 'truth' for works of literature. But it will be clear that I am asserting in this chapter that a sort of indirect correspondence to fact does indeed also occur, so that there are at least two requirements for truth in literature: (1) inner self-consistency, and (2) some degree of correspondence to external reality. Not that this second requirement should be taken at face-value: mere crude realism has often less to tell us about reality than David Lindsay's *Voyage to Arcturus*. For just as a metaphor is a means of revealing hitherto unnoticed aspects of a referent, so an allegory is a means of revealing hitherto unnoticed aspects of the world in general. The requirement of 'truth to experience' must not be thought of as a precept or an ordinance to be rigidly applied like that of Socialist Realism. We should normally balk not at fantastic characters like Caliban or fantastic worlds like that of Arcturus, but at characters and worlds which do not have a density, solidity and variousness in some degree equivalent to that of the world we know. We object, that is, to characters like Hercule Poirot and worlds like those of Michael Moorcock. For the world we know is not made of one-dimensional cardboard, and we have a shrewd suspicion that even an alien planet's substitute for cardboard, exotic though it may be, is an equally unsuitable material from which to construct little green men.

Let me add in parenthesis that I am not of course objecting to 'flat' characters. As E. M. Forster (1962, pp. 75 ff.) so justly argues, there is a right and proper place for such characters in fiction. Nor must we always require 'roundedness' from even some of a book's characters. Those of *Candide* are all flat, and flat for a reason: the book has other qualities which commend it, and which demand flatness of its protagonists. And Lindsay's characters are also devoid of true personality. If, however, one manages to read past the awkward and absurd melodrama of the first chapter, one begins to see that it is in the fantastic machinery of his Arcturan world that a convincing vigour and intensity can be found. Let us not be too dogmatic, then. I am merely pointing out that the criterion of adequacy to experience is one that in practice we apply, and that this amounts to a criterion of correspondence with some aspects of the various and many-faceted real world. As R. W. Hepburn argues, this may be vouch-safed us as 'a quality of wonderment, of surmise and of openness to new possibilities that cannot, however, be fully determined or fully conceptualized'.[9] It follows that if a novelist's world is narrowly mechanical and predictable, it will not satisfy the criterion of ade-quacy. For the openness and variousness of the real world and our inability to reduce it to rigid formulas, are among its most striking characteristics.

The capacity of works of fiction to present us with dense, detailed and suggestive canvasses, albeit canvasses of the imagination, consti-tutes fiction's advantage over history or reportage. We can allow, indeed we demand, that our novelists evoke something like a full range of facts, events and human reactions, so as to give us a sense of experience. For, as I argued in chapter 6, we do not have to worry about the literal truth of what we are being told, only about its plausibility. If I read, in a popular biography of Napoleon, that 'he turned to Josephine and whispered hoarsely, "Chérie, I love you," ' I may rebel against this as mere invention, and only too tediously plausible at that. But in a novel we pass beyond the requirement of *truthfulness* to known and documented facts (which are necessarily few in number) to the demand for a *fullness of truth*—where truth is defined as adequacy. Experience contains an infinity of unrecorded detail. And in the pretence of fiction, the recorded 'facts' may be as many or as various as we like. We invent sufficient detail to give an impression of reality, sufficient detail to suggest the density of real experience. The constructed referents of fiction therefore differ from the real referents of history in that (1) the latter have to be histori-cally accurate, and can contain only what is known. But (2) when we can *construct* our referents, we can inject more reality into them.

We can solve the question whether literature refers, therefore, by defining reference more realistically. Tzvetan Todorov, for instance, points out that there are two diametrically opposed views on poetic discourse: one (Frege's) is that it does not refer; the other (Genette 1968) asserts roundly that its reference is more explicit than that of prose, that it seeks to evoke, to render the object more acutely present to the mind, and hence in a sense to refer more definitely. Todorov however does not adjudicate between these two views: he leaves them contradicting each other puzzlingly, and merely hazards the guess that different epochs have different definitions of poetry.[10]

It would be equally true to say that different poets have different definitions of poetry; that there are different types of poem; and that different forms of reference may occur within the same poem. In Dylan Thomas' poem a greater degree of reference to experience was produced *directly*, by dint of stating explicitly a mesh of connected connotations. In short, (1) a work of art may refer more fully and directly to experience than normal discourse does.

Secondly, we have considered those works of literature where there are fictional characters and worlds. Of these we may say that there is merely a surface disagreement between Frege and Genette: they are both in a sense right. For (2) clearly 'Don Quixote' never had any corresponding referent in the real world. But of course this is a naïvely superficial statement. 'Don Quixote' is a constructed referent: he refers to a set of human characteristics that are very much a part of the real world. Thus (3) fictional referents do indeed refer, though indirectly. And we must add that this indirect reference allows a writer the freedom to recreate the infinite detail of experience, and hence to refer to the real world more fully and (paradoxically) more directly than any work of fact or reportage can.

The confusion of writers such as Todorov is easily explicable. In the case of Thomas's poem, it is evident that the poem refers. The apparent counter-instance, that of a figment of Homer's or Goethe's imagination, is puzzling because it does not directly refer. The controversy is understandable; but the notion of indirect reference easily resolves it.

Amputating the Referent[1]

Peut-être devons-nous parler encore un peu plus bas,
De sorte que nos voix soient un abri pour le silence
[Perhaps we should speak still more softly
Making our voices a shelter for silence]
(Jacques Réda *La Voix dans l'intervalle*)

IT IS EXTREMELY HARD, then, not to refer to the world. Nonetheless, ingenious attempts have sometimes been made. One method is to engineer total identification of word with referent. An example of this is the well-known 'readymades' of Marcel Duchamp. He would purchase a perfectly commonplace object, such as a hat-rack or a shovel, and sign it, thereby in some sense turning it into a work of art. One way of looking at these objects would be to say that the hatrack is an image (i.e., sign) of itself (i.e., the referent). We then no longer have the normal situation (figure 13),

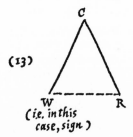

but an abnormal situation where sign and referent are telescoped (figure 14).

For it is clear that in such a case the sign and the referent are absolutely identical, the one with the other. Art's function as standing for something in the outside world is definitively short-circuited.

Another, better known, way of attempting to evade the conditions of the semiotic triangle is to make the referent of a sentence the sentence itself, as in the famous liar antinomy. It will be remembered that Epimenides, a Cretan, is supposed to have asserted: 'All Cretans are liars'. If this is taken to mean that all Cretans invariably lie all the time, then it is clear that the statement refers also to Epimenides' present statement. A still clearer case would be to assert: 'This sentence I am now pronouncing is a lie'. The sentence would then be true only if it were a lie, and a lie only if it were true — which is self-contradictory. That it is self-contradictory has usually been taken to be the puzzling thing about it. For it appears to contradict the law of Excluded Middle, that a thing cannot both be true and untrue at the same time. It will be clear however that the semantic situation in such a sentence is extremely odd, and that it is no odder than in such a sentence as 'The sentence I am now pronouncing is true,' despite the fact that in this latter case the L of E M is not infringed. Moreover it is not the same as with 'The *last* sentence I pronounced is true'; for here, the words point to other words, but they in turn presumably point outside themselves. No, our puzzlement is due to the apparent total identification of word with referent: the diagram used above would be an accurate picture of this situation too.

Some modern philosophers have wanted to eliminate such paradoxes by saying that a meaningful and well-constructed statement cannot refer to itself. Intuition would suggest that, whether or not it is 'well-constructed', such a statement is certainly meaningful; for we can understand it.[2] What is puzzling about it is not that it is meaningless. For the assertion that Epimenides' sentence is a lie is clashed against the implication of this assertion that it is true, and so on. We can perfectly well understand both statement and implication, as also the implications of that implication. Though we may not be able to conceive of an infinite regression, we can at least grasp *that* such a regression ensues.

It must be admitted that the views both of philosophy and of common sense are attractive here, and I should like to take up a position midway between them. For, if we apply the semiotic triangle to the sentence 'This sentence I am now pronouncing is a lie', we find (as I said above) that the referent is the sentence itself, *and nothing else.* The normal situation of word and concept referring outside themselves to some event, or simply some other statement, has been short-circuited. The relationship word-concept is present, and to that extent the statement has meaning. For this is one of the meanings of meaning defined in chapter 2. But to the extent that there is no referent external to the sentence itself, there is absence of meaning (for the relationship concept-referent is also an element of meaning). The statement 'This sentence I am now pronouncing is a lie' is empty of meaning to just this extent, as indeed is the twin statement 'This sentence I am now pronouncing is true'. Epimenides' original statement however is slightly different. For the reference is not only (1) to his own statement; it also, and in addition to this, refers (2) to all the other statements of all other Cretans. And though we may take this to be a rather large claim, it is at least not paradoxical. We may thus distinguish between sentences that are exclusively self-referring, and those that also refer outside themselves.

In all these cases we can readily suspect some kind of trick: we know instinctively that there has been some semantic sleight-of-hand, even though we may not always be able to see how and why. But there are more sophisticated cases than this—also less entertaining ones. Such a modern novel as Philippe Sollers' *Nombres* is, one assumes, self-referring or at least intended to be so; but this comes among the less entertaining instances of the trick, and is strictly unreadable. Indeed, it is clear that the more closely a work of art coincided with the 'ideal' situation of being totally self-referring, and the less it referred outside itself to anything except its own verbiage, the less interest of any kind it could possibly hold.[3] A more interesting case is the poetry of Stéphane Mallarmé, which according to the theorists of *Tel Quel*[4] is also an attempt to eliminate the referent.[5]

That Mallarmé was seeking in some sense to achieve this effect is suggested by some of his statements—or at least they could be interpreted this way. In the following famous dictum, for instance, he seems to be suggesting that the poet's task is to evoke the pure idea of a flower, not refer to any real flowers—to evoke, in short, the concept in the reader's mind, shorn of its relation to any referent: 'Je dis: une fleur!' he writes, 'et, hors de l'oubli où ma voix relègue aucun contour, en tant que quelque chose d'autre que les calices sus, musicalement se lève, idée même et suave, l'absente de tous bouquets.'[6] [I say: a flower! and out of the oblivion to which my voice relegates any contour, inasmuch as something other than known calyxes, musically there arises, the idea itself and fragrant, the one absent from all bouquets.] As we have seen, the idea that when an abstraction is spoken of, there is no referent, is a view that some writers on the subject have held;[7] Mallarmé's poetic language would similarly be language amputated from its referent, as in figure 15.

Though I am not necessarily convinced that this was in fact Mallarmé's view of his own language, the case for it seems worth

(15)

arguing. The reader should take it as a possibly fruitful suggestion rather than my firmly held belief. If this was his purpose, it was based on the famous distinction he made between the language of prose (or *reportage*) and that of poetry (which would then be the language of 'pure ideas' à la Plato):

> Narrer, enseigner, même décrire, cela va et encore qu'à chacun suffirait peut-être pour échanger la pensée humaine, de prendre ou de mettre dans la main d'autrui en silence une pièce de monnaie, l'emploi élémentaire du discours dessert l'universel *reportage* dont, la littérature exceptée, participe tout entre les genres d'écrits contemporains. A quoi bon la merveille de transposer un fait de nature en sa presque disparition vibratoire selon le jeu de la parole, cependant; si ce n'est pour qu'en émane, sans la gêne d'un proche ou concret rappel, la notion pure.[8] [Narrating, demonstrating, even describing, this is all right even although to communicate human thought it would suffice everyone perhaps to silently take or put in someone else's hand a coin, the elementary use of discourse serves that universal *reportage* in which (except for literature) all types of contemporary writing share. Yet what is the good of transposing a natural phenomenon into its vibratory near-disappearance according to the play of speech; if it is not so that from it should emanate, without the annoyance of too close or concrete a reminder, the pure idea.]

Thus poetry would be the language of the pure idea, isolated from the world. Later in the same passage, Mallarmé speaks of 'cet isolement de la parole' [this isolation of speech] which is taken to its most extreme point by the language of poetry.

The prose poem *Le Nénuphar blanc*[9] is a parable of this situation: Mallarmé imagines himself rowing a boat into the estate of a woman friend. He thinks he hears her footstep; but he refuses to raise his eyes and see the real woman, preferring to remain with a purely mental image of her . . . or of an ideal, imagined face which he has substituted for her. Without a word or a glance, he turns the boat and rows away. His language at this point is instructive: 'Si vague concept se suffit: et ne transgressera le délice empreint de généralité qui permet et ordonne d'exclure tous visages . . .' [So

vague a concept is sufficient to itself: and shall not transgress the
delight imbued with generality which allows and orders to exclude
all faces. . . .] In short the generalized concept is preferable to any
particular referent, even if that referent be the face of one's mistress!

This kind of attitude was a commonplace of Symbolism. One
thinks of Axel and his mistress committing suicide rather than sully
the purity of their ideal with actual physical love-making; and of
Huysmans' character des Esseintes deciding against visiting London
—because the reality of that city could never live up to his dreams
of it. In *Le Nénuphar blanc* Mallarmé writes: 'A quel type s'ajustent
vos traits, je sens leur précision, Madame, interrompre chose installée
ici par le bruissement d'une venue, oui! ce charme instinctif d'en
dessous que ne défend pas contre l'explorateur la plus authentique-
ment nouée, avec une boucle en diamant, des ceintures.' [What
type your features are, Madam, I feel their precision interrupting
something produced here by the rustle of an arrival,[10] yes! that
instinctive charm from below that is not forbidden to the explorer
by the most authentically tied of girdles with a diamond buckle.]
The language in which this is couched is most interesting: for it is a
language of sexual euphemism ('ce charme instinctif d'en dessous',
the 'explorateur' and the girdle). To satisfy the demands of reality
would be a kind of defloration: the ideal depends for its existence
upon the real being denied. Semantically the situation is an extremely bizarre one: we might term it a dread of the destruction of
the concept by the referent. The world must be rejected lest it
destroy the contents of the mind.

If one takes the view of Plato or Plotinus that there is a realm of
perfect forms or ideas from which the ordinary world of things is
derived, reflecting that more perfect world in an imperfect and distorted fashion, then no doubt a Mallarmean fear of the world of
experience is justified. To most of us, however, an attitude like
Mallarmé's must come under suspicion of being neurotic and life-
rejecting. The doors and windows of the self are locked and barred.
Such purity is, as Michel Tournier would say, the 'malign inversion'
of innocence.[11] And one may even wonder if Mallarmé's curious
death (he was stifled by a 'glottal spasm' of possibly psychological
origin) does not have some connexion with this apparent hostility to
ordinary reality. It is as if, at the last, even air was forbidden entrance
to the inner sanctum of his self. Of course, this is the merest speculation, and I advance it with some trepidation and the greatest caution.
It would require very close investigation of Mallarmé's entire

psychological history, and for this I have no space here. Perhaps the most that Mallarméans would be willing to accept is that there was a side of the poet that could be called life-rejecting, evinced above all by the 'Hérodiade' (on which he was, by the way, working again at the very end of his life). But in any case, language is learnt in practice through a double contact with other people and with experience. Its source is so much the world that it must be almost impossibly difficult to seek to isolate it from that world.

But let us give some examples of how Mallarmé might be held to have attempted this task. Firstly, one of his methods of amputating the concept from its referent is his characteristic preference for abstractions. For, whereas it is almost a commonplace of criticism that metaphors tend to present the abstract in concrete terms, Mallarmé's tendency is to reverse this: he prefers to present the concrete in abstract terms. Thus 'wings' become 'flight' (*vol*), 'death' becomes 'the fatal law' (*la fatale loi*, p. 67), 'surround' becomes 'circumvent' (*circonvenir*, p. 285); for the latter is more abstract because one circumvents by non-concrete means, but surrounds by concrete ones. And the Great Bear is strangely dissolved into the phrase 'De scintillations sitôt le septuor'.[12] Of course, as we have seen, abstractions do not have direct concrete referents, but they do have indirect ones. At least we might say that the concept, in an abstraction, can seem one remove further from reality.

Secondly, there are Mallarmé's characteristic images of absence and negation. Some instances which spring to mind are the tomb in 'Sur les bois oubliés . . .' which 'Hélas! du manque seul des lourds bouquets s'encombre' [Alas! is loaded with only the absence of heavy wreaths], and the lines 'Le transparent glacier des vols qui n'ont pas fui' [The transparent glacier of flights that have not fled], 'Ma faim qui d'aucun fruit ici ne se régale/Trouve en leur docte manque une saveur égale' [My hunger which feasts here on no fruit/ Finds in their learned absence an equal flavour], and the phrases 'creux néant musicien' [a hollow music-making nothingness], 'musicienne du silence' [musician of silence] and 'aboli bibelot d'inanité sonore' [abolished bauble of sonorous emptiness]. Or, in 'Toast funèbre', the lines:

> Vaste gouffre apporté dans l'amas de la brume
> Par l'irascible vent des mots qu'il n'a pas dit[13]
>> [Vast gulf produced in the mass of mist
>> By the irascible wind of words he has not spoken],

where the non-existent words which Gautier has not spoken blow a nothingness in the near-nothingness of mist: an amazing almost-treble negative. Mallarmé is particularly fond of this technique, and we may explain it by saying that negating a word seems to evoke the concept in the mind, but to deny the referent any external reality: the negative appears to sever the link between concept and the outer world.

Thirdly, we have ambiguity, which is perhaps Mallarmé's fundamental technique. Consider the image in 'Triptyque III':

> Mais, chez qui du rêve se dore
> Tristement dort une mandore
> Au creux néant musicien
>
> Telle que vers quelque fenêtre
> Selon nul ventre que le sien,
> Filial on aurait pu naitre.[14]

[But within one who gilds himself with the dream, there sadly sleeps a mandola, a music-making hollow nothingness—such that near some window, out of no belly but its own, one might have been born a son.]

Like all later Mallarmé, this is highly obscure. It is described by Noulet as 'an allegory of birth, of aborted creation, of the dominating passion of an absent work'.[15] A son could have been born from the big belly of the mandola; as a sound could have been produced from it. The poet prefers the potential birth, the potential sound: creation is held in suspense. And the imagery itself suggests that the birth will never take place; for births depend upon more than one 'ventre': one cannot be born from oneself, but needs the assistance of the outside world.

But let us look more closely at the image of the 'creux néant musicien'. A mandola's sounding-box (like that of a guitar or a violin) is of course hollow, full of air; and it is the vibration of this apparent emptiness that is largely responsible for producing the instrument's sound. It is, in short, an emptiness which produces music. This is a highly suitable metaphor for Mallarmé's own ideal in poetic imagery: 'A quoi bon la merveille de transposer un fait de nature en sa presque disparition vibratoire selon le jeu de la parole, cependant; si ce n'est pour qu'en émane, sans la gêne d'un proche ou concret rappel, la notion pure.'[16] [Yet what is the good of transposing a natural phenomenon into its vibratory quasi-disappearance according to the play of speech; if it is not so that from it should emanate, without the annoyance of too close or concrete a reminder, the pure idea.] It may well be that the poet is referring in the first instance to the sound waves of ordinary speech when he writes 'vibratoire' (vibratory). But clearly he is recommending that this characteristic of speech should be used, for his own higher purposes, by the poet. Perhaps he is saying that normal speech abandons one of its potential capabilities when it abolishes a referent into pure sound, pure vibration . . . but then proceeds to point (as normal speech always does) to that same referent. But the poet's task is to evoke the Pure Idea. And he continues: 'Je dis: une fleur! et, hors de l'oubli où ma voix relègue aucun contour, en tant que quelque chose d'autre que les calyxes sus, musicalement se lève, idée même et suave, l'absente de tous bouquets.'[17] [I say: a flower! and out of the oblivion to which my voice relegates any contour, inasmuch as something other than known calices, musically there arises, the idea itself and fragrant, the one absent from all bouquets.] At this point in his account of language, in fact, the poet takes over, and evokes the Pure Idea of a flower, the generalized concept of 'flower', which no *particular* plant will satisfy.

I want to contend that this is how Mallarmé feels words function when they are brought to a high pitch of ambiguity, and when their referents are highly uncertain. When language is ambiguous, the context no longer allows us to attribute a single positive sense to the concept (or to a single sector of the concept): our attention roams over various of its possible areas. I am reminded of I. A. Richards' remarks on those lines of Shakespeare where Octavius Caesar gazes at the dead Cleopatra:

She looks like sleep,
As she would catch another Antony
In her strong toil of grace.

'Where,' asks Richards, 'in terms of what entries in what possible dictionary, do the meanings here of *toil* and *grace* come to rest?'[18] Mallarmé, more abstractly, conceives this uncertainty, this poetic ambiguity as fining out the reference, succeeding nearly in abolishing it, amputating the concept from all its possible referents. He wrote to Viélé-Griffin: 'Tout le mystère est là: établir les identités secrètes par un deux à deux *qui ronge et use les objects*, au nom d'une centrale pureté.'[19] [The whole mystery is there: to set up secret identities by a two-by-two which *gnaws objects and wears them away*, in the name of a central purity.]

Objects, then, or referents, are to be eroded and abolished by the poetic process. And perhaps the 'deux à deux' which Mallarmé mentions here is to be understood as the use of contradictions. An instance would be given by Jean-Pierre Richard's observation: '*Nue*, par exemple, signifiera aussi bien *dénudé* que *nuage*. Aucune osmose

possible entre ces deux acceptions. Et pourtant on sait que pour
Mallarmé le nuage évanoui dénude. . . .'[20] [*Nue*, for instance,
will mean both 'bare' and 'cloud'. An osmosis is not possible between
these two interpretations. Yet one knows that for Mallarmé the
vanished cloud denudes. . . .]

Perhaps the intention is that, unable to give two mutually incompatible concepts any one interpretation, we should allow our
minds to hover in a no-man's-land of uncertainty between them.

Another example might be the word 'vol' in the opening line of
Mallarmé's sonnet to Méry Laurent:

> La chevelure vol d'une flamme à l'extrême
> Occident de désirs pour la tout déployer
> Se pose (je dirais mourir un diadème)
> Vers le front couronné son ancien foyer . . .[21]
>> [The hair, flight of a flame at the extreme
>> Occident of desires to spread it/her completely out,
>> Settles (I'd call it the dying of a diadem)
>> Around the crowned forehead, its old hearth . . .]

Méry's red hair is compared to a flame; literally, she unbinds it to
make love; metaphorically, its flight symbolizes the blaze of desire.
After love-making, she coils the hair neatly back on her forehead
again: the fire dies down. This is certainly the primary meaning of
'vol'. But it can mean 'theft' as well as 'flight', which gives us overtones of Prometheus' theft of divine fire.

We might also take these three lines from the sonnet 'Quand
l'ombre . . .':

> Oui, je sais qu'au lointain de cette nuit, la Terre
> Jette d'un grand éclat l'insolite mystère,
> Sous les siècles hideux qui l'obscurcissent moins.[22]
>> [Yes, I know that far off in (or from) this night, the Earth cast
>> (or casts away) the unaccustomed mystery of a great brilliance,
>> under the hideous centuries that darken it less.]

The poem has opened on an image of darkness. The sun has gone
down; it is night, and the poet is oppressed by fears of oblivion and
of a failure of poetic creation. In the two tercets, however, he re-
asserts images of light which manage to survive despite the en-
compassing darkness:

> L'espace à soi pareil qu'il s'accroisse ou se nie
> Roule dans cet ennui des feux vils pour témoins
> Que s'est d'un astre en fête allumé le génie.
>> [Space, always identical to itself whether it expands or negates
>> itself, rolls in this monotony insignificant fires (i.e. stars, like

sparks lit from the blaze of the setting sun) as witnesses that the genius of a festive star has come alight.]

I want to concentrate on the second line of the first tercet: 'la Terre/Jette d'un grand éclat l'insolite mystère . . .' [The Earth casts (or casts away) the unaccustomed mystery of a great brilliance]. We may interpret this as follows: (1) 'Seen from far out in space, the Earth casts a brilliant light.' 'Insolite mystère' is then in apposition with 'grand éclat', and means the strangeness and wonder of genius. But we might also remember that the night is still present in the last part of the poem, and that when one side of the Earth is lit by the sun, the other is in darkness. Mysteries too are usually thought of as dark. It is therefore possible to interpret the line as meaning: (2) 'The Earth casts *away* its darkness into space.' The 'mystery' is then 'unaccustomed' or paradoxical, because it is the shadow caused by light—caused, that is, by light falling on the other side of the Earth. And this interpretation is perhaps partly supported by the fact that, if 'des feux vils' are the stars, it is only at night that one can see them.

If these two interpretations are accepted, they nonetheless amount to the same statement. For the Earth's light is also asserted by saying that it 'casts away' its darkness. And it may be that 'mystery' obtains a third meaning, which subsumes both the others. It is an amalgam of dark and light, a mysterious contradiction indeed; and therefore stands for the conflict of light and dark, survival and death, creation and destruction, which is the subject of the poem. There is no total victory over darkness, but a partial one is asserted. The 'hideous centuries' obscure the Earth's light *less*; and the festive blaze of light survives as 'insignificant fires'.

In the final analysis, then, we have a single interpretation. But there is certainly a clash between the individual meanings which go to make it up. I want to ask at this point if it is possible to hold both contradictory meanings in the mind at once. Jean-Pierre Richard's remark about no 'osmosis' being conceivable between the two senses of 'nue' suggests that at least sometimes, in Mallarmé, similar conflicts of sense cannot be simultaneously apprehended. What does the reader feel? Can he contemplate two mutually incompatible 'pictures' at once, seeing them both, or is his mind in the position of our visual faculties when we contemplate the famous picture shown in figure 16? Here, we see alternately the profiles of a face and of a vase. And, as if there were some switching mechanism in the brain, they succeed each other: we cannot see both at the same time. Still more importantly for my argument here, what would

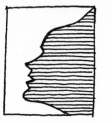

(16)

Mallarmé's own answer to this question have been? Jean-Pierre Richard points to the frequency of the image of 'scintillation' or flickering in his work, and quotes two strange lines of an unfinished sketch: 'Toujours que de ne pas perpétuer du faîte / Divers rapprochements scintillés absolus.'[23] [. . . not perpetuating sundry absolute scintillated comparisons of the crest.][24] This suggests that the different interpretations of an image are meant to *succeed* each other in Mallarmé like a succession of flickers, or of different facets of a jewel. And, according to Richard again,

> Le mot se rêve ici comme un cristal prismatique, composé d'un certain nombre de facettes, et mis en rapport de réflexion lointaine avec d'autres mots-prismes. Chaque facette contient un sens possible: mais ce sens ne s'allume que s'il éveille, loin de lui, son homologue . . . Le remplace aussitôt un autre rapport, tout aussi fulgurant et fragile, établi avec un autre mot. Avec nous le sens semblera donc jouer à cache-cache; il sera à la fois ici et là, partout et nulle part: 'papillon blanc, celui-ci à la fois partout, nulle part, il s'évanouit.'[25] [The word is dreamed of here as a prismatic crystal, composed of a certain number of facets, and put in a relationship of distant reflexion with other prism-words. Each facet contains a possible sense: but this sense lights up only if it arouses its far-off twin . . . It is replaced at once by another relationship, just as fragile and sparkling, established with another word. The sense thus seems to play hide-and-seek with us; it is at once here and there, everywhere and nowhere: 'a white butterfly, at once everywhere and nowhere, it vanishes'.]

This reminds me of my image of the torch-beam of attention scanning the area of the concept, seeking the appropriate sense. So long as the torch-beam cannot come to a halt—and whatever is the actual source of the ambiguity—interpretations come and go, the different facets of the word 'flash' successively.

Thus Mallarmé writes:

'Les mots, d'eux-mêmes, s'exaltent à mainte facette reconnue

la plus rare ou valant pour l'esprit, centre de suspens vibratoire:
qui les perçoit indépendamment de la suite ordinaire, pro-
jetés, en parois de grotte, tant que dure leur mobilité ou
principe, étant ce qui ne se dit pas du discours: prompts tous,
avant extinction, à une réciprocité de feux distante ou pré-
sentée de biais comme contingence.'[26] [Words, of themselves,
are heightened to many a facet recognized as the most rare or
valuable to the mind, centre of vibratory suspense: which (i.e.,
the mind) perceives them independently of their normal order,
projected as if on the walls of a grotto, as long as their mobility
or principle lasts, which is not what is said of discourse (i.e.
normal *reportage*): all quick, before they go out, to glitter
reciprocally at a distance or aslant as contingency.]

The mention of an unusual order suggests that he is thinking above
all of his fourth method for achieving ambiguity, namely his own
strangely ambivalent and contorted syntax. For this prevents our
interpreting his meaning immediately as we would in prose, prevents our imposing one sense upon it. But the image of flickering
light passing across the jewelled crystals on a cave wall, can equally
well describe the effect of all those techniques of Mallarmé which
favour ambiguity.

I hope I am not going too far if, contemplating this image of
Mallarmé's, I cannot help remembering Plato's parable of the
prisoners in the cave, dimly perceiving on its walls the shadows of
the pure ideas they cannot directly see.

At this point we must remember our mandola, and indeed all the
other Mallarméan music-makers. Scintillation is a sort of vibration,
and in the passage just quoted, Mallarmé speaks of 'the mind, that
centre of vibratory suspense'. Scintillation or vibration, however we
conceive of it, it would seem that we are intended to be conscious
above all of a succession of 'harmonics', of overtones. The referent
is vibrated out of existence; a 'fact of nature' is 'transposed into its
vibratory quasi-disappearance' by ordinary speech, and it is upon this
effect that Mallarmé founded his verse, which 'a lieu au-delà du
silence que traversent se raréfiant en musiques mentales ses éléménts,
et affecte notre sens subtil ou de rêve.'[27] [Verse takes place beyond
the silence that its elements traverse, rarefying themselves into
mental musics, and affects our subtle or dream sense.] The effect is
to evoke a 'pure idea'—or at least to give the illusion of evoking it.
In 'Toast funèbre' this whole process is perhaps ascribed to Gautier—
but if so, then Mallarmé is referring in reality to his own aesthetic
and his own practice:

Le Maître, par un œil profond, a sur ses pas,
Apaisé de l'éden l'inquiète merveille
Dont le frisson final, dans sa voix seule, éveille
Pour la Rose et le Lys le mystère d'un nom.[28]
[The Master has, by his profound vision, on his way appeased
Eden's uneasy miracle, whose final throb, on his lips alone,
evokes for Rose and Lily the mystery of a name.]

We may interpret roughly as follows: the manifold and changeable
world (Eden) is turned into a mysterious essence by the words of the
poet. As in the statement quoted above, all particular flowers are
abolished in favour of the capitalized essence of Rose and Lily. And
here again vibration is in question: as the last vibration [le frisson
final] dies, the essence of the flowers is evoked. As Jean-Pierre
Richard too points out, 'C'est ici la vibration ("l'art exquis, de *vibrer*
selon la *note* exacte de l'objet") qui finit par se dégager en vapeur,
en "la *vaporeuse arrière*-musique *subtile*" . . . tels vers ont "une
charme à eux" qui "est d'évoquer la sensation d'un instrument qui
ne requiert pas le toucher, *mais s'exhale*, encore et surtout, quand
on l'a posé".'[29] [It is here vibration ('the exquisite art of vibrating
according to the object's exact note') which ends in vaporizing itself,
in 'subtle vaporous after-music' . . ., such lines have 'their own
charm' which 'is to evoke the feeling of an instrument which doesn't
need to be touched, but still and above all *exhales itself* when it has
been laid aside.'] Or, as I said above, the referent is vibrated out of
existence.

But can this really happen? Mallarmé himself talks of a 'quasi-
disappearance'. And one might make two objections. First, although
I daresay the ordinary logical mind might have great difficulty in
holding two clashing, let alone two contradictory, images in view at
the same time, and although no doubt our optical nerves persist in
switching firmly from vase to face and back again, yet perhaps the
poetic mind does not have to behave like this. Is it not possible to
hold in sight two mutually incompatible images—in sight of one's
imagination, that is? It might even be a particularly valuable
exercise to do so. Besides, even in the poem where we gave two
opposite senses to 'mystère' and two or three conflicting senses to the
line in which it occurs, all these senses can be subsumed in a total
sense in which a conflict of contraries, light and dark, is imagined,
and a partial victory of light suggested. Some of the details may be
contradictory, but this in fact excellently communicates the conflict
within the poet's own mind and emotions.

My second objection is more radical. As this discussion shows, a

Mallarmé poem is 'about' something. And that something is a part of the world. It is also no doubt a part of the mind; but the mind too is a part of the world. Sunset, death, survival, creativity, these are all perfectly normal referents. Ambiguity of reference, well and good; but its total disappearance seems hard to conceive of. And one would normally assert that if a reference is ambiguous, that is, refers to more than one thing, then it does just that, and refers to *more* than an unambiguous reference does.

Even such a barely tangible poem as 'Triptyque III' is 'about' a potential happening (Mallarmé's possible but as yet unwritten poetry; and also about his language which does not quite 'make a sound' because it does not quite have a referent); and it can stand, as a proverb or parable can in the more down-to-earth realm of facts, for any potential event which it would fit. At the very most we might call its reference 'merely potential', like a spanner that can be fitted onto anything of appropriate shape, size and material. But potential reference is a perfectly ordinary feature of language, as when we say, 'Well, if you *did* go to the auction, you'd be able to pick up something cheap.'

Or is 'Triptyque III' self-referring, like the sentences I quoted at the start of this chapter? Could we paraphrase a part of its meaning as 'If only I were able to write what I am now writing'? If so, that would be only a part of its meaning. The poem also refers outwards, to the rest of the poet's potential work. If it is self-referring, it comes into the category of *not* exclusively self-referring statements that I established above. And we all know what happens in the normal world of discourse when we meet an antinomy like Epimenides': we discount what is paradoxical in it, we accept only what seems reasonable. In the case of Epimenides, we accept only the external reference (and indeed, only as much of that as seems plausible). 'Ah yes,' we say, 'he can't have meant that. He must have meant that most Cretans often tell lies. But not that they always do, or that he is lying now.' 'Triptyque III' must be interpreted in a similar way: it refers outwards.

Mallarmé's attempt to amputate concept from referent is doubtless the most brilliant of all such attempts. But ultimately it cannot succeed. We are all earth-bound mortals, and to us words do refer and must refer; and if they often do not do so directly, they certainly always belong to a universe of discourse in which they do so either indirectly or potentially. In the light of this fact, we may even wonder whether my speculations in this chapter are really well founded.[30] I leave the decision to the reader.

Two Philosophical Fallacies

To prove that A = B ; let A = B ; therefore A = B.   (Eric Temple Bell)

What indeed would be the use of an equation, if it only asserted that a thing named A is the same thing as a thing named B ?
(Professor D. J. Bohm 1963, 32)

WE HAVE NOW DISCUSSED abstract referents, fictional referents, non-existent referents, the correspondence of referents to concepts, and various attempts to detach concept from referent. We have mentioned the problem of literary adequacy. These considerations should take us directly on to consider the question of truth more deeply. There is also the knotty problem of metaphoric referents: but this is so near to the heart of poetry, that it is best left till a later stage. Let us, before proceeding, consider a couple of philosophical fallacies where the semiotic triangle may give us some welcome assistance.[1]

For a number of such fallacies have arisen, even in recent philosophy, from the failure of philosophers to analyze meaning into its proper constituents. For instance, Linsky discusses the following famous philosophical conundrums:

1. George IV and Scott: If *a* is identical with *b*, whatever is true of the one is true of the other, and either may be substituted for the other in any proposition without altering the truth or falsehood of that proposition. Now George IV wished to know whether Scott was the author of *Waverley*; and in fact Scott was the author of *Waverley*. Hence we may substitute *Scott* for *the author of Waverley*, and prove that George IV wished to know whether Scott was Scott.[2]

2. Venus, and the Morning and Evening Stars: Consider the proposition 'Venus is the morning star'. Are we saying that 'Venus' and 'the morning star', different though they may be, both refer to the same thing? At one time, Frege tells us,[3] he thought that this view was correct. But he abandoned it because this analysis seemed to turn the proposition 'Venus is the morning star' into a statement about our use of words . . . This conclusion, however, is unacceptable because surely it is the fact that Venus is the morning star which makes our proposition true, and this fact has nothing to do with how we agree to talk.

We could not make it otherwise by using *words* differently! Neither can we make it so by talking the way we do!

We are forced to another alternative. When we say 'Venus is the morning star' it is the planet Venus which is said to be identical with the morning star. Nothing is said about the designations 'Venus' and 'the morning star'. But here too a difficulty arises. We are not saying that *two* things are identical, for if we were, our proposition would be false. No *two* things are identical. But if we are not saying that two things are identical it seems that for our proposition to be true, we must be asserting of one thing that it is identical with itself. Then, however, it is difficult to see how our proposition can be informative, for everybody knows that Venus is identical with Venus.[4]

And so on. Frege therefore concluded that 'it was because the two expressions, "the morning star" and "the evening star" had the same reference that "The morning star = the evening star" was true, and because these two had different senses that it was not a trivial thing to say.' On this Linsky comments: '(This) seems to invite the objection that the two expressions "the morning star" and "the evening star" do not refer to the same thing.'[5] And 'it would be absurd to suggest that when (I say) The Evening Star I am not referring to a planet but to a "sense", whatever that might be.'[6]

Linsky's whole discussion of this problem is thoroughly confusing, and no doubt the reader is by now thoroughly confused. Let me say right away that the source of the confusion is (first) the application of algebraic formulas such as $x=y$ to normal human language,[7] and (secondly) the failure to distinguish between different uses (and consequently different senses) of the phrase. What might be meant by it? (1) It might be a question of nomenclature, in which case 'The Morning Star is The Evening Star' would mean 'We can say "MS" or "ES": they both relate to the same concept and referent.' But a more interesting case is (2) when one is informing someone who didn't previously know that MS and ES were 'identical'. What is the linguistic situation here? Frege has given a hint with his 'different senses'. For it is clear that to the person being informed, there were previously two stars, MS and ES. There were consequently two concepts and two (presumed) referents. The statement 'The MS is the ES' identifies the two referents with each other, as also the two concepts. In short, the statement is not one of *identity*, it is one of *identification*. The simple algebraic equation $MS = ES$ overlooks that fact that the two are not felt to be the same until they are *identified*. The concepts fuse, if you like: but the process of fusion is an event.

However, this is not the whole story. For a Greek there were different connotations, some of them mythological, attaching to the Morning Star (Phōsphoros) and the Evening Star (Hesperos). There are even different connotations for us, since the terms 'morning' and 'evening' are different. Therefore, as far as connotations and overtones are concerned, our sentence does not even *identify*, let alone suggest *identity* (although it certainly ensures that some of the connotations will in future be interchangeable).

But in any case even the identification of the *denotations* is not total. For MS is a 'division' of Venus: it is most properly used of Venus seen in the morning; and ES is another 'division' used of Venus in the evening. From the point of view of various sightings of the supposed referent, the planet Venus (R), they refer to sightings on quite separate occasions. From the point of view of the inner divisions of the denotation 'Venus' (C), they are separate connotations of it.

This is not at all the same thing as $x = y$; and to say that it was would entail us in saying that, for instance 'sky = night sky', or 'George IV in 1779 = George IV in 1780' or 'day = night' or 'black = white'. For all these are divisions of 'the same thing'. And Linsky, in his discussion of this problem, does in the end draw entirely the right moral: 'Only the logician's interest in formulas of the kind "$x = y$" could lead him to construct such sentences as "The Morning Star = The Evening Star" or "Hesperos = Phōsphoros".'[8] The logician is bewildered because he assimilates language (in its purely denotative and referential aspect at that) to algebra; and then goes on to forget not only the linguistic situation in practice, but every linguistic situation in principle.

As for our other conundrum, 'George IV wished to know if Scott was the author of *Waverley*. He therefore wished to know if Scott was Scott,' again no-one but a logician would be confused, for it is only he who reduces the linguistic situation to a simple equation. It is true of course that *sometimes* 'author of *Waverley*' can be used as a stylistic device to avoid saying 'Scott' too often. But that is neither here nor there in the present instance: George IV wasn't using it that way. Once again we have complete confusion here between identity and identification: how is George IV supposed to know this fact before he is told it? Philosophers are in difficulties because they insist on reducing the separate (and various) functions of both phrases ('Scott' and 'author of *Waverley*') to a single unique function: that of pointing at a single referent. One modern logician, Quine, starts with the assumption that George IV *did* want to know whether Scott was Scott; but, since this is patently absurd, he then goes to the opposite extreme, and concludes that in 'George IV wanted to know whether Scott was the author of *Waverley*', the person Scott (R) is not referred to either by 'Scott' or by 'the author of Waverley'. On the other hand, George IV (R) *is* referred to, for any other expression (such as 'His Majesty') could replace 'George IV' without changing the truth of our sentence. This is the principle of absolute identity and indifferent replacement taken to an insane extreme.[9] Russell, in his discussion of the same sentence, takes what is ultimately a rather similar way out. He asserts that the phrase 'the author of *Waverley*' '*per se* has no meaning'[10]—this is apparently because it has been 'broken up' (i.e., is not expressed in the form 'Scott wrote *Waverley*').

The confusion over identity is seen at its best on page 229. Russell writes: 'It is plain that when we say "the author of *Waverley* is the author of *Marmion*", the *is* expresses identity.' Now the *is* would only express identity, were *Waverley* and *Marmion* the same book. Russell might as well say that the sentences 'I got up at 8 a.m. this morning' and 'I had breakfast at 8.20' have the same meaning on the grounds that *I* refers to the same person.

The way out of this muddle is self-evident: the phrase 'author of *Waverley*' itself refers. It refers (1) to a novel, and (2) to someone writing it. This someone 'is' referentially Scott (once someone is sure it is), and 'is' conceptually Scott (but not till George IV knows it is). Once again identity and identification have been confused; once again referent and concept have been mistakenly equated. To put this whole referential relationship in indirect speech ('George IV asked . . .' etc.) is simply to put it in touch with yet another referential relationship. In short the paradox is artificially created by the inappropriate imposition upon language of notions of logical identity, combined with total disregard for context and indifference to the actual speech situation.

This last difficulty (that of reference in indirect speech) has been avoided by saying that the law of identity does not hold in 'intentional' sentences, that is in sentences like 'George IV *believed that* Scott was the author of *Waverley*'. For we cannot tell if 'Scott' and 'the author of *Waverley*' are the same here unless we know whether George IV knew who Scott was. He might have thought he was James Hogg, for instance. Frege therefore identifies the reference of a clause in *oratio obliqua* with its 'sense', that is (as I should put it in my terms) with the conceptual content for George IV of 'Scott is the author of *Waverley*.'[11] For George IV, however, this clause has reference in the ordinary sense of the word, and we must beware of making it sound as if the subordinate clause 'that Scott was the author of *Waverley*' has no reference: such a solution would seem quite unnatural.

We should seek the most natural solution possible, and so we might try applying the semiotic triangle here too. If George IV thought that Scott's *name* was Hogg, but otherwise knew who he was, then for him to 'believe that Hogg was the author of *Waverley*' means that he was making a false equation of word ('Hogg') = concept ('Scott') = referent (Scott). One of the three links is incorrect, namely the link between word and concept. If, on the other hand, George IV knew who Hogg was, and in addition thought he was the author of *Waverley* and of all Scott's other books too, then the equation word ('Hogg') = concept ('Hogg') = referent (Hogg) is totally correct. It is simply the ascription to the referent Hogg of other referents, that is, writing all those books, which is incorrect. This shows that we have to establish in all cases whether word corresponds to concept and concept to referent; and we also have to establish whether other referents too are being correctly ascribed. And naturally, where reported speech or thought is involved, at least two sets of referents, concepts and words are involved, namely, our own and those of the reported speaker. In these cases, therefore, we have a double problem.

This further illustrates the main point I have been trying to make here, which is that dilemmas over identity can only be solved by taking into account all the factors involved when we assert in language what we so loosely call 'identity'. Actually a whole series of relationships are involved in the assertion of 'identity'. When we say that 'Scott is the author of *Waverley*' we are asserting a series of so-called' identities', namely that (1) the word 'Scott' corresponds to our concept 'Scott', that (2) our concept 'Scott' corresponds to the referent Scott; and that (3) the referent Scott at certain points in time performed certain actions which can be termed 'the referent: authorship of *Waverley*'.[12] It is clear that if *any* point on this chain breaks down it falsifies our statement—but in a different way and with different effects depending on which link in the chain is broken. Equally clearly none of these links constitutes an assertion of identity in the strict sense of the word. The word is not identical with the concept, nor the concept with the referent; the word *signifies* the concept, the concept *refers* to the referent. As for the referents Scott and 'author of *Waverley*', these are not identical either. For when I say 'Scott', I may be referring to Scott as a continuous person with a long history from birth to the present moment, in which case his writing of *Waverley* is a segment of his life, a segment (we might say) of the continuous referent Scott. We must not confuse 'identity', in the ordinary sense of the continuing historical identity of an individual, with the logical sense of identity (that is, with the absolute identity of $1 = 1$). And the only case in normal language when we use 'author of *Waverley*' to mean 'Scott, the continuous historical personage', is when we are using it as an elegant stylistic variation, to avoid repeating the man's name too often. This is the only case where these two referents are identical.

Two conclusions might be drawn from my brief discussion of these paradoxes: first, a proper understanding of the complexities of meaning in something of the way I have formulated it, is extremely helpful in clarifying our minds, and would indeed be of considerable service to philosophers. I have not in fact been engaged in these pages in a pointless multiplication of entities. Secondly (and more importantly), the very existence of these paradoxes, and the difficulties certain logicians have had in dealing with them, powerfully suggest that we can take these difficulties as a *reductio ad absurdum* of the pretensions of conventional logic to have anything useful to say about language. There is nothing new in such an observation, of course; Strawson points out in his *Introduction to Logical Theory* that logic is a simplified intellectual tool that has far fewer categories than ordinary speech, and is thus comparatively deficient in representing different causal (and other) relationships.[13]

What I think should be sufficiently clear from the foregoing arguments, and what philosophers have so far been insufficiently aware of, is that unless the true complexity of the structure of meaning is appreciated, and an attempt made to deal with it on something like the lines suggested, linguistic fallacies can hardly be avoided, at least some of the time. I am not of course going to accuse all philosophers everywhere of being invariably confused about meaning, but it would certainly help to make confusion rarer if we could formulate an adequate *theory of meaning*, one which takes into account the full complexities of language. 'Meaning' in philosophical texts is all too often left undefined. It is assumed to exist where we *speak* of its existing, not to exist where we do not. But the usages of English are those of only one language among thousands. Besides, to leave the matter like this, is to leave 'meaning' totally vague, intuitive and intangible. There must therefore be a clear definition that we can get a firm grip on.

In setting about this task, we must listen to Frege, Strawson and J. L. Austin;[14] we must also listen carefully to the modern linguist.

But literature too has its lessons to give us, and with these the philosopher is not usually concerned; and the linguist's attitude to literary texts tends, as we shall see, to be elementary and evasive. For a full account of how language works, we have also to attend to traditional semanticists like Stern and Ullmann, and to literary critics like Richards and Empson.

Part Two

SEEING AND
SAYING

*

Mere Recognition

Reason . . . is never aware of its hidden assumptions.

(L. L. Whyte 1962, 25)

Children are dumb to say how hot the day is,
How hot the scent is of the summer rose,
How dreadful the black wastes of evening sky,
How dreadful the tall soldiers drumming by.

But we have speech, to chill the angry day,
And speech, to dull the rose's cruel scent.
We spell away the overhanging night,
We spell away the soldiers and the fright.

There's a cool web of language winds us in,
Retreat from too much joy or too much fear:
We grow sea-green at last and coldly die
In brininess and volubility.

(R. Graves *The Cool Web*)

HOW RIGID ARE THE frames of reference our minds work by? How much of reality do they conceal from us? We talk of 'a sense of reality'; but how dependent for it are we on unconscious linguistic assumptions? We should not, I think, discount these lines by Graves as entirely poetic hyperbole.

In a fascinating investigation by Bruner and Postman,[1]

experimental subjects were asked to identify on short and controlled exposure a series of playing cards. Many of the cards were normal, but some were made anomalous, e.g. a red six of spades and a black four of hearts. Each experimental run was constituted by the display of a single card to a single subject in a series of gradually increased exposures. . .

Even on the shortest exposures many subjects identified most of the cards, and after a small increase all the subjects identified them all. For the normal cards these identifications were usually correct, but the anomalous cards were almost always identified, without apparent hesitation or puzzlement, as normal. The black four of hearts might, for example, be identified as the four of either spades or hearts. Without any awareness of trouble, it was immediately fitted to one of the conceptual categories prepared by prior experience. One would not even like to say that the subjects had seen something different from what they identified.

With longer periods of exposure, the subjects began to show hesitation over the anomalous cards, however, and then still more hesitation, until eventually, and often quite suddenly, they would begin to identify them correctly.

Moreover, after doing this with two or three of the anomalous cards, they would have little further difficulty with the others. A few subjects, however, were never able to make the requisite adjustment of their categories. Even at forty times the average exposure required to recognize normal cards for what they were, more than 10% of the anomalous cards were not correctly identified. And the subjects who then failed often experienced acute personal distress. One of them exclaimed: 'I can't make the suit out, whatever it is. It didn't even look like a card that time. I don't know what colour it is now or whether it's a spade or a heart. I'm not even sure now what a spade looks like. My God!'[2]

Novelty, Kuhn comments, is only slowly recognized, is greeted with resistance; it is only gradually and painfully that the need for new conceptual categories is recognized. And he says of this experiment, 'Either as a metaphor or because it reflects the nature of the mind, that psychological experiment provides a wonderfully simple and cogent schema for the process of scientific discovery.'[3] As an instance of this, he cites the discovery of Uranus by Sir William Herschel:

On at least seventeen different occasions between 1690 and 1781, a number of astronomers, including several of Europe's most eminent observers, had seen a star in positions that we now suppose must have been occupied at the time by Uranus. One of the best observers in this group had actually seen the star on four successive nights in 1769 without noting the motion that could have suggested another identification. Herschel, when he first observed the same object twelve years later, did so with a much improved telescope of his own manufacture. As a result, he was able to notice an apparent disc-size that was at least unusual for stars. Something was awry, and he therefore postponed identification pending further scrutiny. That scrutiny disclosed Uranus' motion among the stars, and Herschel therefore announced that he had seen a new comet! Only several months later, after fruitless attempts to fit the observed motion to a cometary orbit, did Lexell suggest that the orbit was probably planetary.[4]

By this and other instances, Kuhn suggests that, just like ordinary folk, scientists tend to see reality in terms of their own conception of it.[5] The evidence strongly suggests that we naturally tend to classify, categorize, and stow away information according to a previously established frame of reference; that we have considerable natural resistance to changes in this frame of reference; and that there are many people (perhaps they are even the majority) who find it excessively hard, or even impossible, to accept such changes.

What above all else serves to create and stabilize the frames of reference we use is language. In a striking image the great Swiss linguist Saussure compares word and concept to the two sides of a single sheet of paper: you cannot, he writes, cut one without cutting the other;[6] and writers on language have often observed this apparent inseparability. The word seems somehow to stabilize the concept, so that we are never sure of holding on to our concept at all until we find the word that crystallizes it, so to speak, out of the fluid mass of our developing thoughts. As Linnaeus said, 'Nomina si nescis, perit et cognitio rerum'.

The mention of Linnaeus may remind us of one of the functions that has been claimed for the Arabic language. It seems that it contains an enormously rich vocabulary for plant and animal varieties. According to one authority, for example, Arabic contains no fewer than 5,744 names for the camel. It has consequently been claimed that the study of Arabic can advance our knowledge of natural history and physiology.[7] In such a case as this, language guides our thoughts, stabilizes fine distinctions, and allows us to manipulate them.

Abstract thinking, it has been asserted, could not be carried on at all without the use of words (or similar symbols, such as algebraic formulae, etc.). Kurt Goldstein seems to be quite clear that his experience with cases of brain-damage bears this out: '. . . language is not only a means to communicate thinking; it is also a means to support it, to fixate it. Defects in language may thus damage thinking.'[8] But I should not of course wish to assert the absolute dependence of concepts on words. Indeed, it is perfectly clear that thinking processes of many kinds can be carried on without them, as the experiments of Köhler with chimpanzees abundantly prove. What, I think, is at least clear, is that the words we use to categorize experience can subtly slant our apprehension, and certainly our memory, of that experience.

For instance, in an interesting pre-war experiment, subjects were presented with a number of drawings or figures and asked to sketch them from memory immediately afterwards.[9] These figures were all extremely simple, but also all extremely ambiguous. At the time the figure was shown, it would be described as (in one case) 'rather like the sun' or 'rather like a wheel'; as (in another) 'rather like a 4' or 'rather like a 7'. As one might expect, the clear tendency of the subjects was for their sketch of the figures to resemble the description they had heard of it. The objectivity of their visual memory was in short affected by the name that had been given to the figure. If, then, people tend to see what they expect to see and to reject what they do not expect (as we have just seen in the case of the playing cards and of the planet Uranus), they also tend to see as they are told to see and to assimilate each individual perception to a verbal category.

An even more striking instance is related by Koestler. He writes:

> In one of his experiments, Carl Duncker . . . set his experimental subjects the task of making a pendulum. The subject was led to a table on which had been placed, among some miscellaneous objects, a cord with a pendulum-weight attached to its end, and a nail. All he had to do was to drive the nail into the wall and hang the cord with the pendulum-weight on the nail. But there was no hammer. Only fifty per cent of the experimental subjects (all students) found the solution: to use the pendulum-weight as a hammer.
>
> Next, another series of students, of the same average age and intelligence, were given the same task under slightly altered conditions. In the first series the weight on the table was attached to the cord, and was expressly described to the students as a 'pendulum-weight'. In the second series, weight and cord were lying separately on the table, and the word 'pendulum-weight' was *not* used. Result: *all* students in the second group found the solution without difficulty. They took in the situation with an unprejudiced mind, saw a nail and a weight, and hammered the nail in, then tied the cord to the nail and the weight to the cord. But in the minds of the first group the weight was firmly 'embedded' into its role as a 'pendulum-weight' and nothing else, because it had been verbally described as such *and* because visually it formed a unit with the cord to which it was attached. Thus only half of the subjects were able to wrench it out of that context . . .[10]

The anthropologist Benjamin Lee Whorf tells us that he was once employed by a fire insurance firm. While investigating various cases of fire, he was often struck by the fact that they were not entirely accidents, but had rather been caused by people misreading a situation and attributing to it a meaning that it did not really have. He cites, for instance, 'a tannery discharging waste water containing animal matter into an outdoor settling basin partly roofed with wood and partly open. This situation is one that ordinarily would be verbalized as "pool of water". A workman had occasion to light a blow-torch nearby, and threw his match into the water. But the decomposing waste matter was evolving gas under the wood cover, so that the setup was the reverse of "watery". An instant flare of flame ignited the woodwork, and the fire quickly spread into the adjoining building.'[11]

If Whorf's analysis of this accident (and of a number of others) is correct, it would seem that the workmen at the tannery had been led astray by conceiving of the situation *in the wrong terms.* The pool was assimilated to water. And water of course does not burn (this is one of its connotations). He cites another case where the inflammable material was spoken of as 'limestone'. The accident occurred because of the understandable belief that 'stone', again, does not burn.

What does this tell us about the normal use of language? The pool was categorized as 'water': in short it was filed away in a certain mental pigeon-hole. It ceased to be a relevant feature of the environment, as far as any fire-precautions went. It could be safely forgotten; until a workman casting around for somewhere to throw his match makes the mental connexion 'water—puts out matches.' Then . . . disaster. The story neatly illustrates a characteristic feature of ordinary language: the attachment of a word or concept to an element in our experience allows us (via the generalizing factor) to file it away, to pigeonhole it, to place it in a certain particular frame of mental reference. It also illustrates a further feature of ordinary discourse: its capacity on occasion to deceive us. We are not usually deceived so disastrously, of course. But the possibility remains.

A second story of Whorf's illustrates a further point.

In parts of New England [he tells us] Persian cats of a certain type are called Coon cats, and this name has bred the notion that they are a hybrid between the cat and the 'coon' (raccoon) . . . I know of an actual case, a woman who owned a fine 'Coon cat', and who would protest to her friend: 'Why, just look at him—his tail, his funny eyes—can't you see it?' 'Don't be silly,' quoth her more sophisticated friend. 'Think of your natural history! Coons cannot breed with cats: they belong to a different family.' But the lady was so sure that she called on an eminent zoologist to confirm her belief. He is said to have remarked, with unwavering diplomacy, 'If you like to think so, just think so.'[12]

Here, I think, we are safe in saying we have a case not just of decep-
tion but of downright wilful *self*-deception. We are on occasion only
too willing to have our prejudices flattered. And normal language,
vague and unanalyzed as we like to leave it, serves us only too well
in this respect. The accidents of etymology, a chance concatenation
of sound, the emotional overtones we sense in words: these all too
easily serve us as excuses. One remembers Cinna the Poet, mistaken
in *Julius Caesar* for the conspirator of the same name, and torn in
pieces by the mob for his name: 'It is no matter, his name's Cinna;
pluck but his name out of his heart, and turn him going.'[13] What's
in a name, indeed! A great deal when we work by the crude definitions of ordinary language, which classify all Jews as Jews, thereby
bringing every antisemite's prejudice to bear on each individual Jew.

Even the grammar of a language, it has been suggested, may slant
out understanding of experience. Whorf,[14] again, contrasts our Indo-
European tendency to think in terms of *objects* with the Hopi tendency to think in terms of *events*. One is reminded of the traditional
Western philosopher's tendency to ask such questions as 'What is
Beauty?' And perhaps indeed this is because of our tendency to talk
of events as if they were things. Thus, Austin notes: 'We ask ourselves whether Truth is a substance (the Truth, the Body of Knowledge), or a quality (something like the colour red, inhering in
truths), or a relation ("correspondence")', and adds in a footnote:
'It is sufficiently obvious that "truth" is a substantive, "true" is an
adjective and "of" in "true of" a preposition.'[15] And Poincaré has
suggested that chemists were misled into centuries of fruitless research in an attempt to discover some *substance* which might correspond to the *substantive* 'heat'.[16]

According to Whorf, in Hopi there is a preference for using verbal
forms where English uses subject and predicate. 'The waves are
breaking' (subject 'waves', predicate 'are breaking') seems to suggest that there are such things as waves, distinct from the water in
which they occur. But the Hopi for this is a verbal form 'walalata',
which Whorf glosses somewhat absurdly as 'there is a repeated slosh-
ing'. Hopi in fact is rich in verbal terms for vibrations; and Whorf
wonders whether reality will not in fact eventually be found by
scientists to conform rather to the Hopi grammar of events than to
Indo-European grammar of nouns and verbs: will it perhaps be found
to be a sort of *field* devoid of *objects*?[17]

Whorf, of course, is right: this is exactly the sort of thing that
modern quantum physics tells us about the ultimate nature of
reality.[18] Which is not of course to claim that the Hopis were on the

point of developing a quantum theory. It is, after all, only when assumptions are *questioned*, that technical or scientific progress can begin. Nor is the point here that the Hopis are right and we are wrong; but rather that the normal way in which they and we take language for granted (for it reflects the mind's way of looking at reality) leaves us half unaware of that reality itself.

Whorf's theories had at one time a considerable vogue. But they have also been much criticized by various writers,[19] and are now generally rejected. Max Black, for instance, in his article 'Linguistic Relativity', does not attack Whorf's notion of a 'cryptotype' (that is, an unconscious linguistic structure or pattern), but simply objects that native speakers of Hopi (or for that matter English) are not *consciously* aware of cryptotypes. For example, no English speaker is consciously aware that we can only prefix 'un-' to transitive verbs of a 'covering, enclosing and surface-attaching meaning,' like 'fastening, unfastening; doing, undoing'. True. But Whorf's case rests upon the *unconscious* effects of our speech categories: if we were *conscious* of their effects we would be able to rise above them.

And this is my point here. It is at least *possible* that Whorf's basic theory is correct: this basic theory is that language conditions our view of the world. Various attempts have been made to establish that speakers of different languages do have such a different view of things. Perhaps not a great deal of success has been reported.[20] However, some suggestive experiments have been made, particularly one which seemed to show that colours were actually 'seen' differently by speakers of Zuñi and English.[21] And (to take another example) one may well wonder, with Anthony Burgess, 'whether Malay can be democratized . . . The feudal structure of Malay society has had a remarkable effect on the language. Words appropriate to the common man cannot be used in connexion with a ruler—sultan or raja. I walk (*jalan kaki*—"go with foot") but the Sultan must *berangkat*. I eat (*makan*), but the Sultan *santap*. I sleep (*tidor*), while the Sultan *beradu*.' And this is apparently true of much of the rest of the vocabulary.[22]

Similar observations might be made of Japanese, or of any other language like it where a different vocabulary is used by the two sexes. It is said that one can often tell that a foreign serviceman has learnt his Japanese from the women he has slept with; for he uses the female forms of the words.[23]

Similarly, it is a commonplace of international diplomacy that different nations do not necessarily find it easy to communicate the 'same' ideas. Thus Edmund S. Glenn writes:

Soviet diplomats often qualify the position taken by their Western counterparts as 'incorrect' *nepravilnoe*. In doing so, they do not accuse their opponents of falsifying facts, but merely of not interpreting them 'correctly'. This attitude is explicable only if viewed in the context of the Marxist-Hegelian pattern of thought, according to which historical situations evolve in a unique and predetermined manner. Thus an attitude not in accordance with theory is not in accordance with truth either; it is as incorrect as the false solution of a mathematical problem. Conversely, representatives of our side tend to propose compromise or transactional solutions. Margaret Mead writes that this attitude merely bewilders many representatives of the other side, and leads them to accuse us of hypocrisy, because it does not embody any ideological position recognizable to them. The idea that there are 'two sides to every question' is an embodiment of nominalistic philosophy, and is hard to understand for those unfamiliar with this philosophy or its influence.[24]

It might be thought that this problem is a purely ideological one. After all, surely the words into which the terms used by the two sides are translated 'mean the same thing'. But this is precisely Glenn's point. Such words may have the same denotations, but their connotations are different. In the rest of his long and interesting article, he goes on to analyze, throughout a day's work at the United Nations Assembly, certain French, Russian and English equivalents, and to show that the connotations of these words, *and therefore their precise sense*, depend on the political and philosophical worlds of those who use them.

All this is not to say that 'translation is impossible'. Or rather, I should say, translation *is* quite clearly impossible if by it you mean that for one word in one language (with all its manifold connotations) there will always be another in another language with exactly the same set of connotations. 'Cathedral' in English and 'catedral' in Spanish have apparently the same denotations;[25] but since the experience of cathedrals which goes into our use of these two words is slightly different in the two countries, the connotations (or some of them) cannot fail to be somewhat different. However, it is also clear that by taking enough trouble and spending enough time on the problem, one can always translate anything into another language accurately enough for normal purposes.[26] This may, as Glenn shows it does at the United Nations Organization, depend on the careful spelling out of those relevant connotations which differ.

Max Black's assertion that 'the admitted possibility of translation from any language into any other renders the supposed relativity of such systems highly dubious' will not do. At the level of a very close and precise attention to connotative meaning, translation in fact disproves Black's point.

I am not attempting to support Whorf's argument in its strong form, that is to claim that the basic world-views of two languages may be so different that their speakers conceive of reality in different ways . . . though, as a matter of fact, Whorf's view has its attractions for anyone who knows at least two languages with any degree of profundity.[27] And it must be added that one of the difficulties which researchers have found in attempting to prove his view is this: that the moment two observers from different cultures are presented, in an experimental situation, with, say, a set of colours to distinguish, they are immediately put on their guard: their attention is aroused, and they will no longer be in their normal position of *automatically* classifying these colours according to the normal categories of their own language. Of course the facts are the same for both of them; and of course they are likely to be seeing these facts (as far as their eyesight is concerned) in the same way. In the circumstances it is in fact highly remarkable that the experiment related by Brown[28] succeeded at all. So that it is much stronger evidence for Whorf's view than has usually been admitted.

All this, however, perfectly suits the argument that I am putting forward here, which is not that two different speakers may have two different world-views and be *incapable* of rising above the frameworks that their languages impose upon them, but merely that one of the functions of ordinary language is to classify information for us; and that *until our attention is drawn to it* we normally take the way our language classifies it for granted. Max Black's remark, quoted above, that we are not conscious in English of the rule about the prefix 'un-' (and of many other such rules), so far from disproving Whorf's point, simply proves mine. And this is why, when we meet some foreign turn of phrase which is utterly different from those we are used to, we may be surprised and then delighted. Take for instance the Quechua, who refer to the future as being 'behind' them, and to the past as being 'in front'. A moment's thought will show us why. For we can see what is in front of us, not what is behind us; and we can 'see' the past, but not the future. Such a jolt to our accepted categories is prettily revealing.

Briefly, my case is this: ordinary language normally functions as a system to classify experience, to assimilate it to a consistent, well-understood scheme of categories. As Paul Valéry says of ordinary discourse, it dissolves into its meanings, there is nothing left of it: we say that we have understood, and we pass on to the next sentence.[29] But there is a world of connotations lurking behind our briefest word; and one experience which reveals this to us is when we consider the problem of translation, place ourselves on the fence between two languages, and observe how they never quite fit. The clothes they make in France have a slightly different cut; and in China they wear blue dungarees.

The Language of Science

Proof is an idol before whom the pure mathematician tortures himself. In physics we are generally content to sacrifice before the lesser shrine of *Plausibility*.   (Eddington, 337)

Nature and Nature's laws lay hid in night;
God said, 'Let Newton be!' and all was light.
It did not last. The devil shouting, 'Ho!
Let Einstein be!' restored the *status quo*.
                                    (A. Pope & J. C. Squire)

THE IMPRECISIONS OF NORMAL language may serve advertisers and politicians well enough. But if we are interested in precision, or ascertainable truth, or increasing the expressible content of experience, other ways of talking must be sought. In this respect it is clear that there are two privileged languages: that of science and that of art.

It might be thought amazing that I mention both in the same breath. For science has certainly the greater cachet, the greater pretensions to truth, and indeed has visibly transformed the world we live in within the last century. We shall see however that it has no monopoly of truth, and that though its truths may be said to be more certain than those of literature, this is because they are truths of a very different kind. The poetic and the scientific modes of speech are both necessary to us; and to question either of them is absurd; for it would be (as Ogden and Richards remark) 'as though a dispute arose whether the mouth should be for speaking or for eating'.[1]

What *is* the type of knowledge presented to us by science? May we call it 'truth'? 'A proposition,' says Wittgenstein, 'must restrict reality to two alternatives: yes or no. In order to do that, it must describe reality completely' (4.023). And later, 'Propositions can represent the whole of reality . . .' (4.12 *Tractatus*). Does science conform to these requirements?

To answer this we do not have to be able to answer the question 'What is reality?' For it is self-evident that reality is not the same thing as the words in which we talk about it—or even as the mathematical equations by which we symbolize it or the pictures Wittgenstein would have us draw of it (verbally, in his case). We cannot describe reality as it is; for our descriptions of it are of different order from reality itself: the word is not the concept, nor is the concept the referent. It is therefore already evident in principle that an accurate description of reality is impossible.

Moreover a description of reality can never be complete. Friedrich Waismann remarks correctly on the

> *essential incompleteness* of an empirical description. To explain more fully: If I had to describe [this] right hand of mine which I am now holding up, I may say different things of it: I may state its size, its shape, its colour, its tissue, the chemical compound of its bones, its cells, and perhaps add some more particulars; but however far I go, I shall never reach a point where my description will be completed: logically speaking, it is always possible to extend the description by adding some detail or other.[2]

A little reflection will, I think, show this to be evidently true. Waismann goes on to contrast the case of objects in the phenomenal world with cases like a 'triangle' or a pattern such as is given by musical notation, where description can be complete—complete, that is, so long as one does not take one's triangle to completely represent some object in the real world, or one's sheet of music to completely reproduce an actual performance. Clearly, completeness can be claimed for descriptions of this kind only because they are restricted by definition.

We may conclude that a description of reality may never, in principle, be either *accurate* or *complete*. Nonetheless, scientific discourse is often quoted as the fullest account we have of it. So let us explore what happens when we confront reality; and what happens when the scientist confronts it in his turn.

Faced with a complex of sensory data, says Henry Margenau, we interpret it as an object of a certain sort: we *reify* it: we look at it and pronounce it to be 'a desk' or 'a tree'. In so doing, we classify each individual (and essentially different) object, by fitting it into its normal linguistic category. I have already commented on this feature of language, though presumably it antedates language. It would seem reasonable to suppose, for instance, that the rabbit running for its life across the meadow has successfully managed to classify certain 'sensory data' into a fox—or at least into a danger. Yet each fox is different; and the circumstances under which the rabbit meets a fox are subtly different on each occasion. In short we and the rabbit generalize from experience. And when I use language I generalize by using public words, which omit not only the essential differences between different trees *as seen by me*, but also the essential differences between my notion of trees and yours. I concentrate on the likeness of my tree to other trees.[3] As Margenau puts it: 'What we encounter in purely sensory experience is ineffably complex and multiple; every attempt at dividing it into individual parts is artificial and arbitrary.[4]

This is a first step along the road of abstraction. But a further step, or series of steps, is necessary before such objects can be treated scientifically. We must rationalize, and reduce the object to concepts which can be treated in a rational way; that is to a set of concepts capable of being treated as 'pointer-readings', and hence measurable, treatable in mathematics, etc. For only thus can we manipulate them. And only thus can others manipulate them and arrive at the same (or similar) results to those we obtain ourselves.[5] Thus, Newton's apple must be thought of as a 'mass', and 'mass' must be defined in a special way, so that everyone will be clear about its definition. Not only is the element of individuality removed from the object, but so also is our actual experience of it.

> Newton's apocryphal experience in the orchard at Woolsthorpe led him easily to the object, apple; assigning *mass* to the apple, however, was another step. By taking it Newton was enabled to formulate laws of motion, the law of universal gravitation, and so forth. Now it is to be observed that mass is something very specific, not seen or even felt, something that requires careful definition in terms of data. What interests us here is the circumstance that adoption of the idea 'mass' again lands us in rational territory where theoretic procedures are possible, which are not possible among the bare elements of Nature. And the way by which we got there is *different* from that which led us to reify the apple. Mass, though not part of Nature, has some intuitable aspects; but it lies somewhat further from Nature than does the apple.[6]

And Margenau continues by explaining that 'mass, force, energy, sound, light, etc.' are not the same concepts in science as they are in ordinary parlance.

Upon this basis, Margenau explains, science proposes theories that have certain metaphysical requirements, which he lists as (1) logical fertility, (2) multiple connexions, (3) permanence and stability, (4) extensibility of constructs, (5) causality, and (6) simplicity and elegance. These theories must further be testable against experience, that is they must be empirically verifiable.[7] This verifiability entails, certainly, further comparison with Nature: but what is being verified is of course only what *can* be verified; which by the nature of scientific concepts is those concepts themselves. We are always several steps away from Nature; and the object *itself* is invariably omitted.

Probably the most vivid account of the nature of scientific knowledge ever penned is Eddington's famous account of an elephant sliding down a slope. He writes:

> Let us then examine the kind of knowledge which is handled by exact science. If we search the examination papers in physics and natural philosophy for the more intelligible questions we may come across one beginning something like this: 'An elephant slides down a grassy hillside . . .' The experienced candidate knows that he need not pay much attention to this; it is only put in to give an impression of realism. He reads on: 'The mass of the elephant is two tons.' Now we are getting down to business; the elephant fades out of the problem and a mass of two tons takes its place. What exactly is this two tons, the real subject matter of the problem? It refers to some property or condition which we vaguely describe as 'ponderosity' occurring in a particular region of the external world. But we shall not get much further that way; the nature of the external world is inscrutable, and we shall only plunge into a quagmire of indescribables. Never mind what two tons *refers* to; what *is* it? How has it actually entered in so definite a way into our experience? Two tons *is* the reading of the pointer when the elephant was placed on a weighing-machine. Let us pass on. 'The slope of the hill is 60°.' Now the hillside fades out of the problem and an angle of 60° takes its place. What is 60°? There is no need to struggle with mystical conceptions of direction; 60° *is* the reading of a plumbline against the divisions of a protractor. Similarly for the other data of the problem. The softly yielding turf on which the elephant slid is replaced by a coefficient of friction, which though perhaps not directly a pointer reading is of kindred nature . . . And so we see that the poetry fades out of the problem, and by the time the serious application of exact science begins we are left with only pointer readings. If then only pointer readings or their equivalents are put into the machine of scientific calculation, how can we grind out anything but pointer readings? But that is just what we do grind out . . . The whole subject matter of exact science consists of pointer readings and similar indications.[8]

Let us briefly sum up our findings: science is powerless (and does not pretend) to deal with the data of experience *as such*; it abstracts from these data *constructs*, which are capable of receiving clear definition, general assent (and therefore contain no private elements of the experience), of being consistent, and of being manipulable in

science's own terms. It follows from the requirement of clear definition and general assent, that scientific statements should be trans-
latable with no loss of sense from one language into another. And
naturally science is totally uninterested in any emotional overtones
the language it uses may possess (or possesses in other contexts).

It will by now be sufficiently clear that science does not represent
the whole of reality. Only a definition of reality in such terms that it
deliberately excludes anything that science is not qualified to talk
about (and this is circular), can possibly lead us to the early Witt-
gensteinian position of its propositions 'describing reality completely'.[9] This is what Wittgenstein does at the start of his *Tractatus*,
by insisting that 'The world is the totality of facts, not of things'.
Unfortunately, as Wittgenstein himself of course realized, we none
of us actually *live* in his 'logical space'; so that to disregard 'things' in
favour of 'facts' is not a practical possibility save in science and philosophy. Moreover, science is so far from pretending to describe reality
completely that scientists are the first to admit the merely provisional (though progressive) approximation of their systems to reality.
Moreover, even in principle, as we have already seen, it is unlikely
that any 'complete' picture of reality can ever, in the nature even of
reality as it is narrowly defined by science, be achieved.

The statements of science, then, are not statements about the
whole truth. Parts of the whole are by definition inaccessible to
science. Moreover, the statements of science, even about those parts
of the whole with which it properly concerns itself, are in the nature
of things *rough*. For (1) they are *generalizations*, and (2) they are
provisional.

To take the first point first: the statements of science are generalizations. On the basis of these generalizations, science has achieved an
amazing record of success in manipulating nature and in predicting
events (the two are fundamentally the same, since it is no good
developing, say, a new brand of wheat if one cannot tell in advance
what its behaviour is likely to be). However, probably no scientific
theory has ever had 100 per cent success in prediction, and doubtless
none ever will. Not that we need 100 per cent success most of the
time, of course, except if we are concerned with an individual case.
But it is precisely individual cases which we *cannot* predict.[10] To
illustrate this, consider the history of the planet Vulcan.

After the discovery of Uranus (1781),[11] astronomers set about
plotting its orbit. Discrepancies were discovered in this orbit, which
led some scientists to the hypothesis that there might be a further
planet outside Uranus. Two mathematicians, J. C. Adams and U. J. J.

Le Verrier, independently of each other calculated in what region of the sky such a hypothetical planet might be found. And indeed the new planet (Neptune) was duly found on 23 September 1846, only a brief while after the search had been instituted. In this case, the right hypothesis was applied to the situation; and the result was one of nineteenth-century astronomy's most celebrated triumphs.

In passing, however, we might note that Neptune was found near the edge of the region calculated: an interesting example of the margin of error implicit in scientific predictions.

Having, with Adams, tracked down Neptune, Le Verrier felt confident that he could apply the same principles to the observed discrepancies in the orbit of Mercury. Having analyzed fifty reported sightings of small bodies transiting the sun, he 'based his calculations on six observations, dating from 1802, 1819, 1849, 1850, and 1861, which could be related to one and the same body . . . The discovery of a new planet, christened Vulcan, was duly announced and a further transit predicted for 22nd March 1877. But the planet failed to show up, nor has it been seen since. The "incident" is considered closed: there is no Vulcan.'[12]

This seems on the whole[13] to illustrate the question of choosing the right theory to apply to a problem. The irregularities in the orbit of Mercury are these days explained by a theory which was not of course in existence in Le Verrier's day. 'The orbit of Mercury itself is in slow rotation, and its perihelion moves forward, or *precesses*, by 43″ per century. This is the amount predicted by General Relativity and is regarded as a confirmation of Einstein's improvement on Newton's Universal Gravitation.'[14]

Similarly, the observed shift into the red area of the spectrum of light rays received from distant galaxies, a shift which is greater the farther the galaxies are away, is usually held to demonstrate that the more distant a galaxy is, the more rapid the speed of its movement away from us. It is most realistic however to attach probability to such a theory, rather than certainty: for other explanations seem possible, if certainly less probable, and have sometimes been put forward. There is no question that the Doppler effect *can occur*, of course, in principle: the question is whether it does so *in this case*.

As for cases of prediction such as weather forecasts, it is clear that circumstances of a certain kind usually produce effects of a certain kind: but we can never predict such effects with 100 per cent certainty, for our grasp of the circumstances is never complete enough.

It must also be noted that science is not normally very good at predicting the *unexpected*. With tomorrow's weather, it is safe enough, for rain and sun are familiar conditions; with unknown planets we may again expect it to be helpful, for planets are familiar objects. But if we take an apparently familiar concatenation of events which has in the past produced a highly unfamiliar result, such as the world population explosion or the present threats of ecological disaster, it is clear that scientists have been no more successful at predicting outcomes than Whorf's workman was when he threw his lighted match into a pool of inflammable gases. Both these problems look in principle as if they might quite easily have been predicted; but no-one did so until they were already with us; and it was not until the late 1960s that prophets of ecological disaster ceased to be regarded by the qualified scientist as cranks and ignorant dilettantes. It is all too easily forgotten that, even to the extent that science *does* achieve logical rigour, it is applied by mere human beings; and that however impressive a scientific system may be, it can only answer those questions that human beings think to ask it. In science, as in all human activities, it is posing the right questions that is the really important step. Thus Fleming's discovery of penicillin lay dormant for years, simply because it was not what he had expected nor what he was actually at the time looking for. And in the end it was not he who came to apply it.

In such cases as the above, blame is not usually attached to the *theory* for its inability to predict with absolute accuracy: for we are not sure which theory to apply; or the theory may be accurate only within its own rough limits; or the theory may be adequate enough, but the scientist is looking only in one particular direction. Often, however, the discovery of new evidence leads us to amend a theory radically, or scrap it all together. Perhaps the best known instance of this is the failure of Newton's principles to explain certain phenomena in the field of light; and the ultimate acceptance of Einstein's theory of relativity in place of Newtonianism.

Newton's laws are still applied of course: for they are accurate enough for many purposes. But we may reasonably say of them that they seem to be *rougher* than Einstein's principles, and that the latter constitute (or seem to constitute) a more all-embracing account of the behaviour of Nature. There is no guarantee however that Relativity is the last word on the subject, and it has indeed been questioned by a number of people. As Margenau writes, 'one cannot follow the development of optics, the changes in our conceptions of heat, sound, electricity, chemical affinity, combustion, the firmament, or our notions about the human soul without being impressed by the multitude of ways in which Man has endeavoured to link

Nature with reason. Nor can one maintain, in view of such evidence, that the method now in vogue has any likelihood of being ultimate.'[15]

Science, then, in many of its activities, claims to predict only within rough limits. And in principle *any* theory is capable of being amended or scrapped. Nor do the metaphysical principles lurking behind all scientific hypotheses possess any greater stability than the hypotheses themselves. As we have seen, the absolute validity of *causality* has recently broken down, at least within the confines of microphysics; and St Thomas Aquinas' postulate of compatibility of revelation and scientific method, Descartes' insistence on the identity of what is formally established with what is materially perceived,[16] are metaphysical principles which have been abandoned by modern science.'[17] The immutability of metaphysical principles too is a myth.

It may well be asked where this leaves scientific truth? It leaves it subject to roughness, incompleteness and uncertainty, just like ordinary statements—though naturally to a much smaller degree. Scientific statements of 'fact' are *incomplete*, because they involve abstraction from experience, are restricted by what science can talk about, and therefore leave out any other elements there may be in an experience; they are *rough* wherever a margin of error enters into them, as it normally does; they are *provisional* wherever they depend on a theory which may need amending at some future date. Certainly the statements of science are *less* subject to uncertainty than ordinary statements. But this higher degree of certainty is due to science's higher degree of abstraction from experience. For this provides stable concepts through which the scientist may check and recheck his predictions, without having them falsified by the vagaries of individual interpretation.

Science, in short, is a matter, not of certainty, but of probability. And it may be worth noting in passing that one of the metaphysical principles which the scientist employs when assessing the probability of two rival theories, is the principle of simplicity and elegance. Margenau writes: 'Most embarrassing among the metaphysical requirements is . . . the postulate of simplicity. . . . When two theories present themselves as competent explanations of a given complex of sensory experience, science decides in favour of the "simpler" one.' As he goes on to say, the victory of Copernican heliocentric astronomy over the Ptolemaic system with the earth at the centre of the universe, is often cited here. For Copernicus, by placing the sun at the centre of the planetary system, was able to reduce Ptolemy's complicated set of 83 'epicycles' to a mere 17. 'Simplicity,' writes Margenau, 'was early recognized as a guiding motive in research. Occam's razor is perhaps the most celebrated device for effecting it: "Non sunt entia multiplicanda praeter necessitatem." . . . Planck, Einstein and Cassirer, among many, have avowed [this principle] fervently. . . . There is also an aesthetic element, closely allied with simplicity, to be discerned in the metaphysics of science. Some discoveries are pretty, some are beautiful and awesome; the scientist often employs these words to express his aesthetic satisfaction . . .'[18] Such considerations as this, then, condition the scientist's judgment of what is 'most probable'.

Thus, the words 'This is true' on the lips of a scientist do not literally mean what they appear to do: they mean simply 'This is true within certain limits and with certain reservations,' or 'This is as true as we can know at the moment,' or 'This is the most probable explanation', or at most 'This is almost certain.' And this indeed is no mean claim. But as for supposing that we can call science to stand like a witness in the box, and tell us 'the truth, the whole truth, and nothing but the truth,' that would be a claim that is in the nature of things impossible.

Ravens, Postage Stamps, and the Grand Old Duke of York

> As far as the laws of mathematics refer to reality, they are not certain;
> and as far as they are certain, they do not refer to reality.
>
> (Einstein 1922, 28)

FOR PHILIP WHEELWRIGHT, THE absolute antithesis of poetic discourse is logic, the 'stenolanguage'[1] par excellence. Its basic postulates he sees as being four: (1) the law of identity ('A is A'); (2) the law of non-contradiction ('A is not at once B and non-B'); (3) the law of excluded middle ('A is either B or not B'); and (4) the law of sufficient reason ('Whatever is true must have a sufficient reason why it is true').[2] I suspect that Wheelwright is correct in putting logic at the opposite pole from poetry; but I also want to argue here that the usages neither of ordinary language nor of science necessarily correspond to the principles of logic, and that we do not have a simple opposition between the irrationalities of the poet and the rationalities of almost everyone else . . . or, as Wheelwright would perhaps prefer it, between the reasonableness of the poet and the rigidities of everyone else.

Indeed the first point, that ordinary language is poles apart from logic, will be granted easily enough. Suzanne Langer's introductory textbook on logic is typical in identifying logical meanings with those 'elements and relations' within meaning which have been defined and enumerated explicitly, as by scientists. Logic, she says, rules out 'all associated ideas which . . . are the subjective, personal context of our propositions . . .'[3] This in effect means that logic reduces and diminishes the meanings or ordinary speech. Ordinary speech is woolly and emotional, and logic takes out the wool and the emotion, leaving us with a set of firmly defined concepts and relationships.

However, more than the merely woolly and emotional has been left out. Gilbert Ryle is fond of pointing out that formal logic deals mainly with those expressions like 'not', 'and', 'all', 'some', 'a', 'the', 'is', 'is a member of' and so forth, which 'are like coins which enable one to bargain for any commodity or service whatsoever'.[4] You cannot tell from them what the topic of discussion is. He therefore terms them 'topic-neutral'. He points out, however, that not all the topic-neutral expressions of normal speech are utilized in logic. Logic thus does not embrace the whole even of the purely logical elements of language. Still less does it embrace the whole of the meanings of philosophy, since 'pleasure', 'memory' and 'seeing', however we scrape away at them, attempting to remove the grime of human contact, will still never fit into the pure logician's system.[5]

One may readily agree that messy human concepts such as these are outside the scope of logic. But what of the meanings of science? Surely it seeks, at least ideally, to approach the generality and rigour, the formal beauty of a mathematical or logical system? And it is not uncommon to find writers asserting that scientific and logical thought are practically the same thing. Suzanne Langer's *Introduction to Symbolic Logic*, for instance, terminates with the suggestion that Newton's concept of gravitation and Freud's concept of the unconscious mind were both the products of logical thinking.[6] But we shall see in the next chapter that products of the creative imagination such as these have often nothing whatever to do with logical processes—though logical processes may certainly be used in testing them. Logic is a useful tool; but it is far from being the foundation of science; and its relation to reality is more distant than that of science, which is itself, as we have seen, an abstraction from and selection of certain aspects of reality. Logic, we may say, is an abstraction from and selection of certain aspects of philosophical and scientific reasoning.

Let us first examine so apparently universal a principle as the Law of Excluded Middle. Aristotle enunciates this in the fourth chapter of Book Γ of the *Metaphysics*: 'It is impossible for anything at the same time to be and not to be.'[7] Let us suppose, says Aristotle, that someone wished to reject this view. He cannot hold a view which contradicts the law of contradiction without assuming the validity of the law itself: for otherwise he is not even denying Aristotle's statement. His only alternative must be silence. But this is absurd: 'for such a man, as such, is from the start no better than a vegetable.'[8]

Aristotle is of course correct. It is impossible to conduct any discussion, to state any case or question any view without assuming the validity of this law. Yet its universal applicability in all and every instance may well be doubted, no less in science than in the slipshod world of ordinary discourse. When I argue that the Waverley Monument, at a certain moment in time, either was or was not standing, this may seem incontrovertible. 'There can be no two ways about it,' as we commonly say: it cannot be both standing and not standing. One might ask of course which it was when it was only half built. But the logician's usual reply to this is that we shall decide what we mean by 'standing': the Waverley Monument is 'standing' from the moment it has reached a certain height—or that its final stone is added—or that it has been declared open by the Lord Provost. It will be seen that two-valued logic does not agree with the rime about the Grand Old Duke of York and his ten thousand men: 'When they were only half-way up they were neither up nor down.'

It may be objected that this is purely a question of definition. But indeed this is the point. 'Is' and 'is not' are flatly contradictory; but when we have to deal with a progression from 'is', to 'is not', are we to preserve this strict contradiction? Or are we to posit an intermediate term, or terms? Are we to say for instance that while the Monument was being built it was 'undecidable' whether it was standing or not? Less artificially, what is one to do about a scale of progression from black to white? We may preserve an absolute two-valued contradiction ('Black is not white') by defining 'black' as all shades up to the mid-point, and 'white' as all shades beyond it. But it will be seen that this contradiction depends upon our defining it thus. By defining the scale of black-to-white in this way, we build the absolute applicability of the Law into our statements. But we may choose to give a definition which will leave an intermediate term, 'grey', or a number of intermediate terms, or a fringe of uncertainty. We may choose, that is, a logic in which 'true' still contradicts 'untrue' but in which there is an intermediate position, 'undecided'. But if we choose a two-valued system, containing only the terms 'true' and 'untrue', we cannot make this system finer and more precise than our definitions themselves. If we cannot decide, even for argument's sake, where the dividing line between black and white comes, then the Law will be of no use to us in cases falling within this area of disagreement. The Law holds *if and to the extent that* it is possible to define the two contradictories so that they exclude each other.

We must, by the way, be quite clear what constitutes a contradiction. A modern philosopher remarks that the statement about 'the lady who came home in a sedan chair and a flood of tears' is meaningless.[9] This is of course because 'in' is ambiguous. But what then are we to make of this sentence culled from a still more eminent philosopher: 'Mr Wisdom may be sympathetic towards a policy of splitting hairs to save starting them'?[10] (I hasten to add that the Mr Wisdom in question is no allegorical personage, but an English philosopher.) In short, ambiguity does not in itself destroy meaning. For otherwise:

    1 meaning = 1 meaning

but:

    2 meanings = 0 meaning.

And indeed, in this particular case, the young lady in question is a character in Dickens' *Pickwick Papers*; and so far from being meaningless the suggestion given by the phrase is that she has 'put on' her flood of tears just as she has 'got into' her sedan chair: in short, the flood of tears is—one might almost say 'a vehicle'. And this is practically a third meaning!

In this particular case the notion that uncertainty cannot be allowed, because things either must or cannot be so, has been inappropriately extended to include linguistic ambiguity. But ambiguity of this kind is not contradictory in the sense that even a rigorous application of the Law of Excluded Middle would require. For to be 'in' a sedan chair and 'in' tears are not mutually exclusive by any conceivable definitions of the terms in question. And there is no uncertainty in the listener's mind: he knows perfectly well the meaning of the sentence.

In this case, then, the philosopher himself has been confused about the meaning of 'contradiction'. In the next, he is quite clear about this; but on the other hand he pretends that the definition which he chooses to give to the word 'possible' is not his definition but is part of nature, or at least of language or thought. In short, he confuses the dicta of Aristotle with the laws of thought.

Evidently uncomfortable with the idea of *degrees* of possibility, Ian Hacking wishes to argue that things are *either* possible *or* impossible.[11] This, he claims, is because we do not *say* [sic] 'more possible' or 'less possible'. We do, he admits, say 'very possible' and 'barely possible'. But 'some imagined state of affairs can be barely possible, not because it has a low degree of possibility (whatever that would be) but because it only barely makes the grade of being possible.'[12] But there is just as much difficulty in imagining something 'barely making the grade of being possible' than in its having a low degree of possibility. There is nothing to prevent me, even if Hacking's argument about usage is right, thinking of 'possibilities' just as I think of 'likelihoods'. For we normally do speak of things being 'more or less likely'.[13]

However, Hacking is wrong to assert that we do not ever talk of degrees of possibility: 'No-one asks, "What is the possibility of that?"'' he asserts roundly.[14] But this is quite untrue: one frequently hears such a sentence as 'What's the possibility of your being there this afternoon?' If a philosopher is going to base his arguments on the usages of ordinary language, he should at least take the trouble to get them right. Or could the explanation be that things are 'either possible or impossible' in American English, but have 'degrees of possibility' in British English? Whatever Hacking's answer to this might be, the question itself demonstrates that his argument is about words, not concepts or referents. Our ability to conceive of degrees of possibility between the absolutely possible and the absolutely impossible, is not ruled out of court by the usages of language. If I wish to define 'possibility' as entailing a continuous number of degrees (exactly like 'likelihood'), I am at perfect liberty to do so. Hacking is of course likewise entitled to define 'possible' in any way he wishes: but he is not entitled to claim that it may only be defined in that way and in no other. Still less is he entitled to claim that no other way of defining it is conceivable.

It is likely that Hacking's confusion here is due to overmuch affection for the Law of Excluded Middle. But whether that is so or not, this brief discussion illustrates that the Law does not govern thought absolutely, for we can easily conceive of its being to some extent limited. And indeed we can apply the Law only to the extent that we can agree on definitions of our terms: the precision of its applicability depends upon the precision we give these definitions. It follows therefore that if there are limits also to our capacity to define, the Law's universal applicability is limited to just that extent.

And there are indeed such limits. The Quantum Theory asserts that certain facts are undecidable because of the ultimate haziness of Nature itself. In an engaging discussion between 'Mr Turquer and Mr Rossette' in a modern work of many-valued logic, the following exchange occurs:

Mr Rossette: . . . Nevertheless, I do believe that there are some actual statements which are possibly neither true nor false.

Mr Turquer: You know you are being ridiculous. I challenge you to produce such a statement.

Mr R: Well, suppose that when the janitor arrives we ask him if he is in this room. No doubt he will reply in the affirmative and with complete assurance, but if the question is repeated as he leaves and while he is passing through the door, then he will certainly be flustered and unable to give an answer.

Mr T: Oh, that is no problem, for all we need to do is inform the janitor of the necessity of specifying some boundaries to the room . . . [and] the centre of gravity of [his] body . . .

Mr R: How should this be done in an acceptable scientific manner?

Mr T: Perhaps the best method would be to specify the collection of atoms which constitute the janitor's body, and using their positions calculate the exact centre of gravity of this body.

Mr R: But the janitor's body is at a temperature which can be estimated, so we can estimate the thermal velocities of the atoms which compose his body. [Now] does not the principle of indeterminacy assert that if we have any information whatever of the velocities of atoms, then exact information concerning their positions is impossible? If so, we could not give an exact definition of the centre of gravity of our poor janitor's body.[15]

The existence of such uncertainties in modern science leads the physicist Henry Margenau to observe:

Nor do we discern anywhere within the methodology of science convincing cause for the preference enjoyed by two-valued logics. Aristotelian logic was the first type available and has been used almost exclusively by scientists so far. There is no reason why it may not be abandoned at some future time. Experience cannot prove or disprove directly the law of the excluded middle (*tertium non datur*); hence it is certainly subject to tentative denial. But one thing, though it is sometimes advocated by scientists as well as philosophers, cannot be done. One may not assume that *tertium datur* in certain domains of science, such as the theory of probability and the quantum theory, and then proceed to use the conventional form of mathematics elsewhere without major scruples . . . For many of the accepted results of mathematics have so far been obtained only with the use of two-valued logic and may be inconsistent with the basic tenets of many-valued calculi; compatibility must first be proved. This is particularly true for all results established by the method of *reductio ad absurdum*, which fails when there are more than two truth values. [And he adds:] . . . The mathematics now used in physics (e.g., the differential calculus, operator theory) are not on the friendliest terms with logic, even with two-valued logic . . .'[16]

And for instance Reichenbach among others has proposed a three-valued logic (where the values are True, False and Indeterminate) which he claims fits quantum theory better than the traditional logic of the excluded middle.[17] Normal two-valued logic, in fact, is an idealization: its limits may be broad, but limits it does have.[18]

But neither Reichenbach's three-valued logic, nor his probability logic,[19] could possibly constitute a complete grammar of the thinking process. He says himself, 'if we want to say that logic deals with thinking, we had better say that logic teaches us how thinking *should* proceed and not how it *does* proceed.'[20] But this statement of his is misleading, for he does not really mean to say that thinking 'should' always proceed logically, as his very next sentence shows: 'This formulation, however, is susceptible of another misunderstanding. It would be very unreasonable to believe that we could improve our thinking by forcing it into the straitjacket of logically ordered operations . . . It is rather the results of thinking, not the thinking processes themselves, that are controlled by logic.'[21]

We shall see these remarks clearly confirmed in the next chapter. And of course they point to an essential difference between scientific and logical discourse: the latter is (even in its many-valued forms) a narrowing and simplification of the former. But it may be doubted if logic totally governs even 'the results of thinking'. Its grasp is too narrow for that: it can give an accurate account of some thought-processes, but not of others; and (invaluable tool though it is) it has to be used with circumspection. In a recent lengthy critique of conventional logic and its claims to properly appraise the statements of science, Romano Harré establishes that it omits a good deal of the meaning of scientific statements. This he claims to be so even in the case of such relatively simple statements as taxonomic generalizations, such as 'All birds are feathered' or 'All swans are white'.

Suppose, he says (1) the scientist finds some creatures that in other respects resemble birds, but which have no feathers. He may (2a) conclude that 'having feathers' should not have been included among the characteristics of birds; or he may (2b) make 'not having feathers' the prime characteristic of a new sub-family, featherless birds. In both cases formal logic recognizes only the superficial conclusions, in the following schemata:

I.   From 'Some S are not P is true'
         we conclude
     'All S are P is false'

II. From $(\exists x)(Gx \mathbin{\&} \sim Fx)$
         we conclude
     $\sim (\forall x)(\sim Gx \vee Fx)$

In other words formal logic will show us only that the proposition 'All birds have feathers' has been denied: and that we may not hypothesize that absence of feathers prevents a creature from being a bird. The different steps that may proceed from these conclusions, that is, steps 2a and 2b above, are not specified by this conventional logical scheme.

What, asks Harré, is missing from logic's account of the situation?

The problem is not hard to solve. What is missing is what, as a matter of fact, the expression 'bird' *means*. Scientific reasoning depends for its cogency upon two necessary conditions:

(a) That the *forms* of premises and conclusions are related according to the rules of formal logic: that is, that the acceptable formal relations hold between premises and conclusion.

(b) That the expressions used in premises and conclusion are related according to the appropriate rules of linguistic usage: that is, that acceptable intensional relations hold between the non-logical components of premises and conclusion.

Condition (b) is, says Harré, outside the domain of traditional formal logic. And he concludes that

for taxonomic generalizations formal logic provides an outline or framework of inference, but what happens in any particular case is determined by . . . considerations external to traditional formal logic.[22]

If we choose for instance solution 2a, namely to remove 'having feathers' from the definition of 'bird', we shall in effect have altered the meaning of 'bird'. Logic does not provide for this eventuality.

Harré's discussion of Hempel's paradox[23] is still more enlightening. The paradox may be stated as follows. The proposition 'All ravens are black' is logically equivalent to 'Whatever is not black is not a raven'. Now according to Nicod's criterion of confirmation in the sciences, a general statement is confirmed to some extent by finding that it has instances: 'All ravens are black' is confirmed to some extent by finding ravens which turn out to be black. But, says Hempel, if a general statement is confirmed by certain instances, then any general statement equivalent to it is confirmed by those same instances. Hence not merely would a black raven confirm our original hypothesis (that all ravens are black), but a white dove or a green lizard would equally well do so. For they confirm its logical equivalent, namely that 'Whatever is not black is not a raven'. It follows that a researcher seeking to verify the truth of the statement 'All ravens are black' might do so not merely in the conventional way, by finding a number of ravens and observing that they were black, but equally well by finding a number of non-black objects and observing that they were not ravens. If it were raining, therefore, I should have no need to step outside my front door in search of ravens: I could content myself with counting two red curtains, four blue walls, a green tooth and a yellow highlight on a pewter tankard: all these would equally well confirm the thesis that 'All ravens are black'.

This, commonsense would suggest, is manifestly absurd. Yet Hempel, after several pages of discussion, gives up the fruitless attempt to confute himself and concludes that his paradox has to be taken seriously: since logic affirms that counting red curtains, blue walls and green teeth serves the same purpose as counting black ravens, it must therefore be so: 'the impression of a paradoxical situation,' he writes, 'is not objectively founded: it is a psychological illusion.'[24] It is, however, a psychological illusion that science itself shares. Why is it that ornithologists do not go around counting green teeth?

This paradox has occasioned the spilling of vast quantities of ink.[25] It has been made to look even more paradoxical by those who have pointed out that a green tooth can be shown by exactly the same reasoning to be a confirming instance of 'All ravens are white' or 'All ravens are red' or any other colour one likes. It might well be asked, how can an object's discovery increase the probable truth of two contradictory hypotheses?

One might also ask, how would a researcher whose sole interest was to avoid disproving that 'All ravens are black' set about doing so? He would no doubt studiously seek out objects that were not ravens, and if he were really careful about it he could probably avoid seeing a raven almost permanently. Would such a procedure constitute confirmation?[26] Commonsense would assert that 'seeking to prove' and 'seeking not to disprove' are two quite different activities. In considering Hempel's paradox, then, is it wrong to leave out the researcher's intentions? And is this difference in intention between someone looking for proof and someone earnestly trying not to disprove, not somehow reflected in our two logically equivalent sentences, 'All ravens are black' and 'Whatever is not black is not a raven'? For the focus of interest seems to be different in the two sentences. They may be logically equivalent, but do they mean the same thing?

This question may sound strange. And the paradox can be given some further appearance of reasonableness when one considers the following, superficially similar case. A firm employs a number of typists, some of whom are known to have red hair. We wish to find out if all these red-haired typists are married. Instead of going to each one and asking her if she has a husband, we might equally well obtain a list of all the unmarried typists (the equivalent in Hempel's paradox of all the non-black objects) and then visit *them* to check the colour of their hair. Clearly this solution is perfectly feasible, and would settle the validity of our hypothesis just as well. But equally clearly, we are here dealing with a set which has very few members. In the case of ravens, however, there is an enormous disparity between their numbers and the number of non-black things. And here, as some writers point out, is a possible reason why scientists do not go about counting green teeth: at the very least, checking on non-black objects would be grossly inefficient.

But this is not quite the question at issue. No, the question is whether a green tooth would somehow be a 'confirming instance' of the blackness of ravens. It can be argued that a green tooth would not, in any practical context, confirm so well as a black raven; but that it still might confirm, albeit more weakly, since it reduces by one the totality of unknown non-black objects.[27] This assumes, however, that there *is* such a finite totality of non-black objects, and the assumption seems very questionable. *For what is to count as an object?* Is my red curtain an object? Certainly. But are the thousands of threads of which it is composed also objects? Equally certainly. Is the yellow highlight on my pewter mug an object? And if by altering the lighting I turn it into a blue highlight, is that yet another object?

I am afraid therefore that, unless some ingenious definition of 'object' can be provided, the totality of non-ravens in the world might reasonably be held to be infinite.[28] As is well known, $\infty - 1 = \infty$, and the totality of non-ravens cannot be reduced by glimpsing even seventy-five million green teeth.

Even if this difficulty were avoided, however, the operation would remain purely mathematical. We should still find it difficult to see why finding a green tooth would make all ravens being black more probable *except* in so far as our finding the green tooth eliminated one of a finite set of alternative possibilities. Our feeling that Hempel's paradox is a paradox, is thus probably due to a dim sense of the absence of causal connection between green teeth and black ravens. And this leads us directly to Harré's solution. He substitutes green emeralds for black ravens, but the principle is not of course affected.

Harré's argument is that a scientific law is not purely statistical. We do not count red-haired typists, find they are married, and then posit a law stating that 'All red-haired typists are married,' unless we have a theory, say, that red hair is genetically connected with great culinary talent, so that unmarried redheads are all proposed to constantly from an early age by the most eligible men, and their chances of remaining spinsters by the age of eighteen are nil. That is to say, a scientific law is not of a purely contingent nature: it explains, it suggests causes, it posits a mechanism. As Harré says:

> If I am to accept the statement that all emeralds are green . . .
> as being of the nature of a law, and so of being capable of
> supporting predictions [about] the colour of unexamined

instances, I must not only have knowledge of specimen-instances, but I must also have some idea, it may only be through a model, of the generative mechanisms at work in the differential reflection of light by gem stones. That is I must have some idea why it is that something which has the defining properties of an emerald, that is a certain chemical composition and crystalline structure, is green. When the contrapositive of the original statement (i.e., 'All non-green things are non-emeralds') is formed, it relates, not to emeraldness and greenness, but to non-greenness and non-emeraldness. To make that equivalently law-like, we should have to produce some sketch or model of the mechanism by which, whatever it was that constituted the non-greenness of things, produced their non-emeraldness. And of course, since negated properties are not really attributes at all, the question of the nature of the mechanism by which one comes to be associated with the other is otiose. So contrapositives [do not confirm exactly as the original statement does], since in the process of contraposition the mechanism which lies behind the lawfulness of the original general statement is just lost. This is so even of a very simple world. Suppose that there are only two kinds of things in the universe, emeralds and rubies, and only two properties which anything may have: being red or being green. Contraposition of 'All emeralds are green' yields 'All red things are rubies.' So a red ruby must, it seems, be equally confirmatory of both. Yet once again a moment's reflection shows that the connection between chemical nature and colour which would have to be sketched to supplement the instance-statistics of the emerald statement, will not necessarily do for the ruby statement. In this case, where the sorts of things in the world are restricted to the same natural kind, we might argue that the same sort of mechanism operated in both cases. But if the world consists among other things, of crows and shoes, which can be either white or black, then the mechanism by which crowhood and blackness are associated is genetic and biochemical, while the reason that white things are shoes will surely be a matter of fashion, and so call for a sociological explanation, or some such.[29]

Harré goes on to enunciate the principle: 'For any statement which purports to state a law or a strong connection between states, properties and so on, contraposition, or any other logical move that involves the use of negated predicates, is forbidden.'[30]

As Rutherford is supposed to have said, 'There is physics, and

there is stamp-collecting.' Scientists do not busy themselves counting
the number of one-eyed Irishmen currently engaged in scrubbing
Wigan Pier, unless they have a theory about it. They do not busy
themselves with apparently accidental concatenations of properties
unless they suspect they are not really accidental. 'Whatever is not
black is not a raven' certainly *follows* from 'All ravens are black', but
in the former statement the most important part of the implications
of the latter has been omitted, namely the genetic and other reasons
for its truth.

We have reached the surprising conclusion that two statements
which (by conventional logic) are equivalent, do not necessarily
have the same meaning. They may (and do) follow from each other,
but their conceptual content is to some extent different. My question
about the intentions of ornithologists a few pages back, and whether
these intentions were in any way hinted at by our two statements
about ravens, was a reasonable one after all. And of course, in
traditional logic, p⊃q and ~p⊃~q are formulated differently. A
different operation is being performed, logically equivalent though
the two operations are.

It will be readily admitted that (1) 'All ravens are black' has, as
its main focus of reference, ravens. It does not directly refer to non-
ravens. It may also, even on the lips of a non-scientist, as it certainly
will on those of a scientist, imply or require an explanation.[31] (2)
'Whatever isn't black, isn't a raven' is more difficult to visualize
in actual use. Probably the following possibilities are the main ones:
(2a) two people are about to look actively for ravens, and the possibility of sighting an object of a different sort is being faced. In this
case however the intention of looking for ravens is implied by the
statement, for it implicitly 'writes off' as uninteresting and irrelevant anything that isn't a raven. The main focus of reference is
therefore still ravens. An intention to search for non-ravens is certainly not implied, even though such objects are also being referred
to. The second possibility is (2b) rather unnatural: it implies an
interest in non-ravens (rather a difficult thing to imagine), or perhaps more likely a deliberate avoidance of ravens, as in the case of
our ornithologist who wished to avoid disproving the blackness of
ravens, and so sought to see no ravens at all. In (2b) therefore, the
main focus of reference is different from both (1) and (2a), as are
also the implications of the statement. Clearly therefore, (1), (2a)
and (2b), though logically equivalent, are not fully equivalent in
meaning, in either scientific or ordinary discourse.

Similarly, Rozeboom claims that 'All ravens are black', 'Whatever is not black is not a raven' and 'Everything is either a non-raven or black' 'are not commonsensically understood to mean the same thing' and he concludes that 'two prima facie equivalent statements may project different patterns of inductive implications and must accordingly be suspected to assert different propositions.'[32]

And this need not surprise us too much. Some linguists tell us that no two different sentences of a natural language are absolutely equivalent. They might say, for instance, that the 'theme' of 'All ravens are black' is 'All ravens'; and that the 'theme' of 'Whatever is not black is not a raven' is 'Whatever is not black'.[33] This is precisely what we have just discovered, namely that the focus of reference of the two sentences is different. But it must not be said that conventional logic is faulty in this respect. Contraposition is one of the operations that formal logic finds enormously useful and fruitful. But the equivalence of contrapositives is, we have found, a *limited* equivalence: they are equivalent up to a point: they can be made equivalent only by leaving out of their meanings whatever in them is *not* equivalent. And if that is tautologous, well and good: logic, like mathematics, is a tautologous system.

It is a part of Hempel's own defence of his paradox that we must regard the two statements (1) 'All ravens are black' and (2) 'Whatever is not black is not a raven' as synonymous; for, he says, if we do not, we are making confirmation depend on the *way* the hypothesis is formulated, and not on its *content*. Harré's reply to this is in effect that a large part of the content has been left out of statement (1) in reducing it to a logical statement; and that had this not happened the two could not be regarded as strictly synonymous. Of course confirmation must depend on the content of the hypothesis; but logic has left that content out.

Romano Harré treats Hempel's paradox as a *reductio ad absurdum* of the claims of traditional formal logic to embrace and exhaust the logic of the laws of nature and the meanings of science. Just as science (as we saw in chapter 11) simplifies and abstracts from the multifariousness of experience, so logic simplifies and abstracts from science. It is immensely useful, of course; but in this particular instance it is useful rather as too small a spanner, when applied to too large a nut, shows us that we need a larger spanner.

As a mode of discourse, then, logic is not the language of science. It is a part of that language, and indeed it is from one point of view an idealized form of that language, since it constitutes an increase in abstraction and formalization over the abstraction of science itself. Since the simplifications of logic are narrower and more restricting, however, the language of science cannot be *reduced* to logical state-ment. And we may leave the final word to Henry Margenau: 'We may now properly judge the transition from meaning to language to logic. Something vital is sacrificed in every one of the steps involved, and the loss is greatest in the field near perception. This is why logical positivism, in so far as it restricts itself to an analysis of scientific language, can never do complete justice to science: it must forever talk about propositions, where the scientist concerns himself with meanings that are prior to propositions.'[34]

Scientific Discovery

> I have had my solutions for a long time, but I do not yet know how I
> am to arrive at them.   (Karl F. Gauss, quoted in Koestler 1964, 117)

> The ancient Peruvian language had a single word *hamavec*—for both
> poet and inventor.   (Koestler 1964, 265)

THUS, LOGIC DOES NOT properly represent the reasoning element
in the scientific process. Still less does it represent the process of
scientific *discovery*, at least where that discovery is to connect
phenomena in a way never previously envisaged.

According to an age-old tale, Hiero, the tyrant of Syracuse,
commanded a votive crown of pure gold to be placed in a temple
of the immortal gods. But gossip concerning the goldsmith led
him to suspect that silver had been mixed in its construction,
and he requested Archimedes to determine, without injuring
the crown, whether or not this was the case. While taking a
bath, Archimedes noticed that his limbs were unusually light
when in the water, and that in proportion as his body was im-
mersed in the tub, water ran out of it. A method of resolving the
problem forthwith became evident to him, and leaping out of
the tub in great joy, he returned home naked, shouting as he
ran, 'Eureka, Eureka'.[1]

The solution to the problem is childishly simple—once it has been
found! But it requires that Archimedes should make a mental connexion between phenomena which had never previously been connected. And seeing things in a new light is perhaps the most difficult
mental act of all. It is to be noticed that there is nothing logical in the
process of *discovery* itself (though the process of *validation* of the
discovery may be eminently logical—and indeed in Archimedes'
own account, is so). What occurs is a sudden act of *insight*, due to the
instantaneous meshing of two hitherto separate complexes of meaning. Or, as Koestler calls them in the handy terminology of his *Act of
Creation*, separate *matrices*. The new problem of the golden crown is
suddenly associated with the everyday experience of seeing the bath-
water rise as one lowers oneself into it: matrix enmeshes with matrix; and, hey presto, a new discovery is made!

Koestler's account of scientific discovery is brilliant, detailed and massive, and one cannot do better than follow him. (Readers who doubt this should consult the note.)[2] He calls this process of connecting matrices 'bisociation', and discerns a similar process at work in both humour and the arts. In humour for instance a pun can plausibly be described as the point where two different matrices mesh. Thus he cites Freud's description of the Christmas season as 'the alcoholidays'. Here the meaning as it were pivots upon the syllable 'hol' and moves off in a new and unexpected direction. Or there is the tale recounted of Napoleon, that one of his first decrees after coronation was to confiscate the estates of the House of Orleans. A contemporary wit remarked: 'C'est le premier vol de l'aigle'.[3] Or let me quote Pope's lines on the turbulent Cambridge critic Bentley:

> Where Bentley late tempestuous used to sport
> In troubled waters, but now sleeps in port.[4]

The pun is here doubly supported, by 'waters' and by 'port'.

All three of these examples are interesting because both matrices are held in mind at the same moment. We get an ironic and highly meaningful clash, therefore, between the idea of the glorious *flight* of Napoleon and his *theft*: the witticism is (as Koestler says) a perceptive comment. Similar remarks might be made of the other two puns.

But the same process occurs in normal humour. Koestler is fond of quoting the following example:

> Chamfort tells a story of a Marquis at the court of Louis xiv who, on entering his wife's boudoir and finding her in the arms of a Bishop, walked calmly to the window and went through the motions of blessing the people in the street.
>
> 'What are you doing?' cried the anguished wife.
>
> 'Monseigneur is performing my functions,' replied the Marquis, 'so I am performing his.'[5]

It is not the unexpectedness of the Marquis's action that produces laughter, Koestler points out: or rather, not that unexpectedness *alone*: it is the fact that two different codes of behaviour, (1) the husband's, and (2) the bishop's, have become entangled. They clash. Two 'matrices' are associated (or rather bisociated) in a grotesque and surprising fashion.[6]

In the arts, Koestler sees the process of bisociation basically as 'the infinite being made to blend with the finite'.[7] But he also points out that the process of metaphor, that fundamental element of poetry, itself involves bisociation.[8] This is evidently true when Browning writes:

> The wild tulip, at the end of its tube, blows out its great red bell
> Like a thin clear bubble of blood.

the two images, the flower and the blood, are blended; and the flower takes on something of blood's life, life's fragility, and the vivid and painful beauty of both life and of fragility.

The difference here from Archimedes' Eureka process is that the poet does not go on to verify, to reduce to a rational system, to reach a single carefully defined conclusion. But the initial step, the act of bisociation, is apparently the same.

In Science, the Eureka experience is by no means as rare as one might suppose, says Koestler, if one thinks of scientists as sober men of fact, 'with computers for brains'. The most startling advances in science have frequently come about in the most irrational and subjective way. It is true that we verify the hunches of science after the event; but this is not the point: without the initial irrational hunch, there would be nothing to verify. Scientists are usually well aware of this themselves. And Max Planck writes in his autobiography that the pioneer scientist must have 'a vivid intuitive imagination for new ideas not generated by deduction, but by *artistically* creative imagination'.

Many such cases are too well known to require much elaboration. I will instance only two. The interested reader can find a further selection in Koestler and in Beveridge. My first example is Freud's hypothesis of the sublimation of instincts. According to his own account, he saw a funny cartoon in *Fliegende Blätter*, the one-time German equivalent of *Punch*. It consisted of two pictures: in the first a little girl was herding a flock of goslings with a stick. In the second she had grown up into a governess, and was herding a flock of young ladies with a parasol.[9] This instance involves of course analogy: it is a similar case to Archimedes' own Eureka experience.

Our second involves analogy too: but in this case the unconscious takes a hand! I refer to the famous discovery that Kekulé made by falling asleep at the fireside:

> I turned my chair to the fire and dozed, he relates. Again the atoms were gambolling before my eyes. This time the smaller groups kept modestly in the background. My mental eye, rendered more acute by repeated visions of this kind, could now distinguish larger structures, of manifold conformation: long rows, sometimes more closely fitted together; all twining and twisting in snakelike motion. But look! What was that? One of the snakes had seized hold of its own tail, and the form whirled mockingly before my eyes. As if by a flash of lightning I awoke . . . Let us learn to dream, gentlemen.[10]

This intuition of Kekulé's turned out to be one of the cornerstones of modern science, namely that the molecules of certain organic compounds are not open structures, but closed chains resembling the snake with its own tail in its mouth.

It is clear that in none of these cases was deductive reasoning the prime mover. And Koestler notes that according to an inquiry conducted by the American chemists Platt and Baker, 83 per cent of those scientists who answered their questionnaire claimed frequent or occasional assistance from unconscious intuitions.[11] We are dealing here with the leap of the mind into a region outside the sphere of pure logic. These instances clearly demonstrate the necessity of imagination and intuition in science, just as in the arts. But, as we have already seen, it is not merely imagination that is common to both: both have as their basis what Koestler calls the bisociative process: the association of two hitherto separate 'matrices'.[12]

In the arts, of course, the double-think that results—the seeing of two separate things as one—is left unresolved. We do not, when told that Reagan and Goneril are ravening wolves, reduce the two deadly sisters to wolves; nor do we reduce the wolves to the two sisters, and say, 'Ah, he just means Reagan and Goneril.' We have to stay with our doublethink.

In science the situation—or the emphasis, at least—is different.
> The billiard ball model of gas molecules, for instance, consists of a collection of balls moving at random and colliding with each other and with the walls of the vessel, and the behaviour of such a system is already known and expressed in mathematical theory, independently of the experimental results about gases with which it is compared. This means that further ramifications of the theory of colliding billiard balls can be used to extend the theory of gases, and questions can be asked such as 'Are gas molecules like rigid balls or like elastic ones?', 'What is their approximate diameter?', and so on. Progress is made by devising experiments to answer questions suggested by the model.[13]

The doublethink in question is thus the relation between model and reality explored and resolved point by point (as nearly as experimental evidence can resolve such problems). And the model is used to establish a hypothesis, which is a probable approximation to the facts.[14] This exploration of the literal applicability of the model looks like a total resolution of the doublethink, perhaps. But no: the scientist must remain aware that his model is just a model,[15] though in the normal experiment with a tested and tried theory he will not have this awareness in mind as an audience must when seeing Lear.

In modern science, however, cases of very striking unresolved ambiguity do occur. In the modern theory of light, for instance, light is thought of for some purposes as being of the nature of particles—but as like waves for other purposes. These two models appear to be mutually exclusive; but since neither by itself gives a complete explanation of the behaviour of light, we need both at once: 'The concept of complementarity is meant to describe a situation in which we can look at one and the same event through two different frames of reference. These two frames mutually exclude each other, but they also complement each other, and only the juxtaposition of these contradictory frames provides an exhaustive view of the appearances of the phenomena.'[16] It has been said that the human imagination has broken down at this point; for although some authorities have suggested that light consists of 'wavicles', it is difficult to think what these might be. The imagination is thus confronted by an 'impossible object', like a square circle, or the pictures of M. C. Escher. One is reminded of Plotinus, who apparently held that it was salutary to adopt two contradictory models or metaphors of the same phenomenon—on the ground that one was thereby reminded that one's models were in fact merely models.[17] Science here is being completely unlogical, and, if I may say so, most reasonable and poetic. The situation is almost like that of the poetry reader, holding 'tulip' and 'bubble of blood' in his mind at the same time.

But in the case of the tulip and the bubble of blood, it is quite clear which is vehicle and which is tenor; the parallel is thus not entirely accurate. A more exact instance would be Rimbaud's brief poem 'Marine':

Les chars d'argent et de cuivre—
Les proues d'acier et d'argent—
Battent l'écume,—
Soulèvent les souches des ronces.
Les courants de la lande,
Et les ornières immenses du reflux,
Filent circulairement vers l'est,
Vers les piliers de la forêt,
Vers le fûts de la jetée.
Dont l'angle est heurté par des tourbillons de lumière.
[Chariots of silver and of copper—
Prows of steel and of silver—
Scour the foam—
Tear up the stumps of the thorns.
The currents of the heath,

> And the huge ruts of the ebb-tide,
> Flow away in a circle towards the East,
> Towards the pillars of the forest,
> Towards the posts of the jetty,
> Whose corner is battered by whirlwinds of light.][18]

Here either a landscape is being described in terms of a seascape—
or the reverse—or rather it is both at once.

The strict and total application of the logical mentality to science,
then, would have damaging and stultifying results. For (1) the
exercise of insight and intuition is as vital to the physical as it is to
the human sciences. Beveridge quotes the views of an earlier philosopher of science with approval:

> Among the obstacles to scientific progress a high place must
> certainly be assigned to the analysis of scientific procedure which
> logic has provided . . . It has not tried to describe the methods
> by which the sciences have actually advanced, and to extract . . .
> rules which might be used to regulate scientific progress, but
> has freely re-arranged the actual procedure in accordance with
> its prejudices. For the order of discovery there has been sub-
> stituted an order of proof. [19]

And (2) logic cannot by its nature do complete justice to science, let
alone to the raw experience from which science is an abstraction. On
this second point, and for the sake of emphasis let us listen to
Margenau again:

> A pure abstraction is always easy to define: as an example, the
> mathematical concept of a group may be considered. Its defini-
> tion is complete and adequate, for there is never any doubt as
> to whether a set of quantities forms a group. Denotatively given
> things,[20] on the other hand, always elude precise definition.
> When they are to be incorporated in a logical system, either
> they function as undefined elements or else generous allowance
> for uncertainties must be made. If a dog be defined as a four-
> legged mammal with numerous other characteristics, all of
> which are specified, then a difficulty arises every time a three-
> legged dog is encountered.
>
> There is this inherent logical diffuseness in all parts of the
> immediately given, *and it is important that this be clearly recog-
> nized.* Because of it one may deem it questionable whether for-
> mal logic can ever ingress far enough into the spontaneous
> elements of experience to give a satisfactory account of them . . .
>
> We may now properly judge the transition from meaning to
> language to logic. Something vital is sacrificed in every one of

the steps involved, and the loss is greatest in the field near perception. That is why logical positivism, in so far as it restricts itself to an analysis of scientific language, can never do complete justice to science; it must forever talk about propositions, where the scientist concerns himself with meanings that are prior to propositions.[21]

It will by now be apparent that I have denied a large number of the things that literary people are commonly supposed to want to say about science. And indeed I am inclined to think that despite the great changes that have affected science since the sixteenth century, the Renaissance way of looking at art and science as two branches of the same thing, in opposition rather to rigid philosophical systems than to each other, still contains more than a grain of truth. Both art and science share the vital characteristics of creativity, adaptability and fluidity.

For instance, we have seen that (1) the creative processes of science bear a striking resemblance to those that operate within the arts; (2) the purely logical mentality is one of science's tools, which it has to keep within the bounds of reason; (3) the scientist does not pretend to catch the whole of reality in his net. No scientific mesh is so fine that the subatomic particle will not in some respects escape it. And in science's net it is only the measurable, the rational, the general and the abstract that can be caught: the solidity and substance of the real world is a fish that always gets away.

Scientific discourse is one of our privileged languages; but it becomes so by substituting for the vaguenesses and imprecisions (but nonetheless solid reference) of ordinary language, the abstractions of mathematics and of quantum mechanics, and for the fluid, shifting and continuously adjustable usages of ordinary words, certain agreed, closely defined and at least temporarily fixed special definitions. Of course, this is a matter of degree. I have already pointed out more than once that (4) too much rigidity will kill a hypothesis dead, even in science. I have also pointed out (5) that the scientist's picture of the world is a provisional one, and that (if he properly understands his own discipline) he does not claim absolute certainty—nor will he ever be able to claim it.

On the other hand, of course, he *seeks* it. This is well put by Bronowski, who says that the scientist *looks* for truth, but *finds* only knowledge; and that what he fails to find is not truth, but certainty.[22] Is is also clear that when science is *expounded*, it is presented with the maximum of clarity and precision.

Of course it is true [writes Bronowski,] that when scientists write out their findings, they try to rid their language of ambiguity and make it exact... (Science's) aim is to display the discovery definitively, and place it in the network of axioms and laws, so that everyone can then reason about it unequivocally. It must be so, in order that the consequences of the new discovery may be logically deduced, and tested in specific instances . . . The exposition displays the state of science at that moment as a complete and closed system, wholly contained in (that is, deducible from) its axioms and laws. The man who has to act now on present scientific knowledge has to accept that as an instruction, as a machine does. This is the nature of science as a mode of knowledge. It must be testable in action . . . But the thinker and experimenter does not have to accept the present state of science as closed, and its exposition as complete. He is free to work in the thinking language, and to explore its ambiguities to his mind's content.[23]

It will be seen that this amounts to a provisional acceptance, for the sake of clear experimental testing, of clarity, certainty and precise definition. But by the very fact that science itself admits the principles of ambiguity, uncertainty and the haziness of the real world, it is clear that it at once leaves room for the very different methods and ambitions of the arts, and—more interestingly—actually *validates* them.[24] Science is concerned with what (so far) is known and what (so far) can be said; but at the same time it admits the existence of the unknown and the unsayable. Science shuns ambiguity; but at the same time it asserts it to be a law of nature. 'Whereof one cannot speak,' writes Wittgenstein, 'thereof one must be silent.' (*Tractatus*). But on the contrary: whereof we cannot speak, thereof we beat on drums, sing, dance round the campfire, paint bison on cave-walls, or (more recently) compose symphonies, write novels, plays and poems. Whereof one cannot speak, thereof one creates art.[25] And indeed art would be hard to justify if one could not claim that it said things unsayable by science or philosophy or the average speech of average men.

Rĕcreation and Rēcreation

> People living by the seashore grow so accustomed to the murmur of the
> waves that they never hear it. By the same token, we scarcely ever
> hear the words we utter . . . We look at each other, but we do not see
> each other any more. Our perception of the world has withered away,
> what remains is mere recognition.
>
> (Shklovski 1923, 11, quoted in Erlich, 150)

BUT HOW IS THIS to be achieved? Surely the unsayable is by definition unsayable? And if it may be admitted that music for example
achieves a mode of discourse which in some sense communicates
what cannot be spoken in words, surely this is precisely *because* it
does not use words?—because it is a non-verbal language?

And indeed, this is the fundamental problem. We have seen
(chapter 10) that one of our most common tendencies is to take experience for granted by fitting it into ready-made categories; and
that ordinary language is particularly apt to bring this about. And
this is hardly surprising, since the very nature of language automatically performs this for us: there is, as we have seen, a built-in
'generalizing function': the moment we name a particular tree 'a
tree', we thereby assimilate it to all other trees. We can see this process happening to Yves Bonnefoy in the following anecdote:

Je m'imaginerai, ou me rappellerai . . . que j'entre un jour
d'été dans une maison en ruine et vois soudain, sur le mur, une
salamandre. Elle a été surprise, elle s'est effrayée et s'immo-
bilise. Et moi aussi, arraché à ma rêverie, je suis prêt à me lais-
ser retenir. Je regarde la salamandre, je reconnais ses traits
distinctifs, comme l'on dit,—je vois aussi ce cou étroit, cette
face grise, ce cœur qui bat doucement.

Eh bien, plusieurs chemins se sont ouverts devant moi. Je puis
analyser ce que m'apporte ma perception, et ainsi, profitant de
l'expérience des autres hommes, séparer en esprit cette petite
vie des autres données du monde, et la classer, comme ferait le
mot de la prose, et me dire: '*Une* salamandre', puis poursuivre
ma promenade, toujours distrait, demeuré comme à la surface
de la rencontre.[1]

[I shall imagine, or recall . . . my entering a ruined house
one day and seeing suddenly on the wall a salamander. It has

been surprised, has taken fright and 'freezes'. I too, roused from my daydream, am willing to be detained. I look at the salamander, I recognize its distinctive traits, as they are called, . . . I see also its slender neck, its grey mask, its heart beating gently.

Well, several paths are open to me. I can analyse what my perception shows me, and thus, profiting from the experience of others, separate this little life from the other data of the world, classify it as the language of prose does, and say to myself: '*A* salamander', then continue my stroll, still absent-minded, remaining only on the surface of my encounter.]

Here we have the classificatory function of prose at its normal work: the generalizing function has taken over: *the* salamander has become *a* salamander, has been assimilated to the mental categories of the human observer, who continues along the well-trodden paths of his own internal *mappa mundi*. Any particularity in the experience has been erased. Moreover nothing has happened to alter in the slightest degree the pre-existent pigeon-holing system in the observer's mind.

It is clear that a considerable amount of reading matter (we do not usually call it literature) operates exactly like this. Indeed, it would be surprising if it did not, for the purpose of such writers as Ian Fleming, Agatha Christie, Patricia Robbins and countless others is simply to relax the mind, to entertain, to flatter expectation or prejudice, to provide the promised stimulation and no other. It is perfectly clear that the writers of these works produce them to a formula. Not that there is anything wrong with this: we need such relaxation as we need sustaining cups of tea, holidays at the seaside, games of football and comfortable sofas. Such works are rĕcreative.

To show this process in action we cannot do better than turn to the exceptionally clear-headed account of how to write romantic fiction given by Claire Ritchie, authoress of *Bright Meadows, The Heart Turns Homeward, Hope is My Pillow* and many other works. In her *Writing the Romantic Novel* she proffers invaluable advice to aspiring writers: 'Remember . . . that the primary aim of every romantic novelist is to make her readers FEEL. Generally speaking, they do not want to be worried, nor made to think deeply—a romance should be an emotional experience, not a lesson.'[2] In her concern that readers should not be worried, she goes so far as to say that the Eternal Triangle is 'not a suitable subject for a romance'.[3]

She is however insistent on a principle to which writers of the intellectual novel would equally firmly assent—namely, that the reader should not be told but shown. Character must be revealed through action, conversation and situation. But what kind of character? Here Miss Ritchie is entirely lucid and instructive. 'You are naturally anxious to make your people definite and recognizable—as opposed to the 'stock' character or type—but do not select someone so unusual or peculiar as to be outside the recognition and understanding of an ordinary reader. If you do this—in an attempt to make that character outstanding—you will fail. Your men and women must be people whose desires and motives are recognizable as those of ordinary human beings. The universal appeal is absolutely essential.'[4]

Miss Ritchie is quite clear how this universal appeal is brought about: the complexity of the characters is to be limited: 'Some people —have two or more equally strong—and possibly conflicting character-traits. These are usually the characters in the straight, as opposed to the romantic novel, because that inner conflict in their natures will necessarily make them rather too complicated for the protagonists in a relatively simple and straightforward story, such as a romance.'[5] She therefore recommends what she calls 'Number 1 Characters', who have some single dominant trait. She is careful to say that these must not be made into 'types' or 'stock characters'. But it is equally clear from the examples she gives that this is merely a matter of degree: a narrow range of easily recognizable traits, working inside the limits of rigid social convention, are the restrictive boundary within which all her characters are framed.

The means used are, of course, also those calculated to give the reader the consoling atmosphere of familiar emotion set in a familiar setting. 'If you want to suggest a coming estrangement or parting, a casual mention of the clouds drifting up from the horizon, or the deepening of twilight shadows, as the two characters involved walk and talk together, will effectively heighten the mood.'[6]

Rĕcreation, however, is not all; and a hint of what may be wrong with it if indulged in to the exclusion of all else may be given by the reply of a young wife and mother to an interviewer who asked if she would like more sexual detail to be introduced into the texts of her favourite romantic novels: 'Oh no,' she said, 'I like reading about something nice, not like real life.'[7] And thus, Claire Ritchie herself, in an evidently sincere outburst, complains: 'Today, there are far too many novels dealing with vice, lust, immorality of every kind, and abnormality. Practically every branch of fiction has been invaded by this interest in corruption, though there are notable exceptions— books written by those authors who refuse to dabble in muck for the sake of attaining riches and notoriety. The romantic novelist is almost alone in presenting a picture of true love, decent and honorable conduct, and the happiness which is the result of these "old-fashioned" things.'[8]

The best answer to this sort of thing is probably to be found in a short story of Evelyn Waugh's entitled *Period Piece*, in which the main character, Lady Amelia, 'had grown increasingly fond of novels . . . of a particular type. They were what the assistant in the circulating library termed "strong meat" and kept in a hidden place under her desk.' Lady Amelia's companion is evidently ill at ease reading this kind of literature to her employer, and comments upon one novel:

'Well, it was very sad, wasn't it?'

'Sad?'

'I mean the poor young man who wrote it must come from a terrible home.'

'Why do you say that, Miss Myers?'

'Well—it was so far-fetched.'

'It is odd you should think so. I invariably find modern novels painfully reticent,' [comments Lady Amelia, who then proceeds to illustrate the point by recounting the story of some old friends of hers who, as she caustically observes,] 'came from anything but terrible homes'.

The element of moral shock, in some intellectual literature, is but one method of disturbing the reader's comfort. An even more general and fundamental one is suggested by the universal complaint that reading highbrow literature is 'hard work'. Or if readers do not complain that it is hard work, they misinterpret it utterly—and often in the most absurd kind of way. I am reminded of the subjects in the psychological experiment who could not make out the black hearts suit. Thus, more than one of my students, faced with the problem of interpreting Baudelaire's 'Crépuscule du matin' for the first time, has written (and doubtless will continue to write) that 'Baudelaire is trying to say' (I like that 'trying to say') 'that life in great cities like Paris is ugly and immoral, and he regrets the beauties of the countryside' (*sic*: there is of course nothing in the poem about the countryside).[9] A number of things could be said about this. First, that 'trying to say' perhaps indicates a subconscious irritation with the difficulty of interpreting even this fairly conventionally phrased poem; the writer wonders perhaps whether Baudelaire wouldn't have done better to express himself clearly in prose. 'Trying to say' in fact is a way of claiming that 'Baudelaire really means *this*, and I shall now put it in plain English'.

But, more interesting and important than all this is the interpretation of the poem as a whole. Clearly, these students have been brought up on a few clichés about nature poetry; they imagine that poetry is concerned with beauty; and they identify beauty with the countryside, probably with Wordsworthian lakes and fells. Now it is not so much that the students feel they must at all costs force this poem into the straitjacket of the genre 'moralizing nature poem'; it is rather that they cannot see anything, even when it is in front of their noses, that does not conform to their pre-existent habits of thought. To this kind of reaction I vastly prefer that of another of my students, equally puzzled, but who at least had grasped one of the basic reasons for her puzzlement: Baudelaire, she complained, was a *demoralizing* poet. And indeed he is: he does not offer the consolations of pastoral beauty, religious certainty or human happiness; he is obsessed with pain, ugliness and death. How unhealthy of him! And indeed this kind of thing is perhaps the reason why the ordinary man tends to think of poets and their like as being unhealthy, unstable, ultra-sensitive and excessively prone to alcoholism and suicide.

As far as the *adequacy* of the poem itself is concerned, it is clear that experiences are immeasurably more complex than the language of ordinary discourse seems to give them credit for. We have already seen Waismann asserting, correctly, that an empirical description can never be complete: however far I go in describing an object, I can always add still more—which is as much as to say that something will always be left unsaid. It is in principle impossible totally to describe an empirical object.

But that is another question, which we may touch on later. The point at issue here is that it is the function of poetry precisely to do the unexpected; its language must at all costs not conform to one's expectations of it; it must by some means or other bring off the mysterious conjuring trick of using the words of ordinary language in such a way that the process of ordinary language, the filing-away, pigeon-holing and classifying of the world into safe, well-understood categories, can no longer occur. The problem is to depict or suggest experience both (1) adequately and (2) in such a way that the experience in question cannot just be shrugged off.

But not only is it impossible to *complete* a description; it is also extremely difficult to sketch out a *partial* one which will adequately enable us to recognize the object in question if we do not already know what it is. We normally overlook this difficulty because we normally deal with terms for objects with which we and our interlocutors are already familiar. When I pronounce the word 'horse', you understand me because you have seen horses many times before. But I should have a difficult task describing one to you if you were, say, a man from Mars. Similarly, if it is notoriously difficult to describe a horse to a man from Mars or a bicycle to Julius Caesar, these tasks are not outlandish and tricky pieces of misapplied ingenuity. We meet with this particular problem whenever we have to describe one contemporary human being to another.

Suppose I am to meet someone I have never seen before: the meeting is arranged by phone. I try to describe myself. Easy enough, one would think: my face is perfectly familiar to me: I see it every day in the glass. Yet language, as we know in such instances, is incapable of doing the trick. One has to fall back on vague approximations: 'Er, dark hair, a beard, glasses,' or resort to wearing a flower in one's buttonhole. Guillaume Apollinaire recounts how when he first came to London he had arranged to be met at the station by a friend he had never seen. The friend agreed to wear a white carnation in his buttonhole so that he could be recognized. On his arrival at Victoria, Apollinaire gazed up and down the station, and could see *nothing but* young men wearing white carnations. He therefore hailed a cab and set off for his friend's house, where he found him still in bed.

The anticlimax of this story is neither here nor there. What matters is that this is what we do in literature too, when faced with the problem of doing the impossible: describing someone. We put a metaphorical flower in his buttonhole, that is we disturb the expectations of the reader by an odd concatenation of words, arouse his attention and jog his imagination. 'Mr Calverley,' writes V. S. Pritchett, 'had curling black hair, and looked gentle, savage and appealing.'[10] There is just a slight jolt there; an extended description contains far more:

> Dogged, with its slight suggestion of doggish, was the word for Mr. Pollfax. He was short, jaunty, hair going thin, with jaunty buttocks and a sway to his walk. He had two lines, from habitual grinning, cut deep from the nostrils, and scores of lesser lines like the fine hair of a bird's nest round his egg-blue eyes. There was something innocent, heroic and determined about Mr. Pollfax, something of the English Tommy in tin hat and full pack going up the line. He suggested in a quiet way — war.
> He was the best dentist I ever had.[11]

This is the conventional way to describe someone, conventional that is for the novelist. There are no modernist 'excesses'. But one could enumerate the 'jolts': 'Dogged... doggish. Jaunty buttocks. Cut deep. The fine hair of a bird's nest. Egg-blue eyes.' The odd concatenation of 'innocent, heroic and determined', the association of his peaceful pursuits with war . . . and war suddenly with dentistry. A beautifully calculated series of buttonholes.

There are in fact two points here: the first is that literary discourse must be more adequate to the complexities of experience than normal utterances are; the second is that this can only be achieved by abstracting from experience not merely the things which are normally so abstracted, but others too. 'What is not verbally odd is void of disclosure power,' says one writer.[12] And it is clear that such a Joycean phrase as 'he kissed the plump mellow yellow smellow melons of her rump' is both odd and pretty strong on disclosure power. Oddness performs two functions: it suggests complexity; it is also the means by which the normal process of pigeon-holing is avoided. Oddness interrupts *and* complicates this normal process. And many modern poets have elevated oddness into their prime principle 'A poem,' says Wallace Stevens, 'should almost successfully resist the intelligence.'

These conditions are in fact strongly suggested by the linguist's dictum that the less predictable an utterance, the more meaning it has.[13] Clearly if unpredictability is carried far enough, it interrupts the normal process of understanding: and this is the poet's task. At all costs the normal process of pigeonholing must be prevented. Those who have written on literature and literary discourse from a modern linguistic point of view have often perceived this. The Russian Formalist, Shklovski, wrote 'People living by the seashore grow so accustomed to the murmur of the waves that they never hear it. By the same token, we scarcely ever hear the words we utter . . . We look at each other, but we do not see each other any more. Our perception of the world has withered away, what remains is mere recognition.'[14] And he observed that the omnipresent principle of imaginative literature is to stimulate our awareness of the world by injecting oddness into language. Shklovski therefore recommends that literary discourse 'should have a strange, surprising quality; in practice it is often a foreign language'.[15]

Jakobson puts the same point as follows: 'The function of poetry is to point out that the sign is not identical with the referent. Why do we need this reminder? . . . Because along with the awareness of the identity of the sign and the referent (A is A_1), we need the consciousness of the inadequacy of this identity (A is not A_1); this antinomy is essential, since without it the connexion between the sign and the object becomes automatized and the perception of reality withers away.'[16]

But this is by no means a recent discovery. In the ninth century, the Indian poetic theorist Ānandavardhana was already making very similar statements.

[Ānandavardhana] says that beautiful ideas in poetry are of two kinds: literal (*vācya*) and implied (*pratīyamāna*). The latter is something like charm in girls which is distinct from the beauty of the various parts of the body; this implied sense is something more than the literal meaning and depends on the whole poem, and not merely on its parts. The expressed sense is invariably an idea; but the suggested sense may be of three kinds: an idea, a figure of speech, or an emotion. This suggested sense is not understood by those who merely know grammar and lexicon; it is understood only by men of taste who know the essence of poetry.[17]

It is clear that Ānandavardhana recognized the function of difficulty in poetry: his statements on this seem to have resembled those of Cohen: 'The definite purpose of the *lakṣaṇā* [approximately, metaphor) 'is to help in the process of suggestion. In *lakṣaṇā* there is a break in the flow, due to the incompatibility, and the listener has to think about the possible interpretations; thus the *lakṣaṇā* stimulates our attention to the suggestive elements that formed the motive in resorting to the metaphorical expression.'[18]

An example he gives is that of the word 'Ganges'. This suggests purity and sanctity. Its use in metaphor gives us pause, so that we register the suggestions inherent in it.[19] In other words it is the interruption of the normal process, which produces the poetic effect.

E. H. Gombrich, in a recent lecture,[20] discussed similar departures from regularity in visual patterns, and gave as one particularly striking example, a diagram of a stepped pyramid, in which however there is an irregularity in the succession of steps (figure 17). It is

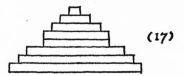

(17)

almost impossible to take one's eyes away from the two level steps in the pyramid's centre, for they constitute an almost 'irritating' disruption of the expected pattern.

Similarly, a recent French writer on the language of poetry, Jean Cohen, claims that the main purpose of metaphor in poetry is to interrupt the normal processes of understanding.

Si la métaphore est nécessaire, si la poésie est art, c'est-à-dire artifice, c'est parce que le code notionnel est le code usuel. Le signifiant renvoie d'entrée de jeu l'usager au sens notionnel. [That is, the Word normally is 'understood' in a cognitive way.] Le poète ne peut pas dire simplement 'la lune', parce que ce mot suscite spontanément en nous la modalité 'neutre' de la conscience. Et c'est pourquoi la prose est 'prosaïque', et c'est pourquoi la poésie est art. Pour susciter l'image émotionnelle de la lune, le poète doit recourir à la figure, il doit violer la code, il doit dire: 'cette faucille d'or dans le champ des étoiles', parce que ces mots, précisément, selon le code usuel, ne peuvent ainsi s'associer.[21] [If metaphor is necessary, if poetry is art, that is artifice, it is because the cognitive code is normal. The signifier (i.e. the Word) immediately evokes in its user the cognitive sense. The poet cannot simply say 'the moon', because this word automatically evokes in us the 'neutral' mode of awareness. And this is why prose is 'prosaic', and why poetry is art. To evoke the emotional image of the moon, the poet must resort to figurative language, he must violate the code, he must say: 'that golden sickle in a field of stars', precisely because words cannot, according to the normal code, be thus associated.]

And Cohen sees the interruption of the normal decoding process as the basic principle of poetry. By this means, for instance, were free verse even an *entirely* arbitrary breaking up of language into chance lengths, it would still be justified. 'L'écart mètre-syntaxe est visé comme tel.'[22] [Divergency between metre and syntax is intended as such.] And Cohen writes out 'Hier, sur la Nationale sept, une automobile roulant à cent à l'heure s'est jetée sur un platane. Ses quatre occupants ont été tués' [Yesterday, on the A 7, a car travelling at 70 miles an hour collided with a plane-tree. Its four occupants were killed], first as prose, and then as verse, thus:

Hier, sur la Nationale sept
Une automobile
Roulant à cent à l'heure s'est jetée
Sur un platane
Ses quatre occupants ont été
Tués.[23]

As he rightly remarks, this is not poetry. On the other hand, somehow the quality of our attention is altered by the new disposition of the words on the page, as if a different voice were speaking the phrases, or as if certain elements of the utterance had altered slightly in significance. Hence, just as 'la poésie. . . est de l'antiprose,'[24] so 'le vers, c'est l'antiphrase'.[25] [Poetry is antiprose. Verse is antisentence.]

Chapter Fifteen

Apparency and Some Varieties of Oddness

A fool sees not the same tree that a wise man sees.   (Blake)

A) APPARENCY

WHAT IS THIS DIFFERENT quality in our attention? Let us return to our image of the language as a classificatory system, a vast filing cabinet containing thousands of drawers.[1] Let us suppose that each word in the language is printed on the front of a drawer. (Each word also has a *place* in the system.) In a sense the word constitutes the handle of the drawer, for we can pause at a word, open the drawer and look inside: that is, we can consider 'what the word means', define it, enumerate its connotations and so forth. For the connotations are the content of the word.

But it is clear (it has indeed often been remarked upon) that in normal speech we do not linger upon words; we do not open every drawer and look into it. And it is also clear that despite what was said at length above about the failings of language in this respect (beginning Part II), this is also a necessary function of language: it is a virtue as well as a failing, for it enables us to use words like counters without having to meditate upon the actual content of each of them, but concentrating upon their structure and interrelationships.[2]

In poetry however our intention is different: as we said above, more of the experience has to be communicated. And this is done by forcing the reader to abandon his usual practice (which is simply to glance at the word on the front of the drawer); to understand the word's use, he has to open the drawer and at least glance inside. Consequently we may define poetic language as language in which certain chosen connotations are more than usually present to the mind. *Poetry is the language of the open drawer.* And this is doubtless why onomatopoeia is vulgarly thought of as particularly poetic: for it *directly* arouses awareness of certain connotations of the object when we read (and inwardly hear): 'The old dog barks backward without getting up' (Frost) or:

> So smooth, so sweet, so silv'ry is thy voice,
> As, could they hear, the Damned would make no noise,
> But listen to thee (walking in thy chamber)
> Melting melodious words to lutes of Amber,

or

Dont la serrure grince et rechigne en criant.   (Baudelaire)
Onomatopoeia imitates (in its rather conventionalized way)[3] the
sounds of nature: it thus makes certain referents seemingly more
apparent to us. But so of course do many other verbal techniques;
and this ability of language to (seemingly) 'show' us experience—
rather than merely 'refer' to it—I shall term *Apparency*.

Both in meaning and derivation this term is not far from the rhetoricians' *Enargia*. That term meant making visible or brilliant, and
is sometimes translated as 'illumination'. This, as Rosemond Tuve
insists, is not concerned with mere decoration, or the adding of de-
tachable 'beauties' to a work of art. Among Renaissance theorists,
she quotes Chapman on the topic, in terms which seem singularly
apt to my argument here: 'That, *Enargia*, or *cleerenes of represen-
tations*, requird in absolute Poems is *not* the perspicuous delivery of
a lowe invention; but high, and harty invention exprest in most
significant, and unaffected phrase; it serves not a skilfull Painters
turne, to drawe the figure of a face onely to make knowne who it
represents; but hee must lymn, give *luster, shaddow, and heightening*; which though ignorants will esteeme spic'd, and too curious, yet
such as have the iudiciall perspective, will see it hath, *motion, spirit
and life* . . .'[4] Chapman's deprecation of mere recognition in favour
of figures that are instinct with life is fundamentally the same distinction as I have tried to make between pigeonholing on the one
hand and apparency on the other.

And, making due allowances for the different purposes of Quintilian, we can see the same basic concern in his remarks on this topic:

> But by what means, it may be asked, shall we be affected, since
> our feelings are not in our own power? . . . What the Greeks
> call φαντασίαι we call *visiones*: images by which the representa-
> tions of absent objects are so distinctly represented to the mind,
> that we seem to see them with our eyes, and to have them before
> us . . . Hence will result that ἐνάργεια which is called by
> Cicero *illustration* and *evidentness*, which seems not so much to
> narrate as to exhibit . . . ἐνάργεια forces itself on the reader's
> notice. It is a great merit to set forth the objects of which we
> speak in lively colours, and so that they may as it were be seen;
> for our language is not sufficiently effective, and has not that
> absolute power which it ought to have, if it impresses only the
> ears, and if the judge feels that the particulars . . . are merely
> stated to him, and not described graphically, or displayed to the
> eyes of his mind.[5]

Let me make it clear from the start that this is not purely a *sensory* question: I mean that it is not a question purely of making *sense data* more 'apparent' to the mind. It is a superstition of modern Anglo-Saxon critical theory that poetry 'is not a language of counters, but a visual concrete one. It is a compromise for the language of intuition which would hand over sensations bodily. It always endeavours to arrest you, and make you continuously see a physical thing, to prevent you gliding through an abstract process.'[6] That is of course T. E. Hulme speaking, and very misleading it is! It must be remembered that Hulme had not brought his meditations on language to a final and considered conclusion, and perhaps this accounts for the imprecision of his language here. And of course I should assent to his remarks about poetry not being a language of counters, and to its always endeavouring 'to arrest you'; and also to its preventing you 'gliding through an abstract process' *provided that an important qualification is made*: namely that the 'abstract processes' in question are those involved in the generalizing factor, in classifying, or in abstracting from experience in the way science, philosophy, politics, etc., do. For as I. A. Richards accurately points out in his *Philosophy of Rhetoric*, to extend the taboo on abstraction to the use of all abstract words is quite unwarrantable.[7] What of such lines as:

Th'expense of spirit in a waste of shame
Is lust in action . . .

or

If music be the food of love, play on,
Give me excess of it; that, surfeiting,
The appetite may sicken and so die.

It will be clear that this superstition was not one that Shakespeare shared! No, if the function of poetry is to achieve 'apparency', then there is no reason why this should not be defined as an awareness of the experience in its *widest* sense, including feelings as well as sense data—not to mention also those 'thoughts' for which John Donne is customarily so highly praised.

One seeming difficulty with 'apparency' is that there is nothing at all to prevent me, when reading a scientific treatise for example, from pausing at any word whatsoever—at the word 'oyster' for instance—and making chosen aspects of the oyster as present as I can to my mind. The question is, however, whether the language is so constructed as to *compel* (or at least prompt) me to do so. And this of course brings us back to the principle of 'oddness'. In the next section of this chapter I shall list a number of the ways in which language can be made to give us pause. This is a vast topic, and I shall make no attempt to be methodical, still less exhaustive.

B) SOME VARIETIES OF ODDNESS
1. Rhythmic

a) *Divergency from Prose Rhythms.* Any poem in traditional metre illustrates divergency from the rhythmic norm of prose.[8] Whether mere versification *as such* can have any effect other than merely to warn us 'Look out! Here comes a poem!' and thereby put us in the frame of mind which we think appropriate for attending to poems (whatever that may be), is a controversial question. Can it be, as some have said, that a sort of trance-like state supervenes? At least one writer who takes this view, however, takes also a suspiciously dismissive view of free verse. Could it be that he likes being *lulled*? And if so, this attitude is closer to escapism than to artistic appreciation, rĕcreative rather than rēcreative. I should prefer to think that conventional metre imposes a time-scale of its own upon language, slowing its pace, and concentrating our minds upon the word and its phonic associations and not purely upon the denotative aspect of the concept, as in prose. (Thus we rarely notice alliteration in prose, but the rhythms of verse emphasize it.)

b) *Divergency within regularity.* But a rhythm of this kind always establishes its own pattern, so that divergencies from this pattern can themselves give us pause. A well-known example is the slowing and hence concentrating effect of the shorter fourth line, and its long vowel sounds in,

> Ah, what can ail thee, wretched wight,
> > Alone and palely loitering;
> The sedge is withered from the lake,
> > And no birds sing.

c) *Divergencies from regularity.* The Laforguian variety of free verse, imitated by Eliot, is perhaps essentially an extension of (1b) into a universal principle. The verse of Laforgue and Eliot is properly seen as a continual departure from, and a continual return to, stable traditional form: As Eliot himself wrote, 'The ghost of some simple metre should lurk behind the arras in even the "freest" of verse; to advance menacingly as we doze, and withdraw as we rouse. Or, freedom is only truly freedom when it appears against the background of an artificial limitation.'[9]

1   Blocus sentimental! Messageries du Levant! . . .
> Oh! tombée de la pluie! Oh! tombée de la nuit,
> Oh! le vent! . . .
> La Toussaint, la Noël, et la Nouvelle Année,
> Oh, dans les bruines, toutes mes cheminées! . . .
> D'usines . . .

> [Sentimental blockade! Levantine steamers! . . .
> Oh, the falling rain, the falling night,
> the wind! . . .
> Hallowe'en, Christmas and New Year,
> Oh, in the drizzle, all my chimneys! . . .
> Factory chimneys . . .]   (Laforgue, *Derniers Vers*, I.)

2   Our only health is the disease
   If we obey the dying nurse
   Whose constant care is not to please
   But to remind of our, and Adam's curse,
   And that, to be restored, our sickness must grow worse.

(Eliot, East Coker, IV.)

In the first example a sudden brevity followed by a pause, in the second, a slow increase in length, jolt and concentrate our attention.

In more radical free verse, every phrase has its own rhythm, every phrase is a divergency, has to be felt and weighed by the reader's awareness of rhythm. A divergency *from what?* We must feel there is an underlying rhythmic pulse, even if this is impossible to scan, or even sketch. Prose chopped into lengths will not convince us that it is free verse, as we saw in the case of Cohen's traffic accident. If verse is a music, it is certainly more like jazz than classical music, in that it presupposes a basic underlying rhythm (audible in verse only in the mind's ear; whereas the drums or the double bass keep it steadily audible in jazz), above which the actual verbal or melodic line moves in syncopation. Children in school may singsong: 'Shall Í compáre thee tó a súmmer's dáy?', but some more natural solution is intended. One possibility (one of many, just as the actual realizations of a jazz chorus are numerous) is: 'Sháll I compáre thee to a súmmer's dáy?' But keeping the basic pattern constantly in mind so that the verse can be felt to move across it while still remaining rooted in it . . . like a tree swaying in the wind.[10]

It is more exact to compare verse rhythms with jazz than with classical music, because the classical score divides the bar into regular lengths and into regular subdivisions of those lengths. For this very reason perhaps, syncopation of a more than rudimentary sort is comparatively rare in classical music. In jazz, on the other hand, the basic rhythmic principle is like that of verse: it is syncopational. Jazz exists in the tension between two rhythms, a rock-steady beat stated or implied, and a wide range of variations round that beat. These rhythmic variations include not merely the more obvious kinds of syncopation, such as the 'Scottish snap', which are easy enough to notate — but more subtle syncopations and stresses which it would be hard or impossible to express in a written notation. Thus the accent may be placed just before the beat or just after it, or other devices such as 'attack' or intensity may be used. It will be clear that in most of these ways jazz resembles the free variations of the spoken word much more than traditional Western European music does. And this is no accident, for jazz instruments are not played with the pure, clean tone taught in European conservatoires, but as if the human voice were speaking through them. Thus, a jazz-player may growl, whisper or shout through his instrument, and in any case may vary his tone and inflection as the speaking voice habitually does. It was said that 'eighty-five per cent of what Lester Young says on the sax you can understand'.[11] The comparison of jazz and spoken verse is thus strikingly exact: we may express their rhythms in precisely the same terms by saying that, in both, all the voice's subtleties of inflection and rhythm are employed in tension and syncopation against an underlying steady rhythmic pattern.

Free verse would then most resemble free jazz, where the basic rhythmic pattern may be in constant movement and not, in any case, audible (just as the mind's ear cannot usually scan free verse). G. S. Fraser remarks on 'a beautiful passage at the end of *Hugh Selwyn Mauberley* (where) one comes on... ambiguities of scansion, that seem nevertheless to be tied to a firm grasp of traditional metrics. Should one scan in a Hopkins fashion, allowing for feet of four syllables to one syllable? Is it:

'Or through/ dawn-/ mist

The grey/ and rose

Of the/ jurid/ ical

Flam/ ingoes,

with alternating lines of three and two feet? Or is it:

'Or through/ dawn-mist

The grey/ and rose

Of the jurid/ ical

Flam/ ingoes,

with two main beats to a line? The uncertainty begets the delicacy.'[12] He is right, though in fact other solutions are possible, and I should even prefer one of them. But the point is that we listen for the rhythms with a peculiar concentration, like the eye scanning not *one*

Gombrich pyramid but a series of them. The words themselves thereby obtain much more attention than we should grant them were our
interest in their rhythms not aroused.

The converse may occur, however. Occasionally one meets a poem
that is so carefully notated, so exactly 'scored', that one feels there
can be only one possible reading of it. Such a poem is Cummings':

ygUDuh

    ydoan
    yunnuhstan

    ydoan o
    yunnuhstan dem
    yguduh ged

    yunnuhstan dem doidee
    yguduh ged riduh
    ydoan o nudn
LISN bud LISN

    dem
    gud
    am

    lidl̸yelluh bas
    tuds weer goin

duhSIVILEYEzum[13]

The inarticulate grunts of prejudice are here so exactly reproduced
that our attention is fully alerted and our reaction fully controlled.
Of course a part of the technique is that Cummings' strange spellings,
while necessary to the exact reproduction of the sounds of his
speaker's voice, also force our attention to concentrate on those
sounds. But we can also say that, whereas poetry often achieves
apparency by the ambiguities of its rhythms, here it is their absolute
unambiguous precision which has the same effect.

More usual, however, are those uses of free verse where the
rhythm and its syncopations direct our attention onto particular
words, and lead us to give them more weight than we should normally accord them. This kind of thing can be briefly and simply illu-
strated by these lines from MacCaig:

    Why, when I praise you, when I tell you
    Some not much decorated truth,
    Do you look as if a stone, dropped
    From your hand, fell
    Upwards? . . .   (*Questionnaire*)

We strongly register the words 'dropped' and 'fell', since they have strong stresses isolated by other strong stresses ('stone' and 'hand') on their left, and by the traditional rhythmic pause of a line-end on their right. Each meaning thus reinforces the other . . . and is then as strongly contradicted by the surprising 'Upward', itself isolated at the beginning of a line by the pause that follows it. These factors help us to 'notice' what is happening, and underline its strangeness.

John Hollander[14] gives a splendid series of examples of apparency effected by the position of words around the line-ending. Milton, he points out, often ends a line with a word which seems to suggest a completed meaning . . . but the enjambement then carries us on to give a different interpretation to the words. Thus, 'Of Mans First Disobedience, and the Fruit / Of that Forbidd'n Tree . . .' contains what he aptly terms a 'ghost image': for the last word of the first line ('Fruit') can be interpreted as 'fruit of disobedience' . . . until we move on to the next line. This, according to Hollander, is a frequent technique in Milton, as in other poets. An interesting modern example occurs in Laforgue's *Derniers vers* no. 1:

Oh, dans les bruines, toutes mes cheminées! . . .
D'usines . . .
    [Oh, in the drizzle all my chimneys . . .
    Of factories . . .]

In the context of the previous lines, where a blockade (a blockade of feeling) and packet-boats from the Levant have been mentioned, we might interpret these 'cheminées' as the funnels of the steamers. The feeling would then be an uncertain mixture of regret for their absence or of relief for their presence (have they or have they not succeeded in breaking through the blockade?). But 'cheminées' also suggests the homely smoke of house chimneys rising through the mist, or, even more cosily, the fireside warmth within the house: 'une belle cheminée' means a fine blaze in the fireplace. These pleasant suggestions linger only a moment, however, before they are overturned and abolished by the words 'D'usines', with their grim industrial connotations. Warmth is dispelled by bleakness, made bleaker still by this sudden reversal.

2. Dispositional (and Visual)

The traditional gap at the end of a line of verse indicates a pause, or is at least a sort of bar-line cutting the poem's rhythms into lengths like a musical score. Disposition and rhythm are usually closely connected. But some poets have thought the lay-out of the poem *as such* to be an important factor; and we have already seen what Cohen has to say about it. Carlos Williams's much-discussed little poem 'The

Red Wheelbarrow' is a case in point, though perhaps spacing the words out like this also has a rhythmic function in that it may slow up our reading of them:

> so much depends
> upon
>
> a red wheel
> barrow
>
> glazed with rain
> water
>
> beside the white
> chickens.[15]

I must first mention Williams's choice of words. As far as this goes, barely two 'odd' turns of phrase (or metaphors, or images and so forth) can be distinguished here: 'glazed' is a metaphor, certainly, but hardly a very odd or striking one; though for the writer to say 'so much depends . . .' is no doubt much odder and more striking. It serves to direct our attention to the words of the poem. Which we then find to be ordinary language or at least very close to it. Here we have simplicity, the commonplace and the direct presenting themselves for close inspection. The oddness here is in fact the *lack* of oddness presented in a context where oddness is *de rigueur*. If poetry is expected not to be prosaic, the prosaic poem will itself appear odd.

The other point which can be made here[16] is (once again) Cohen's point: spacing the poem's words out like this has a strange effect on our attention to them. Words are separated from each other unnaturally (unnaturally, that is, from the point of view of ordinary speech, writing, grammar, syntax and semantics), in an effort to force our attention onto them, as upon the separate elements in a picture.

Whether this particular poem works as such, whether we do in fact see the redness, whiteness, wheel, barrow, wheelbarrow, rain, water and rainwater as distinct particular experiences making up this total experience, is another question. I am inclined to think that we do not; that the technique is here too simple a trick, that poetry here has been fined down too much—to only two of its elements, namely versification (à la Cohen) and the shock effect of prosaïcity. In this case, therefore, the trick can be seen through, and we should rapidly tire of hundreds of poems whose only claim to poetry lay in these two elements.[17]

However, just because it does achieve such narrow simplicity of technique, this Williams poem is instructive. For we can see through it one of the reasons for the apparently odd way in which the expert modern free-versifier chops up his lines. Take for instance another stanza from Norman MacCaig: part of his 'Frogs':

> Above all, I love them because,
> Pursued in water, they never
> Panic so much that they fail
> To make stylish triangles
> With their ballet dancer's
> Legs.

Here, however, the rhythmic element intervenes again. The pause imposed upon our reading of this poem between 'ballet dancer's' and 'Legs', by interrupting the smoothness of natural speech, concentrates attention on both phrases. And 'Panic' likewise gains force and pressure from its syntactical amputation from 'never'. It can only benefit the poem to add weight to our attention in this way. . . *so long as* the words themselves have sufficient strength to support this additional weight. And this is plainly the failing of Williams and the success of MacCaig in this instance.

3. Phonic

Rime and alliteration are a basic divergency from the usages of common or scientific discourse, where we usually disregard the element of *sound*, except perhaps where cacophony is to be avoided. Where these techniques serve the purposes of onomatopoeia, they are no problem: they arrest our attention for a reason that we can easily enough distinguish. But many unpractised readers embark on imaginative attempts to impose onomatopoeia willy-nilly on as many lines of verse as possible. Thus I have heard the opening lines of one of Baudelaire's *Spleen* poems,

> Je suis comme le roi d'un *p*ays *p*luvieux,
> Riche mais im*p*uissant, jeune et *p*ourtant très-vieux . . .
>
> > [I am like the king of a rainy country,
> > Rich but impotent, young but senile . . .]

described as containing *p*-sounds which, according to my interlocutor, represented the sound of falling rain. Perhaps slightly less implausibly (for these things are always a matter of degree), the pattern of *v*'s (and *f*'s) in these lines:

> *V*oilà le sou*v*enir eni*v*rant qui *v*oltige
> Dans l'air troublé; les yeux se *f*erment; le *V*ertige
> Saisit l'âme *v*aincue et la pousse à deux mains
> *V*ers un gou*ff*re obscurci de miasmes humains
>
> > [You see intoxicating memory float
> > In the turbid air; your eyes close; Vertigo

> Fastens with both hands on your soul, thrusts it
> Towards a chasm foul with human vapours.]

has been described to me as 'symbolizing' the mistiness (and dizziness) of which the poet is speaking here.[18]

Onomatopoeia depends upon the sense of *analogy*, and as I said above this is a matter of degree. Does: 'The murmur of innumerable bees' sound like bees? (The answer is usually Yes, up to a point.) Does: 'So smooth, so sweet, so silv'ry is thy voice' sound like a woman singing? Does: 'He clasps the crag with crooked hands' sound rough and craggy? (It will be seen we are already embarked on the perilous waters of synaesthesia.) Does the last line of Carl Sandburg's little poem:

> The voice of the last cricket
> Across the first frost
> is one sort of good-by.
> It is so thin a splinter of singing.

sound tiny, minute, fading?

In short there is (i) *'true'* onomatopoeia, and there are all sorts of degrees between it and an onomatopoeia which depends upon our prejudices about the overtones of certain sounds. We often say, for instance, that 'k' is 'hard', 'f' is 'soft', 'i' seems little,[19] and 'a' big . . . and so forth. And there does seem to be evidence for supposing that at least some of these prejudices (if that is what they are) are universal among human beings. This we might call (ii) *'natural'* or *'synaesthetic' sound-symbolism* (for it evidently depends upon analogies that cross the frontiers of our senses).

There is a variety of sound-symbolism (iii) that is to some extent built into the language, which again differs from one language to another, but which can hardly be said to rest upon any onomatopoeic or synaesthetic analogy. Such (in English) is the combination *fl*, which seems to symbolize moving light in such words as 'flame, flare, flash, flicker, flimmer', etc. ; or *sn*, which Bloomfield described in *Language* as expressing three types of experience: 'breath-noises' (sniff, snuff, snore, snort), 'quick separation or movement' (snip, snap, snatch, snitch) and 'creeping' (snake, snail, sneak, snoop).[20] The first of these cases is onomatopoeic; but the other two are of the kind described here, and which we might term 'contingent' sound-symbolism. The *sn* or *fl* combination is a kind of rudimentary morpheme (i.e., an isolable element of meaning); and this remains true whether its basis is onomatopoeic or accidental.

For it presumably is accident that brings this latter sort of micromorpheme about. As Marchand says, 'In *fl-* there is nothing to suggest flying or flowing movement, but in the co-existence of *flow*, *fleet*, *flutter*, *fly*, *flee*, *float* (all Old English) lies the germ of all the new words expressive of movement which were coined in Middle English.'[21]

This leads us to another point. For, according to Marchand and Jespersen, the pronunciation of old words can be affected, and new words formed, on the basis of micro-morphemes. Marchand notes for instance the creation of *splutter* (1677), *splash* (1715), *splatter* (1784) and several others presumably on the basis of *sputter* and *plash*.[22]

It has often been remarked that for these various effects to be made to work in a poem, the first requirement is that the *meaning* of the lines must support them. For example, as Frost noted, if we replace 'the murmuring of innumerable bees' with 'the murdering of innumerable beeves', the effect is destroyed. But when the requirement of relevant meaning *is* observed, the poet may extend the sound-symbolism of his language in all the three ways I have just described:

(i) *onomatopoeic*. The 'true onomatopoeia' of 'murmur' is combined with 'innumerable' and 'bees' (neither of which are onomatopoeic in normal language) to give a 'true onomatopoeic' effect to the whole line.

(ii) *synaesthetic*. The synaesthetic symbolism of roughness and ruggedness by 'kr' in 'crags' is combined with 'clasps' and 'crooked' to give a synaesthetic effect to the whole line.

(iii) *contingent*. It is a sort of extension of this type of phonic effect when we hear the tedious old rime 'love/dove/above'—as if all three words shared a common element of meaning as well as a common sound. Similarly with such puns as Armand Robin's delightful: 'Je devais manger, lentille par lentille lentillement'. But these are obvious cases. Perhaps the most persuasive (as also the most effective) are instances such as the intercommunication of meaning and sound in masterpieces of 'word-painting' like Eliot's 'Virginia':

> Red river, red river,
> Slow flow heat is silence
> No will is still as a river
> Still. Will heat move
> Only through the mocking-bird
> Heard once? Still hills
> Wait. Gates wait. Purple trees,
> White trees, wait, wait,
> Delay, decay. Living, living,

> Never moving. Ever moving
> Iron thoughts came with me
> And go with me:
> Red river, river, river.

For there is nothing red or riverish about the word 'red', or the word 'river'. There is nothing 'still' about the word still, and still less about 'will' or 'hill'. But the poem nonetheless persuades us momentarily that there must be. Somehow we are led to concentrate on the sounds, and through them on the picture, as if word-form or word-image symbolized it in a more direct way than via our semiotic rectangle, as if indeed the base-line of the rectangle were filled in partially, as it is with onomatopoeia proper.

And perhaps this explains in part our pleasure with the sound-structures that alliteration presents to us. When Lowell writes:

> The fountain's failing waters flash around
> the garden. Nothing catches fire.   (*The Public Garden*)

we may feel as if the words involved in this alliteration of *f*'s *inter-communicate*. The elements of the picture are connected somehow, act upon each other. Patterns doubtless may be purely abstract, and we find pleasure even in such patterns. But, as with a painting by Miró or Klee, give us half a chance and we glimpse a face in the circle, an acrobat balancing upon a tightrope, or merely a snowstorm of lilac paint. And so did Klee, as his titles indicate. My student, then, who wanted to hear rain in Baudelaire's 'pays pluvieux' was not *entirely* wrong: she was mistaking a sense of structure, rightness and aptness (due to the natural tendency to grasp connexions as meaningful), for something more sensuous, more rational and more describable.

(iv) We must add, then, to our account of sound-symbolism, a fourth element, in which (to tell the truth) nothing is being symbolized: our pleasure in *abstract patterns*, particularly when these interfere with and syncopate across the basic verse-pattern. For though regular sound-patterns (such as one gets in traditional Welsh verse)[23] are of course 'odd' in that they constitute a departure from prose usage, an irregular pattern of sound, such as in practice alliteration almost always is, constitutes a further 'oddness'. Alliteration may be entirely abstract, or it may give a sense of semantic connexion between the words it links. But in any case, it is attention-drawing, and hence (whether or not we may attribute any *stateable* meaning to it) contributes to apparency.

4. Levels of discourse

Poetic discourse has often impressed itself on its readers as odd because it affected an unusually 'noble' or 'lofty' manner. Examples of this are the eighteenth century, with its preference for calling a spade an agricultural implement—or rather a plague of rats a 'furry tribe' —, the elevated style of Victor Hugo, or the dignified splendours of Saint-John Perse. But then, of course, along comes Wordsworth with his prescription of the common speech of men, or Corbière with his deliberate parody of, and onslaught on, the verse of Hugo:

> Oh! combien de marins, combien de capitaines
> Qui sont partis joyeux pour des courses lointaines
> Dans ce morne horizon se sont évanouis! . . .
>
> Combien de patrons morts avec leurs équipages!
> L'Océan, de leur vie a pris toutes les pages,
> Et, d'un souffle, il a tout dispersé sur les flots.
> Nul ne saura leur fin dans l'abîme plongée . . .
>
> Nul ne saura leurs noms, pas même l'humble pierre,
> Dans l'étroit cimetière où l'écho nous répond,
> Pas même un saule vert qui s'effeuille à l'automne,
> Pas même la chanson plaintive et monotone
> D'un aveugle qui chante à l'angle d'un vieux pont.

> > [Ah! Countless are the mariners and captains
> > Who set off carefree for a distant voyage
> > And vanished on that sinister horizon! . . .
> >
> > Countless the masters drowned with all their crew!
> > The Sea ripped out the pages of their lives,
> > Scattered them in a gust upon the waters.
> > And none shall know their fate, sunk in the deep . . .
> >
> > Nor yet their names: not even the humble stone
> > Between the narrow graveyard's echoing walls,
> > Not even the willow sheddding autumn leaves,
> > Not even the plaintive murmur of a song
> > Sung by a blind man on an ancient bridge.]

> (V. Hugo, 'Oceano nox')

> Eh bien, tous ces marins—matelots, capitaines,
> Dans leur grand Océan à jamais engloutis...
> Partis insoucieux pour leurs courses lointaines,
> Sont morts—absolument comme ils étaient partis.
>
> Allons! c'est leur métier; ils sont morts dans leurs bottes!
> Leur *boujaron* au cœur, tout vifs dans leurs capotes . . .
> —*Morts* . . . Merci: la *Camarde* a pas le pied marin;
> Qu'elle couche avec vous: c'est votre bonne femme . . .
> —Eux, allons donc: Entiers! enlevés par la lame!

Ou perdus dans un grain . . .

Un grain . . . est-ce la mort ça? la basse voilure
Battant à travers l'eau!—Ça se dit *encombrer* . . .
Un coup de mer plombé puis la haute mâture
Fouettant les flots ras—et ça se dit *sombrer.*

—Sombrer. —Sondez ce mot. Votre *mort* est bien pâle
Et pas grand'chose à bord, sous la lourde rafale . . .
Pas grand-chose devant le grand sourire amer
Du matelot qui lutte.—Allons donc, de la place!—
Vieux fantôme éventé, la Mort change de face:
La Mer! . . .

[So all those sailors—shipmates, captains, tars,
Were swallowed up for ever by the Sea . . .
Departing carefree for their far horizons,
They died—exactly as they had set out.

So what? It's their job: they died with their boots on!
Hearts fired with rum, alive in their sou'westers . . .
Died? . . . No, Madam Death's a landlubber;
She's your old woman; let her sleep with you . . .
But as for them: Complete! Carried off by the waves!
    Or lost in a squall . . .

A squall . . . Is that a proper name for death?
The leaden sea pounds in, the topsails sprawl
Flat on the water—The boat's capsized . . . Or the
    rigging
Drags through the surge—That's foundering.
Foundering.—Plumb that word. Your *death* is a pale
    phantom
Beside the broad grim smile of a sailor
Fighting the gale.—Ahoy! Give way! That stale
Old bogey, Death, tears off its mask—The Sea!]

For when the sonorous beauties of a particular style are no longer felt as odd, when they go stale and no longer carry the weight of apparency they used to, an injection of colloquiality will refresh us, give us back a sense of 'oddness', enable us to feel that the realities of experience are again being grappled with, not classified into oblivion. We have thus the paradox that the need for poetic discourse to violate the code of language, explains also a poetic discourse that is not noticeably poetic.

Well, this is at least a *partial* explanation. For it is also clear that

Corbière would claim his language to be not only less automatic (and hence more real), but also more real *in its own right*. And he has cunningly incorporated the two poles of language between which his poem exists, into the poem itself: it exists as the tension between them, as the rejection of one (comparatively false) in favour of the other (comparatively true). Corbière's ironic technique itself ensures a continuing sense of freshness; for the norm against which his language is to be considered 'odd' is given us in his misquotations from Hugo.

    5. Syntactic

a) *Accepted 'poetic' order*. Here I have in mind such conventionally acceptable distortions of prose discourse as:

    Look, stranger, on this island now
    The leaping light for your delight discovers,
    Stand stable here
    And silent be,
    That through the channels of the ear
    May wander like a river
    The swaying sound of the sea.   (Auden, *Seascape*)

In prose (and leaving some of the very odd semantic uses alone) this might go: 'Look now, stranger, at this island that the leaping light discovers to delight you; stand stable here and be silent, and let the swaying sound of the sea wander like a river through the channels of your ear.' Which so utterly destroys the effect of these beautiful lines that I am almost tempted to use another example: it reads indeed like a bad translation from Aeschylus. But which illustrates perfectly how poetry is a matter of the exact word in the exact place. It is not of course only a matter of 'the swaying sound of' the rime and rhythm, so perfectly under control in Auden's lines here; it is also a matter of the order of clauses, giving emphasis, tension and release.

b) *Syntactic distortion*. Under this heading we may put such deliberate ambiguities as (according to Laura Riding and Robert Graves) Shakespeare's Sonnet no. 129. In a now classic study they pointed to the modernization of the spelling of the original editions of Shakespeare, and by placing a modern version side by side with the original, demonstrated that the latter's ambiguous punctuation supported a wealth of interpretations. The texts set side by side are richly suggestive in themselves:

1   Th'expense of Spirit in a waste of shame
     Is lust in action; and till action, lust
     Is perjured, murderous, bloody, full of blame,

Savage, extreme, rude, cruel, not to trust;
Enjoy'd no sooner but despisèd straight;
Past reason hunted; and, no sooner had,
Past reason hated, as a swallow'd bait
On purpose laid to make the taker mad:
Mad in pursuit and in possession so;
Had, having and in quest to have, extreme;
A bliss in proof, and proved, a very woe;
Before, a joy proposed; behind, a dream.
    All this the world well knows; yet none knows well
    To shun the heaven that leads men to this hell

2   Th'expence of Spirit in a waste of shame
    Is lust in action, and till action, lust
    Is periurd, murdrous, blouddy full of blame,
    Sauage, extreame, rude cruell, not to trust,
    Injoyd no sooner but dispised straight,
    Past reason hunted, and no sooner had
    Past reason hated as a swollowed bayt,
    On purpose layd to make the taker mad.
    Made In pursut and in possession so,
    Had, hauing, and in quest, to have extreame,
    A blisse in proofe and proud and very wo,
    Before a joy proposd behind a dreame,
        All this the world well knowes yet none knowes well,
        To shun the heauen that leads men to this hell.[24]

The kind of use Graves and Riding made of this observation can be
sufficiently—and persuasively—shown by quoting their remarks on
line ten of the sonnet:

The comma between *in quest* and *to have extreame* has been
moved forward to separate *have* from *extreame*. The line originally stood for a number of interwoven meanings:

1. The taker of the bait, the man in pursuit and in possession
of lust, is made mad, is made like this: he experiences both
extremes at once (What these extremes are the lines following
show.)

2. The *Had, having, and in quest*, might have been written in
parentheses if Shakespeare had used parentheses. They say, by
way of interjection, that lust comprises all the stages of lust: the
after-lust period (*Had*), the actual experience of lust (*having*),
and the anticipation of lust (*in quest*); and that the extremes of

lust are felt in all these stages (*to have extreame*, i.e. to have extremes, to have in extreme degrees).

3. Further, one stage in lust is like the others, as extreme as the others. All the distinctions made in the poem between *lust in action* and lust *till action*, between lust *In pursut* and lust *in possession* are made to show that in the end there are no real distinctions. *Had, having and in quest* is the summing up of this fact.

4. The *Had, having*, separately sum up *possession*: that is, the *action* of lust includes the *expence of Spirit, the waste of shame*. The *in quest*, naturally refers to *In pursut*.

5. It must be kept in mind throughout that words qualifying the lust-business refer interchangeably to the taker (the man who lusts), the bait (the object of lust) and lust in the abstract. So: *Had* may mean the swallowing of the bait by the taker, or the catching of the taker by the bait, or 'lust had', or 'had by lust'; *having* and *in quest* are capable of similar interpretations.[25]

Whatever the scholars' view may ultimately be of ambiguities of punctuation (and hence of syntax) in the Shakespearian era, it is clear that this is a technique that can be used by poets—and has most certainly been so used in modern times. It is well known that the fashion of leaving poems unpunctuated was set in France by Apollinaire, who, while his first collection, *Alcools*, was already in proof, went through it removing all the punctuation. He was in certain quarters accused of gimmickry. Yet it cannot be denied that, taken seriously, the absence of punctuation often produces interesting ambiguities. These lines for instance:

> Que tombent ces vagues de briques
> Si tu ne fus pas bien aimée
> Je suis le souverain d'Egypte
> Sa sœur-épouse son armée
> Si tu n'es pas l'amour unique
> > [May these waves of bricks fall
> > If you were not beloved
> > I am the king of Egypt
> > His sister-wife his army
> > If you are not the one and only love]

produce at least for a moment, a certain hesitancy in the reader as to the 'correct' punctuation. Thus, it is possible to take the third line with the second one, or with the fifth one, or with both. It is also possible to read it as it stands, on its own (for the only punctuation in

this poem is given by line-endings). And in that case the poet's pro-
testation of a guiltless love is evidently being denied! The fact that
this is supported by the imagery in these lines, which is indeed of
something guilty and sordid, with overtones of violence, merely sup-
ports this point. Uncertainty of syntax can thus strengthen the suggestions already present in the imagery. And I think we may, with
this evidence, accept that removing punctuation was no gimmick.

Syntactic distortions of all kinds were a favourite device of E. E.
Cummings. And indeed the semantic force of Cummings is usually
slight. Read:

> it may not always be so; and i say
> that if your lips, which i have loved, should touch
> another's, and your dear strong fingers clutch
> his heart, as mine in time not far away; . . .

and you have a highly conventional piece of poetry in early twentieth-century Georgian poetic diction—were it not for the punctuation—and that doesn't amount to much, for we have none of the
subtleties that, say Apollinaire achieves, in his case through suppressing it. Cummings indeed achieves semantic interest (elsewhere)
almost solely through distorting grammar, syntax and punctuation
in an immediately obvious way. For instance:

> here's a little mouse)and
> what does he think about, i
> wonder as over this
> floor(quietly with
>
> bright eyes)drifts(nobody
> can tell because
> Nobody knows, or why
> jerks Here &, here,
> gr(oo)ving the room's Silence)this like
> a littlest
> poem a
> (with wee ears and see?
>
> tail frisks)
>
>   (gonE)
> "mouse",
>   We are not the same you and

Which will do, I think, to make the point. Very little of the effect of
this is due to meanings being altered by 'oddness' in anything but a
very arbitrary way. And to defer to the criterion of J. P. Thorne, that
perhaps deep structure has to be altered before the poem becomes

worthwhile, deep structure is certainly not altered in *this* poem.[26]
On the other hand:

> anyone lived in a pretty how town
> (with up so floating many bells down)
> spring summer autumn winter
> he sang his didn't he danced his did.

looks more like an alteration in deep structures. But this doesn't
necessarily correspond to depth in the poetry. Naturally so, for 'deep'
in the phrase 'deep structure' merely means 'underlying', and has
no necessary connexion with profundity. 'Anyone lived . . .' may be
deeper than the mouse poem, but only relatively. For anyone can
see how the trick is done: by formula: place a few words in an unfamiliar grammatical category, and there you are:

> nobody stairs up who the came treads
> (rockabye everytwo sleep their dream)
> wish by chimney and snow by dark
> he reined his deer he stockinged his fill.[27]

But I do not wish to condemn what is after all a charming poem. The
method is the same as John Berryman's 'Homage to Mistress Bradstreet', where the distortions of syntax:

> so squeezed, wince you I scream? I love you and hate
> off with you. Ages! *Useless*. Below my waist
> he has me in Hell's vise.
> Stalling. He let go. Come back: brace
> me somewhere. No. No. Yes! everything down
> hardens I press with horrible joy down . . .

more extreme even than those in the rest of the poem, express the imposition of a new rhythm on the body of a woman giving birth . . .
and pressure and violence and pain. The violence done to language
corresponds to the sense. The structure of the experience seems to be
reflected in the structure of the language.

6. Semantic

Such figures of speech as simile, metaphor, metonymy, cata-
chresis, synecdoche, zeugma, etc, come under this heading. Each of
these is evidently 'odd', in that there is a clash between context and
figure. Thus, in Eliot's:

> His soul *stretched tight* across the skies
> That fade behind a city block,
> Or *trampled* by insistent feet
> At four and five and six o'clock   (Prelude IV, *Prufrock*)

the words are unusual attributions to the extent that we should
normally call them metaphoric. As usual this is all a question of

degree, since for the soul to be 'trampled' is less unusual than for
it to be 'stretched tight across the skies'. (For we say 'He trampled on
my feelings' or 'He rode roughshod over my objections.')

Unusual attributions are not by any means always metaphoric,
however. Few lines in English poetry are so striking or so well
known as the opening of *The Waste Land*:

> April is the cruellest month, breeding
> Lilacs out of the dead land, mixing
> Memory and desire, stirring
> Dull roots with spring rain.
> Winter kept us warm, covering
> Earth in forgetful snow, feeding
> A little life with dried tubers.

April is here literally the 'cruellest month', and winter did literally
keep us warm (though in both a physical and an emotional sense).
Yet these attributions are certainly surprising.

The same passage will also serve to illustrate the 'odd' effect that
can be given by unusual juxtapositions: '. . . Breeding lilacs out of
the dead land, mixing/ Memory and desire . . .' are both literal or
nearly so. But they pass from nature to man and back again, so that
we feel that memory and desire are attributed also to nature, and
death and painful renewal also to man.

All this is sufficiently obvious not to need any exposition. I shall in
any case return to the question of types and degrees of metaphoric
language in chapter 16. We might reasonably here however explore
the question whether semantic oddness is all that is needed to produce poetry, or whether the question is more complicated.

And of course, like most questions, it is more complicated. It is
evident that a mere unusual concatenation of words, like the linguist's favourite 'Colourless green ideas sleep furiously' or 'Asleep
children the are' are not poetry. It is true of course that some arts of
poetry have recommended this sort of thing. 'Colourless green ideas
sleep furiously', for instance, could be a quite typical case of the
Surrealists' favourite game 'Cadavre exquis'.[28] However, as André
Masson put it when talking of another not dissimilar Surrealist
technique: 'Automatic writing is like fishing: you may pull in a fine
fish; you may catch nothing but an old boot.'

The same is equally true of less extreme images. We must feel that
their oddness is acceptable, not in any flatfooted way of course, but
because it is adequate to the poem's sense.[29]

When for instance Ted Hughes begins one of his best-known
poems 'Terrifying are the attent sleek thrushes on the lawn,' we are

distinctly jolted. But I think we give assent to the image—or do so, at least, by the time we have seen that Hughes admits the other side of appearances ('those delicate legs'), neatly observes the head-on-one-side stance of the thrush ('a poised/ Dark deadly eye'); and when we remember to brush up our own observation (the birds act 'with a start, a bounce, a stab'), and accept the worm's eye view of things: 'Overtake the instant and drag out some writhing thing'.

On the other hand, the same poem falters briefly in its second stanza. Hughes writes:

Is it their single-mind-sized skulls, or a trained
Body, or genius, or a nestful of brats
Gives their days this bullet and automatic
Purpose? Mozart's brain had it, and the shark's mouth
That hungers down the blood-smell even to a leak of its own
Side and devouring of itself. . . .

Is the 'genius' put in for the sake of putting in Mozart? And is Mozart put in for the sake of assimilating him to a shark? This is odd, certainly; and too odd for its adequacy, I should guess. Perhaps the oddness of comparing Beethoven's mind to a shark, might have seemed more accurate. But Mozart, of all composers, is not like that; and Hughes, of all poets, is not a Mozartian man. The image is ill-chosen, and falsifies the reality it seeks to represent. The principle of oddness, that is of violence done to our normal perceptions, may not be indulged in arbitrarily.

Linguists have sought to deal with this problem in a characteristic way: they function as usual on a non-semantic level, and seek the explanation in mere pattern, disruption of pattern, and a further pattern within that disruption. According to Bierwisch, poetry is distinguished from merely arbitrary deviations from the norm of common speech by its habit of producing a regularity within irregularity. 'Brecht made clear that the assumptions of a metrical scheme and its simultaneous violation can be a special poetic medium. But here too the violation must be regular; it cannot rest upon mere whim.'[30] This sounds reasonable, the more so as we have already seen Eliot recommending that free verse should constantly suggest a regular pattern of metre. When Bierwisch applies the principle to the semantics of poetry, however, one is not so sure: '. . . mere ungrammaticality is not sufficient . . .' (Here he means by un-grammaticality, semantic abnormality, as the reader may see by consulting the relevant passage.)[31] '. . . mere ungrammaticality is not sufficient: . . . [Sentences] achieve poetic effect only when the deviation has a specific regularity as its basis, when they stop being

merely violations of the grammatical rules. This means that poeti-
cally effective deviations must be explicable in terms of rules of
deviation which themselves specify the conditions and form of the
deviations.'[32]

Now this will not do at all. It is insufficient for a poet to write his
own deviant grammar, so to speak, and proceed to apply it in a consistent way. For we should end up with this kind of thing being
presented as poetry:

> Asleep children the are,
> Cupboard the in toys all the are,
> Come sandman the has,
> Town the all over fallen darkness has.

This is extremely deviant and extremely regular. It is also extremely
pointless.

At first sight Bierwisch might be offered a way out by Thorne's
suggestion that only if the deep structure of language is affected, can
worthwhile poetry be produced.[33] This is a much better way of looking at things, but it still will not do, I believe, for the following
reason: it would leave us unable to distinguish between parody and
the real thing. (And indeed I suspect that the principles that linguists apply to literature are all inadequate to avoid this problem.)[34]
Henry Reed's deservedly famous parody of Eliot has all the characteristics required of it by linguists: its deep structure is deviant in a
consistent way. Yet this is insufficient to explain why it is not a
perfect Eliot poem. And indeed it nearly is so!

Chard Whitlow
(Mr Eliot's Sunday Evening Postscript)

As we get older we do not get any younger.
Seasons return, and today I am fifty-five,
And this time last year I was fifty-four,
And this time next year I shall be sixty-two.
And I cannot say I should like (to speak for myself)
To see my time over again—if you can call it time:
Fidgeting uneasily under a draughty stair,
Or counting sleepless nights in the crowded tube.
There are certain precautions—though none of them very
                                                    reliable—
Against the blast from bombs and the flying splinter,
But not against the blast from heaven, *vento dei venti*,
The wind within a wind not able to speak for wind;
And the frigid burnings of purgatory will not be touched
By any emollient.'[35]

No grammar of semantic distortion is going to be able to explain why *The Waste Land* or the *Four Quartets* are great poetry, whereas this is great parody. For its greatness as parody resides precisely in its closeness to Eliot, in the devilish subtlety of its perversion of his style.

And this perversion is so exact that Eliot is capable of committing it himself. Reed takes us disquietingly close to such lines as

> And indeed there will be time
> To wonder, 'Do I dare?' and, 'Do I dare?'
> Time to turn back and descend the stair,
> With a bald spot in the middle of my hair . . .

and

> I grow old . . . I grow old . . .
> I shall wear the bottoms of my trousers rolled.
> > (*The Love Song of J. Alfred Prufrock*).

and

> Time present and time past
> Are both perhaps present in time future,
> And time future contained in time past

and

> You say I am repeating
> Something I have said before. I shall say it again.
> Shall I say it again? (*Four Quartets*).

Can the principle of regularity within irregularity explain *that*?

What then is the explanation? Semantic, certainly. But the difference between *Chard Whitlow* and *Burnt Norton* is not explicable by claiming patterned deviance for the one and arbitrary deviance for the other, for both are patterned. Nor is it very easy to claim that the two patterns are different. We have the same mixture of incongruity and nostalgia in *Prufrock* as in *Chard Whitlow*:

> Shall I part my hair behind? Do I dare to eat a peach?
> I shall wear white flannel trousers, and walk upon the beach.
> I have heard the mermaids singing, each to each.

Even if linguists could invent a 'grammar' for producing semantic absurdity, it would clearly be too blunt an instrument to explain why we just barely accept *Prufrock* and just barely reject Reed. For degrees of absurdity depend upon what particular absurd images are chosen, and the way they fit into the total poem. But what determines our decision that:

> It is, we believe,
> Idle to hope that the simple stirrup-pump
> Will extinguish hell,

is more absurd than some of the phrases in *Prufrock*? Or fits its context worse? Our decision is made on the grounds of our experience of the particular object and the particular word, the 'stirrup-pump' or 'white flannel trousers', the 'draughty stair' or 'bald spot'. For the connotative structure of each word is individual,[36] and differently apprehended in each different context. *It is beyond the reach of formulas.*

I am not saying, of course, that regularity within irregularity does not occur. On the contrary, it is this that determines recognizable style, whether in Homer, Lucan, Webster, Racine, Pope, Sterne, Poe or McGonagall. But the inclusion of the two last in this list sufficiently demonstrates my point. As a criterion of *poetic effect*[37] mere pattern within deviance is not enough.

One broad distinction which we might, however, make, and which would at least be a help in certain cases of regularity within irregularity, is a distinction between *full and empty ambiguity*. Let me quote four brief passages:

1   Je fis un feu, l'azur m'ayant abandonné,
       Un feu pour être son ami,
       Un feu pour m'introduire dans la nuit d'hiver,
       Un feu pour vivre mieux.

       Je lui donnai ce que le jour m'avait donné:
       Les forêts, les buissons, les champs de blé, les vignes,
       Les nids et leurs oiseaux, les maisons et leurs clés,
       Les insectes, les fleurs, les fourrures, les fêtes.

       Je vécus au seul bruit des flammes crépitantes,
       Au seul parfum de leur chaleur;
       J'étais comme un bateau coulant dans l'eau fermée,
       Comme un mort je n'avais qu'un unique élément.

              [I made a fire, for the blue sky had abandoned me,
              A fire to be her lover,
              A fire to penetrate the winter's night,
              A fire to live better.

              I gave her what day had given me:
              Forests, bushes, cornfields, vines,
              Nests and their birds, houses and their keys,
              Insects, flowers, furs, festivals.

              I lived by the sole sound of crackling flames,
              By the sole scent of their warmth;
              I was like a boat foundering in sealed water,
              Like a corpse I belonged but to a single element.]

                                        (Eluard vol. I, 1032–3)

2 *Combat*
Ta langue de fourmi desséchée
sur l'arête d'une brique
en face.
Arbre
aux noires feuilles velues,
chien trotteur.
Bouquet sevré d'un batteur d'odeurs,
ton chagrin,
plus aride que l'amour
sur le dos encrassé du matin.

Tiens-toi, pertinent!
on fouille tes sables.
Devant ton mal:
débris des os.

Qu'importe!
Dans ce lieu répudié désert,
nulle phrase ne pourra fléchir
l'élan de ton combat,
petit peuple,
les mains dressées vers ce bec,
désormais vautour
et jusqu'aux cimes,
oiseau de proie!

> [Your dried ant's tongue
> on the crest of a brick
> opposite.
> Tree
> with hairy black leaves,
> loping dog.
> Bouquet parted from a whisk of odours,
> your chagrin,
> more arid than love
> on morning's dirty back. etc.]

(Garelli *Brèche*, 33–4).

3   Yes but he's not the sort who'd wait
    Except to look at her, to—let the
    Recognize her, to one who has ju
    Passing into the enemy camp,
    Sewn into your white thread
    'Come now, that's nothing
    Very good talking abou
    Of clothes distributed   H
    Badly 'get as far upstre   I
    Distance as far as possible   D
    Moment to leave again let's   D
    Ning! Wearing a pair of pants on   E
    Sumptuous hostess looking, here   N
    Colonialist, farmer or master of the ho
    Ass having laughed a lot. (Lexicon, p. 92 ff. like Pleynet
    'Hostess remaining leaning at the level she can see that she
                                                        can't be
    Taken again in the position of a supine poem-reader
                    (Denis Roche, trans. Martin 1972, 179.)

4   riverrun, past Eve and Adam's, from swerve of shore to bend
    of bay, brings us by a commodious vicus of recirculation back
    to Howth Castle and Environs.
        Sir Tristram, violer d'amores, fr'over the short sea, had
    passencore rearrived from North Armorica on this side the
    scraggy isthmus of Europe Minor to wielderfight his penisolate
    war: nor had topsawyer's rocks by the stream Oconee exag-
    gerated themselse to Laurens County's gorgios while they went
    doublin their mumper all the time: nor avoice from afire
    bellowsed mishe mishe to tauftauf thuartpeatrick: not yet,
    though venissoon after, had a kidscad buttended an bland old
    isaac: not yet, though all's fair in vanessy, were sosie sesthers
    wroth with twone nathandjoe. Rot a peck of pa's malt had Jhem
    or Shen brewed by arclight and rory end to the regginbrow
    was to be seen ringsome on the aquaface.
                            (Opening of *Finnegan's Wake*)
        To interpret the poem by Eluard (1), we have to attribute a very
    general sense indeed to each of its main images. *Feu* for instance is
    meant to recall everything that is warm, above all figuratively warm:
    all those traditional metaphors for fire, such as love, friendship,
    security, companionship, hearth and home, shelters against the cold
    (which is of course also a metaphor of the same wide-ranging sort),

a light in darkness. Similarly for *azur*, *jour*, *nuit d'hiver*, etc. This is a technique that Empson calls 'ambiguity through vagueness'.[38] The possible senses of the word 'fire' are, one might say, hardly restricted at all by the context: it is allowed to send out waves in a large number of directions.

The dangers of this technique reside precisely in this vagueness. In the Racinian use of *feu*, we have practically a one-for-one correspondence between *feu* and *amour*. The clarity is total. Here, however, the metaphor is as if encircled by a halo of different interpretations: the vehicle stands for a number of different, though associated, tenors. One might think that the word would therefore 'resound' more, be more powerful by virtue of the larger number of associations it suggests. But just as waves may become superimposed on each other and mutually destroy each other, so the associations given by a word may become *too* numerous: the more senses there are, the weaker each one appears, until they are nearly obliterated in what Mallarmé called 'their vibratory almost-disappearance'. Clearly, this point has not yet been reached in Eluard's poem: it is in fact powerful and emotionally evocative: it is a case of *full ambiguity*.[39]

In the poem by Garelli (2), we are fortunate in having the comments of its author, himself no mean theorist in the matter of poetry. He explains the opening lines of the poem thus:

Bien sûr, ce n'est pas l'idée d'une fourmi à la langue desséchée, posée de face sur l'arête d'une brique qui évoque l'idée de combat. Le détour serait bien compliqué et son effet . . . minuscule! Il s'agit d'un problème tout autre: rendre présente une certaine dimension du monde, irréel sans doute, mais constituée par la réalité du texte et qui révèle dans son accomplissement que le monde est aussi un combat. Dès lors, il s'agit de présenter de manière concrète une structure du monde concentrant en elle les notions d'agressivité, d'opposition, de rupture. Or l'image d'un homme à la langue acide dressé face à moi surgit et sa présence m'obsède comme l'image fabuleuse d'un tableau de Chirico. Comment dans l'univers du langage manifester mieux son apparition brusque que par une apostrophe? . . . C'est donc l'apostrophe avec son jugement péjoratif: 'ta langue de fourmi desséchée' qui porte en elle-même l'idée d'un combat et non le simple contenu conceptuel du texte.[40] [Naturally it isn't the idea of an ant with a dried tongue confronting one on the crest of a brick which evokes the idea of combat. This would be very complicatedly devious, and of negligible effect! The problem is quite different: to summon up a certain dimension of the world, doubtless unreal, but established by the reality of the text and revealing in its accomplishment that the world too is a combat. Consequently the question is to present in a concrete manner a structure of the world concentrating in itself the notions of aggression, opposition and rupture. Now the image of a man with an acid tongue confronting me comes to mind, and his presence obsesses me like the fabulous image of a Chirico painting. In the universe of language, how could one manifest his sudden appearance better than by an apostrophe? . . . It is thus the apostrophe along with the pejorative judgment 'your dried ant's tongue' which implies the idea of a combat, and not the mere conceptual content of the text.]

Let us pause and consider these remarks. Clearly we must agree that what he calls the 'conceptual content' of the text, that is, what I should call its denotative content, may be largely irrelevant to its poetic effect: what counts are the connotations. But are the connotations that Garelli desires sufficiently evident here? Not all correlatives are objective. And the connexions which Garelli desires to emphasize are only three in number: (i) the acid tongue; (ii) a sudden appearance symbolized by the apostrophe; (iii) the pejorative judgment given by the phrase 'Ta langue de fourmi desséchée'. But this is insufficient. These connotations are thin, slight and excessively abstract; they are not assisted by the context; and I think it is true to say that they would never have occurred to us had we not read Garelli's explanation of them first!

Garelli goes on to appeal to sound-effects and syntax:

Mais d'autre part, la sonorité acide et aiguë de la syllabe finale 'mi' de fourmi, renforcée par l'aridité et l'âpreté du mot 'arête', puis par le mot monosyllabique 'brique', qui ponctue comme une masse coupante le deuxième vers, accentue cette structure agressive de l'apostrophe . . . Enfin, le rejet au troisième vers de la locution 'en face' rompt le rythme de la phrase en même temps que le sens logique de la proposition dont on attend le verbe est suspendu. L'attente et le malaise propres à l'inquiétude d'un combat naissent donc de la structure matérielle et syntaxique de ces trois vers. Mais au lieu de rencontrer un verbe permettant de liquider ce malaise, voici que le lecteur tombe à la ligne suivante sur le mot 'arbre' qui aggrave la rupture de sens initial.[41] [But besides, the sharp and acid sonority of the final syllable 'mi' of *fourmi*, reinforced by the dryness and harshness of the word *arête*, and by the monosyllabic *brique* , which punctuates the second line like a shearing weight, accentuates the aggressive structure of the apostrophe . . . Lastly, the postponement till the third line of *en face* breaks the rhythm of the phrase, at the same time as it suspends the logical sense of the proposition, whose verb we are expecting. The suspense and unease proper to the alarms of a combat are thus produced by the material and syntactic structure of these three lines. But instead of coming upon a verb which could resolve this unease, the reader meets in the next line the word 'tree', which worsens the initial rupture of meaning.]

This short passage is a model of textual explication. Unfortunately however, it applies not to the text we have before us, but to some ideal version of it existing only in the author's mind. 'Rupture', perhaps yes; a certain roughness of sound, no doubt; a disruption of syntax, certainly. But the multiplicity of radically different experiences which these phenomena could symbolize makes it impossible for us to assimilate them solely to a 'Combat'. Garelli has forgotten that the connexions between sound-effects and meaning are notoriously subjective, and 'ambiguous' in the sense of being undecidable. We do not have sufficient guidance from the semantics of the poem: its 'objective correlatives' are too subjective; so many possible senses are offered us that none is indicated. This is a case of *empty ambiguity*.

Our third example is even more clearly a case of no connexions being given. Indeed, its point is its arbitrariness, for Denis Roche is an anti-poet concerned to mock the conventions of poetry. Here I think we can more properly talk, not of empty ambiguity, but of simple emptiness.

No doubt the example from *Finnegan's Wake* (4) is more controversial. But it is also clearer, for enormous effort has been expended by critics on unraveling the multiplicity of senses that each individual word may be assumed to have. Thus Joyce's portmanteau word *venissoon* may be a conflation of *vain, vein, veinous, vinous, on, venison, very soon, Venitian, Venice's son, Venice's sun, Venus's son, Venus's sun, penis's son, Phoenix's son, vanishing,* etc.[42] Whether this goes too far or not, and whether the interaction of these many portmanteau words in context fines down their senses to an acceptable degree of ambiguity, is doubtless a controversial question. But it is controversial, I believe, because some readers will feel that so complex and multifarious an ambiguity loses itself in vagueness: the waves of meaning interfere with each other, and an empty ambiguity results; whereas others will claim a density and plurality of meaning that can be defined as 'full'.

I am not concerned to decide this question here, but merely to emphasize the conclusion that our brief examination of an Eliot parody had already suggested. Oddness must be supported by adequacy. These passages by Eluard, Garelli, Roche and Joyce, all have distinct stylistic characteristics of their own; each presents us with a different kind of pattern within deviance. But it is not this that makes us react to them with interest, excitement, distaste or indifference. It is whether they present us with a complexity that is full or one that is empty; it is whether they do or do not have apparency for us. They are all odd. And they are all odd in a partially regular way. Their oddness jolts our attention. Their regularity constitutes a semi-private language that we can learn to interpret. But that language must offer a content. The function of oddness is to provide apparency, to fill out the hasty schema of experience that ordinary language sketches for us. It is not to empty that sketch even of those few outlines it already held.

c) IMPOSED APPARENCY

It might well be argued that I have still not shown how apparency can be *forced* upon the reader. And indeed, just as I remarked above that it is possible for me to pause at the word 'oyster', when reading a scientific treatise, and make chosen aspects of that creature present to my mind; so I can read Eluard's lines:

Notre vie tu l'as faite elle est ensevelie
Aurore d'une ville un beau matin de mai
Sur laquelle la terre a refermé son poing
[You made our life, it is buried/ Dawn of a town one fine
morning in May/ On which the earth has shut its fist.]

as saying merely 'She is dead and I am very sad'; or Shakespeare's:

It seems she hangs upon the cheek of night
Like a rich jewel in an Ethiop's ear

as 'I find that girl rather attractive'. I can insist, that is, at all costs on imposing the classifying attitude upon even the most resistant of language.

And this, of course, is what the majority of average readers obstinately persist in doing. It can hardly be denied that this is very unreasonable of them. When Hopkins writes:

No worst, there is none. Pitched past pitch of grief,
More pangs will, schooled at forepangs, wilder wring.
Comforter, where, where is your comforting?
Mary, mother of us, where is your relief?

he is clearly not saying 'Holy Mother of God, why do I feel so miserable this morning?' However, if a reader were to insist, in the teeth of all the verbal evidence, on reading poetry in this way, there is a further technique that a poet can use to dissuade him. He can remove the denotative element; he can make it impossible to read the poem at all save *via* connotations.

This is, so to speak, the converse of Eliot's famous 'objective correlative'. It will be recalled that he writes: 'The only way of expressing emotion in the form of art is by finding an "objective correlative"; in other words, a set of objects, a situation, a chain of events which shall be the formula of that *particular* emotion; such that when the external facts, which must terminate in sensory experience, are given, the emotion is immediately evoked.'[43] In the process to be described here, the statement itself is left inexplicit, and the only equivalent for it is to be found in an objective correlative for the emotion attached to it; then the statement can be reconstructed (or guessed at) only *via* the emotion evoked. Or to put it less rebarbatively, the poet abandons statement for suggestion. For it is the emotion attached to statements that he values, not the statements themselves. For nothing is easier than to sweep a statement under the carpet like a cutting from a newspaper; and then the fine dust of emotion is lost too, along with any individual quality that the statement may have had.

Let us take an example from a modern Swiss poet, Philippe Jaccottet:

> Tout à la fin de la nuit
> quand ce souffle s'est élevé
> une bougie d'abord
> a défailli
>
> Avant les premiers oiseaux
> qui peut encore veiller?
> Le vent le sait, qui traverse les fleuves
>
> Cette flamme, ou larme inversée:
> une obole pour le passeur   (*Airs*)

> [At close of night
> when the breath sighed
> a candle first
> had guttered
>
> Before the first birds
> who still keeps vigil?
> The wind that crosses rivers knows

This flame, or inverted tear:
an obol for the ferryman]

Nothing could be further from the poetry of concrete description affected by our modern British poets, like Hughes or MacCaig. There is no picture. For T. E. Hulme is not a figure in the French Pantheon. And it should be remembered that Mallarmé's ambition was to 'reprendre à la *musique* son bien': to steal poetry's lost magic back from music, not from the painters. If there is a picture it is of the vaguest and most general kind, a diagram, a misty sketch-map. There is an effort towards particularization only in a grammatical sense: '*la* nuit', '*ce* souffle', '*une* bougie', '*cette* flamme'. And this suggests that these concrete but familiar words (too familiar indeed to be so very concrete) have a mysterious importance. They are presences, we feel, of an importance beyond their literal sense. Moreover the general is explicitly present in the poem: '*les* premiers oiseaux', '*les* fleuves'. And at the centre of the poem is a question: '*qui* peut encore veiller?'

One consequence of this is that the French poem appears at first sight much more obscure than, say, the Hughes poem I quoted from above p. 188. We can readily 'understand' the details of Hughes' poem. His description of the shark, for instance, is powerful and highly coloured, but immediately comprehensible. There is nothing in Jaccottet's brief poem to understand in this way at all. The sensory associations of the words Hughes uses are important in his poem, at least as a first requirement; the English reader likes to visualize things, and to be sure that his poet has seen them, weighed them, observed them with meticulous attention: these are an English poet's testimonials, they bear witness to his respect for the well-known sensory qualities of the English language.

We might phrase this differently by saying that in Hughes' poem, the words have inner and outer connotations, (as well as psychological overtones: hardness, toughness, violence, etc). But in Jaccottet's poem, everything (or almost everything) is psychological overtone. It is, I suppose, just possible (though it is not of course Hughes' intention) to remain at the surface of his description. In Jaccottet's poem, there is no such surface: we must lay ourselves open to the psychological overtones it presents us with, or give up the attempt to 'understand' it. And this of course is the reason for the poem's being written in the way it is: there is only one path into it: an emotional and psychological rather than a sensory one. The poet insists we take that path and no other. Obscurity is his weapon, it forces us to read the poem in the correct way or not at all.

For, although we might take the first line: 'Tout à la fin de la nuit' literally, we are prevented from doing so with 'ce souffle': 'This breath' should mark a precise reference to something gone before. But in this case there is no such item to refer to: the demonstrative, one can only assume, is being used for the purpose of emphasizing the words, giving them a strange importance. Similarly 'Une bougie d'abord/a défailli' leaves us ignorant of any precise reference. These phrases present us with puzzles: we are left uncertain even whether they are literal or metaphoric. An even more explicit puzzle is given later in the phrase 'qui peut encore veiller?' Who indeed? What sort of person, creature or thing? And what kind of watch or vigil is being kept?

The poem is thus a kind of puzzle. And to a puzzle we require a key. We are indeed duly given one in the final line: 'une obole pour le passeur'. This allusion to the coin given to Charon to ferry a dead person across the river of death into Hades, at once enlightens us. Night, flame, breath, wind and tear, and the mysterious watcher (but *is* there a watcher?) can therefore be read in the context of a death. As context, in prose, controls the precise sense of words, so context here controls the precise associations intended.

These associations are in fact manifold. There are hints of a wake (the candle, the night, the watcher); but these will not take us far in a factual direction, for though in this sense these words may be 'literal', no certainty is given about whether a death has, is, will, or maybe simply might, occur. Our attention is, or should have been, riveted upon the words of the poem—gives them more weight than words in prose would have—largely on account of the 'puzzle' element. Emotional associations are clearly necessary. The candle and its flame, symbolic of life and death; the breath (transmuted perhaps into a wind in line 7), symbolic also of life, or of a parting breath; the strange association of wind with Charon (for both 'cross rivers'): these associations go some way towards resolving the puzzle. We may say that the poem is about a death, possible, actual or feared; that the elements of it are both literal and metaphoric: the candle's guttering may be a life being extinguished; the wind that of a spirit passing. And life and grief are strangely equated in the last line but one, and equated also with the 'sop for Cerberus', the obol, the offering to the Gods, which is, after all, such a little thing, a penny, a tear, a hope. All these uncertainties are themselves elements in the poem: they cast across it the twin shadows of doubt and fear.

Of course this leaves the poem still vague and mysterious, still obscure, in this sense that we can more certainly say what it *evokes* than we can decide what it is *about*. But if its function is therefore to arouse a feeling (akin to a child's unreasoning fear of the dark, or the cold shiver down the spine when, as we say, someone is walking on our grave), then this remaining obscurity is understandable. Our normal, rational vocabulary for feelings is notoriously sparse and scanty. 'Love' covers a multitude of virtues, and 'hate' a multitude of sins. The words for our emotional categories are merely words for categories: just as calling a tree a tree assimilates it to all other trees, wipes out its differences from all other trees, so 'love' can cover all kinds of feeling from D. H. Lawrence's *bête noire* of 'sex in the head' to Phèdre's murderous passion.

In short, in Jaccottet's poem, the *feeling* is precise. Describing or rationalizing about it is difficult not because of any lack of precision in the feeling, but because our descriptive and rationalistic vocabulary is unfitted to such a task. For, once again, we are here in the presence of a particular experience. Words, used in their normal function as classificatory devices, necessarily miss this particularity. A different function has to be imposed upon them: or rather, our attention to them must be of a different quality, so that more of the experience seems to be communicated by them than is normally the case.

But principally, let us note how this particularity is arrived at. (1) It is not by way of drawing attention to particular details, as in Hughes. It is the psychological experience which is particular (and general), not the sensory one. (2) Nor is it by telling us anything. It is the feeling that matters, not the information.

But if we want information, if we really want to know 'what the poem is about', we cannot approach it except through connotations. We must ask 'What do flame, breath, wind, rivers suggest emotionally? What are their overtones?'[44] We have to put together the data we are given for ourselves, form it into a meaningful whole by ourselves. Basically, though Eisenstein was writing of montage, and though the technique of montage is most akin to that of juxtaposition,[45] his words here may equally serve to underline this point —and to complete this chapter: 'The strength of montage resides in this, that it includes in the creative process the emotions and mind of the spectator. The spectator is compelled to proceed along that self-same creative road that the author travelled in creating the image. The spectator not only sees the represented elements of the finished work, but also experiences the dynamic process of the emergence and assembly of the image just as it was experienced by the author.'[46]

On Metaphor

According to Hobbes, we abuse words when we use them metaphorically—that is in other senses than they are ordained for. It is, however, quite clear that if we do not use them metaphorically, we shall not use them at all.   (Urban, 178)

A) HOW METAPHOR OPERATES

IT IS A STRANGE paradox that the process which enables us to assimilate new objects to previously established categories, so that we can call a salamander a salamander, and no longer see it in its full mysterious particularity, is the very same process which poetry employs in dislocating and breaking down such categories, such indifference to the individuality of phenomena. For, as most writers on poetry seem to have asserted, it is *metaphor* that is poetry's fundamental means of achieving this end. But metaphor, as we shall see, operates through the generalizing function.

For how are objects classified? We may assume that the process is *either* that having learnt the term 'dog' in relation to a particular dog or dogs, we then extend it to other objects which we learn are to be seen as similar (or which we ourselves see as similar)—*or* that we learn that objects with certain features in common are to be called 'dogs'. Which occurs (and probably both occur) does not really matter for the purposes of the present argument. For in both cases we can say that the distinguishing marks of individual dogs are suppressed. Each dog-owner of course knows his own animal perfectly: Bonzo has certain distinguishing marks (i.e., his name has certain connotations) which make him a different dog from Gip fifty yards down the road. Let us say that 'Bonzo' has connotations $a \ldots w$, 'Gip' connotations $d \ldots z$. It is by virtue of $a \ldots c$ that we recognize Bonzo as an individual; and by virtue of $x \ldots z$ that we recognize Gip. The other connotations $(d \ldots w)$ are those by virtue of which we recognize both dogs as 'dogs'. (It may be noted, in passing, that of course proper names, as is shown clearly here, possess (when we have attached them to particular individuals) *more* connotations than common nouns. They have in short more *intension*. On the other hand their *extension* is 1.)

Thus classification involves the suppression of connotations that attach to individuals: we have in mind their similarities, not their differences. Similarly, when a term is extended in a metaphorical usage, still more connotations are suppressed. Or this is at least the case with such hoary old talking-points as 'lion' for 'brave man', or 'leg' for 'table-leg', etc. In this latter case, let us assume (for the sake merely of simplicity) that 'leg' normally contains two connotations: (1) locomotion and (2) a (vertical) support. Then the locomotive element is suppressed in our applying it to 'table-leg'. It will be seen that the process whereby we extend terms into their metaphoric range is not in principle different from that whereby they are in the first place used to classify, in their literal sense.[1]

But *is* 'leg' (for the leg of a table) a metaphoric usage? Max Black, in *Models and Metaphors*, gives a list of questions (p. 25) that remain to be settled about metaphor, for example (1) 'How do we recognize a case of metaphor?' and (2) 'Are there any criteria for the detection of metaphors?' It will be plain from my remarks here[2] that I regard literal and metaphoric as a matter of degree. There are all sorts of gradations between the use of 'leg' as referring to a human leg, and, say, the 'leg' of a journey. Now it is perfectly possible to *differentiate* between the use of 'leg' for a human leg and, say, a wooden leg. For everyone will agree that the criteria, that is the connotations, are different in the two cases. But how is one to come to a decision whether both or one of these uses is 'literal'? And this is the problem. The usual definitions of literality are irritatingly vague: they assert that an expression is literal if it is normal, or 'proper'; or they talk of an 'essential difference' between the two referents, the name of one of which is being applied to the other. But what is an 'essential difference'?[3]

Thus, Gustaf Stern, in *Meaning and Change of Meaning*, approvingly quotes Stählin to this effect: 'Metaphors are figures of speech in which a referent is designated by the name of another referent in such a fashion that (1) the transfer does not involve an essential identity of the two referents, (2) the designation is taken from another sphere of experience than that to which the actual referent belongs, and (3) the process of transfer is not expressed.'[4] Condition (3) is of course quite straightforward: it simply refers to the absence of a term such as 'like', 'as' or 'such as', that is to the metaphor's not being technically a simile. The expression 'sphere of experience' however is very vague, as Stern notes. And so is the word 'essential'.[5]

Need this, however, worry us? In practice we seem to get along perfectly well with a great deal of loose talk about literal and metaphoric. And I suspect the situation is similar to that obtaining between 'mountains' and 'hills'. Nobody is going to establish a definition stating that 'henceforth we shall call anything over 3,000 feet a mountain, and anything 2,999 feet 11.9 inches or less a hill'. Still less is anyone going to assert that 'the literal use of a term shall be when two referents have thirty connotations in common, the metaphoric when they have twenty-nine or less'. For I have already given reasons for supposing that connotations are not enumerable. Moreover, they are certainly not all definable, as John Stuart Mill himself asserted: '. . . it is clear that the word man, besides animal life and rationality, connotes also a certain external form; but it would be impossible to say precisely what form; that is, to decide how great a deviation from the form ordinarily found in the begins whom we are accustomed to call men, would suffice in a newly-discovered race to make us refuse them the name of man.'[6]

The idea then that we might ever establish a clear and precise definition of literal and metaphoric, is just a pipe-dream. On the other hand, we can certainly express an opinion about the *degree* of metaphoricality or literality as between two uses of a term, just as when faced with what geographers call two outstanding natural features, we are more likely to apply the word 'hill' to the smaller of them, and 'mountain' to the larger. Thus everyone will concede readily enough that 'leg' applied to part of a table is more metaphoric than 'leg' applied to a human leg; though whether they would agree that 'leg' in 'table-leg' is 'in fact' a metaphor is another matter.[7] In short, if theoreticians wish to define metaphoric and literal in such a way that the two terms are totally distinct and have a clear dividing line between them, they will only be able to do so by (1) an arbitrary act of decision, and (2) a different arbitrary decision *in each case*. We may therefore give this firm though doubtless frustrating reply to Max Black's problem, and pass on with clear consciences to a consideration of metaphor itself.

One of the most impressive studies of metaphor this century is contained in Gustaf Stern's *Meaning and Change of Meaning*. He illustrates the theoretician's traditional talking-point, 'lion' for 'brave man', with the following diagram:

	I	II
Word:		*lion*
Meaning:	'a brave man'	'lion'
(Speaker's apprehension	$\alpha\,\beta\,\gamma$	$\gamma_1\,\delta\,\epsilon$
of the referent)		
Referent	The man	The lion
	$a\,b\,c$	$c_1\,d\,e$

'In Referent I,' he writes, 'only three main characteristics are designated, in order not to complicate matters unnecessarily. Of these c is assumed to be the quality of courage. In the lion (Referent II) there are also three characteristics, of which courage is one, but since it appears in another aspect in a lion, I have given it the symbol c_1. In a corresponding manner, the meanings, that is to say, the subjective apprehension of the referents, are given each three main elements, of which γ and γ_1, respectively, correspond to the qualities of courage in man and beast.'[8] It will of course be clear to the hearer that a particular man is being referred to: *his* connotations will not be suppressed. On the other hand, irrelevant connotations of 'lion', 'as the yellow colour, the nocturnal habits, the tail, etc, are inhibited; they would be merely disturbing.'[9]

It will be clear that the process has the effect of high-lighting the element that both terms are supposed to have in common, namely, courage.[10] However, the courage of the lion has a particular quality of its own: it is thus not merely 'courage' that is attributed to the man by the use of the metaphor, but a particular quality of courage.[11] Moreover, at least so far as the hearer is concerned, 'the remaining elements of meaning of *lion*, perhaps especially the emotive elements or an awareness of the sphere to which the primary referent' (i.e., the lion) 'belongs, are evoked more or less, forming a background or fringe to the actual referent.'[12] (. . .) 'The essential point is that we experience the actual meaning of the metaphorical expression, and of the context in which it is placed, and simultaneously also something of the primary meaning of the phrase or word. The fusion of the latter elements with the actual meaning and the actual context constitutes the metaphor.'[13] Something of the flavour of the *vehicle* (the *lion*) is carried over to the *tenor* (the *man*).

This fusing of the two elements of metaphor, vehicle and tenor (in the account given here, *lion* is the vehicle or metaphoric term, *brave man* the tenor, or literal or real term), has been noted by a large proportion of modern writers on the topic. One of the most important statements to this effect is Max Black's remarks in *Models and Metaphors*.[14] Max Black

> speaks of metaphor as a filter. In 'man is a wolf' 'man' is seen as the principal subject; 'wolf' the subsidiary subject. 'Wolf' has a 'system of associated commonplaces or true and false literal uses . . . These literal uses commit a person in a speech community to certain beliefs . . . To deny a commonplace is to create a metaphor, e.g. as in 'man is a wolf'. The literal or implied assertions of 'wolf' are then made to fit 'man'. A new system of commonplaces for 'man' is then determined and

organized on the basis of wolf commonplaces. Metaphor is regarded as a filter or screen of commonplaces. The principal
subject, man, is 'seen through' the filter of the subsidiary subject or metaphor, wolf.[15]

It will be clear that if this view is correct, then we have here a clear
case of bisociation in Koestler's sense. Max Black calls his theory an
'interaction theory of metaphor'. For the filter works both ways: man
is regarded as wolf-like, but the wolf may also be regarded as more
man-like than usual.[16]

Perhaps this theory of metaphor can be made clearer by quoting
Max Black directly:

Suppose I look at the night sky through a piece of heavily
smoked glass on which certain lines have been left clear. Then
I shall see only the stars that can be made to lie on the lines
previously prepared upon the screen, and the stars I do see will
be seen as organized by the screen's structure. We can think of
a metaphor as such a screen and the system of 'associated
commonplaces' of the focal word as the network of lines upon
the screen.[17]

A rather similar image is used by Stanford in his discussion of
Greek Metaphor: 'Metaphor is the stereoscope of ideas. By presenting
two different points of view on one idea, that is by approaching a
word through two different meanings, it gives the illusion of solidity
and reality.'[18] Or, as I should say, apparency.

We need therefore a slightly different diagram from the one that
Stern proposed in 1931; we need a diagram in which the denotation
'wolf' is superimposed on the denotation 'man', thereby bringing out
appropriate connotations in both 'man' and 'wolf', and causing them
to interact (figure 18). Which connotations of the vehicle are

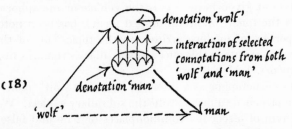

(18)

brought out by this process? In favourable circumstances, any that
fit the tenor.

Thus, Ramsey describes

a metaphor whose possibilities I first realized when Sir George
Clark developed them . . . in an informal speech at Oxford

some years ago. The head of an Oxford college, said Sir George, is often thought of as a figurehead. Now what is a figurehead? It is a colourful, decorative but somewhat wooden personality, well to the front, representing the ship to the outside world. But it might be said that a figurehead is also virtually useless, needs pushing from behind if ever it is going to move at all; and yet everyone admits that if a storm breaks, it is the figurehead who bears the worst of it.[19]

This is a particularly useful example, because Sir George Clark has taken the trouble to spell out the connotations of his metaphor for us. But usually in poetry the connotations are not spelled out: we are given the task of feeling them for ourselves, as in the folksong 'Bonnie Ship the Diamond':

Along the quay at Peterhead the lassies stand around
With their shawls about their heads and
                              salt tears running down:
'I'll never weep, my bonny lad, although I'm left behind,
For there's not a rose in Greenland's ice
                              to make you change your mind.'

'A rose' for 'a girl' is the most faded of traditional metaphors. But it is refreshed by (1) the fact that there are literally no roses in Greenland's ice, (2) the contrast of roses with ice, which immediately makes us feel once more the grounds for the metaphor: the association of roses with summer, and therefore with warmth (which is suggested by their colour too), their 'complexion' and 'bloom', their fragility, and so on. Vehicle and tenor interact once more: the more so as we cannot here abolish the vehicle (rose) in favour of the tenor (girl) as the literal-minded might have us do. For there are literally no roses in Greenland's ice, as I observed above, so that 'rose' is both literal and metaphoric. This is of course a special type of metaphor; but I use it here because it is the clearest possible instance of Black's 'filtering' mechanism or Stanford's stereoscope: it is like looking at a rose with one eye and a girl with the other, and holding them both in focus.

Now that we have a model for the working of metaphor, we may clearly show how a metaphor may be supposed to produce 'apparency'. Let us take a simple case, a dead metaphor like 'the nose of an aeroplane'. Normally, we use this term without ever thinking why: we apprehend it literally as we do such terms as 'aileron', 'cockpit' or 'strut'. We may however guess that when this expression is first used to someone who has never heard it before (a child for instance), the process of understanding it goes something like this:

' "Nose": he must mean that bit at the front that is shaped like a nose.' This process is rapid, no doubt barely conscious, and, with such readily comprehensible and straight-forward metaphors, occurs almost instantaneously. We might picture the process as in figure 19.

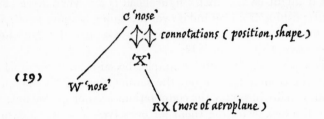

(19)

However aware the hearer is of these connotations, word and referent *cannot be connected except* via *them*. It is only they that can form a link between the normal uses of 'nose' and the actual object referred to. Unless they are present in some way in the mental process of understanding that 'nose'='front of aeroplane', then it is impossible to see how the term 'nose' in this context (or any other metaphoric term in any other context) could be understood by the hearer at all. (I am of course assuming here that the speaker is not pointing at the plane's nose, and that he is allowing the hearer's knowledge of the connotations of 'nose' to locate the referent for him. This is a perfectly natural situation. It is clear on the other hand that if a new or unknown word were used—or if the metaphor were obscure— the speaker would have to point to the referent in some way, unless the context was sufficiently clear. But that is a different case.)

With further uses of the word 'nose' in the context of aeroplanes, however, it becomes quite familiar and normal; and, as we say, the metaphor 'dies'. We can explain this by saying that the process of understanding 'nose' has become more direct: we no longer have to think of it as referring to the front of an aeroplane only through the connotations of 'frontness' and 'shape': we now think of it as being the natural term to use, and the connotations become merely implicit.

We need therefore a term midway between 'implicit' and 'explicit', to describe those connotations which, in a first use of 'aeroplane's nose' or 'tail' or 'wing', are actually evoked, are present in the mental process, have not, like an appendix, degenerated and been bypassed, do not therefore lie totally dormant and unconscious. We might call them 'interplicit' (for they are not explicit, nor are they so implicit as to be imperceptible; and they form a mediating link). Apparency *is* the making apparent of connotations, and this is why so many writers have thought metaphor to be the basis of poetry. We can now see precisely why. When a term is extended into a new context, or used as a metaphor, it forces into consciousness—or at least into the fringes of consciousness—certain connotations, makes them 'interplicit'. Thus the term is not apprehended as a mere conceptual token of the referent, and has to be understood as possessing a certain content, namely those connotations. When Browning calls a tulip a 'bubble of blood', all those connotations which justify his comparison are forced into the margins of consciousness. Our awareness of the flower is given a content.

But this is not all. Metaphors like the 'nose' or 'tail' of a plane are very easily grasped by the reason: the connotations on which they depend are of a simple and schematic kind. With the 'tail' of an aeroplane, for instance, even at a first hearing of the term there is no problem in assimilating tenor to vehicle. For the connotations ('rearness', 'appendage', 'function') fit perfectly, and are simple to define. (I assume that 'shape' will in this case be rejected as a connotation, since an aeroplane's tail seldom bears much resemblance these days to the real tails of real birds. Even if it did, however, we should clearly not be required by ordinary language to fit the two conflicting appearances together in any complex way: the tail of a plane and the tail of a bird are similar only superficially, and we could easily take their main point of resemblance to be their similar positions, at the back of both planes and birds.)

Less easy to categorize and pigeon-hole, however, are those connotations which seem both more descriptively accurate and less clearly defined. We must remember the imprecision of most shapes (other than schematic shapes such as 'square' or 'triangle'). When Lowell writes of 'yellow dinosaur steamshovels',[20] the actual appearance of dinosaurs and steamshovels has to be contemplated and compared in imagination. We have to imagine both tenor and vehicle, and fit them over each other, 'picturing' both at once. Similar remarks can be made about Allen Tate's lines 'Long shadows of grapevine wriggle and run / Over the green swirl.' Hence the sense of reality and solidity that an image like this provides. The connotations that link tenor to vehicle are a set of visual experiences that cannot be reduced to mere language. The link is experiential, not just linguistic. Similarly, with Browning's comparison of the tulip to a 'bubble of blood', we mentally compare redness with redness: we have to imagine the colour, and this is an irreducible sensation. And again, when we read the biblical line:

'[The war-horse] saith among the trumpets, Ha, ha,' (*Job* 39, 25) our attention is forced onto auditory sensations, the neighing of horses, shouts of laughter and triumph, and the shrill discord of trumpets. We can now see just how important it is for poetry that (1) connotations are not merely linguistic but experiential, and that (2) language cannot be understood without a vast range of experience of the real world—because it is on such experience that meaning itself depends.[21] Poetry's ability to transmit a sense of reality is due to the fact that the connotations it evokes are not merely linguistic but may be elements of our remembered experience. And they may of course belong to any element whatever of our experience, not merely to the sense data.

For many images are even less easily consigned to the mind's pigeon-holes than those examples already given. The 'dark backward and abysm of time' is still less tangible, still less capable of being neatly defined. Again, the two 'objects', tenor and vehicle, have to be held in consciousness and contemplated together. A metaphor like this, or like Robert Lowell's 'The Lord survives the rainbow of his will', so conflicts with normal categories that it forces us to bring to our contemplation of it a considerable amount of our past experience of both tenor and vehicle. Hence the sense of revealing depths that such a metaphor gives us.

And it would follow that poetry which depends mainly on verbal wit, like that of Cummings, is less profound than poetry which forces us to compare actual fragments of sensation, like Tennyson's 'Eagle';[22] and that this again is less profound than poetry which makes 'interplicit' our emotions and attitudes. For in this last case we may assert, and assert literally, that deeper levels of our awareness are actually being stirred.

This, then, is true apparency: when our attention is forced onto the connotations—not onto connotations seen superficially as abstract categories, but onto our awareness *of the things themselves.* I think, therefore, that we have made a considerable discovery: we have solved the age-old problem of *ut pictura poesis.* It has always been said that poetry could 'show' us reality; but we have now discovered *by what mental process* this occurs.

B) DEGREES OF ASSOCIATION

The two examples of 'figurehead' and 'rose' used above, one of them witty, limpid and explicit, the other rapid, compressed and emotive, might logically lead us to consider different classes or types of metaphor. This is an immensely complex subject, and one of the reasons for its complexity is doubtless that the metaphoric process is so

deeply embedded in language itself, that one might usefully look at
metaphor from all those standpoints one uses in surveying linguistic
processes in general. The strange thing is, however, that although
vast quantities of ink have been spilt on the question of classifying
the metaphor, most of this effort has been directed towards ideational
content, rather than form or structure.[23] Christine Brooke-Rose's
Grammar of Metaphor is a splendid exception,[24] and contains some
invaluable insights. It is not, however, so much a grammar *of*
metaphor as an investigation (in great and sensitive depth) of the
way the grammatical function of metaphors affects their meaning.
I should like, therefore, to make a few tentative suggestions myself,
partly so as to give some kind of basis for thinking about the differences between scientific and poetic discourse, partly so as to con-
solidate and expand on what other writers have said.

The first classification I want to recall, or rather recast, is one of
degree of association between vehicle and tenor. I base myself upon
James Liu's remarks in *The Art of Chinese Poetry*. He distinguishes
four types of 'compound images':

> First of all, there are compound images which simply put two
> objects side by side without making any overt or covert com-
> parison[25] between them; then there are those which liken one
> thing to another; then those which describe one thing as if it
> were another; finally those which attribute to an object qualities
> not normally attributable to it. These images differ from one
> another in degree rather than in kind: they represent various
> stages of the same mental process—that of connecting two
> things. We may designate these stages juxtaposition, compari-
> son, substitution, and transference, respectively.[26]

The reader may be ready to predict that I shall give broad assent
to this analysis of 'degrees of association'; for he will by this time
have observed that I dislike rigid distinctions. But Liu's has, I feel,
several genuine advantages. It will be recalled for example that
Wellek and Warren mention, as two of the 'basic elements' in our
conception of metaphor, that of analogy, and that of double vision.[27]
If we accept Liu's analysis, these are two different degrees of the
same process—or rather, if we approach a metaphor from the standpoint of its logical (or emotional) justification, that is if we look at it
in the light of comparison, we may judge it to be based on analogy,
just like a comparison. But if we approach it from the other end of
the scale, that is in the light of those startling modern images where
there is no apparent ground for comparison at all, we shall judge it
to be true 'double vision'. Thus, Eliot's famous:

the evening is stretched out against the sky
Like a patient etherised upon a table.
or
The worlds revolve like ancient women
Gathering fuel in vacant lots.

are, interestingly enough, similes. Yet they are among the most
striking and effective images in *Prufrock*, for they achieve that
double vision which is supposed to be characteristic of the extreme or
dissonant type of metaphor. At one end of the scale we have faded
metaphors like the 'leg' of a table, where the analogy is so complete
that any sense of double vision has completely departed—until,
that is, the hypersensitive Victorian lady starts to clothe her table-
legs in bloomers; at the other we have apparent similes like Eluard's
'The world is as blue as an orange', where contradiction masquerades
as comparison. But even with a double vision as contradictory as this,
there is overlap, connotations are exchanged, vehicle and tenor are
seen in the light cast by each other.[28]

Juxtaposition is a typical Chinese poetic technique (and indeed,
according to Liu, in Chinese poetry before Tu Fu, comparison,
substitution and transference were relatively little used. We might
use one of Li Po's poems to illustrate it:

Song of War

Before the Peak of Returning Joy the sand was like snow.
Outside the surrendered city the moon was like frost.
I do not know who blew the horns at night,
But all night long the boys looked toward their homes.[29]

Each line is a separate statement, a separate image. Yet each line
interacts with the others. The process is of course assisted in the
first two lines by the characteristic Chinese technique of parallelism,
which underlines the poet's intention that we should connect his
images into a new totality.[30] And of course parallelism is one of the
techniques used in ordinary prose to show a connecting link (though
without actually stating the type of link). One thinks of proverbs
such as 'Feed a cold and starve a fever' or 'Spare the rod and spoil the
child'.

My first example, then, is already one stage removed from mere
simple juxtaposition, which we might illustrate by:

O westron wind when wilt thou blow
That the small rain down can rain?
Christ that my love were in my arms
And I in my bed again.[31]

As Archibald MacLeish comments: 'Here the two little scenes of

wind and weather and love and bed are left side by side to mean if
they can. And they do mean. The poem is not a poem about the one
or the other. It is not a poem about weather. And neither is it a poem
about making love. The emotion it holds is held between these two
statements in the place where love and time cross each other.'[32]

For the mind is a machine for making connexions. Eisenstein
wrote:

> . . . two film pieces of any kind, placed together, inevitably
> combine into a new concept, a new quality, arising out of that
> juxtaposition. This is not in the least a circumstance peculiar to
> the cinema, but is a phenomenon invariably met with in all
> cases where we have to deal with the juxtaposition of two facts,
> two phenomena, two objects. We are accustomed to make,
> almost automatically, a definite and obvious deductive generali-
> zation when any separate objects are placed before us side by
> side. For example, take a grave, juxtaposed with a woman in
> mourning weeping beside it, and scarcely anyone will fail to
> jump to the conclusion: *a widow*.[33]

And he illustrates this principle of 'montage' from Pushkin, by the
poet's selection of details in the episode of Kochubei's execution: a
scaffold dismantled, a priest praying, a coffin being loaded onto a
wagon.[34]

In juxtaposition, then, we have two objects, two statements, two
images side by side. Our minds naturally adduce a connexion
between them. This connexion may be easily stateable, as in Eisenstein's example of the widow; or it may be much harder (MacLeish
would say impossible) to put into words, as in the 'Westron Wind'.
In parallelism, the connexion is stronger: the two images begin, we
might say, to move across each other: 'The Peak of Returning Joy'
and 'the surrendered city' gravitate together.

The next stage in the process towards metaphor is *comparison*, or
simile. Here the connexion of analogy is stated literally, with a word
such as 'like' or 'as' or 'such as'. In 'Song of War', 'sand like snow'
and 'moon like frost' are of course similes. This process needs no
comment here.

Fourthly, we have metaphor proper. Here one word is substituted
for another. Typical metaphors in Chinese are 'stars' for 'eyes', or
'snow, frost or water' or 'moonlight'.[35] At this point the two images
have moved together completely: Black's filtering process begins to
operate.

So far Liu's categories have been syntactical. The comparison,
implied or explicit, between one image and the other, is expressed by

syntax, by (1) juxtaposition, (2) parallelism, (3) comparison and (4) substitution. His last category, however, that of 'transference', as he calls it, is syntactically the same as 'substitution'. It is only from the semantic point of view that we can distinguish between substitution and transference, by judging, for instance, that in his example from Tu Fu, 'At the fourth watch, the mountains disgorge a moon',[36] an unusual attribution has been made. For mountains do not have mouths. Now this is a semantic matter, and no longer a syntactic one. We may describe it by saying that there is contradiction between some of the connotations of vehicle and tenor.

In modern poetry such contradictions are taken to surprising lengths. Hugo Friedrich, for instance, speaks of 'semantic dissonance',[37] and cites Ungaretti's 'deaf screams of the mirror'. It is not hard to find such images as these in modern poets:

> Once it was the colour of saying
> Soaked my table the uglier side of a hill.

and

> If my head hurt a hair's foot
> Pack back the downed bone. If the unpricked ball of my breath
> Bump on a spout let the bubbles jump out.

writes Dylan Thomas. Nor does Liu mention the fact that tenor and vehicle may (in some European poetry, at least) actually contradict each other denotatively, as in Góngora's

> milagroso sepulcro, *mudo coro*
> *de muertos vivos*, de ángeles callados,
> cielo de cuerpos, vestuario de almas.
> [Miraculous tomb, mute choir of living dead, of silent angels, heaven of bodies, robing-room of souls.]

Rather similar effects to these may be achieved with certain complex images, as in these lines from Baudelaire,

> Cher poison préparé par les anges! liqueur
> Qui me ronge, ô la vie et la mort de mon cœur![38]
> [Beloved poison prepared by angels! Liquor that corrodes me, O my heart's life and death!]

where (1) the first image is a complex metaphor the elements of which have some contradictory connotations, and (2) the final image equates two directly contradictory denotations, life and death.

I think therefore that we should amend Liu's classification. It really has two aspects, the syntactic and the semantic. Syntactically, we may distinguish four stages in the movement away from literality: (1) juxtaposition; (2) parallelism; (3) comparison; (4) Substitution.[39] Each of these four stages asserts a stronger degree of identity between the two phenomena in question. Semantically, on the other hand, there may be widely differing degrees of correspondence and dissonance between the items being compared. It is evident that the two aspects, synactic and semantic, do not go hand in hand. I have already quoted two or three surprising similes, for instance, where the things being compared are very unlike, or even contradictory. When Eluard writes: 'La terre est bleue comme une orange' [The earth is as blue as an orange] a line that he follows with the confident assertion, 'Jamais une erreur les mots ne mentent pas',[40] [Never a mistake words don't lie] we have a comparison where the things compared are denotatively incompatible. It might look at first sight as if Eluard has practised a favourite Surrealist trick of replacing one word with another torn quite out of context: as if on top of an original line 'The earth is *round* as an orange', Eluard had gummed the word 'blue'. The line has however been much discussed, and generally held to be highly successful. It deserves our attention.

Why did Eluard not write 'La terre est une orange bleue'? This is a metaphor, and metaphors are usually said to be more effective than similes. Not in this case however. For it is perfectly possible to imagine a blue orange; and there is nothing impressive about the phrase: it suggests roundness, smallness, the blueness of the earth as seen, perhaps from a great distance. But the colour orange has thereby been reduced in importance; and the colour blue, though the clash with the orange makes it stand out more than it would normally do, has not somehow the mentally dazzling quality that it has in the original line.

The secret of the line is, I suggest, in the word 'comme'. It is impossible to imagine an object that is as blue *as* an orange; for oranges are *not* blue. There is thus a total clash at the exact point where one would expect the simile to be supported. The very basis of comparison is itself a contradiction in terms. The result of this is that neither term is abolished to the benefit of the other: the mind's eye goes on hopelessly clashing together blue and orange. An extremely vivid effect is thereby produced: the two colours do not cancel each other out, but set each other off, succeeding each other perhaps rapidly in the mind's eye like the famous black and white pictures of Edgar Rubin, which switch back and forth from vase to face to vase.[41] This line of Eluard's is in fact a spectacularly successful example of foregrounding the connotations present in the words, making us 'open the drawer' as I put it above. And he is right to add: 'Jamais une erreur les mots ne mentent pas'.

I suppose we might say, 'Ah yes, but then *comme* is a metaphor'.

But that is too much of a trick. Besides, surprising and yet effective semantic dissonance can be produced with the technique of juxtaposition too, as Philip Wheelwright shows when he quotes the lines:

> My country 'tis of thee
> Sweet land of liberty
> Higgledy-piggledy my black hen.[42]

This he calls an instance of 'the creation of new meaning by juxtaposition and synthesis.'[43] He also quotes Pound's:

> The apparition of these faces in the crowd;
> Petals on a wet, black bough.

Now I am not sure that these lines are not a simile: 'apparition' after all is ambiguous, suggesting both 'appearance' and a pallid ghost-like effect. But in that case, even if Wheelwright's example is ill-chosen for his own purposes, it will serve as another instance of a surprising comparison.

I think we may therefore view the *degree of association* between the elements of an image as being the effect of two factors: *syntactic* and *semantic*. This view has several advantages. It places metaphor proper in a context of types of syntactic association, and it therefore does not tie one down to asserting its sole importance as some critics, forgetting their early Chinese poetry, have come dangerously close to doing. It thereby allows us to harmonize the views of those who see metaphor as paramount with the views of those, like Archibald MacLeish, who see juxtaposition as the prime poetic technique.[44] The two are simply different degrees and stages in the same process. On the other hand, if we claim that semantic connexion and dissonance are not controlled purely by the syntactic form of the words, but are to a large degree independent of it, and interact with it, we are saved from such sweeping generalizations as: metaphor is always 'better' than simile, or to claim that it is more 'violent'. For there are clearly cases like Eluard's blue orange or Wheelwright's black hen where simile and juxtaposition are as dissonant and startling as you like.

This approach may also clarify what I feel to be a certain degree of confusion in Philip Wheelwright's distinction between 'epiphor' and 'diaphor'. He claims that these are two distinct types of metaphor, and he explains them as follows:

> Epiphoric metaphor starts by assuming a usual meaning for a word; it then applies this word to something else on the basis of, and in order to indicate, a comparison with what is familiar . . .
> 'Life is a dream': here the idea of life, which is the tenor of the sentence, is relatively vague and problematic; whereas a dream

is something of which, and the waking up from which, everyone has memories. Accordingly dreaming can be offered as a semantic vehicle for those possibly similar aspects of life which it is desired to bring to the attention. Similarly, 'God is the Father', 'the milk of human kindness', 'his bark is worse than his bite', and so on; countless such examples . . . come to mind.[45]

Here the use of a word is *extended*, the generalizing function employed.

As for 'diaphor', as we have already seen, he defines this as 'the creation of new meaning by juxtaposition and synthesis'. And apart from

> My country 'tis of thee
> Sweet land of liberty
> Higgledy-piggledy my black hen.

which is indeed juxtaposition in a *syntactic* sense, and Ezra Pound's 'In a Station of the Metro', also already quoted, which I suspect of being a simile (or at least a demi-simile), he quotes Gertrude Stein's 'Toasted Susie is my ice-cream' and 'A silence a whole waste of a desert spoon, a whole waste of any little shaving . . .' 'One could cite examples at random from Miss Stein's voluminous compositions',[46] as he says; and I imagine that Edith Sitwell would be almost as good an example. But there is a danger here of confusing syntax with semantics. Wheelwright's criterion of distinguishing 'epiphor' from 'diaphor' is purely a criterion of the degree of violence done to normal meaning, and his own very acute awareness that the process of normal understanding has been radically altered. The examples he gives from Gertrude Stein are, formally, metaphors, for they are substitutions, some of which go as far, no doubt, as pure collage— but their syntax is metaphoric, even if we may be hard put to it to interpret their sense.[47]

c) SIMPLE, ANALYTIC AND SYNOPTIC

ψυχῆς πείρατα ἰὼν οὐκ ἂν ἐξεύροιο, πᾶσαν ἐπιπορευόμενος ὁδόν· οὕτω βαθὸν λόγον ἔχει. [No matter how far you go, you cannot reach the limits of the soul: it has such depth.]   (Heraclitus)

The other type of classification of images[48] which I want to adumbrate briefly here depends on two connected factors: (1) the number of connotations which the two elements of the image seem to have in common; (2) the degree to which these connotations are explicit, or could in principle be made explicit. These are very awkward matters to deal with, since connotations are neither enumerable nor totally definable, and since there are subjective differences between readers. As Arqueles Vela remarks, metaphor is too diverse to establish any rigid classification or nomenclature.[49] For, as I observed in chapter 4, no regular types of connotative structure can be supposed to obtain: the ramifications of meaning are infinitely diverse. It might however be useful for our purposes to attempt a loose definition of certain extreme (and hence relatively clear) cases.

Faded metaphor I shall define as a metaphor where we think of the denotation only—where the connotations of the vehicle are disregarded. I am not sure that we need a special term for this, as faded metaphors fall into two very familiar categories, the dead metaphor and the conventional metaphor. In common usage such terms as the 'tail' and 'nose' of an aeroplane, the 'toe' of a peninsula, the 'leaf' of a book or table, and such expressions as 'There were *loads* of people there,' are dead metaphors—dead, that is, until someone starts drawing attention to them as I am doing here. In a similar way, the moment Sir George Clark starts to draw attention to 'figurehead' it comes alive. Conventional metaphors are 'Through a glass, darkly,' 'The wages of sin,' or simply 'rose' for 'girl', 'stars' for 'eyes' and 'the fire of love'. These are perhaps not so dead as the tails, toes and noses mentioned above, since their users are probably aware of choosing a term that is not *totally* ordinary. However, where a metaphor has no apparency, we may say it is faded: that is, the connotations of the vehicle are either not observed or barely noticed.

Narrow and *Tenuous metaphor* have in common the fact that the connexion between vehicle and tenor is either single or as near to single as makes little difference. Vehicle and tenor have, in short, only one (or barely more than one) connotation in common. An example of narrow metaphor in ordinary speech would be 'The hair of the dog', where the connexion with taking another drink for a hangover occurs, so to speak, at a single point. (The allusion is of course to the old notion that the burnt hair of a dog was an antidote to its bite, and the single connotation in question could be defined as 'Similia similibus curantur'.) Besides being narrow, this metaphor is also conventional—conventional, that is, if one realizes it is a metaphor at all, for inquiry confirms that the vast majority of its users have no idea what, if anything, the connexion might be between dogs and mornings after nights before.

In narrow metaphor there is no sense of clash between those other connotations of tenor and vehicle that do *not* correspond: we do not pause to compare the dog's hairiness and the taste of Campari, for instance, and conclude that they have nothing in common. Tenuous metaphor, however, is a narrow metaphor where we do sense other connotations thronging round the ground of comparison, and these other connotations clash. The best examples are from literature, and the best in literature from the post-Renaissance period. When Donne writes:

> But as some serpents' poison hurteth not,
> Except it be from the live serpent shot,
> So doth her virtue need her here, to fit
> That unto us; she working more than it.[50]

(this is a simile, of course, but the same observations apply to all degrees of association) the liveness of the serpent is to the effectiveness of its poison as the presence of the woman is to the working of her virtue, and there seems at first sight to be no other ground of comparison than this single one. We cannot compare a woman's virtue and a serpent's venom in respect of their effects, for instance, or of their emotional overtones.[51] However, I should not define this simile as tenuous, but as narrow, for irrelevant overtones are carefully suppressed by the apparently formal and logical presentation of the simile ('But as . . . except it be . . . so . . . to fit that unto us . . .'). And even its narrowness is moderated by the fact that one may remember Jesus's advice to his apostles to be 'wise as serpents and harmless as doves'.[52] There is, in other words, a further connexion between virtue and serpents.

A proper case of tenuous metaphor is given by such images as:

> I am no poet here, my pen's the spout
> Where the rain-water of my eyes runs out
> In pity of that name, whose grief we see
> Thus copied out in grief's hydrography.

For can it be said that Cleveland's pen is in any sense a 'spout' — save in the one narrow sense he intends? Similarly,

> And now where're he strayes,
> Among the Galilean mountaines,
> Or more unwellcome wayes,
> He's followed by two faithfull fountaines;
> Two walking baths; two weeping motions;
> Portable and compendious oceans.

> (Crashaw, *Saint Mary Magdalene*)

The objection to this kind of thing is of course that, though the central ground of the comparison is clear, the vehicle brings with it a number of connotations which it is impossible to put out of one's mind, and which clash disastrously with the poet's intention.

Analytic metaphor is where the appropriate connotations of the vehicle are enumerated by the writer, as in Sir George Clark's 'figurehead' or Donne's famous 'compasses' image:

> If they be two, they are two so
> As stiff twin compasses are two,
> Thy soul the fixed root, makes no show
> To move, but doth, if th'other do.
>
> And though it in the centre sit,
> Yet when the other far doth roam,
> It leans, and hearkens after it,
> And grows erect, as that comes home.
>
> Such wilt thou be to me, who must
> Like th'other foot, obliquely run;
> Thy firmness makes my circle just,
> And makes me end, where I begun.
>
> (*A Valediction, Forbidding Mourning*)

This is evidently the technique employed with such scientific models as the billiard balls discussed in chapter 13 (p.153). A scientific analogy of this kind serves to pose the question: 'In what ways is phenomenon x (fairly well understood) like phenomenon y (less well understood), and in what ways unlike?' The analogy is then explored, and the ways in which x and y resemble each other are established with as much certainty and precision as possible. Of course, as I have frequently observed, certainty and precision are never total; moreover, with really useful models, the range of potential connotations may not be enumerable (p.60). However, when the scientist is engaged on a particular task, he will seek to limit the range of application of his analogy to the particular purposes he has at the time.[53]

In the case of science, each connotation that is thus explicated should be clear, simple and as near as possible fully understood. It should be spelled out in full detail. In the case of poetry, however, each connotation may well itself imply a wealth of connotations: it may itself be multiple, as the overtones of the shadows of Donne and his mistress are in 'A Lecture Upon the Shadow' or as his 'Compasses' are.

Analytic metaphor in Cleveland shows another way in which this type of metaphor may be treated. Here, each listed connotation of the central image approaches tenuousness (in the sense meant above), for there is a clash between other possible connotations.

> My sight took pay, but (thank my charms)
> I now impale her in mine arms,

(Love's Compasses) confining you,
Good Angels, to a circle too.
Is not the universe strait-laced,
When I can clasp it in the waist?
My amorous folds about thee hurled,
Like Drake I girdle in the world.
I hoop the firmament and make
This my embrace the zodiac.
  How would thy centre take my sense
  When admiration doth commence
  At the extreme circumference?

(*To the State of Love, or, the Senses' Festival*)

This tenuousness is, I think, particularly sensible in lines 5–6 and 7–8, and we are not far from absurdity. Yet these lines are so bursting with wit and energy that one cannot dislike them.

In analytic metaphor, the image is analyzed, its connotations are listed, it is, so to speak, laid out flat on the page. The majority of poetic images, however, are much more like the 'rose in Greenland's ice': they are simply presented to us as such, but in a context which arouses our awareness of the intended connotations. A number of these interact at once and we feel them in a moment of time, as a totality, in combination with each other, that is *synoptically*. In the first case it is possible to separate vehicle from tenor, and lay it on the dissecting table. In the second, we may feel that it does a violence to the metaphor to dissect it, to divide the rose into its petals.[54]

But in any case, this may be impossible. After all, I barely scratched the surface of the implications of 'Rose = Girl', and the vast number of connotations that may be involved in an image is suggested by such exercises as Empson's account of the senses of 'Brightness falls from the air': there is almost a page and a half of this, and it is not untypical of Empson's explications.[55]

In the most extreme of cases, the image stands for so much that we cannot explicate it, only give rough pointers to its meaning. This is often called a symbol. As Christine Brooke-Rose remarks, 'when Eliot mentions Madame Sosostris' cards, *the drowned Phoenician Sailor, the Lady of the Rocks, the man with the three staves, the Wheel, the one-eyed merchant, the Hanged Man*, these . . . turn out from the general context . . . to be symbols of all sorts of ideas which have kept exegetists in happy employment.'[56]

I do not want to spend space on this point, for the notion of ambiguity has been much discussed and widely accepted. I merely want to point to the fact that, as we move from faded metaphor through analytic metaphor to synoptic metaphor, and finally to that most complex of all images, the symbol, we are moving from a situation where the connotations are single, or few, or to some extent enumerable, to a situation where they could not possibly be enumerated, and where indeed many of them may be unknown or unconscious. The most spectacular example of an unparaphraseable symbol in all literature is perhaps chapter 42 of *Moby Dick*, where the narrator spends eight pages or so discussing 'The Whiteness of the Whale':

> What the white whale was to Ahab, has been hinted; what, at times, he was to me, as yet remains unsaid.
>
> Aside from those more obvious considerations touching Moby Dick, which could not but occasionally awaken in any man's soul some alarm, there was another thought, or rather vague nameless horror concerning him, which at times by its intensity completely overpowered all the rest; and yet so mystical and well-nigh ineffable was it, that I almost despair of putting it in a comprehensible form. It was the whiteness of the whale that above all things appalled me. But how can I hope to explain myself here; and yet, in some dim random way, explain myself I must, else all these chapters might be naught.
>
> Though in many natural objects, whiteness refiningly enhances beauty, as if imparting some special virtue of its own, as in marbles, japonicas, and pearls; and though various nations have in some way recognized a certain royal pre-eminence in this hue; even the barbaric, grand old kings of Pegu placing the title 'Lord of the White Elephants' above all their other magniloquent ascriptions of domain; and the modern kings of Siam unfurling the same snow-white quadruped in the royal standard; and the Hanoverian flag bearing the one figure of a snow-white charger . . . and though among the holy pomps of the Romish faith, white is specially employed in the celebration of the Passion of Our Lord; though in the Vision of St. John, white robes are given to the redeemed, and the four-and-twenty elders stand clothed in white before the great white throne, and the Holy One that sitteth there white like wool; and yet for all these accumulated associations, with whatever is sweet, and honourable, and sublime, there yet lurks an elusive something in the innermost idea of this hue, which strikes more of panic to the soul than that redness which affrights in blood.

And so on for eight pages, ending thus:

> . . . pondering all this, the palsied universe lies before us like

a leper; and like wilful travellers in Lapland, who refuse to wear coloured and colouring glasses upon their eyes, so the wretched infidel gazes himself blind at the monumental white shroud that wraps all the prospect around him. And of all these things the Albino whale was the symbol. Wonder ye then at the fiery hunt?

It is clear that in a case such as this, the word 'white' cannot be separated from its multifarious meaning: the tenor needs its vehicle, for it is so multiple, so complex and all-embracing, and above all so deeply embedded in the unconscious as well as the conscious mind, that we should be left with too dark and impenetrable an enigma without the solidity of an image to hold on to. As the clear listing of connotations becomes less possible, so the vehicle becomes more inseparable from its tenor, becomes at once more mysterious and more necessary. Novelists like Melville and poets like Jouve find symbols invaluable for exploring their own inner caverns, as some psychologists find them invaluable for making the hidden spaces of the psyche visible.

Nous avons connaissance à présent de milliers de mondes à l'intérieur du monde de l'homme, que toute l'œuvre de l'homme avait été de cacher, et de milliers de couches dans la géologie de cet être terrible qui se dégage avec obstination et peut-être merveilleusement (mais sans jamais y bien parvenir) d'une argile noire et d'un placenta sanglant. Des voies s'ouvrent dont la complexité, la rapidité pourraient faire peur. Cet homme n'est pas un personnage en veston ou en uniforme comme nous l'avions cru; il est plutôt un abîme.[57] [We now know that there are, hidden inside the human world, a myriad other worlds which Man has spent his whole life working to conceal, myriads of strata in the geology of this terrible being obstinately and perhaps wonderfully (though never with complete success) struggling to disengage himself from black earth and blood-congested placenta. Paths open up terrifyingly complex and steep. Man is not a personage dressed in a suit or a uniform, as we had thought; he is more like a bottomless pit.]

A symbol is a cloak thrown over darkness to give it shape. Though of course the cloak must be of suitable colour, form and weight.

Taxonomy and Feeling

> *To a Pragmatist*
> You say a splash of water
> Means itself, and nothing more.
> Well then, what it means to me
> Means itself, and nothing less.
> The one is as real as the other,
> Though I'd no more sit by the fire
> With a splash of water
> Than you'd wash your face with a meaning.
>
> One day you're going to drown
> In a splash of meaning.
> It won't be much, but your feet
> Won't find the bottom.
>
> (Norman MacCaig *Surroundings*, 25)

WE ARE NOW AT last approaching the point where some kind of distinction between poetic and other modes of discourse might be sketched. First, however, let us consider some instances of different types of discourse. For this purpose I shall take examples that are as similar as possible: I shall compare an entry in a dictionary and a taxonomic description with what is probably the nearest approach to such discourse ever penned by a literary man: the poetic taxonomy of Francis Ponge.

To begin with, here is part of a general description of the apricot:

> *Apricot* . . . The apricot, in a general view, is one of the earliest of our wall fruits, and next in esteem to the peach. The ripe fruit is second to no production of our gardens for jam or other preserves: it makes a delicious liqueur, and gives a delicious flavour to ice; it excels all other garden fruits, in both beauty and agreeableness, for the purposes of pastry; and it possesses the recommendation, when used as a dessert, of being pleasantly astringent to the palate and somewhat strengthening to the stomach. But the over-ripe fruit is divested of a large proportion of its aroma and its other elements of delicious flavour, and is clammy, comparatively insipid, and not so easy of digestion . . .[1]

If we put this side by side with Ponge's long description of the apricot:

La couleur abricot, qui d'abord nous contacte, après s'être massée en abondance heureuse et bouclée dans la forme du fruit, s'y trouve par miracle en tout point de la pulpe aussi fort que la saveur soutenue.

Si ce n'est donc jamais qu'une chose petite, ronde, sous la portée presque sans pédoncule, durant au tympanon pendant plusieurs mesures dans la gamme des orangés,

Toutefois, il s'agit d'une note insistante, majeure.

Mais cette lune, dans son halo, ne s'entend qu'à mots couverts, à feu doux, et comme sous l'effet de la pédale de feutre.

Ses rayons les plus vifs sont dardés vers son centre. Son rinforzando lui est intérieur.

Nulle autre division n'y est d'ailleurs préparée, qu'en deux: c'est un cul d'ange à la renverse, ou d'enfant-jésus sur la nappe.

Et le bran vénitien qui s'amasse en son centre, s'y montre sous le doigt dans la fente ébauché.

. . . . .

Pour les dimensions, une sorte de prune en somme, mais d'une tout autre farine, et qui, loin de se fondre en liquide bientôt, tournerait plutôt à la confiture.

Oui, il en est comme de deux cuillerées de confiture accolées. . . .[2]

[The colour apricot contacts us first, massed in happy, coiled abandon in the fruit's shape, present miraculously in the pulp's every part, as strongly sustained as its flavour.

Though it's only a little round thing, hanging from the stave almost stemless, lasting several beats on the dulcimer in the scale of oranges,

It remains an insistent, major note.

But this moon in its halo can only be dimly heard, simmering, muted by the felt-soft pedal.

Its brightest rays shine inwards. Its rinforzando rings within.

It is designed to be divided in two: the bottom of an upside-down angel, a baby Jesus on the cloth,

And the Venetian bran massing at its centre, shows under the finger in the opened slit.

. . . . .

In size a kind of plum, but of quite a different grain, not liquefying but turning into jam.

Yes, like two spoonfuls of jam side by side. . . .]

First, we note that there is barely any significant difference in manner between these two passages. For the first passage is taken from a *Rural Cyclopedia* of 1849, and its English is the normal 'degree zero' of the day, seeking no effect other than that of scientific objectivity. The manner is a pointer to the intention: 'Here,' the author is implying, 'is a sober, matter-of-fact account of apricots. I make no attempt to arouse interest, to make your mouth water, but simply to describe and inform. For I know it is for information you have consulted me.'

Ponge's passage is equally sober and matter-of-fact in tone. And we might take this opportunity of reminding ourselves that whereas this tone is normal or even *de rigueur* in scientific or informational contexts, a wide variety of other tones is of course permitted in literature. Ponge is here imitating the tone of sober description. But his content is completely different: though the calm balance and rhythm of his sentences, and their apparently logical and prosaic construction, might lead us to suppose we were reading an entry in a '*Rural Cyclopedia*', his vocabulary gives us instead a rash of metaphors.

If metaphor is the basic stuff of poetry, it is clear that this is poetry. It is equally clear that the *Rural Cyclopedia* avoids all but the most mummified of metaphors. One might make a supreme effort and unearth 'in a general *view*', '*next* in esteem', '*second* to no production', 'it *possesses* the recommendation', but this I think is all unless one is going to set about disinterring the roots of Latin words. As Stanford says, 'dead metaphors tell no tales, except to the etymologist'.[3] It is evident that the writer has no metaphoric intention, that is, no wish to impose the 'stereoscopic' effect upon his readers.

In Ponge on the other hand, even the less striking metaphors, those like *contacte* or *massée*, which one might at first sight think have merely an abstract or denotative meaning, have (on further inspection) a more complex intention. Of *contacte* for instance Ponge himself writes:

'*Contacter* means to make or afford contact. The amusing thing about this . . . is that some weeks ago the French Academy elected a new member.' In an interview with the papers, the new academician was reported as saying: 'I am very happy to be elected to the French Academy, because I shall be able to work on the Dictionary and to defend the French language. For instance there's a word that simply *must* be suppressed, the word *contacter*.' Ponge at first felt rueful, then he collected himself and realized that the word *contacter* was nonetheless precisely the word he wanted: no other would do: it was impossible to remove it from his poem 'because the sonority *contacte* is just what I need for the apricot.'[4]

We may explain these remarks about the sound of the word by suggesting that the insistent *contacting* of tongue and palate during its pronunciation, together with the nasal vowel 'on' must seem to Ponge to suggest the particular quality of the apricot's taste and colour. Taste *and* colour: for the apricot's taste is felt to be as orange as its colour; and the sound of *contacte* must be felt to be as orange as its taste. *Contacte* is of course closely connected with other words such as 'tactile'; and much later in the poem, Ponge makes deliberate use again of a 'k' alliteration, when he writes 'comme de deux cuillerées de confiture accolées'. Hence again a sense of insistent contacting, together with perhaps the slightly gluey sensation of tongue touching palate. But the oddness of the word's use consists also in speaking of a colour 'contacting' us. This anticipates our actual physical contact with the fruit, as we bite into it, just as, confronted with a real apricot, the remembered experience of its taste and its consistency is also a part of our visual experience. *Contacte* suggests, too, the strength of the apricot's colour: seeing it is as physical as touching it or tasting it. Moreover it is not we who, in Ponge's poem, contact the apricot, but its colour which takes the first step, forcing itself upon our attention.

It follows from this plethora of connotations that there is a vast difference in apparency between the two experiences of reading Ponge and consulting the *Rural Cyclopedia*. In the latter there is no attempt to describe the apricot's flavour save in the most general and imprecise of terms. It is 'delicious' (twice); its 'agreeableness' is mentioned; and the closest the writer gets to a description is in the words 'pleasantly astringent to the palate'. Even this, however, is the most general of categorizations. It could have been used of several dozen other fruits; and it is generally clear that the writer's concern is not to describe or evoke the flavour as such, but to say *either* 'It's something that's worth trying' *or* at most to remind us of a familiar experience, not by evoking it, but simply by referring to it. No clearer case could be given of the tendency of ordinary language, when allegedly 'describing' something, merely to refer us to something already known, already familiar, and already classified.

In Ponge's text, it is true, there is only one real attempt to evoke the (over-ripe) apricot's special taste, in the words 'il en est comme de deux cuillerées de confiture accolées'. But appearance, texture, consistency and, above all, colour, are startlingly evoked. *L'Abricot* is in fact a superb exercise in 'describing a bicycle to Julius Caesar'.

Clearly what are contrasted here are principally the generalities
and vaguenesses of ordinary speech as against the particularities of
poetic or literary speech: in ordinary language we are not concerned
to describe or evoke particular experiences in all their detail. A
general statement as to the apricot's being 'delicious', will be
enough to remind someone of its taste or to persuade someone else to
try it. As to the listener's belief in what we say, we are before him
and can carry conviction by our tone of voice, by his knowledge of us
(or of the reliability of the book he is reading), and so forth. The
poet's case is different and more difficult. In his case we seek to relive
in imagination a portion of real experience; we seek if possible to
have our attention drawn to facets of the experience that we had
missed; we seek to penetrate its reality in a way that we do not when
we are merely calculating whether we can grow apricots in our
garden, or when we are eating them and talking to our friends of
something else. If it is experience we demand, we could not be
content with a poet who, asked to 'describe' something, merely points
offstage like the writers of Rural Cyclopedias, and says 'Go and see
what I mean'. Our requirement is to be *shown*. The apricot has to be
brought on stage.

There are times, to be sure, in the course of normal conversation
when we need to be more precise than usual. What if our interlocutor, not knowing the fruit in question, depends upon us to describe
it to him? In certain cases extreme precision might be very important, as it is in distinguishing between certain closely similar
types of mushroom. We should then apply more thought and more
precision to our language than is customary in the flow and approximate gesture of ordinary speech. Our description might become
taxonomic, like a scientist's.

For precision is the hallmark of the scientist. Appealing to him for
a precise description of the oyster, for instance, we might find:

> *Ostrea edulis*, Linnaeus, *Edible Oyster*.
> Shell nearly round, though variously shaped, inequivalve; the
> upper valve flat, or nearly so, with scales or laminae of a
> yellowish-brown; the lower valve convex, and foliaceous, of a
> pale pinkish-white, with streaks of purplish-pink; transversely
> striated. Hinge toothless; ligament internal, of an olivaceous
> brown; beaks small. The interior of the shell white and polished,
> sometimes *the purplish-pink colour of the margins showing
> through*.[5]

Most of the vocabulary is normal enough, though it is supple-
mented by learned words where normal vocabulary is lacking. A

good deal of this description however is incomprehensible to the speaker of normal English untrained in the study of molluscs. He might look up such words as 'inequivalve' or 'laminae' in the dictionary, and receive enlightenment enough, it is true. But what is a 'toothless hinge'? In what sense is 'ligament' used? These questions suggest an important, even vital, fact about scientific discourse: words are used in a more than usually *precise* and *limited* way.

But there is a further point: Yonge interestingly comments on the description given above, that it is 'lengthy'. 'It is fortunate,' he writes, 'that the shells (of the oyster) are so well known because, as indicated in the lengthy description by Lovell quoted above, *precise definition cannot be brief.*' [6] For the scientist is interested on the one hand in precision, but on the other in economy. He is interested, in other words, not in *evoking* the oyster, but in *characterizing* it as briefly as possible. As Kenneth Burke puts it,[7] this system of language is like an address written upon an envelope: it should take the letter infallibly to the correct individual. But it does not describe the individual, except in so far as description is necessary to the finding of him. The words are labels, not handles. They exercise no leverage upon the drawers of language.

But is this true? For at this point the reader may well wonder about the correctness of my statement. Is the scientific description not admirably concrete (in the finest tradition of English poetry)? And is it after all so far from Ponge?[8] In both cases it is 'the oyster' that is evoked, not any individual oyster. In both cases the description is admirably exact. And why should one *not* open the oyster—I beg your pardon, the drawer?

The answer is, as I have said, that one always can. There is no rule to prevent one opening any drawer that one likes and spending hours poring over its contents. The question is whether one is compelled to partly by the language used and partly by intention. The scientific statement has the intention of labelling—of an economical minimum of meaning. The drawer will be opened in the case of seeing a particular oyster. Ponge's intention is quite different: he wishes us to open the drawer, if need be, without ever having seen an oyster in our lives. As he himself says of his poems:

> Ce sont donc des descriptions-définitions-objets-d'art-littéraire que je prétends formuler, c'est-à-dire des définitions qui au lieu de renvoyer (par exemple pour tel végétal) à telle ou telle classification préalablement entendue (admise) et en somme à une science humaine supposée connue (et généralement inconnue), renvoient, sinon tout à fait à l'ignorance totale, du

moins à un ordre de connaissances assez communes, habituelles et élémentaires, établissent des *correspondances inédites, qui dérangent les classifications habituelles, et se présentent ainsi de façon plus sensible, plus frappante,* plus agréable aussi.[9] [It is literary-object-definition-descriptions that I seek to formulate, that is definitions which instead of relating (for instance in the case of some plant or other) to some already understood (or accepted) classification and in general to a supposedly familiar (and usually unfamiliar) science, relate, if not absolutely to total ignorance, at least to an order of quite common, habitual and elementary knowledge, and which set up *brand-new analogies which upset the usual classifications, and are thus presented more concretely, more strikingly,* and also more agreeably.]

But let us turn to another close comparison of scientific taxonomy with, if I may so phrase it, poetic taxonomy: the mistletoe. This time both texts are brief:

1   *Viscum album.* Mistletoe. Evergreen unisexual shrub of a tawny or yellowish colour, usually attached to its host in the form of a pendulous, dichotomously branched, rounded bush two or three feet wide. *L.* opposite, narrowly obovate or oblong, roundish at the apex, $1\frac{1}{2}$ to $3\frac{1}{2}$ inches long, $\frac{1}{4}$ to 1 inch wide, sessile. *fl.* inconspicuous, sessile, in the forks of the branches, often in threes. *fr.* translucent white, globose, $\frac{1}{3}$ inch wide, with one seed embedded in viscous pulp. Europe (including Britain), N. Asia. (E.B. 635.)[10]

2   *Le Gui*

Le gui la glu: sorte de mimosa nordique, de mimosa des brouillards. C'est une plante d'eau, d'eau atmosphérique.

Feuilles en pales d'hélice et fruits en perles gluantes.

Tapioca gonflant dans la brume. Colle d'amidon. Grumeaux. Végétal amphibie.

Algues flottant au niveau des écharpes de brume, des traînées de brouillard,

Epaves restant accrochées aux branches des arbres, a l'étiage des brouillards de décembre.[11]

[*Mistletoe*

Birdlime mistletoe: a sort of nordic mimosa of the fog. A plant of water, atmospheric water.

Propellor-blade leaves and sticky-pearl fruit.

Tapioca swelling in the mist. Starch paste. Curds.

Vegetal amphibian.
Seaweed stranded among scarves of mist, swathes of fog.
Flotsam caught in the tree-branches, at lowest ebb of the
December fog.]

The taxonomic text first: this again strikingly illustrates the tendency
of scientific language to *limit* meaning. To be more precise about
this: *sessile* is defined as 'sitting, as though sitting close, destitute of
a stalk'.[12] In other words, *sessile* has but one relevant connotation.
Globose is 'nearly spherical'. We should note here the necessity of
close definition: were this word in normal use, it might well be much
vaguer in sense (cf. 'roundish'). *Entire*, *opposite* and *pendulous*
illustrate normal words used in a precise (and hence limited)
scientific sense: *entire* means 'without toothing or division, with even
margin'; *opposite* 'set against, as leaves when two on one node'; and
here again we have science's tendency to reduce connotations towards one or two. Similarly with *pendulous*, which simply signifies
that the mistletoe bush *hangs*. In normal usage, the connotations of
'pendulous' are fat and ungainly: one thinks of paunches or an old
woman's breasts. These connotations are indeed so strong that a
literary writer (such as Ponge) would have avoided the word at all
costs unless he had intended just those connotations. Our scientific
text, however, exists in a world of emotionless fact, exact delineation
and hence narrowness of meaning. If the literary writer would
choose 'pendulous' because it says more than simply 'hanging', the
scientific writer chooses 'pendulous' because, ironically, it says *less*.
In his world of discourse, its emotional connotations do not exist—
for they could not possibly be meant! It is chosen because it means
one thing and one thing only.

Where the tendency of a discourse is to reduce connotations to one
or two, we may say that there is a tendency for denotation and connotation to coincide. Those writers who, like Cohen, have suggested
that science uses a denotative language, are therefore working on the
right lines. It is also clear that this is the reason why scientific discourse, as has often been observed, can be translated. The normal
difficulty in translation is of course that the numerous connotations
of a word do not coincide;[13] but if the connotations can be reduced
in this radical fashion, or at the very least carefully delimited by
accepted international definition (as indeed is the case in science)
then the difficulty disappears.

The consequence of these qualities of scientific vocabulary is that
scientific language has a particularly tight and narrow precision,
which gives it both universality and a remarkable capacity to analyze

experience closely. Scientific language is an analytic language par excellence. Of course, by the same token, it is only those elements of meaning that are foreseen by its definitions that are intended, or in any sense contained, by the discourse: my emotive connotations of 'pendulous' are irrelevant to the botanist. Only so much of the feel, appearance and context of the mistletoe is given as may be necessary for our botanist to recognize it and distinguish it from other plants. It would be almost true to say that the mistletoe is conceived of in terms of a Saussurean definition, in which it is the *differences* between one plant and another that count, because it is those differences that are crucial in distinguishing it.[14] The mistletoe, in the botanist's account of it, has so to speak no positive content: it is defined by its differences from other similar parasites.

To say this, however, is definitely to exaggerate. It is perfectly obvious that to say something is 'globose, dichotomously branched', etc., is also to assert positive qualities about it. But the point is worth making, for it shows that to treat literary language in a Saussurean way, by voiding it of its content, and attributing to words only such meaning as they may have in contrast to one another, is clearly mistaken. It is to apply a tendency found in scientific discourse to a discourse which contains the opposite tendency.[15] And the remarks of Ponge himself on the function and purpose of his poems show this unmistakeably:

> . . . ce galet, puisque je le conçois comme objet unique, me fait éprouver un sentiment particulier, ou peut-être plutôt un complexe de sentiments particuliers. . . . Une qualité, une série de qualités, un compos de qualités inédit, informulé. . . . Me voici donc avec mon galet, qui m'intrigue, fait jouer en moi des ressorts inconnus. Avec mon galet que je respecte. Avec mon galet que je veux remplacer par une formule logique (verbale) adéquate.
>
> Heureusement 1° il persiste, 2° mon sentiment à sa vue persiste, 3° le Littré n'est pas loin: j'ai le sentiment que les mots justes s'y trouvent. S'ils n'y sont pas, après tout, il me faudra les créer. Mais tels alors qu'ils obtiennent la communication, qu'ils soient conducteurs de l'esprit (comme on dit conducteur de la chaleur ou de l'électricité). Après tout j'ai les syllabes, les onomatopées, j'ai les lettres. Je me débrouillerai bien![16] [. . . since I conceive of this pebble as a unique object, it gives me a special feeling, or rather perhaps a complex of special feelings . . . a quality, a set of qualities, an unexpressed, unformulated mixture of qualities . . . Well, here

I am with my pebble, which intrigues me, sets unknown processes going within me. With my pebble that I respect. With
my pebble that I wish to replace by an adequate logical (i.e.,
verbal) formula. Fortunately (1) it continues to be there, (2)
my feeling on seeing it continues to be there, (3) Littré[17] is
not far off: I have a feeling that the right words can be found
there. And if they're not, I shall simply have to make them up.
But in such a way that they will be able to communicate, to act
as conductors of the mind (as one talks of conductors of heat or
electricity). After all I have syllables, onomatopoeias and letters.
I shall manage very well!]

Not that Ponge thinks of course that one can ever say *everything*
about an object. His remarks in 'The Practice of Literature'[18] make
this sufficiently clear. But he *is* interested in saying something new,
something until now unexpressed.

Thus, the words in a Ponge poem are there to reproduce the feeling that the poet had when contemplating his subject—or rather his
object. The poem is born of a confrontation between the object and
the poet's sensibility. The object has to be evoked by words in all its
reality—or rather with a higher degree of reality than usual. There
is nothing negative or analytic here: the poet's purpose is rather a
synoptic one: the object in its reality, as a positive experience, is to be
pieced together by the poet's carefully chosen words. 'Il est question
d'en faire un texte, qui ressemble à une pomme, c'est-à-dire qui
aura autant de réalité qu'une pomme. Mais dans son genre.'[19] [It's
a matter of composing a text which resembles an apple, that is to say
which will have as much reality as an apple. But in its own way.]
For the literary artist, the object is *positive*: it is not there merely to
be defined; nor is it there to be manipulated, utilized, or associated
causally with other objects. It is there in its own right, to be grasped,
apprehended and felt.

For this, as described above, Ponge needs and uses the manifold
potentialities of language. In *Le Gui* there is no question of restricting the connotations, but of utilizing and extending them. The poem
opens with the words 'Le gui la glu'. No quasi-scientific equation is
intended: we are reminded perhaps that birdlime is made from
mistletoe; we are reminded too that its fruit is glutinous.[20] But the
words echo each other, are explicitly associated in sound as well as
meaning. These connotations thus gain double support, as if their
overlapping had been foreseen by the French language.

We may even have the feeling that there is something 'sticky'
about the sounds 'le gui la glu', or even something 'mistletoey' about

them. Perhaps it is true that the sounds 'g . . gl . . ' are apt in
some way to symbolize stickiness. But it can hardly be alleged that
they are in any way 'mistletoey'. I think this effect is due simply to
the close association of the two words, operated by their juxtaposition, and this highlights their similarities in sound 'as if' they
shared a hidden morpheme. We are invited to compare them, to feel
them as equivalent. We are invited to fill in any suitable connotations there may be. And this is the true explanation of our feeling
that 'le gui la glu' is an *icon*, that is an expression which actually resembles what it describes. Apart from the onomatopoeic effect of
' . . gl . . ', there is nothing in them that properly speaking *resembles* the mistletoe. It is probably mainly a matter of bringing connotations to our notice, and thus producing 'apparency'.

There are two points about the use of connotations in a poem: (1)
they will be brought out and supported as strongly as possible, as in
the phrase just discussed; (2) we are in effect invited to fill in as
many connotations as will fit the context, for the poet will seek for
words that are appropriate on as many scores as possible. This procedure is very Pongean, as one may judge from the following remarks of the poet:

J'étais en Algérie, dans une maison adossée aux premiers
contreforts de l'Atlas, d'où l'on voyait trente kilomètres de
plaine et la ligne des collines qui bordent la mer, le Sahel, et
cette chaîne de petites collines avait une couleur dont je voulais
trouver l'adjectif, le mot. C'était un rose, un certain rose. Le
couleurs ont des nuances, c'était un certain rose, mais ce rose,
je ne pouvais pas le trouver. . . . D'abord pourquoi voulais-je
en parler? Je n'ai pas pensé, j'ai senti que c'était un rose qui
ressemblait un peu au rose des chevilles des femmes algé-
riennes. C'est une des seules choses qu'on voit de leur peau.
. . . On ne voit presque pas même [un seul] œil, mais on voit
la cheville. Et alors il y avait ce rose. Il y avait aussi un côté fard.
J'ai cherché cette couleur rose, un rose ardent, intense, un peu
violet et j'avais fini par trouver des mots de couleur. Ça ne marchait pas. Rose cyclamen, non, non, rose polisson, coquin, à
cause du fard, à cause du côté sensuel de la chose: ça n'allait
pas. Je mets en fait, je dis que beaucoup de poètes se seraient
arrêtés là. Ils auraient dit: polisson; ça marche. Je ne sais pas
pourquoi ça ne marchait pas. Finalement j'ai trouvé un mot, il
existe, je ne l'ai pas inventé. . . .: sacripant, un rose sacripant.
C'est un mot qui n'est pas très rare en français, qui veut dire un
peu polisson. Sacripant, c'est un personnage qui est un peu

escroc, un peu voleur, un peu . . . pas très catholique, comme
on dit. Sacripant. Le mot me plaît. Rose sacripant. Ça y est.
J'étais sûr que je l'avais. Ça y était. Je suis allé au dictionnaire
après. J'étais dans une petite maison en Algérie, dans la cam-
pagne, je n'avais pas de dictionnaire. Je laisse mon rose sacripant et je vais au dictionnaire plusieurs semaines plus tard.
Sacripant: de Sacripante, personnage de l'Arioste, tout comme
Rodomonte. Rodomonte, qui signifie, «rouge montagne» et qui
était Roi d'Alger. Voilà la preuve. Quand on a ça, on est sûr.' 21
[I was in Algeria, in a house backing onto the first escarpments
of the Atlas mountains, and from which one could see thirty
kilometres of plain and the line of hills fringing the sea, the
Sahel; and this chain of little hills had a colour which I wanted
to find the adjective, the word for. It was pink, a particular
shade of pink. Colours have nuances, it was a particular pink,
but I couldn't find the exact one . . . But why was I interested? I didn't think, I felt it was a pink that was rather like the
pink ankles of Algerian women. It's one of the few parts of
their skin you see . . . You hardly even see one eye, but you
see their ankles. And then it was that pink. There was also the
make-up side of it. I searched for that pink colour, an ardent,
intense, rather violet pink, and I had ended up finding words
for colours. It didn't work. Cyclamen pink, no, no, rogue pink,
hussy pink, because of the make-up, because of the sensual side
of it: it didn't fit. I suggest that a lot of poets would have given
up at this point. They'd have said: rogue, that'll do. I didn't
know why it wouldn't do. At long last I found a word, it exists,
I didn't invent it . . .: *sacripant, sacripant* pink. It's a word
that's not uncommon in French and means a bit rascally. *Sacripant* is someone who's a bit of a cheat, a bit of a thief, a bit . . .
a bit unprincipled, as we say. *Sacripant.* I like the word. *Sacripant* pink, That's it. I was sure I'd got it. It was only later that I
consulted the dictionary. I was in a little house in Algeria at the
time, I hadn't got a dictionary. I let my *sacripant* pink stand
and went to the dictionary several weeks later. *Sacripant*: from
Sacripante, a character from Ariosto, like Rodomonte. Rodomonte, whose name means 'red mountain', and who was King
of Algiers. And that proves it! When you have something like
that, you can be certain!]
Thus we see Ponge insisting, in true poetic style, on finding a word,
a *number* of whose connotations will fit: it must be apt in a number
of ways.

But it should also be added that Ponge has overlooked, or simply omitted to mention, other connotations of his *'sacripant* pink'. At one point of Proust's *A la recherche du temps perdu*, the narrator sees a picture by the painter Elstir of a 'Miss Sacripant': she is dressed ambiguously, half as a young man, her costume is described as 'provocative',[22] and the narrator is quite clear that the picture has immoral sexual overtones. It almost immediately transpires that 'Miss Sacripant' is a younger version of one of the novel's central characters, Odette de Crécy.[23] But Odette, as all addicts of the novel will know, is also the mysterious and nameless 'young lady in pink' of one of the narrator's earlier encounters.[24] And she was a 'cocotte', or courtesan. Ponge's *'sacripant* pink' applies to the body as well as to the dress. Whether Ponge was at any time consciously aware of these additional connotations, they too presumably contributed to his feeling that the image was 'right', as they certainly do to ours. The instinct for accurately sensing the aptness of connotations, even when these remain inaccessible to the conscious mind, is one of the poet's most essential talents.

To return to one of the points I raised at the outset: why does Ponge use the 'flat authoritative factual' tone in these poetic taxonomies of his? Is there not the danger that we might read them in a matter-of fact way? The question reveals its own answer: the objective tone leads us to concentrate on the *object* of description, pebble, frog or oyster, exactly as we concentrate in a scientific description upon the object and not upon our private reactions and feelings. This is part of Ponge's purpose: he wishes to evoke an object, not an attitude. But by the same token, our expectations are disappointed: we meet not with the dispassionate closely defined descriptions of science, but with a vocabulary instinct with human sensory and emotional experience. This human experience is presented to us, in fact, as if it were present in the objects themselves. Thus, Ponge's tone is both an element basic to his purpose and a device whereby 'oddness' operates upon us.

Finally, I do not want to give the impression that Ponge's 'proems'[25] are the essence of poetry, and so to support indirectly the modern British superstition that it is the poet's highest vocation to be constantly rubbing our noses in the stickiest of sense data. I have already argued against this superstitition (see p.169), which has only a partial basis in the nature and practice of English poetry and English poets. There is more to experience than sense data, just as there is more to the world than apricots, oysters and mistletoe; there are also human beings and human feelings, and the poem that was briefly discussed at the end of chapter 15 may serve to remind us of this fact. For my part I have always regretted the insularity that has led so many of our poets to confine their attention almost solely to hedges and ditches, and to turn their backs upon the rich imagery of inner sensation and feeling that is offered by Eliot, Dylan Thomas, and by the whole modern continental and American tradition. I. A. Richards himself distinguished between metaphors that work by resemblance and those whose basis is a common attitude, and we do well to remember that fact.[26] There is an inner world as well as an outer.

The tentative findings of this chapter may now be summed up. Scientific and literary modes of expression are distinguished from others by their precision. Armed with Lovell's description of the edible oyster we can go out on the beach and pick one up. Reading Ponge's description of it, we can visualize it, smell and all, and even imagine those qualms which the inexperienced oyster-eater feels, opening the creature up, and swallowing it live.

But these two precisions are utterly different. The language of scientific taxonomy imposes a closely defined system of qualities upon the world, analyzes, describes, and places them in relation to one another. All that is not previously defined is excluded from their senses. Connotations are thus rigorously reduced to a manageable number: the connotations of 'oyster', to a scientist, *are* the description we have seen above: they are, that is, the criterial connotations, those which allow us to distinguish between it and other molluscs. Each connotation is distinct and definable: at its own level, it is thus almost pure denotation. (It is therefore not surprising that logically minded people like Marckwardt[27] are reluctant to accept the distinction between connotation and denotation.) When the oyster's valves are described as 'foliaceous', this means *leaf-shaped*: there is one connotation only. When the mistletoe is described as 'pendulous', there is again only one connotation.

The poem, on the other hand, invites us to attribute to its words as many connotations as may fit. In some cases, as when a girl is compared to a 'rose in Greenland's ice', we should never come to an end of listing them; and we intuit the metaphor's aptness, since we intuit a number of overlapping connexions. If the apricot is spoken of in terms of a 'felt pedal', we can connect this in several ways with the fruit: its outer skin is a dull orange, muted: it is to the taste of the flesh within as a muted note is to a loud one; and its texture is furry to the touch and tongue, not in any vague way, but almost *precisely* as is the texture of felt.

The words of the taxonomic description, then, narrow down the object's nature to its economical minimum. The words of the poetic description invite us to explore them, to descend into them, to test their sensory and emotional rightness. The one offers us the clarity of a map, its lines firm . . . but skeletal. The other, the deliberate fluidity and indeterminacy of a picture, in all its illusive solidity. In one, the object is not there, though a definition of it is given. In the other, we at any rate may have the illusion of presence.

Three or Four Languages

When I am impelled neither to lay hands on the object immediately,
nor to ticket it for tomorrow's outrage, but am in such a marvellous
state of innocence that I would know it for its own sake, and conceive
it as having its own existence. (Ransom 1941, 45)

A DISTINCTION BETWEEN, ON the one hand, poetry and, on the
other hand, a completely different mode of discourse, variously
described as 'scientific', 'denotative', 'informational' or 'prosaic', is
one of our twentieth-century critical commonplaces. Already in the
nineteenth century Mallarmé distinguished between *reportage* and
literature or poetry.[1] Following in his footsteps, his disciple Valéry
asserted that prose functioned in the universe of cause and effect,
whereas poetry existed in a purely 'harmonic' universe; and he
likened the former to walking, the latter to dancing.[2] I. A. Richards
contrasts the 'scientific use of language' with the 'emotive use'.[3]
Both Valéry and Richards, on the face of it, seem rather to discount
the relevance of poetic discourse to the outside world; though they
both consider it of great value as a mental exercise.

The majority of distinctions of this kind, however, assert that
poetic discourse has a special *quality* of relevance to experience.
Kenneth Burke, for instance, makes a distinction between 'semantic'
and 'poetic' meaning. The first involves fining down and abstracting
from the object referred to; the second involves filling it out, giving
it body. Semantic meaning is (as we saw above) rather like a postal
address: it will infallibly tell you how to get somewhere; but it tells
you nothing about the kind of house you will find when you do so.[4]
Similarly, Pollock contrasts the 'referential symbolism' of science
with the 'evocative symbolism' of literature, and is insistent that
more of the content of actual experiences is present in the latter.
And John Crowe Ransom writes: 'The world of predictability is the
restricted world of scientific discourse. Its restrictive rule is: one value
at a time. The world of art is the actual world which does not bear
restriction; or at least . . . offers enough fullness of content to give
us the sense of the actual objects.'[5] In other words, apparency.

Scientific discourse achieves its high score of predictability, according to Ransom, by a fining down similar to that observed by Burke
and Pollock: 'The validity of a scientific discourse depends in part,

we should say, on its semantical purity. That is, each symbol should refer to an object specifically defined, or having a specific value-aspect, for the discourse; and throughout the discourse it should have exactly that reference and no other. The reference of a single symbol is limited, and uniform. In aesthetic discourse, however, we replace symbols with icons; and the peculiarity of an icon is that it refers to the whole or concrete object and cannot be limited . . . The icon is a particular. A particular is indefinable; that is, it exceeds definition.'[6] Similarly Cleanth Brooks writes that the scientist 'demands an exact one-to-one relevance of language to the objects and events to which it refers. The tendency of science is naturally to stabilize terms, to forge them into strict denotations; the poet's tendency is by contrast disruptive. The terms are thus (in poetic discourse) continually modifying each other, and thus violating their dictionary definitions.'[7]

Philip Wheelwright's contrast between two discourses is very similar. The language of literature is 'tensive' or 'fluid discourse'; that of science is 'block discourse'[8] or 'steno-language'.[9] These last two terms suggest rigidity and narrowness; but we should not take them as derogatory: they suggest once again a one-to-one relationship between word and sense. 'Tensive' language, on the other hand, says Wheelwright, may contain words which have more than one reference, or whose meanings cannot be exactly delineated, or may even involve an acceptable self-contradiction.[10] The 'steno-language' par excellence is 'logical discourse'. And indeed Wheelwright bases a great deal of what he has to say in *The Burning Fountain* on the laws of traditional logic, and particularly on the law of Excluded Middle.

Investigations of poetic and scientific discourse such as I have carried out in this book lead me to agree broadly with the authorities quoted above. There is indeed a different quality to poetic and scientific discourse, and the former relates in a different way to experience. But this is not due—or at least not exclusively due—to a special ethical, emotive or structural factor present in poetry as opposed to other types of language. I must agree with Ransom when he writes:

> A Poem differentiates itself for us, very quickly and convincingly, from a prose discourse . . . [But the differentia] is not moralism, for moralism conducts itself very well in prose, and conducts itself all the better in pure or perfect prose . . . It is not emotionalism, sensibility, or 'expression'. Poetry becomes slightly disreputable when regarded as not having any special or definable content . . . Much more promising as a

differentia is the kind of structure exemplified by a poem . . .
But it is hard to say *what poetry intends by its odd structure* . . .[11]

Ransom therefore appeals (as we have seen) to a distinction between 'symbols' and 'icons' borrowed from Charles W. Morris. An iconic sign, he explains, does not only refer to objects, it also resembles or imitates those objects.[12] But Ransom does not properly answer *how* this 'resemblance' is brought about. And is it resemblance? As Ransom is himself aware, except in the one case of the kind of imitative phonic effects I noted in chapter 15, it is not.[13] For me, apparency is given when language brings its normally hidden connotations to our notice: poetry is rather a matter of reminding than resembling. Once connotations begin to be apparent, we can never finish with the object; and it is *this* that gives us Ransom's sense of the particular. As he says, 'a particular is indefinable; that is, it exceeds definition'. But it exceeds definition because we feel that the connotations cannot be enumerated. Poetry is more an analogy for experience than an imitation of it. It is utterly unlike representational painting, in which light can fairly simply be imitated, because painting itself is of course done with light. Poetry *corresponds* to experience, but the stuff of which it is made is very different in kind.

A further qualification I shall make is that there is a tendency among these writers to confuse ordinary and scientific discourse. This is as much a mistake as to confuse ordinary and poetic discourse. Aldous Huxley is much nearer to the truth—as one would indeed expect from a writer whose knowledge of both literature and science was unusually profound—when he wrote:

> As a medium of literary expression, common language is inadequate. It is no less inadequate as a medium of scientific expression. Like the man of letters, the scientist finds it necessary to 'give a purer sense to the words of the tribe'. But the purity of scientific language is not the same as the purity of literary language. The aim of the scientist is to say only one thing at a time, and to say it unambiguously and with the greatest possible clarity . . . At its most perfectly pure, scientific language ceases to be a matter of words and turns into mathematics.
>
> The literary artist purifies the language of the tribe in a radically different way. The scientist's aim, as we have seen, is to say one thing, and only one thing, at a time. This, most emphatically, is not the aim of the literary artist. Human life is lived simultaneously on many levels and has many meanings. Literature is a device for reporting the multifarious facts and expressing

their various significances . . . (The literary artist) purifies, not by simplifying and jargonizing, but by deepening and extending, by enriching with allusive harmonics, with overtones of association and undertones of sonorous magic.[14]

Thus both science and poetry are privileged languages, each rising above the ordinary in its different way. The meanings of ordinary discourse are not defined in the clear and rigid fashion of science: they have considerable logical imprecision. Nor are they clashed together in the fashion habitual in poetry: they do not present us with poetry's complexity and hence experiential precision. Ordinary language is neither analytic nor synoptic to any great extent. It does not seek to analyze experience (that is dissect it, abstractize from it, and reason about it), but to point to it. Nor does it seek to recreate experience, to imitate or represent it, but again to point to it. Thus, we will be told only so much about a happening as will enable us to picture it for ourselves. This involves ordinary language's picturing things according to a purely conventional scheme, inherent in the grammar of the language and the meanings of the words as they are 'normally' understood by its users.

At this point readers may be tempted to protest that I am making it sound as if ordinary language leaves us cold, without feelings, unable to visualize or react in any way. Clearly this is far from being the case. The reactions of listeners to an ordinary piece of language are usually highly precise. But a distinction must be made: when we react to a piece of news we hear from someone's lips, our reaction is not normally due to the connotations evoked by the *language* our informant uses, but to our knowledge of the *referents* to which he alludes. This distinction between connotations being evoked by *word* and by *referent* is basic to the difference in functioning between common and poetic discourse.

When I hear that someone has been blown up in Ulster yet again, I am moved *because of their deaths*, not (normally) because of the language in which their deaths are described. Ordinary language is being well used when it refers to referents that are calculated to produce the desired effect. In this, good common discourse resembles bad nineteenth-century painting, like *Bubbles* or *The Monarch of the Glen*, where the paintings are like photographs, and vanish into their subjects, so that we react as we would to the subject. C. S. Lewis has argued persuasively that if you treat literary language in this kind of way, that is, imagine it evokes real events, and then react as to those real events, you are reacting self-indulgently. For you would be reacting to something *that was not so*—inappropriately and unwarrantably. You would be 'using' the work of art 'as a self-starter for certain imaginative and emotional activities of your own. In other words you "do things with it". You don't lay yourself open to what it, by being in its totality precisely the thing it is, can do to you.'[15]

I am not of course suggesting that the pain or joy which we feel on hearing some friend relate something painful or pleasurable, is a mere 'self-starter', a mere penny-in-the-slot that starts our own sentimentality going. There *are* of course people who treat the experiences they undergo, or that are reported to them, in precisely this sentimental way, like Evelyn Waugh's old ladies hiding from a revolution on top of a hotel, and, as the cavalry die in the street beneath, sighing to each other: 'Oh, the poor dear horses!' (This indeed is not so much a literary, as a pseudo-literary reaction to life: reacting to real experience as to a penny novelette.) The real content of real experiences imposes its own pattern, its own often more welcome or unwelcome reality than one could have imagined, upon what we hear (as upon what we experience). The point is that experience is at its most valuable (or at its most terrible) when it brings one something new: when an account of an event imposes upon us a fresh pattern of experience, whether because we know the event to be true or because the account itself is an effective recreation of experience, our own experience is enriched. Or, to express this same idea in my terminology, this happens when *apparency* is provided, whether by connotations that are controlled by referents, or by connotations that are controlled by language. Whereas, if we read a book that relies merely upon those connotations that are immediately available to our imaginations, and are not imposed upon us by either events or language, then our reaction is likely to be self-indulgent. The secret lies in the control of connotations: if the author controls them (if they are linguistic), well and good; if lived experience controls them (if they are referential) even better; but if we allow our own concepts to control them (if they are, thus, conceptual and subjective) we are in danger of sentimentality, or are at least experiencing our usual programmed reaction, not attempting to experience something new.

This is exactly what one would expect. The words we read are outside us: they bring us something from the outer world, something beyond ourselves. The experiences we go through act upon us too from the outside: they too bring us something beyond ourselves, enlarging us (and sometimes, alas, diminishing us) in the process, but altering us always. The one apparent exception in fact proves my point. For there are often books (I think everyone knows at least one such book) which, though classifiable as pseudo-literature, though incapable for most of us of effecting a sea-change, though trivial perhaps or sentimental or downright bad, yet speak to us personally with the power that we normally attribute only to a great work of art. This is because they speak for some reason to the beyond *inside* us as *François le Champi* spoke for Proust to the deepest recesses of his own childhood trauma. Here again it is the beyond refreshing the here-and-now, it is something outside us working upon us and altering us. The unconscious too is outside us, outside, that is, our normal awareness.

There is thus a difference between the reader's activity and the writer's in this respect: the writer starts from the basis of concepts, invents new connotative patterns (at the level of the concept): he embeds these patterns in the language he uses (at the level of the word). We, as readers, have to allow these verbal connotations to impose *their* pattern upon our concepts.

What then of the (almost) straight narration that is the mode of the traditional novel? Is this not too simple linguistically to be able to achieve the 'apparency' I should evidently like to claim for it? But novels of course tend more or less to be a narration of lived or imagined experience: they tend to obtain their power from the consistency with which they do so: the novel tends to build up 'a world of its own', as we say. This 'world' may be as fantastic as you like: it may be Swift's Lilliput, Huxley's Brave New World, Orwell's Airstrip One or David Lindsay's Arcturus; this matters little provided it has achieved a certain solidity and reality in our minds, so that when we read, say, the bitter dénouement of *1984*, Winston and his experiences have themselves achieved a certain solidity. Except that they are fictive, they behave like referents in common discourse: we are moved not only because of the language but also *because of the 'events' recorded*, and because of their relationship to other 'events' in Winston's 'life'. It is this of course that makes the simplicity of so many novels' endings so effective. The last sentence of *The Devils* runs 'The verdict of our doctors after the post-mortem was that it was most definitely not a case of insanity.' We are referred back once again to Stavrogin's whole history. Even these calm, apparently detached and matter-of-fact words, so like a legal or medical report, have the apparency of experience—because of the referents that underlie them.

One can see that to achieve the same weight of apparency in a poem, a different technique must be adopted. When poems are short, one has not time to build up a lengthy narrative universe: the language must therefore be denser, odder, more complex. And it should be noticed that the view I take here avoids the dogmatism of asserting that discursive language is *necessarily* lacking in apparency. Otherwise it would hardly be possible to explain how novels give us a sense of life at all.[16]

Like the literary artist, the scientist has to invent a means of preventing his language from being interpreted in a vague and unconsidered way. He therefore adopts a special tone, which I have described as 'the flat but authoritative factual'; he invents new terminology, and uses it, and those apparently ordinary words he employs, in what are evidently strictly and narrowly defined senses. His object is to perceive new categories, to impose them on and thus reanalyze old experience, to fit them into the network of accepted knowledge in such a way that they will harmonize with it, or subtly alter it. His tendency is towards analysis and clarity, away from vagueness; towards unity and simplicity, away from unresolved complexity.

It would however be a mistake to confuse Scientific and Logical discourse. We have seen that although science, in its tendency towards abstraction, towards precisely defined entities and relationships, tends towards the rigidities and certainties of logic, this is only a tendency. Logical discourse is hard and narrow, but, though the relative rigidity of scientific notions is useful to science, too much rigidity as we have seen, would be fatal to science itself. It is in fact precisely modern science's willingness to regard its definitions and concepts as merely provisional, and not as reflecting some divine and absolutely certain order of the universe, that has enabled it to progress. One extreme (logic), if taken too seriously and not as the merely invaluable tool it definitely is, would be as damaging as the other (ordinary imprecision). Logic is a useful systematization and formalization, and therefore impoverishment, of scientific discourse, because it does not take into account the full range of meanings, the full range of relationships, which science does.

If by way of contrast we want an example of poetic discourse being pushed to its ultimate, we might think of *Finnegan's Wake*. Here the number of associations presented by each word approaches the infinite—just as, in logic, the number of meanings presented by a symbol approaches unity. Both systems are equally extreme. One is almost wholly relational and abstract, giving us a logical drought of meanings; whereas the other gives us an associative deluge: excess in either direction tends to destroy meaning, in the one case by contracting it out of existence,[17] in the other by expanding it to the point of explosion, like Aesop's bullfrog.

We might therefore hazard figure 20: the languages of science and literature grow together yet apart out of the same soil: ordinary language. They are both refinements on it: like plants, they take the elements of the soil in which they are rooted, and reassemble them into complex, living, propagating organisms. They yearn towards two opposite types of certainty: the totally fixed, distinct and mathematical in the case of science, the totally mobile, ambiguous and indistinct in the case of poetry. But *medio tutissimus ibis* (the middle way is the safest). Both clarity and obscurity may become so extreme as to be self-defeating.

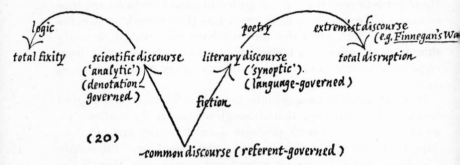

(20)

Though science thus represents a radical improvement over ordinary discourse in the direction of clarity, certainty and general acceptability, it equally clearly achieves this by ascetically denying itself large areas of the total possible range of discourse available to language. We may therefore arrive at two different but complementary definitions of poetic discourse: (1) poetry is the language of the open drawer, language in which more of the content of an experience (more of the connotations) are present; and (2) in poetry meaning attaches to all the features of language; or, conversely, poetry is the tendency to drive to their limit the full capabilities of language.

On the other hand, there is clearly no absolute distinction to be made between these three modes of discourse.[18] When the man in the street says: 'Now come. You don't really mean that. You mean . . .' he is thinking about the language he uses—and the referents to which that language refers—and analyzing them. And when he sang: 'Pack up your troubles in your old kitbag,' he was including the experience of being a soldier among those worries—which is a poetic and non-logical way of dealing with a problem! As always, things are a matter of degree. There are an infinite number of fine gradations between these different types of discourse, just as there are any number of gradations between dissonant metaphor like Anne Hébert's: 'A brazier under the eyelashes sings at full pitch.' and straightforward extension of the word 'sing' in the phrase 'The kettle's singing'.

Thus I do not (strictly speaking) disagree with Isabel Hungerland's statement that 'poetry cannot be marked off from other kinds of discourse in terms of some specific kind of meaning, feature, or function of language predominant in it. All the modes of meaning, features, and functions of everyday language are found in poetry. In brief, the medium of poetry is living language.'[19] By saying this, she nonetheless gives a wrong impression: what distinguishes poetic language from normal language is not that it contains different varieties of meaning, features or functioning, but that it employs all those normal features at a higher level of intensity. Poetry is language where the meaning is packed more tightly than normal.

Linguistics and Subjectivity

Language is too serious a matter to be left to the linguists.

(Deguy 1969, 169)

Even a complete grammar is only the beginning.

(Zeno Vendler 1967, 195)

FOR SOME TIME NOW the devotees of linguistics have been claiming especial virtues for their own approach to literature. In particular they rightly assert that poetry is a part of language: did not Mallarmé himself write to Degas that sonnets are made, not of ideas, but of words? And they also rightly assert that the grammatical categories which the modern linguist uses are more closely analyzed and more subtle than the traditional ones that are usually all the literary critic has at his disposal. (Though of course the linguists themselves have by no means yet decided what form their new model grammar will ultimately take.) They also claim more objectivity, more dispassion, and the virtues of a truly *scientific* approach to language. Let us investigate to what extent these claims can so far be justified.

We have already seen (ch. 14) that a number of eminent linguists have asserted that poetry is a special type of language, a special mode of discourse, in which the 'code of language is violated'. If this is so, an enormous field is immediately opened up to the linguist interested in literature. And those who have taken some advantage of this are those who have made the most interesting statements. These do, however, tend to be statements of a purely *general* kind: little enlightenment on the actual detailed working of *individual poems* has yet been given.[1]

For instance, some suggestive comments of a general kind have been made in various articles by J. P. Thorne. In one he makes the interesting suggestion that 'poems in which the grammar differs from Standard English only in the surface structure are usually bad poems'. And he quotes these lines of Longfellow as an instance:

Have I dreamed? Or was it real,
    What I saw as in a vision,
When to marches hymeneal
    In the land of the Ideal
Moved my thought o'er Field Elysian?[2]

And he seems to believe that in principle a new grammar could be

written for each individual poet.[3] The word 'grammar' here seems
perhaps misleading: but it is certainly true to say that there is something odd about typical poetic phrases such as 'houses are asleep' or
'I have known the inexorable sadness of pencils',[4] though one would
normally say it was the semantic content that was odd. In a sense, to
call 'houses are asleep' ungrammatical is to use the word as 'un-
grammatically' (i.e., as metaphorically) as the phrase it describes. It
is in fact Chomsky who is responsible for this application of 'un-
grammaticality';[5] but one might at first sight suspect that the wholesale extending of 'grammatical' to cover 'semantic' too, is part and
parcel of the twentieth-century linguist's suspicion of anything to do
with meaning. This would be unfair. Modern linguistics has discovered that to distinguish rigidly between semantic and syntactic
aspects of language is impossible; and the current tendency to extend
the meaning of 'grammatical' to cover meaning too, is evidence of a
new willingness to get to grips with meaning. Thus Thorne frankly
admits that 'if the grammar of the language of the poem is such that
Stones live is a well-formed sentence in it, then [these words] too
have changed their meaning'.[6]

It is clear that a grammatical element (in the normal sense of the
term) does very commonly enter into the sundry oddnesses of poetry.
Thorne himself has written about the idiosyncratic grammar of
E. E. Cummings.[7] For it is Cummings' habit to contort grammar to
an unusual (or at any rate an unusually obvious) degree:

anyone lived in a pretty how town
(with up so floating many bells down)
spring summer autumn winter
he sang his didn't he danced his did.

where 'anyone', 'how', 'up', 'so', 'down', 'didn't' and 'did' are certainly performing a number of curious grammatical functions; and
the second line has a particularly contorted syntax. Thorne however
hardly discusses at all *how* these strange usages affect the poet's
meaning. He confines himself to pointing at them, and to hazarding
the guess that a strange new grammar might be written to take
account of them. Meaning extends, one might say, in two directions,
the grammatical and the semantic. Thorne approaches it purely
from the grammatical direction, and then does not move very far
down the path.

It is certainly valuable to point to strange grammatical usages.
Thorne, given his predilections, has chosen a highly suitable poet in
this respect. He plausibly demonstrates the possibility of writing a
grammar to take account of 'anyone lived'. But why does he not

actually *use* this grammar, by elucidating the changes of meaning that Cummings thereby imposes on his vocabulary?

The answer is clear: here, as usual, we have a linguist who is crippled by his own insistence on scientific objectivity. Thorne dare not tread too heavily upon the shifting sand of semantics. Yet it cannot be too strongly emphasized that if there is any point in the linguist's insight of a grammar specially invented by the poet, this point must be found in the fresh *meanings* evoked by these techniques, in the mental *effects* they tend to produce. And this is Hendricks' point in his discussion of Thorne's article. He points out that it is changes in meaning which are the purpose of the poem, not changes in grammar. And Thorne, in his answer, in effect concedes this.[8]

For the pattern of an utterance is of no interest apart from any purpose it may reveal. Constellations such as the Plough are the product of chance alone, and consequently have no interest to the astronomer save for the purposes of orientation; nor did insectologists spend their time studying the flight patterns of the bee until it dawned upon them that these patterns contained a *meaning*. Linguists do not spend their time studying the sound of wind blowing down the chimney, but in dissecting human speech—for the very good reason that it is usually thought to be meaningful.

But if the meaning of a literary text is in question, as indeed it is, then a vast and bewildering world of subjective interpretation opens up before the linguist. He therefore does, in general, as Thorne does. He takes us in detail through the external, grammatical or structural detail of a poem, and gives us a few cool calm tools with which to dissect it. But, having taken us to the very threshold of meaning, he bids us farewell, and tantalizingly leaves us standing there, with fragments of a grammar in our hands, but no lexicon. Thus Cohen too, by the end of his book, has interestingly listed certain methods, certain techniques utilized by the poet: but about the *effects* of these techniques he has nothing to say, save that poetry is concerned to offer us not the 'notional' (that is ideational, rational or denotational) image of (say) the moon, but its 'emotional' image. What this might be, however, we are not told.[9]

The explanation is, of course, that many linguists still feel there is something unscientific about the study of meaning. It is doubtless such scruples as this that lead J. C. Catford, the author of a current textbook on translation, to begin the fifth chapter of that work with the words: 'It is generally held that *meaning* is important in translation.'[10] Few writers reach this pitch of squeamishness, to be sure, but even so too many linguists still prefer to confine their remarks on meaning to a footnote, or a sentence, or at most a paragraph. Sinclair, in 'Taking a Poet to Pieces', is a typical case. He remarks: 'The paucity of lexical comment' (in his article) 'reflects the fact that objective description of vocabulary patterns is still impossible.' He adds, however, hopefully enough: 'Nevertheless, the exercise shows how some aspects of the meaning of the poem can be described quite independently of evaluation.'[11] When one considers this claim carefully, one sees that it could hardly be smaller. All he has in fact demonstrated is the frequency and pattern of certain grammatical categories in Philip Larkin's 'First Sight'; and if I may be allowed, as a literary critic, to evaluate, I should say that though the fine distinctions Sinclair makes might well turn out in some cases to assist the literary scholar, he totally fails to prove this—for the simple reason that he merely enumerates, and quite fails to relate this enumeration to any meanings or shades of meaning that the poem might contain.

Fortunately, Sinclair himself now seems to have recanted his belief in total caution. His treatment of Graves's poem 'The Legs' is a quite different kettle of fish. Here he has explicitly given up the attempt to be 'objective' at all costs, and at one point appeals to 'the common sense and integrity of the analyst' (i.e., himself), *'just as in literary criticism'*.[12] And in consequence his article conveys a number of useful insights.

The greatest sinner of all in these respects is doubtless 'stylostatistics', which involves the counting of adjectives, or images, or articles, or anything else that strikes the statistician's fancy, and which, though it may sometimes give valuable indications as to the authorship of works (and has indeed been much used in this direction), is all too often applied uncritically. It is true, of course, that it is interesting to be told that there are almost no metaphors in the early part of *L'Etranger*, but that suddenly, at the point where Meursault murders the Arab, a mass of metaphors blossoms from the page. But perhaps even a literary critic might have noticed this. It is indeed the sort of thing that literary critics do notice. And on the other hand, as Leo Spitzer puts it, is it really necessary to have numerical data for the high frequency of the word 'love' in poetry?[13]

This kind of attitude (and it is a common one)[14] so far from being scientific, merely evinces a morbid terror of the least glimmer of speculation. It is admirable of course that we should know what the writer considers to be fact, and what he is more hesitant about, and might even attribute to fancy; but without a proper *demonstration* of the value of their approach, such overcautious linguists simply undermine their own case. They present us merely with structures; and the structures in different kinds of verse are yet very similar. Unless a close connexion can be shown to hold between certain structures and certain meanings, the linguist's case is not made; and for this he needs to discuss meaning.

The picture is immediately quite different in the case of Archibald Hill's discussion of 'Pippa's Song'.[15] Here is a writer using linguistic techniques in the service, ultimately, of interpreting and even evaluating a poem. Besides, the article has a special interest in that it discusses, and finally condemns, a previous appraisal of the same poem made by the poet and critic John Crowe Ransom.[16] A comparison should therefore be instructive. Browning's brief poem runs:

> The year's at the spring
> And day's at the morn;
> Morning's at seven;
> The hill-side's dew-pearled;
> The lark's on the wing;
> The snail's on the thorn;
> God's in his heaven—
> All's right with the world!

Ransom complains that the last two lines are a subjective imposition of a human moral and theological attitude upon nature: He writes: 'Pippa's Universal is a feeling of joy, intense but diffused over every act and thought. (She is innocent, and this is her holiday from the silk mills.) . . . We are given to understand that everything is joyful like Pippa, that all nature is animated in the morning light . . . She spends three lines . . . dating the occasion very precisely . . . Then come three details which constitute the concrete: the hillside, the lark, the snail . . . And that would be the poem; except that she must conclude by putting in her theological Universal . . .' This complaint, as Hill points out, is based on a 'structural' analysis of the principal meanings that Ransom sees in the poem: namely, units of time, of concrete experience, and a unit of abstract theological universality. 'If the operating units are valid,' says Hill, 'his statement of the structure and the resultant evaluation follow almost inevitably.'[17] Hill proceeds therefore from his own approach to cut up the poem in a different way from Ransom. He sees the first three lines as parallel statements, culminating in the fourth line; and lines five to seven as parallel statements culminating in the last line. For, he says, lines one to three and five to seven all have the same grammatical structure; while lines four and eight share a different structure: 'noun, copula, and phrasal modifier'.

Hill then paraphrases the structure of the meanings, as follows:

    Large A is at contained B (its best)
    Smaller B is at contained C (its best)
    Still smaller C is at contained D (its best)
      Therefore small X is Y (its best).
    Small E is on F (its best place)
    Smaller G is on H (its best place)
    Large I is in J (its best place)
      Therefore the large scene is at its best.[18]

It will be clear that this analysis is accurate as far as it goes. Hill has thus obtained a complete orderly system of parallelisms from the poem. We shall see other linguists making the same kind of demonstration.

Hill concludes (but we shall have to return to how he comes to this conclusion in a moment) that Ransom is being unfair to the poet: the transition from snail to God to the moral universal in the last line *is* justified. And he ends:

> It remains only to state the differences between Ransom's method and that used here. Ransom is structural in his approach, but uses semantically defined units without having worked through the formal linguistic differentia. His method is therefore similar to that of traditional grammar, where a formal word-class, such as nouns, is defined in terms of the semantic content of the class. In contrast, the analysis given here rests on one of the most basic assumptions in linguistics, that it is form which gives meaning and not meaning which gives form.[19]

It is my belief that all this will not do at all. Hill's critique is at the level of the *structure* of the meanings (how they fit into each other, what their relationships are within each phrase and between phrases, and so forth); and it is clearly valid at that level. Ransom's critique is at the level of the *type* of meaning; and of whether certain types of meaning (philosophical universals) can be supported by other types of meaning (concrete instances), or can even be regarded as producing a poetic effect. And this is a much more tricky affair. It would seem that Hill is assenting to Browning's last two lines, and Ransom is dissenting to them, on two utterly different grounds.

But it is not just that Hill and Ransom differ and might agree to differ. There is something faulty in the basis of Hill's own approach. His analysis of the poem's structure simply cannot lead to his conclusions. For can the *orderliness* of a structure lead us to assent to the *rightness* of a meaning embedded in that structure? Clearly not! For structures can be as orderly as you like without being in the slightest degree convincing. Indeed orderliness in poetic structure is the most commonplace of things: the traditional poem is nothing if not orderly; and the more excruciating products of those nineteenth-century writers lampooned so rightly by Lewis Carroll were of course also perfectly orderly. If the products of both deserve our laughter, the fact is that the laughter is of two quite different qualities. How will an investigation of mere pattern, of mere orderliness, help us when we compare two symmetrical products such as these?

> Twinkle, twinkle, little star,
> How I wonder what you are!
> Up above the world so high,
> Like a diamond in the sky.

and

> Twinkle, twinkle, little bat,
> How I wonder what you're at!
> Up above the world you fly,
> Like a tea-tray in the sky.[20]

Indeed, if linguists wish us to take their structural approaches seriously, perhaps they should turn their attention to the differences between bad poetry, good poetry, and parodies of both. It is not hard to find unmistakeable examples of all three.

Orderliness, then, demonstrates orderliness; but not the quality of that orderliness, or indeed anything else at all. But we may now ask (leaving the question of *pattern*, and embarking on that of *sense*): Can a succession of *concrete* imagery (such as we have in 'Pippa's Song') lead us to assent to the rightness of an *abstract* universal led up to by that structure? Surely yes, at least in certain cases. And this, in effect, is Hill's argument![21] As he himself admits, he takes off his linguist's gown, and dons a literary critic's disguise to refute Ransom. As he himself admits, his previous analysis cannot lead him to any such refutation. Here, in short, he is arguing like a critic, and one may even be disposed to agree with him when he does so. 'Ransom has called the last two lines a well-schooled theological tag. Pippa breaks her strict analogical pattern to bring *snail* and *God* together. [This is not how] theologians talk about God. It correlates, instead, with the way we expect children to talk of Him, in concrete and simple terms.'[22]

But what have we here? Hill, talking of 'concrete and simple terms'! Hill, using Ransom's terminology to refute him! We could not, I think, have a clearer instance of the necessity, for discussing the efficacity of poetry, of using the approaches of literary criticism.

If Hill's defence of Browning is effective, then, it is so *because* it is couched in literary critical language, and is a literary critical approach. But before I adjudicate between Hill and Ransom, I should like to point to two further features of the poem's structure, both unmentioned by both critics. Line four, 'The hill-side's dew-pearled', marks in fact a progression between lines 1–3 and lines 5–6. For hillsides are dewpearled in the morning: the line is both temporal and concrete, and links what goes before with what goes after. Secondly, line 7, 'God's in his heaven', similarly marks a transition, from the concrete details of lines 4 to 6, to the 'abstract universal' in line 8. For it has the same form, of apparently concrete assertion, as lines 5 and 6. It thus may seem to gain support from these previous, dead sure, down to earth assertions. It thus may perhaps justify the poet in going on to make his further assertion: 'all's right with the world!'

Of course if the 'abstract universal' is merely abstract; if it has no support from concrete detail or from the progression of the poem, simply interrupting us like a loud irrelevant sermon in the middle of a sunny morning, then we shall have to agree with Ransom. As it is, it could be said he has overlooked the careful transition of line 7, and the effect that this has in the context of the poem. We might read 'All's right with the world!' in inverted commas, as Pippa's feelings made explicit.

But this is not in fact Hill's argument. For he goes on to talk of Pippa's simple and childlike faith, and its containing 'insights somehow better than those found in the words of the most philosophically sophisticated.'[23] But can we interpret Pippa's words as representing such a 'right view of the world'? And are we not back then with a statement of a universal which (and this is what I feel Ransom's argument really amounts to) goes too far because it pretends to assert a general truth whilst merely in fact asserting a particular feeling? And is this not the well-known failing of shrugging moral complexities off under the guise of an appeal to God or authority or (as here) natural untutored instinct? This view gains support from the poem's context. Browning uses it to moralize from: his two guilty lovers, overhearing Pippa's song, fall to quarrelling; and the whole threatening panoply of a morality of sin and retribution announces its presence. I am afraid that our final conclusion must be that Pippa's song does indeed draw too explicit a moral: it opens on the sunshine and closes on the sermon.

But there is worse. The quarrel between the lovers is not so much a quarrel as a brutal and selfish invective on the part of the man against his mistress. One could well deduce that, if Pippa's proposition creates such cruelty, it is itself in some way inadequate. Yet there is no hint that Browning has anything but total sympathy and admiration for Pippa's starry-eyed innocence. 'All's right with the world' is thus not even true of Pippa: for it symbolizes a purity which is absolutely pitiless, and so equals the cruellest of pruderies. We cannot commend such an inhumane emotion.

I conclude that Hill's view is less persuasive than Ransom's. But whatever view we take of the final line, the fact remains that, despite his disclaimers, Hill's disagreement with Ransom is on the basis of the 'semantic units' they each adduce: Ransom calls the final statement 'a theological universal'; Hill thinks it the justified product of simple faith. It is no good therefore Hill talking of 'form giving meaning'. The point is that, *despite form*, it is possible for the meaning of the last line to over-reach itself.

And we may now proceed to Hill's final remarks: 'Since the two sets of assumptions [his own and Ransom's] are correlated with differing kinds of activity, it is impractical to measure which set is the more reasonable. Fortunately the two analyses can be measured otherwise. They must be assumed to be significantly different, since one cannot be mechanically translated into the other. If different, both cannot be true; one must be more complete, more consistent, and more simple than the other. Evaluation may be left to the reader.'[24] The logicians' assumption of the applicability of the Law of Excluded Middle is here quite blatant—and quite unwarrantable. The fact of the matter is that both Hill's structure and Ransom's structure can be seen in the poem: they overlap, and are, as it were, syncopated against each other. And such syncopation is in fact one of the attractions of the poem. Why then use simplicity as a criterion of truth? Simplicity in explanation is only a virtue where the facts can be fitted into that simplicity. Logical criteria are inappropriate to poetry, where we move in a different world from that of science and Occam's razor. Completeness is more important, and we therefore need both accounts of the poem.

Finally, 'evaluation may be left to the reader'. Yes, and the percipient reader will see that Hill has not used his own system in refuting Ransom, but Ransom's. I think his evaluation is more doubtful than Ransom's, but that is another matter; and I think this brief exploration into the detail of a linguistic approach is indicative of what we shall find everywhere: the tools of the linguist may certainly be valuable; but they will show us only the simplest and most obvious of facts: to interpret those facts, even the linguist needs to abandon his structuralist stance for a while.[25]

We now turn to what is probably the most famous of all linguists' commentaries on poetry, namely, Roman Jakobson's and Claude Lévi-Strauss's discussion of Baudelaire's poem 'Les Chats'.[26] For though it spends most of its time counting adjectives, plural nouns, relative clauses, feminine rimes and so forth, it nonetheless attempts to provide an interpretation. It cannot be too often reiterated that if a linguistic approach to literature is to prove its point, it must tell us what that point is!

Nonetheless, one needs to make certain reservations, though this time they are of a different order. There exists a balanced and moderate assessment of Jakobson's and Lévi-Strauss's article by Michael Riffaterre, and I should assent to most of what he says there. He describes Jakobson as believing that parallelism is the basis underlying poetry: a poem is a verbal sequence wherein the same relations between constituents are repeated at various levels (phonetic, phonological, syntactical, semantic, etc.) This enables one to avoid 'dragging in hard-to-define concepts like non-grammaticalness or departure from the norm'.[27] Riffaterre admits that Jakobson and Lévi-Strauss give 'an absolutely convincing demonstration of the extraordinary concatenation of correspondences that holds together the parts of speech' in 'Les Chats'.[28] And certainly order of various kinds is an important feature of poetry, at least of traditional poetry.[29] What, however, has happened here to Shklovski's principle of oddness? It is clear from Jakobson that such a principle is difficult or impossible to deal with from his point of view. It is only regularities that his brand of science can cope with.

It is therefore no surprise when one comes to read 'Les Chats' to see that these two structuralists have chosen for their exposé one of Baudelaire's more banal and insipid poems.

Les Chats

Les amoureux fervents et les savants austères
Aiment également, dans leur mûre saison,
Les chats puissants et doux, orgueil de la maison,
Qui comme eux sont frileux et comme eux sédentaires.

Amis de la science et de la volupté,
Ils cherchent le silence et l'horreur des ténèbres;
L'Erèbe les eût pris pour ses coursiers funèbres,
S'ils pouvaient au servage incliner leur fierté.

Ils prennent en songeant les nobles attitudes
Des grands sphinx allongés au fond des solitudes,
Qui semblent s'endormir dans un rêve sans fin;

Leurs reins féconds sont pleins d'étincelles magiques,
Et des parcelles d'or, ainsi qu'un sable fin,
Etoilent vaguement leurs prunelles mystiques.

[Fervent lovers and austere scholars share the same love, in
their riper years, for powerful but gentle cats, the pride of the
household, who like themselves are sedentary and sensitive to
the cold.

Friends of learning and sensuality, cats ever seek silence and
dreadful night; Erebus would have employed them as funereal
messengers, could they lower their pride to slavery.

They assume, when they daydream, the majestic poses of
those colossal sphinxes who stretch their limbs in the realms of
solitude, and who seem to be sleeping in an endless dream.

Magical sparks teem in their fertile loins, and particles of
gold, like delicate grains of sand, vaguely fleck their mystic
pupils with stars.][30]

The central image probably carried for the poet a special emotional
charge; for he used it often. But perhaps indeed it had *so* high an
emotional charge that he trusted it too much. The charge was in the
image, for Baudelaire; but for us it must be brought *out*; and this the
poet has not achieved.[31]

'Amoureux fervents' and 'savants austères' are both clichés, and
also constitute a standard opposition; 'puissants et doux' is a conventional oxymoron; 'dans leur mûre saison' is again a cliché, besides
being an elegant evasion of a rather faded kind; 'Ils cherchent le
silence' is not a cliché, but not in any way unusual; 'horreur des
ténèbres' and 'nobles attitudes' are again clichés, and the rime
'funèbres/ténèbres' is a conventional one.[32] I shall not continue; but
it will already be apparent that this is not one of those poems where
Baudelaire amazes and disturbs us with the power or violence of his
imagery.

However, my objection to the Jakobson/Lévi-Strauss analysis of
the poem is not so much that it gives us no hint whether the poem is
successful or not, and hence no criterion for judging poems; for this
was no part of their intention. No, the point is rather that they have
applied a theory of *regularity* to a poem; and the poem they have
chosen is admirably suited to the task, for it is *regular*; but its very
regularity, its conformity to conventional modes of poetry, renders it
relatively uninteresting.

If these remarks of mine are fair, then they constitute a partial
refutation of the Jakobson/Lévi-Strauss approach. Not that Jakobson

and Lévi-Strauss are mistaken in any way about the complex parallelisms which the poem presents us with. It is simply that such regularities are the most commonplace fare of all poetry, and *all traditional poems follow them more or less.* The analysis of Jakobson and Lévi-Strauss therefore amounts to no more than an analysis of those features without which the poem would not (at the particular point in history when it was composed) have been a poem at all. We have certainly had important elements of the poem's nature as a poem (in a general sense) brought out—but not any of its *particular* qualities. But precisely! The poem is relatively banal, and relatively lacking in particular qualities.

Such is the price of objectivity. But *are* Jakobson and Lévi-Strauss objective? One consequence of their avoiding the principle of oddness is that they examine absolutely every detail of the poem, so that nothing is made to appear more striking than anything else. They 'scan everything with an even hand,' says Riffaterre,' and [are] therefore misleading.'[33] From the point of view of a scientist who makes no judgment on subjective human reactions, this is doubtless objective. But in reacting to a poem, it is precisely one's subjective human reactions that count. In the matter of art, it is not objective to ignore the subjective.

Yet they cannot themselves ignore the subjective. For instance, they claim that the use of feminine words for masculine rimes suggests androgyny.[34] The suggestion looks at first sight absurd: how many French poems, after all, contain masculine rimes expressed by means of feminine nouns? An enormous number, surely. And Riffaterre, in his critique, condemns this idea out of hand.[35] Certainly it seems far-fetched. But I mention it here merely to bring out the highly dubious nature of some of the remarks on meaning that the authors make. Their method is inadequate to bring out a poem's particular qualities; yet they are nonetheless not free of subjective judgment.

'Ah!' the objective linguist will say. 'But that is exactly why one should never discuss meanings. The moment you do so, look what happens: prejudice and partialities creep in.' The point is well taken. But the consequence would be without interest.

For what would be the consequence? To count the number of feminine rimes of masculine nouns *without* drawing a conclusion. It is this sort of thing that Halliday does in his article on Yeats's *Leda and the Swan*.[36] There, he merely contents himself with counting certain grammatical categories he finds in the poem. Similar remarks apply to Sinclair's account of Larkin, as we have seen. Linguistics, one is tempted to say, is not happy except when standing firmly on the hard rock of a statistical calculation.

Yet is this a true picture of the case? Upon what authority, after all, do modern linguistic categories depend? Let us quote part of Lyons' account of the importance of Chomsky's book *Syntactic Structures*.

> In it, [says Lyons] Chomsky did not amass a wealth of detail from many languages, but selected a few evident, and in a sense well-understood facts about the structure of a very familiar language (English) and about the nature of language in general, and demonstrated, conclusively, that these facts could not be 'explained' within the framework of current linguistic theory. But in doing so, he set more rigorous standards of 'explanation' than linguists had hitherto been accustomed to. These standards are still somewhat controversial (although a good deal of the controversy is based on misunderstanding). But they have been accepted by many linguists, including some who have rejected the details of the formalization of grammatical theory developed by Chomsky . . . The principles of transformational grammar outlined and discussed in *Syntactic Structures* are simple enough . . . The application of these principles to more than a fragment of the grammatical structure of any one language is far from simple . . .[37]

This is a typical picture of the present state of a field of scientific study. We see that (1) the original theory is based upon a hunch relating to a small and well-thumbed sector of the problem; (2) it is then extrapolated to cover the rest of the field of study; (3) an argument or 'demonstration' is in effect an appeal to other experts in the field; (4) it is rather a question of acceptance of the probable rightness of a point of view than of proof;[38] and (5) that advances upon the mysterious frontiers of knowledge are always controversial.

I think therefore that we should agree with Geoffrey Leech, one of the more convincing linguistically-inclined critics, when he writes: 'In fact, though objectivity may be a theoretical requirement of science, a scientist (particularly in linguistics, if that is to be counted a science) in practice can rely so much on his own intuition for discovery and his own judgment for corroboration, that his method of investigation may prove hardly distinguishable from that, say, of a literary commentator.' And he adds, 'insight or understanding is a much more important goal, in any human endeavour, than being objective. Statements of objective fact (for example, that there are eighty-two occurrences of the word *the* in the fourth canto of the first book of *The Faerie Queene*) can be as inane in the domain of style as anywhere else.'[39]

Leech's example is instructive in practice too. He is responsible for a helpful beginners' course in stylistics, and in his discussion, for instance, of Dylan Thomas's poem 'This Bread I Break',[40] he accepts the need to explicate, and immediately comes up with interesting and worthwhile results. Other linguistically based critics adopt a similar point of view.[41]

For the dream of 'objective description of vocabulary patterns'[42] is after all but a pipe-dream. When we read Reverdy's lines: 'Une lampe s'est allumée/ Dans la maison qui ouvre ses fenêtres/ Les yeux se sont mis à briller'[43] [A lamp has lit/ In the house that opens its windows/ Eyes have begun to shine.] we see the windows as the house's eyes. But on what 'objective' basis? To what extent are lamps and eyes 'objectively' similar? To what extent is their shining similar? Surely only in the context of these three lines would we read 'la maison qui ouvre ses fenêtres' as being the same kind of opening as opening one's eyes? Surely it is only on the basis of one's human experience of seeing houses at dusk, and seeing eyes open— and perhaps also of certain haunting and half-remembered pictures —that one can 'see' and react to this image at all? And if this is how the image works, how much of human experience would have to be fed into the linguist's machinery before he could even begin to 'describe vocabulary patterns objectively'?

Not merely experience, but also literary experience, legend and deep-rooted myth. In 'Départ', Reverdy writes:

> Un cœur saute dans une cage
> Un oiseau chante
> Il va mourir
>   [A heart hops in a cage
>   A bird sings
>   It's going to die]

Even assuming the linguist's machinery were capable of connecting heart with bird, equating them, and interpreting the lines as a fear or warning of death, could it also be programmed to contain such information as the legend of the swan singing before its death? Well, perhaps so; but the psychological *effect* of this reminiscence would still remain outside its grasp. For it is not a question of 'vocabulary patterns', but of a whole wealth of connotation which only the fully fledged human brain can possibly have at its disposal. And with images which strike even deeper, into the unconscious for instance, like some of the more perturbing images of Jouve, the problem is surely even more insoluble.

So, whatever the story may be in mathematics, from a linguistic point of view it is the human brain that is still the best computer. We may, as literary critics, perfectly well continue to do as we have always done: that is, proffer our explanations and interpretations in the continuing context of a critical dialogue with each other and with our readers. For that, after all, is no more and no less than what linguists do among themselves, continually appealing to each other (in effect) for corroboration of what is 'evidently' a correct interpretation of the sense and syntax of an English sentence.

For in this 'evidently' there lurk a quantity of traps. Computers depend totally upon what has been fed into them. Similarly the human brain cannot rapidly achieve results in a field it is unacquainted with. As Leo Spitzer rightly puts it, stylistics depends upon 'talent, experience and faith'.[44] And, as long as his faith is not an absolute, no critic should be expected to apologize for his talent and his experience.

I shall conclude my remarks on the question of whether linguistics may be said to have anything in particular to contribute to the criticism of literature, by pointing out that (1) relatively few linguists have yet tackled the subject; (2) there are however a number of highly interesting comments by linguists. These are mainly of a very general kind, and often relate above all to the differences between different types of discourse. I have discussed some such observations above, in chapter 14, and it will be seen that I think some of these insights are of great value. It must also be said that (3) I think the value of the modern linguistic approach to metrics can hardly be over-rated.[45]

Many of the weapons that linguists are proudest of, however, are strictly useless, since they give us no further information than we had already. I will take just one instance, that of the notion of 'collocation', which is claimed to be a handy way of explaining some of the features of what happens when Dylan Thomas, for instance, writes 'A grief ago . . .'[46]

'Collocation' refers to the kind of vocabulary with which a word is usually associated. Clearly Thomas has here replaced the normal collocative field of the 'a . . . ago' (which would be nouns of time, like 'year', or 'month') with a word ('grief') not usually found here. Just what *effect* this has, however, linguists do not say. As for the (implicit) suggestion that literary critics have overlooked something odd about the phrase, or if they have not, that they do not know what exactly *is* odd about it, well, that is clearly arrant nonsense.

It must also be added that (4) as yet linguists have made little progress towards any meaningful discussion of individual texts; and moreover, (5) where they have done so, it is mainly with the help of normal literary-critical techniques. There are certainly some hopeful signs; and some contemporary French structuralists are already producing valuable work.[47] Such critics however all pay close attention to meaning as well as structure. We should certainly welcome the linguists' new-found interest in literature, but we should insist once more that, if they are to make the really useful contribution we may justifiably expect of them, they will have to lose their prejudices against 'subjectivity', and adopt an approach (perhaps) like Riffaterre's . . . or accept an analysis of the structures of meaning like that suggested in the present book.

Literary Critics and Objectivity

> A text is a mechanism which anyone may use in his own way and as
> best he can: it is not certain that its constructor uses it better than the
> next man.   (Paul Valéry)

THE LINGUIST MIGHT STILL object, however, that even if his own
subject is not without its subjective judgments, and even if the study
of literature presupposes that one should apply the imagination to
texts, this is still unscientific. Isn't the study of literature hopelessly
'woolly'? How can we ever be sure we're right? Why do we contradict each other all the time? And so forth. Moreover, what are we
to make of my own claim (in chapter 17), that poetry was a 'precise'
mode of discourse? In what way can it be so? Are the possible connotations of a given phrase not too numerous even to be controlled by
the poet himself?

This is an enormous topic, and I do not wish to offer a complete
defence. I shall confine myself to a few points. It has been said for
instance that the very concept of poetry working in a connotative
way is open to doubt, because it lets in a chaos of alternative readings
and associations.

For instance Marckwardt writes: 'a particular succession of linguistic experiences, peculiar to a single individual and not likely to
be duplicated, gives rise to certain associative experiences and hence
connotative values which no author could possibly have intended or
anticipated'.[1]

Marckwardt of course overstates his case. It is simply not true
that the *majority* of our experiences with words are in substance
radically different from each other's; and the majority of our connotations for a given word are likely therefore to coincide. As for the
privateness of some connotations, this cannot be denied. But some
control over this is built in, so to speak, by the contextual system of
the poem. We do not attribute to a word overtones which do not suit
its context, but only those which do suit its context. In the properly
constructed poem the context *arouses* those particular overtones
which are appropriate. Thus 'la glu' and 'le gui' mutually arouse
those overtones which fit.

There are of course cases where inappropriate overtones are too
powerful and universal to overlook, as we saw above in the case of the

word 'pendulous', or with the tenuous metaphors of Cleveland. However, *it is precisely the test of a bad poem that it contains such words.* Which indicates, if you like, that the *Rural Cyclopedia*'s description of mistletoe is a bad poem!

In general, therefore, the contextual system of the poem controls the connotations which will occur to the reader—at least to a degree which is in general sufficient. Moreover this system can be depended upon in most cases to continue to protect the poem's barrage of meanings long after the demise of the style in which it was written. A poem is a structure whose elements are mutually supportive. Thus, to give an unusually simple example, Corbière's 'La Fin'[2] provides within it two stylistic poles, the Hugolian grandiose and the Corbièrian direct, whose relative positions from each other we may surely expect to continue to be discernible, whatever developments French will undergo during the next few centuries. This tendency of the elements of a successful poem to interlock and provide a stable structure is often called 'convergence'. Riffaterre comments on the following sentence from *Moby Dick*: 'And heaved and heaved, still unrestingly heaved the black sea, as if its vast tides were a conscience.'

> There is here an accumulation of (1) an unusual Verb-Subject word-order; (2) the repetition of the verb (3) the rhythm created by this ternary repetition (plus the combination of this phonetic device with the meaning: the rise and fall of the waves is 'depicted' by the rhythm); (4) the intensive co-ordination (*and . . . and . . .*), reinforcing the rhythm; (5) a nonce word (*unrestingly*) which by its very nature will create a surprise in any context; (6) the metaphor emphasized by the unusual relationship of the concrete (*tides*) to the abstract (*conscience*) instead of the reverse. Such a heaping up of stylistic features working together I should like to call *convergence*.[3]

As for the author not having 'intended' or 'anticipated' connotations, what would Marckwardt say of Ponge's evidence about 'sacripant'? It must surely be clear that the writer's unconscious intentions are as important as his conscious ones; and that it is more often a feeling of rightness rather than a conscious working out of connotations that leads a writer to put down on paper what he does put down.[4]

The finger of fun is also often pointed at literary critics because they allegedly spend their time contradicting each other's interpretations. This is surely truer of traditional criticism, by which I mean criticism before T. S. Eliot, Robert Graves, I. A. Richards and William

Empson came on the scene. It certainly must be admitted that the spectacle of the three or four universally acknowledged experts on Mallarmé contradicting each other over the interpretation of a phrase is an amusing one. But one of the finest instances of this kind of thing is to be found in *Seven Types of Ambiguity* itself:

It is with a pretty turn of grammar [writes Empson] such as might have been included in my seventh type (of ambiguity) among perversions of the negative, that the Arden editor insists on the variety of associations the word *rooky* had for an Elizabethan audience.[5]

'This somewhat obscure epithet, however spelt (and it should be spelt *rouky*), does NOT mean 'murky' or 'dusky' (Roderick, quoted by Edward's *Canons of Criticism*, 1765); NOR 'damp', 'misty', 'steamy with exhalations' (Steevens, also Craig); NOR 'misty', 'gloomy' (Clar. Edd.); NOR 'where its fellows are already assembled' (Mitford), and has NOTHING to do with the dialectic word 'roke' meaning 'mist', 'steam', etc . . . the meaning here . . . I THINK, is simply the 'rouking' or perching wood, *i.e.* where the rook (or crow) perches for the night.'

Now, of course, the reason an honest editor puts down the other possibilities, as well as the one he is tentatively in favour of himself, is simply that these meanings had seemed plausible to scholars before; might, for all we know, therefore, have seemed plausible to anybody in the first-night audience; might have seemed plausible to Shakespeare himself, since he was no less sensitive to words than they. There is no doubt how such a note acts: it makes you bear in mind all the meanings it puts forward. I cannot now make the imaginative effort of separating the straightforward meaning of the line from this note; I feel as if one was told elsewhere in the text, perhaps by the word *thickens*, or by the queer hollow vowels of *rooky wood*, that the wood was dark and misty . . .[6]

Empson concludes that we must either suppose the work of all these scholars to have been misguided, or assume that the poet's original meaning was complex enough to include all their interpretations.

What, at any rate, seems evident in such a case as this is that we have no rational reason for rejecting any of the senses offered; and that, moreover, the semantic structure of the language is such that, *if* any of these senses is suggested to us *and* it fits, we can hardly fail to bear it in mind.

But modern literary criticism, since Empson, is only too willing to accept such concatenations of meaning. The logical mentality is sometimes offended by the margin that is thereby left to different interpretations. Archibald Hill, for instance, asserts in downright fashion that he will not accept conflicting interpretations, and then puts himself in grave difficulties over Hopkins's phrase 'dapple-dawn-drawn Falcon',[7] since he cannot tell for certain whether 'drawn' means 'delineated' (as with a pencil) or 'attracted'. He nonetheless insists on rejecting one of these meanings, even though he cannot tell which one it should be! This is a clear case of the excluded middle excluding *itself*.

A striking instance of ambiguity with which I am myself concerned, can be found in *Le Cimetière marin*, where Valéry, addressing the sea, calls it: 'Golfe mangeur de ces maigres grillages . . .' [Gulf devouring these thin rails]. Two suggestions had been made by previous commentators as to the sense of the second line here; in my own commentary I combined these and added a third: '(1) the iron railings surrounding each tomb are corroded by the sea-air, . . . (2) the optical phenomenon whereby one looks through narrow railings at the sea, and they seem to disappear against it . . . (3) the cemetery railings, symbolic of death, seem abolished by contemplation of the divine . . .'[8] Obviously the line may reasonably be held to suggest what it suggests, namely at least these three interpretations.[9] In short, ambiguities, or rather sources of disagreement, can be removed by accepting those ambiguities. And this is now accepted modern practice. We tend to subsume conflicting interpretations in a *total* reading. So much, therefore, for literary critics contradicting each other.[10]

On the other hand, private associations do exist; and the author himself may be at fault if the associations his images suggest are too private. A classic instance of a controversy over private associations, namely Edith Sitwell's phrase 'Emily-coloured hands', occurred in the *Observer* a number of years ago.[11] The figure of speech was strongly condemned and just as strongly defended by those who said they knew 'quite well what [they] are like, thin, pale, yellowish, and faintly freckled.' Miss Sitwell herself commented: 'I did not write "Emily-coloured hands," a hideous phrase. I wrote "Emily-coloured primulas", which to anyone who has progressed in poetry-reading beyond the *White Cliffs of Dover* calls to mind the pink cheeks of young country girls." '[12] Now since primulas are perhaps most commonly thought of as *yellow*; and since the associations of the name *Emily* at the time of the correspondence in question were probably rather with aged maiden aunts than with young country girls (for the name had long been out of favour), one feels at first sight that even in the case of Miss Sitwell's original phrase, those who had thin, pale and yellowish associations were 'feeling' the phrase correctly.

However, we have so far been looking at the phrase quite out of context, and the overtones of 'Emily' should (if Miss Sitwell has been doing her job properly) be to some extent controlled by that context. Here are the surrounding lines:

> In Midas' garden the simple flowers
> Laugh, and the tulips are bright as the showers,
>
> For spring is here; the auriculas,
> And the Emily-coloured primulas
>
> Bob in their pinafores on the grass
> As they watch the gardener's daughter pass.[13]

In his discussion of the phrase, Geoffrey Nokes remarks that the pinafores put Emily's age quite beyond doubt: she must be young![14] And Miss Sitwell's own comment on the associations of the phrase are 'Obviously I could not mean yellow primulas, since nobody is of that bright yellow colour.'[15] Kingsley Amis on the other hand, points out that primulas can be of any colour you like — and so, very nearly, can people.[16] But the remark itself is comic: which indicates that Amis is making a mere debating point. And it must be remembered that he is not himself noted for sympathy towards poetry of an even faintly modern tendency.

What then are we to conclude? That to a poet who wishes to 'communicate', as Kingsley Amis roundly asserts Edith Sitwell does not, such extreme private associations as this must be avoided? And yet, is this rather comic misunderstanding either so comic or so serious as the logical mind might take it to be? If, for instance, the phrase 'Emily-coloured primulas' presents itself as containing an invitation to fill in, or rather fill out, the colour for ourselves (and this, *pace* Miss Sitwell, is the only way that in practice it *can* function, *particularly* for experienced readers of poetry), then we must do so; and if Miss Sitwell had wanted more precision in her colour, then she should have chosen another phrase or another name more suited to the likely associative systems of her readers. And if we are then left with a clash between the effects the phrase may have on different readers, this may not be too serious a matter in a poetry such as Sitwell's, which functions in an almost surrealist manner, as if it were indeed inviting us to fill in our associations for ourselves. For some poems are, quite simply, of a less controlled nature than others. Edith Sitwell's is full of a particularly strident energy, which may even be partly due to the particular *in*appropriateness, the particularly energetic *clashes* of sense that she produces.

But even in the most 'controlled' of poems, connotations are to some extent unpredictable, and may vary from reader to reader. Why not? For, if poetry is to achieve some sort of equivalence for experience, it is precisely necessary that all the connotations must *not* be enumerable or predictable . . . or even ultimately definable. For poetry must achieve this equivalence without dispelling the element of mystery and uncertainty which is, as we have seen (p. 128) Margenau confirming, a striking element in all our confrontations with the world. It is precisely because this mystery, and a sense of infinite possibility, infinite potentiality, ultimate unsayability, must remain in an experience, that one must *not* be able to put one's finger on everything that a poem may express: paraphrase must remain impossible: just as in the real world, total paraphrase, total translation, total explanation of a phenomenon in all its details remains impossible, as we have seen, in principle, even for science.

It is therefore perhaps not so much intention which is the criterion (except in so far as the poet's own intention was itself to construct an ambiguous and 'mobile' object)[17] but aptness. It is (at least to some extent) the poem's capacity to remain itself while nonetheless growing and changing which is the criterion of its adequacy. A poem is a machine to make one feel—and we are not certain, said Valéry, whether the poet always uses it better than anyone else.[18] To be capable of making a number of disparate individuals feel, it must indeed be capable of adjusting itself to their disparate systems of feeling. For aptness and adequacy to experience are obviously to some extent subjectively judged.

Total control of connotations is thus not only a pipe-dream; it is not even desirable. If poetry is to offer us analogies for experience, it must be left with fringes of mystery and uncertainty, like the phenomenal world itself; and it must have sufficient flexibility for different minds to be able to stretch it to fit their own measurements. It must have the adaptability of a living organism or of a cloak, not the rigidity of a formula or of a suit of armour.

Bridge Passage

THIS BOOK MIGHT PERHAPS have closed here. But, as in those modern novels where alternative endings are offered to vex us, there are other directions to be taken, and further conclusions that might be drawn. Of these further directions I shall pursue only one. In chapter 13 I wrote that 'despite the great changes that have affected Science since the sixteenth century, the Renaissance way of looking at Art and Science as two branches of the same thing, in opposition rather to rigid philosophical systems than to each other, still contains more than a grain of truth.' This remark has further consequences: it forcibly suggests that art has an important function to perform. The line of this book therefore takes on a Shandean kink at this point, as we move off at a tangent to present a defence of poetry.

*

Part Three

A DEFENCE OF
LITERATURE

*

Real-ativity, or, The Use of Poetry

It is only boots that can be made to measure.   (Brecht)

REJOICE!!
The location of the Centre of Imagination is the latest discovery of
science in The One State. This Centre is a miserable little cerebral
node in the region of the Bridge of Varioli. A triple cauterization of
this node with x-rays, and you are cured of Imagination —
PERMANENTLY!!
You are perfect: you are on a par with machines; the road to one
hundred per cent happiness lies clear ahead. Hasten, then, all of you,
young and old — hasten to submit yourselves to the Grand Operation!
       (Zamyatin *We*)

γίγνεται δὲ ἐκ τοῦ αὐτοῦ τρόπου μισολογία τε καὶ μισανθρωπία. [Hatred of discussion and hatred of men are born of the same process.]
       (Socrates *Phaedo*, 89D)

THE TROUBLE IS, IT'S so difficult to find a quotation. So few people
attack the utility of poetry—in print, that is. It is much more
common to find defences of poetry—or at least of literature as a
whole. And this must surely be for a very simple reason: people who
don't think literature useful don't write books.

Yet it isn't difficult at all to find a quotation—in spoken words.
One proceeds to the nearest pub. One engages in conversation. One
admits (for once: it isn't often one admits this) that one is concerned
in the writing, or the reading, or the criticism or the teaching, of
literature (or any other of the arts will do). And if one's interlocutor
is not embarrassed or overrawed (as, God knows, he sometimes is),
he may eventually, cautiously and with all due politeness, inquire
whether you think that's *work*—well, yes, certainly you put in, that
is you spend or pass, *hours* (not so many as he does, he suspects),
but still, is that *work*?

Théophile Gautier whole-heartedly agrees: 'A quoi bon la musique? à quoi bon la peinture? Qui aurait la folie de préférer Mozart
à M. Carrel, et Michel-Ange à l'inventeur de la moutarde blanche?'[1]
[What's the good of music? What's the good of painting? Who would
be so foolish as to prefer Mozart to M. Carrel, or Michelangelo to the
inventor of white mustard?] For bread is surely preferable to
circuses; and circuses to poems. And the problem is in fact frequently

posed in modern society whenever we have to decide whether we
should spent £15 million on a new cyclotron or £1 million on a new
concert hall—£20 million on the Health Service or £500 on an
Arts Council grant. Of what practical use is art? 'J'ai la conviction
intime qu'une ode est un vêtement trop léger pour l'hiver, et qu'on
ne serait pas mieux habillé avec la strophe, l'antistrophe et l'épode,
que cette femme du cynique qui se contentait de sa seule vertu pour
chemise, et allait nue comme la main, à ce que raconte l'histoire.'[2]
[It is my private opinion that an ode is too thin a garment for the
wintertime, and that one would be no better dressed in strophe,
antistrophe and epode, than the cynic's wife who thought her virtue
a sufficient covering, and went about mother-naked, as the story goes.]

One suspects Gautier didn't really believe these statements of his.[3]
The whole of the preface to *Mlle de Maupin* is a piece of witty and
swaggering rodomontade. 'Un roman a deux utilités:—l'une
matérielle, l'autre spirituelle si l'on peut se servir d'une pareille
expression à l'endroit d'un roman.—L'utilité matérielle, ce sont
d'abord les quelques mille francs qui entrent dans la poche de
l'auteur, et le lestent de façon que le diable ou le vent ne l'empor-
tent . . . L'utilité spirituelle est que, pendant qu'on lit des romans,
on dort, et on ne lit pas de journaux utiles, vertueux et progressifs,
ou telles autres drogues indigestes et abrutissantes.'[4] [A novel, (he
claims,) has two uses: the first material, the second spiritual (if one
may apply such an expression to the novel). Its material use is . . . the
several thousand francs that go into its author's pocket, and ballast
him well enough to keep the devil or the wind from carrying him
off . . . Its spiritual use is that, when one reads novels, one is at rest,
and one is not reading useful, virtuous and progressive journals, or
other such indigestible and stultifying drugs.] And he proceeds to
enter an eloquent plea for the pleasures of life which, he asserts,
differentiate Man more from the lower animals than any intellectual
or moral qualities he may have.

Now it is true that Gautier had no intention of presenting a
reasoned case. As the classic declaration of 'art for art's sake', however, this simply will not do at all. Gautier pretends to attack moralists
on the grounds of the greater good of pleasure—but his charge
against them has (at least in part) moral overtones: for he accuses
them of hypocrisy and envy. As he observes, 'la virginité du capitaine
de dragons est, après la découverte de l'Amérique, la plus belle
découverte que l'on ait faite depuis longtemps.'[5] [the virginity of
the average captain of dragoons is, next to the discovery of America,
the most remarkable discovery that has been made for a long time.]

And as for his assertion that art is useless, a part of his argument is that so little, after all, *is* strictly 'useful', and that contemporary society suffers from a crudely narrow conception of 'utility'.[6]

In the light of all this, one may well agree with the usual view of art for art's sake, and see it as a reaction against the philistinism of the period, an instinctive snatching away of art and poetry from hands which might defile it or destroy it. This is the true explanation of Gautier's cry: 'Il n'y a de vraiment beau que ce qui ne peut servir à rien; tout ce qui est utile est laid, car c'est l'expression de quelque besoin, et ceux de l'homme sont ignobles et dégoûtants, comme sa pauvre et infirme nature.'[7] [Nothing is truly beautiful unless it can be of no use whatsoever; everything that is useful is ugly, for it expresses some need or other, and Man's needs are ignoble and disgusting, like his poor and infirm nature.]

This is almost like stating art to be the supreme value on the grounds that it is *not* the supreme value. And this is what we should expect: the tone of Gautier's essay shows that he is to some extent being deliberately paradoxical.

Not so George Moore, when he writes, elevating his own sensibility into the supreme value: 'What care I that some millions of wretched Israelites died under Pharaoh's lash or Egypt's sun? It was well that they died that I might have the pyramids to look on, or to fill a musing hour with wonderment. Is there one among us who would exchange them for the lives of the ignominious slaves that died? What care I that the virtue of some sixteen-year-old maid was the price paid for Ingres' *La Source*? That the model died of drink and disease in the hospital is nothing when compared with the essential that I should have *La Source*, that exquisite dream of innocence . . .'[8]

So much, one is tempted to say, for dreams of innocence. Art for art's sake, taken to this extreme, is (ironically enough) a clear instance of the double morality of the society it affects to despise. Besides, what kind of picture does this give of art? Surely a trivializing one: by amputating them of human suffering, Moore divests the pyramids of a large part of their meaning; and if that is the case, then he might as well have gone and contemplated cardboard replicas against an imitation sunset. And if I have a charge to level at Ingres' *La Source*, it is precisely that it is a dream of innocence, and nothing more profound, nothing more ambivalent, more tragic and more human. What price an art that disregards the human meaning that art contains? Moore is in fact jibing at the darker overtones of these images. His attitude is revealing for it shows his own distaste for reality.

However, his remarks do have this virtue: save for the fact that Moore has stood the argument on its head (to the detriment moreover of his own sense of balance) this is precisely the dilemma that our man-in-the-pub so clearly perceives: the aesthete's selfish pleasure is in direct contrast with—is accused by—the human suffering of those less fortunate than himself. Now I have no doubt that our man-in-the-pub would willingly admit that his very presence there illustrates the need of human beings to relax and enjoy themselves: he would accept, on the principle that one man's meat is another's poison and that one man's Mozart is another's *Ah Belong tae Glasgae*, that we all have a right to our own favourite form of relaxation. All this, however, does not elevate the intellectual's preferred pastimes of classical music, highbrow literature and pictorial distortion into specially valuable experiences. (And we should be quite clear, by the way, that when we do assert the value of the arts, we are also asserting a special benefit to those who appreciate them— an argument that is hardly likely to appeal to the man-in-the-pub.) A special claim is implied for the arts by the fact that we set up Chairs in Literature, Music and the Visual Arts—but not in Wine-Tasting, Sunbathing and Football-Spectating. In short, if recreation or pleasure is the criterion, then whatever entertains the largest number of people loudest and longest must needs be the greatest art.

One trouble is that most arguments seeking to valorize the arts preach merely to the converted. (This one is no exception.) Another is that it is impossible to *prove* the usefulness of art: I am not aware of any experiment in which one hundred well-read intellectuals have been compared with one hundred vulgarians to either the former's or the latter's discomfiture. And Shelley's 'Defence of Poetry' as promoting the imagination and thereby the human sympathies and the morality of its readers, might plausibly be contrasted with the confusion and pain usually wreaked by his own actions. At most, claims for art's usefulness speak of tendencies in the long run, at many removes from any immediate effect, and hence from any possible verification. Of this kind are the possible uses of art mentioned in Beardsley's careful discussion of this topic:

> 1. That aesthetic experience relieves tensions and quiets destructive impulses . . . (or, as Russell suggested in his Nobel Prize acceptance speech) art may be valuable because it gives scope to this motive, which otherwise, in a civilized society that no longer hunts, sometimes plays its dangerous part in promoting social unrest and war . . .

2. That aesthetic experience resolves lesser conflicts within the
self, and helps to create an integration, or harmony . . .

3. That aesthetic experience refines perception and discrimina-
tion . . .

4. That aesthetic experience develops the imagination, and
along with it the ability to put oneself in the place of others . . .
We may become more flexible in our responses, better able to
adjust to novel situations and unexpected contingencies . . .[9]

This all looks a little speculative, and none of it is likely to convince our average Polonius ('He's for a jig, or a tale of bawdry, or
he sleeps') or our average man-in-the-pub who appeals to the manifest utility of butchers, bakers, candlestick-makers and doctors as
against the manifest futility of tinklers, daubers and scribblers. Yet,
if Beardsley's positive case will not convince him, perhaps a complementary but negative one will make him reflect: for if the en-
thusiasm of readers for their books cannot convince us of their worth,
perhaps the ferocity of certain governments and churches, of certain
individuals, against certain books, and often against almost all books,
may give us pause. If literature cannot be proved to be useful, it has
at least often been feared to be dangerous.

This argument at first sight looks irrelevant. For it is usually
thought that totalitarian governments ban books because of their
content, because of the *ideas* they contain. The German students at
Jena in 1817 burnt books for their unGermanness, McCarthyites in
America withdrew Sartre from government-subsidized library shelves
because he was a 'Commie', the Irish government bans books for
'obscenity', Chinese students during the so-called 'Cultural Revolution' (actually in many respects an anti-cultural revolution) burnt
whole libraries not because they contained poetry, but because they
contained the whole of the pre-Communist culture, its spirit and its
attitudes, Nazis in 1934 burnt Freud, Wells and Upton Sinclair for
their ideas, Russians condemn books for not containing the particular
interpretation of Communist ideology that happens to be modish at
the time . . . and so on. (One is not sure on which side of the
argument to place the first Emperor of China, Ch'in Shih Huang Ti,
who had the literature of China collected and burnt (save for copies
that he preserved in the imperial library)—but exempted books that
dealt with such 'useful' topics as divination, pharmacy, medicine and
agriculture. Did he burn the rest because it was useless? Or because
it was dangerous?)

Yet this is perhaps not the whole truth; for, in the case of the
monolithic political systems of the twentieth century, it has often

been not solely the *content* of a work of art that has brought the wrath of dictatorships down upon it, but also its *form*. Nazism and Socialist Realism are both equally hostile to the techniques of modernism in all the arts, though with strange inconsistency the former called it 'Jewish, bolshevist and degenerate', the latter 'bourgeois, formalist and degenerate'.

I do not believe, therefore, that the virtues of literature reside— or at least not solely—in its content. There is perhaps something in the nature of literature as a mode of communication that stimulates the hostility of bigots and fanatics. And I believe that this something is literature's tendency to militate against simple answers, against hasty judgments, and against rigid systems of thought. For literature is both complex and ambiguous: it is hostile to preordained frameworks of thought; and in this respect it is like science, in which new discoveries tend to build up increasing pressure on the old ways of thinking, until a beautiful new theory is arrived at, which later findings will fit, and which bursts the old theory asunder like so much old and rotten wood.

That literature is complex and ambiguous is indeed an obvious point, which needs little argument to support it. One thinks readily enough of the characters of Proust, of Albertine perhaps, whose character remains inscrutable to the last. Was she guilty of those Lesbian tendencies which the narrator at times ascribes to her? Evidence which comes to light after her death suggests she may even have been worse than he supposed; other evidence suggests that he had suspected her quite wrongly. Neither Proust's narrator nor we, his readers, will ever know the truth. The complexity, mystery and relativity of such characters approaches that of living human beings themselves. Our beliefs about them alter and deepen as the book progresses.

Moral issues are similarly presented in the serious novel as being complex. Jane Austen takes care to introduce Emma with the wry comment that she feels no-one may much like her save herself. We are meant, with Jane Austen's assistance, to pick our way between Emma's mistakes, to judge without ever withdrawing our sympathy, and to learn, in this exemplary way, that there is, in human affairs, frequently a clash between emotion and ideal, between intention and achievement, between what we approve and what we love. Moral ambiguity in more modern novels than this has reached an even more bewildering stage. Northrop Frye observes the commonness of the anti-hero in modern fiction,[10] and we may generalize and say that the modern novelist rarely presents us with characters to whom we could give either unreserved approval or unreserved disapproval. Even for Jason, at the end of *The Sound and the Fury*, one perhaps feels a glimmer of sympathy. Even Camus's Dr Rieux is no hero, but simply a human being attempting to do his job.

These points are generally accepted; they are part of the common fare of criticism. But it might be argued that the characters and moral tendency of a novel are a part of its content; and it might also be asked where poetry comes in. For moral issues are not often paramount in poetry, and when they are the critic may complain of didacticism. It is hard to see a moral tendency in Keats' 'Ode to Autumn' or Shelley's 'Ode to the West Wind'. However, a great deal of this book has been concerned to show that poetry echoes a complexity that normal language cannot cope with—a complexity in the stuff of nature itself, and the further problem of communicating this complexity. There is, in fact, even in the most unmoralistic poetry, an ultimate moral message: namely that truth is not easily arrived at or communicated. The difficulties of understanding poetry (or, for that matter, modernist prose) reflect the difficulties of understanding experience itself.

It is precisely this that is the central value of art, its civilizing use and its ultimate justification. *The very nature of art as a medium* is hostile to simple answers, to views of Man in terms of simple black and simple white, to blissful disregard of the problems of communication and expression, to all facile and dogmatic assertions of truth and falsehood. It is above all the tradition of modernism which implies (rather than explicitly teaches) these truths most clearly. For it is the modern writer who (other things being equal) imposes the greatest burden of comprehension upon his reader, and incorporates the most staggering complexities and ambiguities into his work.

In Lehmann-Haupt's classic study of the visual arts under Hitler and (after the War) in East Germany under the Communists, it is convincingly demonstrated that the architecture, painting and sculpture promoted by Nazis and by Communists alike are to all intents and purposes indistinguishable from those of Hitlerian Strength-Through-Joy. Both exhibit a series of ideally muscular men and women, gazing starry-eyed into a rosy future, and carrying in their hands identical symbols of military, political and industrial might, the flag, the sword, the sledgehammer and the machine-gun. Nazi and Socialist Realist taste is purely representational, and it is representation with a heroic bias. In both these respects it is firmly opposed to modernism, which it frequently castigates as 'degenerate', 'decadent' and 'individualist'. Modernism is commonly referred to by Socialist Realist writers as 'bourgeois modernism': a tendentious term, since though the modern Western intellectual has long since come to terms with modernism, Western society as a whole did so only recently; and the more conservative elements of Western society are still bitterly opposed to it. The picture is quite clear: modernist art has been accepted since its inception by intellectual and artistic circles both in the West and under Communism. It has been opposed under Hitler and in the East by governments and bureaucracies, and in the West by the forces of convention. Superficially, this situation may appear strange:

> We are faced with a seemingly insoluble paradox. The Nazis called modern art Bolshevistic, degenerate, Jewish. The Soviets call it capitalistic, bourgeois, degenerate. The critics in the United States call it communistic, subversive, abnormal. Obviously these things are mutually exclusive. Modern art cannot possibly be all these things at the same time. There is only one conclusion from this absurd dilemma, and it is a matter of the greatest importance: modern art is a powerful symbol of anti-totalitarian belief. It is this by virtue of its nature as the free expression of creative forces—not as a deliberate fulfilment of any political programme. It is not the implementation of an ideology but the inevitable result of a genuine belief in individual freedom.[11]

In short, the fact that conservative forces in the West, in Soviet Russia and Nazi Germany all attack modernism and all appreciate the same kind of vapid representationalism, demonstrates the fundamental identity of all these forces. They are united in their intolerance, in their absolutism, and in their belief in their own complete rightness, come what may.

What is true of the visual arts is equally true of literature. Here, the evidence is occasionally distorted by such exceptional cases as Gottfried Benn's espousal of the Nazi cause, or the Communist tendencies of such writers as Aragon and Eluard. But, by and large, the same picture can be seen. For instance, at the famous Burning of the Books in 1934, Nazi supporters consigned to the flames the works of Einstein, Freud, Gide, Thomas and Heinrich Mann, Proust, Upton Sinclair, Hemingway, Arnold and Stefan Zweig, among many others. Under Hitlerian rule a vast exodus of German writers occurred, and in general it was impossible to get published unless the ruling ethic of the Nazi party was in some sense reflected in one's work.

It is more difficult to generalize about the Russian Soviet experience since it has gone through a number of phases, starting with the relative freedom of the period just after the Revolution. At its worst, during the period of Zhdanovite purism just after the War, it tended towards the wholesale rejection of anything Western. For instance, in a volume of studies published in 1948, and devoted mainly to French and British authors, the list of those French writers attacked comprises practically all the major figures of the twentieth century. The only writers (apart from Russians) held up as models are a few Western 'progressives' who have evidently been selected for their Communist sympathies rather than for their aesthetics.[12] The number of Russian writers attacked or purged, however, was also so great that one might almost speak of an assault on literature itself. As for the great trinity of modernist novelists, Joyce, Proust and Kafka, none of them ever seems to have been *persona grata* in the Soviet Union, at least since the early thirties.

As for philistinism in the West, the Irish censorship is the most amusing example of it. Hardly a major twentieth-century writer has escaped having at least one of his works prohibited for a time. Writers thus banned include Beckett, Faulkner, Genet, Gide, Jaroslav Hasek, Joseph Heller, Hemingway, Aldous Huxley, Joyce, Koestler, Mailer, Malraux, Thomas Mann, Moravia, Nabokov, Proust, Sartre, Mikhail Sholokhov, and Steinbeck.[13] It is true that these are all supposed to have been banned on grounds of obscenity. It is inconceivable however that the motive in some cases at least was not political or religious, as with Shaw's *Adventures of the Black Girl in Search of God* or Upton Sinclair's *Wide is the Gate*. And as a Memorandum submitted in 1944 to the Irish Minister responsible said, 'the result of such . . . banning has been to gain for the Register of Prohibited Publications the alternative title of "Everyman's Guide to the Modern Classics".'[14] Whatever the censors' alleged motives, the effects have been to deny to readers in Ireland, in Nazi Germany and in the Soviet East of Europe large areas of the 'modern experience' in literature.

But is this anything more than a coincidence? Are the largely identical results of these three censorships due to anything more than a very narrow and rigid conception of what is permissible? Is a definite aesthetic discernible? And is it in any way similar in the three cases?[15]

I believe that it is: in all three cases one can discern the workings of the same type of mind: it is a mind that believes that truth is unambiguous, easily accessible and self-evident. Since none of these qualities can in fact be attributed to truth, this sort of mind is necessarily obliged to simplify what is ambiguous, to suppress what is contradictory, and to disparage what is odd, singular and individual. I am not in short asserting common historical origins or influences as an explanation of any similarity we may discover between Nazi and Communist attitudes to literature, but merely a similar cast of mind, a similar attitude to truth, a similar misapprehension of reality.

The earliest instance of the absolutist attitude to art is, I suppose, Plato. As creator of the *Republic*, he concluded that 'only such specimens of poetry as are hymns to the gods or praises of good men are to be received into a city.'[16] Since images of vulgarity, meanness, evil or ugliness may all too easily impress themselves upon the mind, such qualities and characters must not appear either in portraiture or in literature: 'we must speak to our poets and compel them to impress upon their poems only the image of the good, or not to make poetry in our city.'[17] Similarly, only one style of diction, which one might describe as uniform or 'straight', is admissible; a style which is 'mixed', which would be capable of imitating 'thunder and the noise of the wind, hail, axles and pulleys, the notes of trumpets and flutes . . ., the barking of dogs, the bleating of sheep and the cries of birds . . .', and which would use all the devices of voice and language to achieve this—such a style is inadmissible. For, as Plato interestingly remarks, this 'mixed' style would not be 'befitting in our city where no man is twofold or manifold . . .'[18] Thus a synoptic view of truth is rejected. It would seem that, had Plato known the complexities of modern poetry, he would have condemned them, and for the very reason that they are complex.

He is suspicious too of laughter,[19] and of ambiguity: for he complains that poets contradict themselves and each other: they are not clear, and they can be interpreted differently.[20] Plato was of course himself a considerable artist, and it is with reluctance that he exiles his poet: 'we shall do obeisance to him as to a sacred, wonderful and agreeable being; but we shall say that we have no such man in our city, and the law forbids there being one, and we shall anoint him with myrrh, and crown him with a sacred garland, and send him off to another city . . .'[21] Later censors will not be either so reluctant or so humane.

But their attitudes to art are nonetheless basically the same. The key is a basic hostility to anything that is complex or difficult. Thus, Hitler wrote: 'It has often been asked: what does it mean to be German? A great German once replied: to be German is to be clear, which means that to be German is to be logical and truthful. [Therefore] cubism, dadaism, futurism and impressionism have nothing to do with our German people . . .'[22] Another Nazi theorist wrote: '[German artists] wisely renounce all that is too *recherché* and corrupted in advance by excessive intellectual analysis'.[23]

The same demand for clarity, along with an explicit condemnation of 'complexity' can easily be found in Soviet Russia: for instance, in the official criticism of a short Russian war novel, *A Lieutenant-Colonel of the Medical Corps*. The periodical *Zvezda* published (1949) the first instalment only, and its author (who was also one of the editors of the journal) then wrote a letter in which he explained that in view of his readers' 'just criticisms' he had decided to stop the publication of his novel, which needed 'radical reworking from the first chapter to the last'. He wrote: 'It has been pointed out that the hero of the novel, Dr Levin, lived isolated in his tiny circumscribed world, was completely engrossed in his own sufferings, and had no right to be described as a positive character. The *psychological self-probing* of the decadent hero, the *complexity of his attitude towards life*—all this taken together had led to a wrong picture of the life of the hospital and the garrison.'[24]

One important aspect that complexity can take is the revelation of the dark side of experience along with the bright. This was anathema to the Nazis.

> (German artists) no longer care to reproduce the doom-laden monotony of slums, urban wildernesses or sleazy nightclubs. They no longer even assert their right to depict scenes of distress whilst assuming a harshly critical attitude, a mute accusation, a profound pity, so as to appeal to the conscience of society. They are right to adopt the point of view that the artist must not impress by what is negative, but must rather encourage his compatriots towards all that is positive by communicating to them a visible value. Even if corruption is depicted with the best of intentions, one never knows if its magic, emphasized by depiction, may not exercise some baneful influence![25]

In voicing these sentiments, Kauffmann is but echoing the views of his Führer, who had declared: 'Our ideal of beauty must always be *Health*.'[26] Or as Goebbels wrote, 'The Volk visits the theatre, concerts, museums and galleries [because] it wants to see and enjoy the beautiful and the lofty . . . The people approach the illusions of art with a naïve and unbroken joyousness and imagine themselves to be in an enchanted world of the Ideal, which life allows us only to guess at but seldom grasp and never obtain.'[27] Similarly, though violent death was a favourite theme of Nazi novelists, it was always seen in a 'positive' way, depicted as 'heroic sacrifice'.[28]

It was a heroic picture of human experience that the Nazis tried to paint, heroic in this sense that it depicted the true German as larger than life, uncomplicated, sure of himself, the archetypal German hero, fighting against the forces of darkness, that is, Judaism. 'The ideal in art must no longer be romantic, individualist art is no longer interesting. The *hero*, in art, is no longer the problematic tormented individual counting his troubles, but the strong healthy man proclaiming his victories or his defeats, but always in a *heroic* spirit.'[29] Similarly, Josef Nadler calls German literature an 'ideal reflection of our rejuvenated and united nation' and praises eighteenth-century Lower Saxony for having 'conferred on literature a heroic attitude'.[30] A simple black and white morality is the result. Apropos of this, it is said that Hitler's own taste in literature was of a similarly simple kind: 'He reads mostly cowboy and detective stories; though, in a drawer of his bedside table, he also keeps pornographic picture books . . .'[31]

As in Hitlerian Germany, the picture of Man which Russian orthodoxy would like to put about is a *heroic* one. The dark side of life must be hushed up, the petty concerns of everyday experience passed over in silence. Thus in 1934 Radek (at that time a still unliquidated member of the Party hierarchy) attacked both Proust and Joyce as instances of bourgeois decadence. 'He saw the quintessence of Joyce in "his conviction that there is *nothing great in life—no great events, no great people, no great ideas*, and that the writer can give a picture of life by just taking 'any hero any day' and photographing him carefully. *A heap of dung, teeming with worms and photographed by a motion-picture camera through a microscope— that is Joyce.*" '[32] It is characteristic of the situation of literature in Soviet Russia that from that time on there were no further attempts by writers to defend Joyce. Thirteen years later we can hear the same vituperation, the same absolutist ethic on the lips of Zhdanov in his violent attack on a Soviet writer:

> The point of this 'work' of Zoshchenko's is that in it he portrays Soviet people as lazy, unattractive, stupid and crude. He is in no way concerned with their labour, their efforts, their heroism, their high social and moral qualities. He never so much as mentions these. He chooses, like the cheap philistine he is, to scratch about in life's basenesses and pettinesses . . . He is in the habit of jeering at Soviet life, ways and people, as he does in *The Adventures of a Monkey*, and of concealing his jeers behind a mask of empty-headed entertainment and pointless humour.[33]

Again the insistence that any shadows should be eliminated from the uniform brilliance of the lives of the heroic Soviet people. The aesthetics of Zhdanovism are indistinguishable from those of Hitlerism: both preached health, simplicity, optimism, and absolute faith in the ruling party. It is not surprising that in Russia the terms 'objectivity' and 'dispassion' have at times been used as terms of opprobrium.[34]

Humour, too, is anathema to the absolutist mind. We can see Zhdanov, above, attacking Zoshchenko for 'empty-headed entertainment and pointless humour'. He might have been quoting Plato— or Reich-Superintendent Glasmeier who 'sharply opposed the re-infiltration, by way of the "humorous" sketch, of the destructive Jewish spirit into the radio broadcasting system. We cannot have a situation in which the leaders of the movement extol the sacredness of marriage and the ethos of the German soldier, who must risk his life and blood for the Fatherland, while in the evening those very values are insulted and ridiculed in "colorful" entertainment sketches with the corroding sarcasm of so-called variety programmes.'[35] For humour of course undermines the 'heroic' spirit. But the totalitarian mind's distrust of it goes deeper still: humour and irony depend on a sense of balance: the basic structural feature of humour, according to Koestler, is bisociation,[36] or the convergence of two (or more) clashing frames of thought. However trivially, a sense of humour presupposes the ability to adopt a dual standpoint. And this will never do.

The risk the totalitarian runs, of course, is that he may then no longer be able to see a joke, even an unintentional one. For instance, during the Zhdanov era, human feelings often disappeared from literature entirely—with results that conscious self-parody could hardly have bettered. In a typical story of the period, a young man makes a rendezvous with his girl in the woods—and when she arrives first, and has to wait for him, she spends the time wondering if he means to discuss production problems with her.[37] At this stage in Soviet literary history, it was apparently thought that human feelings were merely relics of the bourgeois past. Such is the ultimate result of eliminating 'individualism' by decree from literature.

Linked with the censorship of human feeling[38] is the censorship of sexual feeling. Typical episodes in the Zhdanov period were the criticism of a play by Panfyorov (*When we are Beautiful*) for 'distorting the moral countenance of the Soviet people'. This phrase appears to mean that whereas the play was 'in some respects ideologically sound, it is remiss in suggesting that sexual laxity exists under "socialism". The approved thesis was that such laxity was the characteristic of the decadent capitalist world.'[39] As Yarmolinsky remarks, in the post-war literature 'sex became virtually taboo . . . In a story by Lyashko, printed in 1933, this muscular passage occurs: "Beneath the trees their bodies were intertwined, breast merged with breast, and lip with lip, so that their bones cracked." The 1949 edition substitutes: "They were holding hands, and occasionally their lips brushed." . . . One thinks of George Orwell's remark, in 1984, on the connexion between chastity and political orthodoxy in a totalitarian state.'[40]

The implications and effects of the official Socialist Realist aesthetic have been well (though of course anonymously) described by a contemporary Russian writer: irony is outlawed, cliché rampant, the happy ending *de rigueur*: 'Thus every production of Socialist Realism, even before it is published, is certain to have a happy ending. To be sure, the ending may be sad for the hero who risks all possible dangers in his struggle for Communism. But it is always happy from the point of view of the supreme Purpose which transcends the individual.'[41] Consequently, the Positive Hero becomes 'Socialist Realism's Holy of Holies . . . He is not only a good man, he is . . . without any faults, or, if he has some, they are trivial ones (*à la rigueur* he may sometimes lose his temper) so as to keep up some semblance of verisimilitude, and also so as to have something that can be eliminated in him so as to raise him towards an ever higher political and moral level . . . He knows with certainty what is good and what is bad, he says only "yes" or "no", he never confuses black with white; for him there are no inner doubts, hesitations, insoluble problems, impenetrable secrets; and in the most complex of matters he easily finds a solution, by seeking his end directly.'[42] And the writer notes that the complex heroes of nineteenth-century literature (and even more of our own time) 'appeared much more dangerous than the negative enemy hero, because the enemy *resembles* the positive hero: clear, direct, all-of-a-piece. Only his *purpose* is negative.'[43] Socialist 'realism' is thus in reality an idealism, and the sort of art it produces is a kind of classicism.[44] And in this respect, we may again compare the effects of Nazi doctrine on German art-forms.

This kind of attitude produces of course hilarious effects. A novel by Vera Panova, for instance, 'led to a curious and typical controversy, during which some critics blamed Panova for (her detachment and understatement). One of them complained . . . that Panova did not "decipher" her characters enough, that no sooner did the reader come to like a character than he discovered that the author meant that character to be "negative", and vice-versa, thus "shouldering upon the reader the responsibility for appraising her characters". ' A critic who praised Panova for this quality, for her depiction of 'imperfect people who change and towards whom my attitude changes', was condemned by no less an authority than *Literaturnaya Gazeta* for attacking the proper spirit of party-mindedness.[45]

Later, when the 'thaw' had set in, the poet Mikhalkov lampooned the resulting attitude of mind in a satirical poem entitled 'The Three Portraits'. In it the Great Khan, who has lost an eye and an arm in battle, commissions three painters to paint his portrait. The first shows him advancing into battle with his lost arm and eye restored to him. The Khan exiles him on the ground that he has falsified nature. The second painter has depicted him, however, as he is, with only one eye and one arm. At this the Khan commands his execution: to depict him thus is tantamount to encouraging the enemies of the state. The third painter, however, a wiser man, has drawn his portrait in profile, so that only the remaining eye and arm can be seen. He is rewarded with riches and a state pension. Mikhalkov draws his moral:

> And I've met other painters too
>> Who had this self-same guile:
> They don't paint life head-on, full-view,
>> They paint it in profile.[46]

This type of moral attitude is the very one which, in the respectable bourgeois opponents of Baudelaire, led his advocate Chaix d'Est-Ange to exclaim in 1857: 'The logical conclusion of this morality is that henceforth we are only to write books that are comforting, and tend to show that man is born good and that all men are happy. What contemptible hypocrisy!' Nothing could more clearly indicate the profoundly philistine and bourgeois nature of Communist party censorship. Indeed the aesthetics of this kind of 'Socialist Realism' are clearly identical with those of the popular romance and the Western in all important respects.

Even so admired and in some respects so liberal a mind as György Lukács[47] suffers from this same totalitarian blindness, though in his case it takes a less extreme form. He, it is true, does admire Thomas Mann, Anatole France, Martin du Gard, Romain Rolland, George Bernard Shaw, Ibsen, Lorca, Conrad, O'Neill and Brecht.[48] But the list of modern writers about whom he has at least grave reservations is much longer and contains names as great if not greater: Joyce,

Kafka, Gottfried Benn, Faulkner, Musil, Freud, Beckett, Montherlant, Proust, Gide and Camaus. He agrees with the Hitlerian Nazis in condemning all varieties of modern art.[49] Though, in common with the usual Communist dogmatists, he calls modernism 'bourgeois modernism', most of his criticisms of it are precisely those of Nazism or of the typical western philistine: that modernism presents a picture of a distintegrated personality;[50] that it is chaotic and full of a disagreeable *angst*;[51] that it tends to be 'psychopathological';[52] that it lacks 'meaning'.[53] More perceptively, he objects that modernism 'rests on the assumption that the objective world is inherently inexplicable'.[54] (One is tempted to send Lukács a reading-list in modern science.) And finally, he objects to modernism's lack of interest in history.[55] (It would be truer to say that modernism is not interested in dogmas about history. And actually I am being too fair to Lukács: the word he uses is the loaded one 'historicity'.)

I do not propose to linger on these disappointing and predictable judgments. Suffice it to say that Lukács rejects modernism because it does not have 'perspective';[56] and that this 'perspective' he demands of novelists is either a Communist one, or at least one which regards the Communist account of history as plausible and relevant.[57] It is true that he does not take an extreme Stalinist position: he notes and criticizes the Stalinist tendency 'to suppress the contradictions existing in socialist society, their reduction of "socialist perspective" to childish "happy endings".'[58] Lukács in short does not suffer from the extreme form of the disease: he does not insist on everything being painted in dazzling black and white. On the other hand, the deficiencies of his view are still crippling: the writer's approach must be socio-historical, details not contributing to this overall picture must be omitted, the opinions we are to hold of a work must be clearly discernible.[59] Whilst not going so far as to demand that writers should rigidly adhere to a cops-and-robbers picture of the world, and that all confusions and contradictions should be omitted from this, Lukács nonetheless insists that there is only one basic standpoint from which to view the world. His dogmatism is thus at one remove only. His views could be summed up as: relativism in small things, but not in large.[60] It is characteristic of him—and of the totalitarian mentality in general—that he complains that 'antisocialist forces' have no 'system of ideas'.[61] Which is the same as the complaint of Adolf Spemann that before National Socialism there was no 'clear world view or any clear cultural political aim' to oppose 'decadence' in literature.[62]

But of course the forces of modernism have no 'system of ideas':

they could indeed retort that Socialist Realism has a system, but no ideas, for the system has killed them.[63] Whereas modernism may have no system, but it has at least the ideas. But in any case the charge is an over-simplification. In fact modernism has at any rate a recognizable frame of mind, asserting the importance of the individual, the uncertainty of truth, the difficulty of expression, the variousness and ambiguity of the world. Moreover this frame of mind is, as we have seen, in harmony with the modern scientist's picture of things.

For, if we briefly compare Nazi and Soviet attitudes to twentieth-century developments in science, the result is equally revealing. It might be thought at first sight that these would be quite different, since Nazism always prided itself on being 'anti-materialistic', and Communism, as we know, claims to be a materialism. What we find, however, is that modern science is castigated by both Nazis and Stalinists for the same motive—only that each uses their own preferred insult, 'materialistic' in the one case, 'idealistic' in the other. These apparent opposites are in fact identical in meaning.

The methods of science are methods of free inquiry, free discussion, and the arrival at provisional conclusions on a basis of consensus, and without any requirement to conform to *a priori* 'truths'. The enormous success of modern science confirms the practical value of these methods. Equally certainly, the philosophy that these methods embody is indeed a provisional and relativistic one, whose humility is in striking contrast to the hubris of totalitarian dogma. We should not therefore be surprised when totalitarian states react against science itself, as the Nazis did, and as, under Stalin and Khrushchev, the Russians did. For almost thirty years, the very science of genetics was in Russia considered 'formalistic, bourgeois and metaphysical'.[64] and the fraudulent theories of Lysenkoism were erected into a dogma.[65] After August 1948, cybernetics, relativity, Bohr's principle of complementarity, and Pauling's theory of resonance were, among others, declared reactionary. Zhdanov himself, for instance, attacked Einsteinian science for no longer believing in the comfortingly material atoms of Epicurus.[66]

Of course these extremes are no longer the case in Russia, though Jaurès Medvedev regrets that Russian scientists still have not been given the independence that their vocations require. But it would be false to regard the Zhdanovite and Stalinist assault on modern science as an aberration. It is on the contrary entirely logical, given their premises of an absolute truth and absolute certainty already known and already embodied in the doctrines of the party.

Similarly the Nazi theorist Bruno Thüring attacked Einstein's work as being the antithesis of Kepler and Newton. That he calls Einstein 'materialistic' and Newton 'antimaterialistic' in plain contradiction to the accepted meaning of the words (and in contradiction incidentally to Zhdanov) is neither here nor there. It is the relativism of Einsteinian science, its consonance with modernism in the fields of art and literature, and with democratic and libertarian viewpoints, that Thüring finds objectionable. He clearly recognizes that the underlying philosophy behind all these currents of thought, is the same.[67] I am almost tempted to express my gratitude to Thüring and Zhdanov for so clearsighted an anticipation of my argument.

Einstein's theory of relativity is a sort of allegory of the individual: truth looks subtly different according to one's standpoint. Which is not to say that certain complex formulae may not harmonize these standpoints—but only by not falsifying their validity. Modernism can be seen as a movement which inculcates a proper respect for the complexities of experience, for the doubts and uncertainties which attend our relationships with others and with the world, and for the strangeness and ultimate unknowability of the physical universe itself. It is a state of mind; and in opposition to it we have that other state of mind which holds that truth is more properly written 'Truth'; that it is everywhere ascertainable and certain; that there is only one angle from which it may be viewed; that the world is fundamentally simple; that moral and political views are as clearcut as the theorems of Euclid; that everything is either black or white; that everybody is either good or bad; and that the person holding such views is (it need hardly be said) invariably right.

The position of Tolstoy's *What is Art?* is in many ways similar. Tolstoy establishes, not narrowly utilitarian, but narrowly moral, criteria of artistic value, to the effect that there are only two types of worthwhile artistic creation: (1) art that expresses 'feelings flowing from the perception of our sonship to God and of the brotherhood of man'; (2) and art that expresses 'the simple feelings of common life, accessible to everyone without exception' (p. 164). In the process he rejects practically all contemporary or modernist writing, painting and music, either because it is 'incomprehensible' or because it is 'trivial'. Thus he actually claims he cannot understand [*sic*] the music of Liszt, Wagner, Berlioz, Brahms and Richard Strauss (p. 97). As for Beethoven's Ninth, it does not have anything to 'say' about religious or universal truth, and so is condemned as bad art (p. 173). And indeed a great deal of traditional work is condemned, including most of his own output—and also the tragedy of *Hamlet*, to which it is not entirely clear what his objection is, but the context seems to suggest that he considers it *too complex*. For, since art is like food, and everyone can distinguish good food from bad, art, to be good, must be capable of pleasing everyone (pp. 100–1), and the criteria of good art are 'naiveté, sincerity and simplicity' (p. 90). He consequently declares himself incapable of understanding Baudelaire (pp. 85 ff). There is actually nothing difficult about the poems he mentions—except that the feelings in them are not clear, single, monovalent and conventional, and indeed are good examples of modernist mixing of attractive with repugnant and of dark with light. (One must comment here that Tolstoy's argument is evidently absurd. For if art is not like food, but like science, then the criterion of its pleasures being evident to everyone immediately collapses.)

One must admire Tolstoy's sincere concern for communication with ordinary people, as also his wish for them to participate fully in artistic creation, and his admirable awareness of the aliveness and genuineness of folk art. His is a marvellous dream of art for everyone, a universal brotherhood of culture. Whether because of his own hostility to the principles of modernism, however—or because of the lofty but narrow religious principles which lead him to condemn even works that he loves—his position dangerously resembles the 'absolutist' one I am describing here. For it shares its two main features, namely, the demands for easy intelligibility and for the exclusive depiction of 'the Good', as well as various minor but equally characteristic features, such as a puritanical horror of sex.

Nonetheless, Tolstoy has a saving grace not present in such characters as Zhdanov, McCarthy, Goebbels and Senator Sean Goulding: he seems, at least marginally, *to admit the possibility of his being mistaken* (e.g., p. 170 note). Of such is the Kingdom of Heaven.

It makes no difference to which particular absolutist doctrine any particular person gives credence: whether he is intransigent in an old-fashioned or a new-fangled, a religious or a political way, he will still never agree with those unlike him—or with those like him, provided always that they do not happen to belong to his own sect— or with himself, when (as often happens) he is expected to believe the opposite this year of what he believed last. Paradoxically, though he believes that communication is easy—for the words he uses mean only what *he* wishes them to mean—this very fact makes it impossible for him to communicate, except with those who share identical definitions and doctrines.

To this absolutist mentality there is opposed the flexible, relativistic, provisional view of an artistic and scientific research that is continually in movement, continually refining and revolutionizing its picture of truth.[68] Here, disagreement is the occasion for discussion, and language is a necessity, because definitions are not given in advance. Once we know that understanding each other is extremely difficult, we have no option: we must believe in communication, not excommunication.

We have also to believe in change and indeterminacy: full stops are as much anathema to modern science as they are to Apollinaire's poetry; and science, like Gide's *Faux-Monnayeurs*, reaches only this provisional conclusion: 'Could be continued'. I do not mean of course to suggest that truth itself is relative: it is our human knowledge of truth that is relative, and the ultimate knowability of truth in all its wished-for perfection for ever out of reach. As Popper writes:

> The old scientific idea of *epistēmē*—of absolutely certain, demonstrable knowledge—has proved to be an idol. The demand for scientific objectivity makes it inevitable that every scientific statement must remain *tentative for ever*. It may indeed be corroborated, but every corroboration is relative to statements which, again, are tentative . . . With the idol of certainty . . . there falls one of the defences of obscurantism which bar the way of scientific advance . . . The wrong view of science betrays itself in the craving to be right; for it is not his *possession* of knowledge, or irrefutable truth, that makes the man of science, but his persistent and recklessly critical *quest* for truth.[69]

Hence the great value to science of the play of controversy and the clash of opinion: 'Any assumption can, in principle, be criticized. And that anybody may do so constitutes scientific objectivity.'[70]

But in the arts, it may be asked, is it only modernism that represents this attitude of mind? Are the characters depicted in Dickens, or Jane Austen, or Fielding, or Shakespeare, not just as ambiguous and complex? Is the poetry of Donne, Góngora and (again) Shakespeare, not just as complex? For that matter, what of the ironies of Swift or Pope? Is not all good literature complex by its nature? Why, then, are such writers as these not banned in totalitarian societies?

The answer is (1) that many of them have been. Hitlerian Germany was profoundly hostile to the whole literary past that could not be said to embody in some way its own racialist ideals: so a great deal of it was banned. And in Soviet Russia in the Zhdanov period there was a tendency (as we have seen) to write off all that was not 'Russian', rather as the Nazis wrote off all that was not 'Nordic'. (2) The usual official explanation for publishing the classics in Russia has

been that they depict a past state of affairs, that they are examples of
the march of history. (3) Modernism in every age constitutes art's
spear-point, its cutting edge, the area where our perceptions and our
representation of them in language are being questioned anew.
Properly understood, modernism is the *sine qua non* of our understanding the art of the past: by refreshing our perceptions it enables
us to see the past freshly.[71] As such, it usually takes the brunt of
absolutist assaults on perception and understanding. For the attitudes
of totalitarians tend to be the same as those of philistines the world
over: they are in general willing to accept the great works of the
past—though it may be doubted if they understand them. After all,
the great writers of the Russian *present*, such as Pasternak and
Solzhenitsyn, consistently traditional though they are in form and
style, have not met with any noticeable approval from the Russian
apparatchiki. (4) The literature of the past to some extent acted
under Nazism as a means of propagating anti-totalitarian ideas;[72]
and it has been suggested that it performs much the same function
in modern Russia.[73]

Tempted though he was at times by views that some have called
fascistic, D. H. Lawrence's own novels are far from any absolutist or
simplistic view of truth. And he himself was emphatic that this was
the novel's greatest virtue.

> Now in a novel there's always a tom-cat, a black tom-cat that
> pounces on the white dove of the Word, if the dove doesn't
> watch it; and there is a banana-skin to trip on; and you know there
> is a water-closet on the premises . . . The novel contains no
> didactic absolute . . . For man, there is neither absolute nor
> absolution. Such things should be left to monsters like the right-
> angled triangle, which does only exist in the ideal consciousness.
> A man can't have a square on his hypotenuse, let him try as he
> may . . . Everything is relative. Every Commandment that
> ever issued out of the mouth of God or man, is strictly relative:
> adhering to the particular time, place and circumstance. And
> this is the beauty of the novel; everything is true in its own
> relationship, and no further. For the relatedness and inter-
> relatedness of all things flows and changes and trembles like a
> stream . . . How immoral the absolute is! Invariably keeping
> some vital fact dark! Dishonourable! . . . A theosophist can-
> not be a novelist, as a trumpet cannot be a regimental band. A
> theosophist, or a Christian, or a Holy Roller, may be *contained*
> in a novelist. But a novelist may not put up a fence . . .

The novel is a great discovery: far greater than Galileo's

telescope or somebody else's wireless. The novel is the highest
form of human expression so far attained. Why? Because it is
so incapable of the absolute.[74]

I conclude that if totalitarian governments were really consistent
with themselves, they would ban literature, *all* literature, the literature of the past as of the present, outright. Thus, I need no pressing
to agree with Plato—and to disagree with him emphatically. Literature is dangerous. It is dangerous because it militates against simple
answers, it helps us to understand the complexities of the individual,
language and the world. And in these respects, it is in harmony with
science. Both science and literature are a part of the same culture,
the same humanism. Both equally abhor Gloster's cry: 'Talk'st thou
to me of *ifs*? Thou art a traitor!'

Let us be quite clear about this: it is not merely a question of
individualism versus totalitarianism. Though of vital importance,
that is but the expression on the social and political plane of an even
profounder question: namely, *what constitutes a proper apprehension
of reality*. The Irish censorship, the Nazi auto-da-fé, the Lysenko and
the Pasternak cases, Thüring and Zhdanov's fear of Einstein, all have
the same underlying meaning: of this basic struggle between those
who admit complexity and uncertainty, and those whose truth is
always certain . . . and therefore never true.

Speculative Appendix
The Dangers of Literary Self-Knowledge

ὁδὸς ἄνω κάτω μία καὶ ὡυτή.   (Heraclitus)
The way up and the way down are one and the same.

Il avait incendié de grandes parties de forêt vierge, on le voyait à ses
cheveux et à tous les beaux animaux qui s'étaient réfugiés en lui.
[He had burned great tracts of virgin forest, as could be seen from his
hair, and from all the beautiful animals that had taken refuge in him.]
                                              (Breton 1969, 56, of J. Vaché)

IT WAS SUGGESTED IN the 1960s, by investigators of human
slumber, that *it is our dreams that enable us to sleep.* 'When dreaming
was prevented on successive nights, the subject became irritable and
disturbed . . . When normal sleep was permitted [again], the
proportion of dreaming time went up from [the] normal 20% to
30%—the subject, so to speak, had to catch up on his dreaming.'[1]
Just what the reason for this might be, we do not know. An explanation on the analogy of computer programming, is that during its
periods of dreaming, the brain is perhaps assembling and ordering
the information received during the day. Another answer (as everyone is aware) was given by Freud, who suggested that dreams are
fundamentally wish-fulfilment, a release, in disguised, censored
and symbolic form, of repressions, obsessions and the like. There may
be a parallel in the world of the arts. Are our darker impulses
perhaps released in symbolic form when we watch the horrific
tragedies of Webster, or the repulsive rituals of Genet? Is this what
Aristotle meant by 'purging the emotions by pity and terror'?[2]
    Yet what would ensure their purging? Is it sufficient simply to
release them, to drag them out into the light of day, where one trusts
they will burst like fishes dragged up from the Tuscarora Deep? Is
the model of art as a valve releasing pressure when it builds up too
strongly, not over-simple? Or must some movement towards inte-
grating, harmonizing and subsuming these darker impulses not be
present, either in the work of art itself, or in the attitude of the
reader? Is it logical to claim that a work of art may, on the one hand,
do us good, and cannot, on the other, do us harm? I cannot at the
moment see any way of answering these questions except specula-
tively. So let us by all means speculate.
    One important distinction we must make from the start is between
artist and audience. The effect of a work upon its author may well

not be the same as upon its reader. For if the work represents for its author—as some works do—a sort of harrowing of Hell, then he has different ways of plumbing those depths: perhaps the work may constitute more a re-enactment of his obsessions than an exorcism of them. One thinks readily enough of George Painter's interpretation of *A la recherche du temps perdu*. A part of Proust's guilt had perhaps been that he was, during his mother's lifetime, unable to create the great work of art he hoped for. Another part of his guilt was undoubtedly his homosexuality, which in itself prevented his writing while his mother was still alive: for how could she have accepted it? And it was doubtless based on the one heterosexual love-affair of his life, so to speak: namely his passionate dependence on his mother. Proust's homosexuality is ascribed to Charlus (and indeed to almost everyone else), and inflated into a monstrous symbol of evil and of the impossibility of love. His father is well-nigh abolished, his brother totally so, but his mother is granted immortality—that is, she does not die, in the novel, though her death has then to become that of the narrator's grandmother. And above all it is his mother who is responsible for bringing him salvation in the guise of the tea and the madeleine. Thus Proust, it might be said, sought to create a novel which, like a dream, should be part wish-fulfilment, part redemption.

But as an act of redemption *for Proust himself*, purging him of evil and restoring him to the normal world—that is, considered purely as therapeutic exercise—the book was a failure. Unless one accounts it a success that its completion finally enabled him to die—and to die in peace. The torments of guilt are still there in *Le Temps retrouvé*; and indeed the very writing of Proust's book is the occasion for some of them:

> J'avais beau croire que la vérité suprême de la vie est dans l'art, . . . je me demandais si tout de même une œuvre d'art dont [Albertine et ma grand'mère] ne seraient pas conscientes serait pour elles, pour le destin de ces pauvres mortes, un accomplissement. Ma grand'mère que j'avais, avec tant d'indifférence, vue agoniser et mourir près de moi! O puissé-je, en expiation, quand mon œuvre serait terminée, blessé sans remède, souffrir de longues heures, abandonné de tous, avant de mourir! . . . Il était triste pour moi de penser que mon amour, auquel j'avais tant tenu, serait, dans mon livre, si dégagé d'un être que des lecteurs divers l'appliqueraient exactement à ce qu'ils avaienté prouvé pour d'autres femmes. Mais devais-je me scandaliser de cette infidélité posthume . . . quand cette infidélité . . . avait commencé de mon vivant et

avant même que j'écrivisse? La profanation d'un de mes
souvenirs par des lecteurs inconnus, je l'avais consommée avant
eux.[3] [It was no good my believing that the supreme truth of
life lies in art, . . . I still asked myself if a work of art which
[Albertine and my grandmother] could not know of, could be
a consummation for them, for the destiny of those poor dead
women. My grandmother, whose agony and death I had
watched with such indifference! Oh that in expiation, when my
book was ended, I could die alone, shunned by all, after suffering the long torments of a mortal wound! . . . It made me
sad to think that my love, which I had so clung to, should be
made in my book so independent of any one individual that
different readers would identify it precisely with what they had
felt for other women. But how could I reproach myself for this
posthumous infidelity . . . when it had already begun during
my life, before I ever started writing? One of my memories
would be profaned by unknown readers, but I had myself profaned it long before them.]

Moreover Proust's death, as Painter shows (I believe) conclusively,
bears all the marks of a deliberate (if possibly unconscious)[4] act of
suicide. Having caught bronchitis and suffering from a severe fever,
he went out into the cold and returned worse than ever. The illness
turned into pneumonia, but Proust refused to take his doctors' advice,
or to submit to the expert nursing which was in those days the only
known treatment for pneumonia.[5] Moreover, it is likely that the
figure of death in the form of a dark woman who haunted Proust for
some time before his death, and who appeared to him again in his
last moments, was in part an image of his mother:[6] only death could
redeem him, the book could not achieve this.

Yet for *us*, of course, the redemption *is* present in the book.
Whatever one is to think of involuntary memory as a revelation of
truth or as a spiritual healing (and we may well be sceptical of it, for
if moments of the past are sometimes momentarily restored to
Proust's narrator, they as surely quickly fade), Proust's considerable
skill is exercised in making us 'believe' in it (that is, suspend our dis-
belief) in the context of the book. Moreover, it does not *in itself*
constitute salvation, but is, like the wafer and wine of the Eucharist,
a token, a promise and a sign. It is the book itself that constitutes
truth and redemption. Time is saved through art: the insights of a
human life, profoundly plumbed, the universe as seen through one
writer's distorting glass, and therefore a supplementary picture to
our own one, *this* is the value of *A la recherche*. The book pictures

truth painfully struggled towards, with all its ambiguity, with all its admitted impossibility of final achievement. It is in short a symbol of integration; that in real life its author could not himself achieve this is tragic—but quite another matter.

We have seen, then, that the re-enactment in his art of an author's obsessions may not in the long run be enough to save him. It may indeed be actually destructive. Some of the psychological factors involved are discussed by Jung in his paper 'The Transcendent Function'. This paper recommends the technique of allowing one's fantasies to flow freely onto paper, rather as the surrealists did, or as Jung himself did in such creative works as his *Red Book* and *Septem Sermones ad Mortuos*.[7] According to Jung, 'the advantage that [great artists and others distinguished by creative gifts] enjoy, consists precisely in the permeability of the partition separating the conscious and the unconscious'.[8] In most people, however, the unconscious is suppressed. This of course is advantageous, since our psychic life needs stability and conscious direction. But, since we do not know the contents of the unconscious, we are suppressing what we do not know and 'what under certain conditions might considerably enrich the directed process'.[9] Jung therefore recommends the release of unconscious material lest the conscious process should become one-sided. And here and elsewhere he underlines the dangers of repression: Nietzsche is cited as an example of someone led to disaster by repressing the unconscious;[10] and he warns us that psychic health is dependent on our knowledge of ourselves: to suppress the dark forces in ourselves, to fail to come to some understanding of them, is to leave ourselves defenceless to those same forces, as the Nazis or the Bolshevists were.[11]

Jung therefore recommends the use of 'free association' on paper, the practice of producing or attending to one's inner fantasies, and notes that in the proper state of mind, words and images seem to appear out of silence.[12] The material thus obtained can be treated in two ways: (1) by 'creative formulation', or (2) by 'understanding' it.[13] The former is like the work of the creative artist; the latter like that of the psychoanalyst. The parallel with the practices of the surrealists is not far to seek.

Yet this too involves dangers. Jung notes that patients are often unable to find release from their neuroses if the material that psycho-analysis dredges from them is treated 'merely in a concretistic-reductive sense', that is, if it is treated merely as factual data, whose simple appearance is supposed to cure the patient. The patient must be given insight into his psyche, the material must be treated as evidence for purposeful psychic development on the patient's part: 'Constructive treatment of the unconscious, that is, the question of meaning and purpose, paves the way for the patient's insight into that process which I call the transcendent function.'[14]

These remarks of Jung clearly suggest the dangers, to the artist, of a personal harrowing of hell. As Heraclitus said, 'The way up and the way down are one and the same'; spiritual progress, including the spiritual progress of the artist, involves a descent into the hidden darknesses of the self. But when Theseus descended into the Labyrinth, he drew with him the thread of Ariadne. Sheer abandonment to darkness is deadly: some guiding force must be found which, though facing that darkness, does not allow it to swamp the controlling intelligence. And does not an account of Theseus descending into the Labyrinth *without his thread* sound almost like a description of the doctrines of surrealism? The surrealists trusted implicitly in the wonders of the unconscious: they surrendered themselves to it passively, made themselves simply its spokesmen, its mediums. It is no accident, I believe, that the records of dadaism and surrealism are so full of suicides. 'On se tue comme on rêve', said the first number of *La Révolution Surréaliste* (1925), introducing a symposium on the subject 'Is Suicide a Solution?' And to this question most respondents replied 'Yes'.

As dadaist or surrealist suicides, we may list Jacques Vaché, Arthur Cravan, Jacques Rigaut, René Crevel, Kurt Seligmann and Jean-Pierre Duprey.[15] The first of these was a much admired and regretted friend of André Breton. At the first performance of Apollinaire's *Les Mamelles de Tirésias* he is supposed to have entered the theatre with a revolver in his hand, and talked of firing bullets into the audience.[16] He committed suicide, it seems (if indeed if *was* suicide), by taking an overdose of opium; and the two acquaintances he was with at the time had also, on his recommendation, taken similar doses. Breton hazards the guess that this was a 'practical joke' of Vaché's.[17]

As for Jean-Pierre Duprey, he had created a furore some time before his death by urinating on the Eternal Flame under the Arc de Triomphe. From a psychoanalytic point of view there could hardly be any doubt of the meaning of this gesture: a symbolic attack upon the flame of life, his own life. And to these physical suicides one is tempted to add the spiritual suicide of Salvador Dali as evinced by his admiration for Hitler and by his famous remark, apparently often repeated, 'that railway crashes delighted him so long as the first class coaches were spared'.[18]

Further evidence of the danger to the artist of too passive a descent into his personal hell may be sought—and found—in Alfred Alvarez's *The Savage God*, where he sets up as the supreme masters of contemporary poetry in English what he calls the 'Extremist' school, namely Robert Lowell, John Berryman, Ted Hughes and Sylvia Plath. Alvarez's remarks are very clear-sighted. Hughes, he writes, 'starts with a series of extraordinary animal poems . . . in which he elegantly projects onto a whole zooful of creatures whatever unpredictable violence he senses in himself. Then gradually, *as in a case of demonic possession*, the animals begin to take over; the portraits turn into soliloquies in which murder is no longer disguised or excused; the poet himself becomes both predator and prey of his own inner violence . . . Hughes's other animals were all redeemed, in their different ways, by a certain instinctive grace. In comparison, *Crow is irredeemable: pure death instinct.*'[19] (My italics)

Thus, in this passage Alvarez diagnoses the progressive taking over of Hughes's poetry by the uncontrolled violence of his own unconscious. Of the 'Extremists' in general he says:

> Out of the haphazard, baroque connexions of the mind running without restraints the Surrealists created what is, essentially, a landscape art. In comparison, the Extremist artists are committed to the stage below this, a stage before what Freud called 'the dream-work' begins. That is, they are committed to the raw materials of dreams; all the griefs and guilts and hostility which dreams express only elliptically, by displacement and disguise, they seek to express directly, poignantly, skilfully and in full consciousness. Extremism, in short, has more in common with psychoanalysis than with Surrealism.[20]

This, as a generalization about surrealism, is a little too sweeping. It is perfectly clear that writers such as Duprey expressed their inner darkness without disguise (though of course with all due modernist obscurity). Nor is there much concealment about the agony of Paul Eluard in collections such as *Les Dessous d'une Vie* or poems like 'Sans Rancune':

Larmes des yeux, les malheurs des malheureux,
Malheurs sans intérêt et larmes sans couleurs.
Il ne demande rien, il n'est pas insensible,
Il est triste en prison et triste s'il est libre.

Il fait un triste temps, il fait une nuit noire
A ne pas mettre un aveugle dehors. Les forts

Sont assis, les faibles tiennent le pouvoir
Et le roi est debout près de la reine assise.

Sourires et soupirs, des injures pourrissent
Dans la bouche des muets et dans les yeux des lâches.
Ne prenez rien: ceci brûle, cela flambe!
Vos mains sont faites pour vos poches et vos fronts.

    Une ombre . . .
    Toute l'infortune du monde
    Et mon amour dessus
    Comme une bête nue.

    [Tears in the eyes, griefs of the grieving,
    Griefs without interest, tears without colour.
    He asks for nothing, he has feelings too,
    He's wretched in prison, wretched if he's free.

    It's dirty weather, it's a pitch-black night
    Not fit to put a blind man out in.
    The strong are sitting, the weak hold the power
    And the king is standing by the seated queen.

    As smiles and sighs, curses fester
    In dumb men's mouths and cowards' eyes.
    Touch nothing: if it doesn't burn, it blazes!
    Your hands are made for your pockets and your forehead.

    A shadow . . .
    All the world's bad luck
    And my love astride it
    Like a naked animal.][21]

Any obscurity here, I feel, merely serves to reinforce the poem's despairing power. On the other hand one readily admits, with Alvarez, that not all surrealists were great poets; in a movement the size of surrealism, this is to be expected. However, Alvarez's remarks are interesting in that they show him clearly attributing to his 'Extremist' poets the exploration of unconscious material.

This unconscious material can be deadly. Of Plath, Alvarez writes that she goes even further than the others into 'exploring the nexus of anger, guilt, rejection, love and destructiveness which made her finally take her own life . . . If [this] road had seemed impassable, she proved that it wasn't. It was, however, one-way, and she went too far along it to be able, in the end, to turn back. Yet her actual suicide . . . adds nothing to her work and proves nothing about it.'[22] He then praises the 'Extremists' for their 'determination to confront the intimations not of immortality but of mortality itself, using every imaginative resource and technical skill to bring it close, understand it, accept it, control it . . .'[23]

This, I would submit, is precisely what (with the exception of Lowell) these poets don't do: whilst bringing the death impulse close, and (to their own peril) accepting it, they neither understand it nor control it. For the mere imposition of a poetic form on unconscious material is not control but a heightening of the power of that material. Sheer abandonment to darkness is deadly: the only value in such exploits is to assimilate them to the light of the mind. This we, as readers, are able to do; and this is the value of Plath's work to us—a value of the very highest order. But one can certainly say that the poet's own disaster was so to expose herself to the full power of her own darkness that she lost hold on any counterbalancing impulse. What one misses in Plath is an attempt to subsume the temptations of death, to emerge from the dark tunnel into the light of day, though still carrying the invaluable knowledge of that darkness with her.

Alvarez's own experience has perhaps blinded him to all this. His own survival of attempted suicide, which he recounts in *The Savage God*, has made him attribute a special value to darkness. Not that I am recommending our poets to don rose-coloured spectacles forthwith. Alvarez interestingly tells us how he objected to Sylvia Plath's image 'the nude/Verdigris of the condor' on the grounds of its being 'exaggerated and morbid'; and how he tried to turn the poet's mind away to the more cheerful topics. But the image is utterly accurate. We know perfectly well, and she knew perfectly well that condors are like that, and that the world is like that—and even much worse. And the impulse to evade disagreeable truths may be as dangerous as the counter-impulse to embrace them too affectionately.

And indeed one must agree that darkness *has* a special value: we should be poorer indeed without Plath's *Ariel*. But the value of darkness is that, if we can face it and survive, we can transcend it: the way up is the way down, but only if the way down turns again into the way up may we recommend it as a route. Plath's terrors are not incorporated, by her, into a balanced picture of the world: they simply grow and grow like a monstrous shadow till they blot out that world, and consciousness with it.[24]

Must we then affix a solemn warning to all copies of Plath's *Ariel* or Ted Hughes' *Crow*: 'Read this at your peril'? No: for the artist's case is not the reader's. The former is more constantly, more personally involved in the struggle with his own self and with his awareness of the world than the reader can ever normally be with the works of one writer or with one type of work. Consequently the reader does not run the writer's risks. Normally he turns from the complexity of one individual writer's view of the world, to contemplate the different complexities of other writers' views. The obsession with one single viewpoint—with the books of one writer, or the paintings of one painter, or even with one particular work of art—can sometimes be observed. I remember one such case myself which was with hindsight, I believe, an evidence of psychological peril. Or at least this can occasionally be the case if the writer or painter is himself one-sided. Clearly such an obsession is evidence of a similarly one-sided spirit.

We can therefore offer the beginnings of an answer to such critics as Kenneth Burke and Wayne C. Booth when they instance, say, Gide's Lafcadio, 'that casual and charming criminal who murders to express his—and Gide's—freedom,' and add that 'such fiction assumes "a sophistication on the part of the reader whereby the reader would not attempt too slavishly to become the acting disciple of his author's speculations". It is written for "pious" readers, "not for poisoners and forgers". But is not the notion that one's readers will be morally sound rather naïve? Readers will be human beings with all their sins upon their heads; it is more likely that they will yield to a comfortable identification with Lafcadio's morality—since Gide "insists" upon our sympathizing with him—than that they will be jarred by the inconsistencies in his portrayal into the precise degree of distance that Gide intends.'[25]

Well, there is no doubt something in this. But there would be more in it if a single book impressed us with its own indelible stain once and for all time, just as if calling a man a 'wolf' once made us see all men as 'wolves' thereafter.[26] I would suggest that people who argue like this are often misled by the age-old imagery of purity and corruption, by the metaphor of the indelible stain (used to horrifying effect by Lady Macbeth), or by that of the virgin soul:

Le cœur de l'homme vierge est un vase profond,
Lorsque l'eau qu'on y met la première est impure,
La mer y passerait sans laver la souillure.
[The virgin heart is a deep vessel: When the first water one puts there is impure, the sea could wash over it without removing the stain.]

writes Musset. But what if the human mind does not resemble the hymen of a Vestal Virgin, or a prehistoric river-bed ready to preserve the imprint of dinosaurs' feet for several million years? The human mind is much more complicated than such simplistic models would suggest, and is forever trying to fit new impressions into place among the mass of old ones it already possesses. Certainly a book may produce a strong impression; but that impression will be obliged to compete with the already present tendencies of the reader's mind, which will largely of course not be derived from books.

But even if we were to restrict the argument to books, the solution is very similar. In the first place, literature usually contains sufficient moral complexity *in itself* to turn aside such charges. But where it does not, where it is 'one-sided', sufficient balance and objectivity is given to readers by their exposure to the corpus of literature *as a whole*, to a mass of works by other writers: the nastinesses of Genet's *Haute Surveillance* may be balanced and perhaps outweighed by the zany humour of Ionesco's *Les Chaises*; the nightmares of Plath find an antidote in the tenderness of Cummings. We are not usually first readers of isolated books, and the influence works of art have upon us is more complex, shifting and unpredictable even than those works of art, because they do not influence us in the void but in interaction with each other.

Moreover highbrow literature is difficult, and this (in the present argument) may be accounted one of its advantages. Plath's poetry, I suppose, is largely incomprehensible to people who have not read other poetry; this very fact is likely to ensure that her readers have a considerable experience of different literary points of view behind them, and hence to make it hard for them to read her with that obsessive singleness of mind that might, just possibly, be damaging. The difficulty of highbrow literature ensures a variety of reading experience in its public.

It is thus hard to level the charge of their being corrupting at even very easy and simplistic works, *provided that* they are not someone's sole reading material. But if they are, then the case is quite different. For instance, Frederick Wertham's *Seduction of the Innocent* makes out what seems an almost unanswerable case for the American Crime Comic of the 50's having corrupted and perverted the imaginations of its child readers.[27] But then one would think it likely that those who fall under its influence read little else. The crime comic suffers from all three of the failings I have outlined here: (1) it is simplistic (to excess: its outlook is pre-moral and instinctual); (2) it is easy to read; but, (3) most importantly and crucially, it is often the sole imaginative influence upon those who read it. It is this third failing (the uniqueness of its influence) that renders the first (the crudity of its outlook) dangerous.[28]

The final guarantee of the morality of literature (as opposed to cautionary verses and detective stories) may thus be not merely the complexity of the individual text. It may be that further complexity which is a function of the corpus of literature *as a whole*: literature as a whole forms a relativistic and expanding universe of the mind, or rather of a multiplicity of minds. And if that universe contains many different galaxies, the English, the French, the Russian, the Chinese and many more, then the resulting clash and concord of viewpoints will only be the finer. 'Opposites meet,' wrote Heraclitus, 'and it is from discord that the loveliest harmony is born.'[29]

Notes

Introduction

1. Ayer 1946, 118–19.
2. I speak metaphorically, as do they. A case in point is light, interpreted both as waves and as particles. See below. p. 154.
3. Ibid., 113. Ayer himself finds this extreme position a little dated now. But such views are still far too widely held, and may serve as a clear and emphatic starting-point.
4. As far as I am aware, the first writer to enunciate an Uncertainty Principle (in the context of litera-ture) was Thomas Pollock. He does not however mention the parallel with modern Quantum Mechanics, in which the very act of measuring the *position* of an electron entails a corresponding ignorance of its *momentum*.
5. Robert Pinget in Edinburgh, 7 Dec. 1972.
6. There are many aspects of mean-ing I do not discuss, such as synonymy, hyponymy, incompati-bility, etc.

Chapter One.
How to Avoid Defining a Concept

1. Austin 1963, 6.
2. The diagram is modelled upon Ogden & Richards, 11, though I do not use their terminology, as I find it confusing. Cf. also Lyons 1968, 404 and Ullmann 1962, 55. An interesting recent discussion of this diagram and of improvements which might be made to it can be found in Heger 1969. But his conclusions are not, I think, suited to the dis-cussion of literature; for his improve-ments are of an abstract nature and

do not constitute an adequate model of such factors as connotation, deno-tation, extension, etc.
3. Where I feel that there is danger of confusing word, concept and referent, I shall use the following conventions: 'tree' (w), 'tree' (c), tree (R). There seems no point, how-ever, in irritating the reader with such symbols where the context is sufficiently clear to dispense with them.
4. Cf. Lyons 1970*b*, 33.
5. Fries 1954, 64–5.
6. Bloomfield 1939, 13.
7. Cf. Katz 1972*a*, 63ff., and Chomsky, passim.
8. Skinner 1957, 108.
9. Chomsky 1959, 552–3.
10. Fries 1961, 206–7. Both Fries's articles seek to defend Bloomfield against the charge of being a beha-viourist. Though one must be pleased to find that even behaviour-ists find something faintly dis-creditable in the label, one is bound to say that Fries's defence is no defence at all. It is usually held (e.g. Ullmann 1962, 60, Lyons 1970*b*, ch. 3) that Bloomfield was the person mainly responsible for the disrepute in which meaning was long held by linguists, and it is abundantly clear that his theory was of the pure Jack-in-the-Box kind. It is true of course that Bloomfield was interested in meaning, unlike many of his disciples. But it is also true that there is nothing in his theory to *explain* adequately the semantic data he discusses, and, though his book *Language* has a lot of percep-tive observations to make about

meaning, this simply shows that there is a yawning gulf between his theory and his practice. I must for my part admit to a certain puzzlement about the reluctance of behaviourists to be so called. After all, 'a rose by any other name' . . . Skinner too utters the pious hope (1957, postscript) that the 'black scorpion' of behaviourism will not have raised its ugly head in his book. One thing, however, is clear: whatever Bloom-field, Skinner and their disciples would like to call themselves, it is their views that I am contradicting here.

11. Vendler 1972, 128.

12. Skinner 1957, 115. (His italics, though why he should use them is mysterious.) The whole context beautifully illustrates his deter-minedly abstract jargon. It reads: 'How a word "stands for" a thing or "means" what the speaker intends to say or "communicates" some condition of a thing to a listener has never been satisfactorily established. The notion of the verbal operant brings such relations within the scope of the methods of natural science. How a stimulus or some property of a stimulus acquires control over a given form of response is now fairly well understood. The form of a response is shaped by the contingencies prevailing in a verbal community. A given form is brought under stimulus control through the differential reinforcement of our three-term contingency. The result is simply the probability that the speaker will emit a response of a given form in the presence of a stimulus having specified proper-ties . . . So far as the speaker is con-cerned, this *is* the relation of refer-ence or meaning. There would be little point in using this formula to redefine concepts such as sign, signal, or symbol, or a relation such as reference, or entities common in a

speech episode such as ideas, mean-ing, or information. These tradi-tional terms carry many irrelevant connotations, arising from their use in describing the relation between the speaker's response and the be-haviour of the listener and the con-tingencies of reinforcement imposed by a verbal community.'

13. Lyons 1968, 89. He is writing here of the contribution to linguis-tics of information-theory. He *might* be taken to mean that improbable choices of words are more meaningful within a closed system, i.e., where there are only a finite number of possible alternatives. He himself however seems to interpret his principle in terms of the entire language system, for he writes: 'The more predictable a unit is, the less meaning it has. This principle is in accord with the commonly-expressed view of writers on style, that clichés (or 'hackneyed expres-sions' and 'dead metaphors') are less effective than more 'original' turns of phrase.' (ibid.) This is entirely in accord with my use of the principle here.

14. Unpredictability can only be an index to the *likelihood* of a word being more meaningful: for it may of course simply point to the ravings of a disturbed mind.

15. The early Lyons was an opera-tionalist and anti-mentalist: 'We must reject any theory of semantics the terms of which neither refer to observables nor are reducible to observables. (We must therefore reject) any theory which defines meaning as the relation which . . . the "sign" bears to . . . the "con-tent" . . . and leaves this relation unreduced.' (Lyons 1963, 1) 'I consider that the theory of meaning will be more solidly based if the meaning of a given linguistic unit is defined to be the set of (paradig-matic) relations that the unit in question contracts with other units of the language (in the context or contexts in which it occurs), without any attempt being made to set up 'contents' for these units. This I should mark as one of the principal theoretical points . . . being made in the present work.' (ibid., 59)

16. Haas 1954, 71. Cf. Bloomfield 1935, 142–3, where he too insists on calling inner processes 'non-physical'.

17. Cf. Chomsky 1972, 98.

18. E.g., Wittgenstein 1968, paragraphs 1, 9 & 10, though he has the occasional doubt, e.g. paragraph 138, p. 215e.

19. Ryle 1961, 364.

20. Strawson, 1963, 171. His italics.

21. For an unusually careful attempt to construe meaning as use, see Alston. For a general account, see Rulon Wells 1954. For a refutation, see Katz 1972*a*, 93 ff.

22. Harré 1970, 26–7 (paraphrased).

23. Induction, in Harré's view, is not a mystery, since if we have reason to believe a mechanism is responsible for some regular succession of events, then it is entirely reasonable of us to expect this regularity to continue.

24. An Air-Force base is not, of course, as systemic as a clock; but it is still more systemic than no Air-Force base.

25. Quine 1961, 251.

26. Skinner 1961, 252–4. Elsewhere, he uses Quine's argument. (Skinner 1972, 12).

27. Ryle 1963, 306–7.

28. If question 3 means 'Why is he riding his cycle off down the road?' then there is nothing unreal about it, and the cyclist could give us a perfectly sensible answer. If, however, it means 'How is it that he can tell his body to act in this way?' then a part answer could be given by physiologists. The more difficult part of the question, however, that con-

nected with the traditional concept of 'will', cannot be shrugged off as 'meaningless!' It is both perfectly meaningful and interesting to scientists, as can be seen from the experiments of Neal Miller (1970) where subjects were able to lower their blood-pressures by 'act of will', and of José Delgado, where subjects could be made (by the insertion of electrodes in their brains) to perform acts on which they commented, 'I guess, Doctor, that your electricity is stronger than my will.' (Delgado, 114)

29. Ryle 1963, 291. Mind you, I agree that talk of 'forming the abstract idea of' Contour may often be nonsense. I am certainly unhappy about the way Ryle does it for us here. But, like everything else, it depends how it is done.

30. Morris 1939, 83.

31. That any referent should actually exist *as referred to*, i.e., that the concept should coincide exactly with the referent, is of course an unwarrantable assumption; and *if* it is necessary for Morris's argument, *then* nothing exists as referred to, there are no 'denotata' at all, and Morris's attempt to avoid asserting the existence of abstractions and of concepts ends, paradoxically, in the implication that nothing exists whatever!

32. Baruch 1973.

33. E.g., Pap 1963, 320–4: ' . . . in order to locate an electron with great accuracy, the observer must illuminate it with light of a short wavelength. But the shorter the wavelength, the greater the frequency, and the greater the frequency the greater the energy of the photon that strikes the electron . . . Hence the momentum that the electron supposedly had before the act of measurement took place is altered by the act of measurement.' (321)

34. For the vexed question of images in thinking, see for instance Gardiner 1951, 36–7; I. A. Richards 1926, 117–24; Ogden & Richards, 60 ff.; H. H. Price, 234–97; Gustaf Stern, 49–53.

35. This too is intended metaphorically, and has no necessarily visual implications, though the reader may by all means picture a cat upon a mat if he wants to.

36. Alston 1964*b*, 24.

37. Consider also Kenny's 'thistle-freezer', discussed on pp. 51 ff. Cf. Alston 1964*b*, 23–5 and Katz 1966, 177–85, where these points are fully discussed. Cf. also Leeper 1951, an account of current psychological experiments in concept-formation, where he writes: 'Experiments on inductive concept formation have shown that . . . concepts may be formed, retained and used unconsciously.' (p. 755) By the way, he also concludes that ' . . . concept formation is not determined in simple ways by conditions of reinforcement.' (ibid.) Cf. also H. H. Price, 65–70.

38. This is perhaps not far from Vendler's conclusions: 'A concept . . . appears to be an open proposition, that is, a proposition in which some constituents are left undetermined.' (Vendler 1972, 132) When a conceptual event occurs, these constituents become determined, i.e., a sense in which the concept is being used is established.

39. Katz 1971*a*, 94.

Chapter Two.
The Semiotic Rectangle

1. Ullmann 1962, 56.

2. Besides, there is the danger that if semantics ignores the Referent, it may 'fall prey to an extreme esoteric formalism'. (Werner 1952, 255) Ullmann discounts this. However, it has already occurred in certain quarters: see my article on Julia Kristeva's brand of semiotics, Martin 1971*b*.

3. Lyons 1968, 115.

4. Brown 1958, 9.

5. Goldstein 1942, 161. My italics. Cf. Goldstein 1948, 90.

6. For similar schemes in the West, see for instance Peterfalvi 1970, 75. Cf. also Heger 1969.

7. I do not propose to enter into a discussion about 'permanent words'. Perhaps one should compare Saussure's distinction between *langue* and *parole*, or Chomsky's *performance* and *competence*.

8. Kunjunni Raja 1963, 11–15. His diagram (though not of course his terminology) resembles the one given here.

Chapter Three.
Proper Names and Common Nouns

1. No defence is required for rejecting or redefining the usages of ordinary speech. The English language is not the exclusive repository of the world's wisdom, and I make no apology for not consulting my dictionary on this occasion, as so many modern philosophers do; for dictionaries are not compiled by the Spirit Albion, or even by the spirit of the Ordinary Man. And did not Dr Johnson himself define a lexicographer as 'a harmless drudge'? Progress only comes about in one way: by redefining, by adding to and altering our previously unconsidered assumptions.

2. Price, 34. Quine 1959 contains an essay on 'similarity and kinds' in which he takes similarity as 'fundamental to our thinking', and even says 'A standard of similarity is in some sense innate'. (p. 123)

3. Hebb 1972, 26.

4. See below, p. 35.

5. Neville Cardus of Ranjitsinhji, if my memory serves me aright.

6. Ullmann's semiotic triangle resembles the one given here, and his definition of meaning is: 'Meaning is a reciprocal relation between name and sense' (i.e. between W and C) 'which enables them to call up one another.' (1963, p. 70). He thus contradicts himself when he writes, three pages later, 'Nothing has happened to invalidate Stuart Mill's contention that proper names have no meaning—or, in our terminology no sense.' For this is not so in his own terms.

7. Goldstein 1942, 154 ff. Cf. 89 ff, where it would seem that metaphoric thinking comes also under the heading of Goldstein's 'abstract attitude' and of my 'generalizing function', and may therefore also be lost in similar cases of brain injury. Cf. also pp. 87–8. If someone replies to 'A bird in the hand is worth two in the bush' by 'If anyone has a bird in his hand, (it) must be a tame bird,' then clearly an impairment of the ability to extend instances, to employ analogy, and to comprehend metaphor has occurred. Cf. Goldstein 1948, 61–3, 257.

8. Jakobson 1971, 229–59, 289–333.

9. 'Of the two varieties of figural speech—metaphor, based on similarity, and metonymy, founded on contiguity—,' writes Jakobson of a patient who has lost his ability to perceive similarity, 'only the latter (i.e. contiguity) is used and grasped by him . . . It is questionable whether this breaking down of similarity relations can be ascribed to the loss of an 'abstract attitude', as Goldstein terms it. The metonymical and the metaphorical steps are but two different types of what he calls "abstract behaviour"' (Jakobson 1971, 236). Goldstein, however, seems to use his term 'abstract attitude' above all when talking of impaired perception of similarity, and of inability to understand metaphor. There seems to be no real disagreement, therefore, except over

the aptness of Goldstein's terminology. It must also be noted that Jakobson and Goldstein's remarks support my view of metaphor (see chapter 16A), which I regard as due to extension on the basis of similarity.

10. Ogden & Richards, 187. 'Properties' in this quotation is ambiguous. I must again emphasize that connotations are our *estimate* of the properties of an object.

11. Except that names have *more* properties than nouns, as we shall see.

12. Geach 1957, 70. My italics.

13. Mill, 20. Cf. also Sir Alan Gardiner's discussion of this whole question, 1951, 42.

14. See G. Stern, chapter 7.

15. Valentine 1942, 419–20.

16. Diamond, 95.

17. Thus Valentine shows us the child at a later stage correcting himself so as to restrict his use of a word to its normal range, op. cit., p. 421.

18. That is, when we are using them of someone who is no longer 'a mere name', as Jespersen also says, ibid., 1929, 66.

19. Ullmann 1962, 74.

20. Apart, of course, from bisexual names like Hilary.

21. See chapter 16.

Chapter Four.
On the Structure of Meaning
1. Inadequate definitions can be found for instance in J. B. Carroll 1964, 40–1 (as 'non-criterial attributes') and in Bloomfield 1935, 151–4 (as 'supplementary values').

2. Ogden & Richards, 187.

3. 1946 edition, vol. 22, p. 446.

4. Bally 1940, 195 ff.

5. Parain 1969, 123.

6. Konrad, 70–1.

7. Konrad on Meillet, p. 71. Cf. G. Stern on the shifting content of words.

8. Cf. pp. 123–5.

9. E.g. Lyons 1968, 427. For a very

well-known, highly useful, and detailed discussion of the emotive-cognitive distinction, see Henle ch. 6 (1958).

10. Differences in wave-length are of course an element of 'the nature of things'. Our decision to draw boundaries upon a scale of such wave-lengths is however our decision.

11. Quoted in Hagopian 1968. The original can be found in Robbe-Grillet 1963, 53.

12. Hagopian 1968. Cf. Chomsky 1965, 29: 'artefacts are defined in terms of certain human goals, needs and functions instead of solely in terms of physical qualities.'

13. Brain 1959, 10, 39–40; cf. 1951, 45–6.

14. Robbe-Grillet 1957, 19–20.

15. Ibid., 44.

16. Ibid., 17.

17. This instance is also discussed by Hagopian, loc. cit.

18. Robbe-Grillet 1953, 260.

19. Cf. for further evidence Sturrock 1969, where the connotative and metaphoric element in Robbe-Grillet's novels is fully allowed for and convincingly interpreted.

20. See Kaplan 1954 for a persuasive argument that cognitive and emotive meanings are just two sides of the same coin.

21. Ullmann 1963, 80.

22. Richards 1936, 118.

23. Cf. Jakobson, e.g. 1971 vol. 2, 239–59.

24. e.g. Lyons 1968, 454.

25. Cf. Gardiner 1951, 36. 'We can perhaps best picture to ourselves the meaning of a word such as *horse* by considering it as a territory or area over which the various possibilities of correct application are mapped out.' This corresponds to my first division here.

26. This is *not* the way in which the term is used by modern linguists, e.g., Lyons 1968, 427 ff. But for my purposes it is essential to have a term

for this relationship, and 'sense' seems the obvious one.

27. E.g., Paul Eluard: 'Tout est comparable à tout.' (Eluard vol. 1, 527).

28. Terms such as 'presupposition', 'entailment', etc., are common in linguists' current work on semantics, *passim*, and they can certainly be used to make valuable distinctions, as by Leech in chapter 13 of his *Semantics.* He uses them, however, to discriminate between various kinds of truth entailment, and I am not concerned to make such distinctions here. One distinction I am tempted to make, however, would be as follows: In 'You get a good view through the trees in winter', 'trunks' would be a criterial connotation; 'leafless' and 'deciduous' would be inner connotations. But it is also clearly implied that one is looking through the branches of the trees; otherwise there would be no point in saying 'in winter'. It seems more natural to call this an 'implication' of the sentence as a whole, not just a connotation of the word 'trees'. I shall continue to use the blanket term 'connotation', however, for I do not think any absolute distinction can be made between 'implication' and 'connotation'. For could one not say that 'trees' have here to be interpreted as 'the trees' branches'? And then the denotation 'trees' stands for its own connotation 'branches'. In any case, the question is merely one of terminology.

29. In point of fact, I don't suppose anyone would be likely to misinterpret this sentence. But the point is: Why don't they? And the answer must be, because different interpretations are available to us, and in easy instances like this one, our mind rapidly and unconsciously selects the right one.

30. Cf. pp. 76–7, where it can be seen how, faced with apparent nonsense, we nonetheless naturally seek a plausible interpretation.

31. *The Nature of Mind*, Edinburgh 1972.

32. Landesman 1972, 15.

33. Winograd, 22.

34. Ibid., 23.

35. Cf. p. 63 ff., and Winograd, 26. It will be obvious that my account of the structure of meaning is far from complete. I have not even mentioned such elements of meaning as antonymy, hyponymy or incompatibility, e.g., Lyons 1968.

36. 'Then what is *time*? I know—if no-one asks me; but if I am asked to explain it, I have no idea.'

37. Valéry vol. I, 69, cf. 1317–18.

38. *Notebooks*, 30.5.15.

Chapter Five.
Are Meanings Atomic?

1. Russell 1956, 117 ff.

2. Ibid., 193.

3. Pears, 66. Cf. Hacker, 42.

4. Cf. Bohm 1952.

5. e.g. Bohm 1952, 494.

6. Cf. Bohm 1952, 116–24.

7. Heisenberg 1969, 63–4. 115.

8. Bohm 1952, 166.

9. Ibid., 167.

10. Skinner 1957, 123–4. Cf. the similar statements made by Russell. 1956, 197–8—and his similar conclusion that such a language could not be established.

11. Of course, the attitude is thoroughly 19th century, and no longer corresponds to the thinking of contemporary science.

12. Cf. Ryle 1954, 34–5.

13. Braithwaite, 76.

14. Cf. Pap 1958, 326 ff. Also J. J. C. Smart, 1953.

15. Bondi, 9–10. My italics. Cf. Polanyi 1967, ch. 1 where the basic point is that 'we can know more than we can tell', and that scientific endeavour would become impossible without this fact.

16. Bohm 1952, 169.

17. Paraphrased from Bohm, 169–72.

18. Here is the exception that proves the rule. I am talking here of mental images of a pictorial kind.

19. Bohm 1952, 146–7.

20. Firsoff 1967, 56.

21. Cf. Waismann, 1945 and 1951 for the view that the fluid edges of language, its indeterminacy, are no accident and no misfortune.

22. Bierwisch 1967, 36.

23. As this modern investigation of connotations is termed. See Bendix, Fillmore, Ebeling, Fodor & Katz 1963a and 1964, Katz 1972a, Katz & Postal, U. Weinreich, and a great deal of more recent work too numerous to list.

24. Geoffrey Leech claims that 'having a womb' is not a criterial attribute of *woman*. (Leech 1974, 14) This seems an extraordinary assertion. The criteria for being female are several in number. The absence of one of these criteria might or might not lead us to refuse the name 'woman'. But the absence of two or three of them might well do, and we might then justify our refusal of the name by listing the absent criteria. They therefore clearly are both relevant and criterial.

25. Mill, Book I, ch. II, para 5, p. 23.

26. Leech 1974, 204–5.

27. Ibid., 88–9. 'Connotations', though not his term, is what he means in my terminology.

28. Bolinger 1965, 563–4.

29. Cf. my conclusion on p. 54 above.

30. Much paraphrased and shortened from Cohen & Margalit, 724–5. I am grateful to Professor John Lyons for pointing this article out to me.

31. Beardsley, 143–4.

32. Bolinger 1965, 566–7.

33. Cohen & Margalit, 725.

34. This is merely a manner of speaking: naturally, I assume no such thing as 'atoms of experience'.

35. Bendix, 10–11.

36. Haas 1973, quoting H. L. A. Hart.

Chapter Six.
The Status of the Referent
1. Stern, 31.
2. Ibid., 33, slightly rephrased.
3. Once again, not necessarily an 'image'. Cf. p. 20.
4. For discussion of this, see Wittgenstein 1968, part I, sections 19–20 and George Pitcher, 1964, 'Introduction'.
5. Lyons 1973, 10.
6. Russell 1956, 179.
7. Eddington, 352–3.
8. e.g. Ayer 1946, 121, and Lefebve, 273.
9. Austin 1962, 141.
10. I will mention only three: Russell, discussed in Strawson 1963 and Linsky 1967. I shall not however discuss their views here, since to apply the formula of meaning to the problem puts it in a new and revealing light.
11. Note that in this case 'The King of France is bald' is not nonsense; it *means* 'Nonsense!'
12. That is, he notes our ability to compose new sentences, never invented before, but instantly comprehensible to all speakers of English. Chomsky 1966, 3–31.
13. Kunjunni Raja, 165.
14. Gregory, 32.
15. I cannot pretend to be at home in the modal logician's world (or should I call it a possible world?). Let me refer the reader merely to the introductory account given in Hughes & Cresswell, to the works of Hintikka (especially 1969), and mention the name of Richard Montague.
16. See for instance George Lakoff 1972 and Karttunen 1973. I shall not use Lakoff's principal example ('It's possible that Sam will find a girl and certain he will kiss her') since, like another commentator, I see nothing anomalous in it. It is certain that 'it is certain' would be understood as depending on the possibility of Sam's finding his girl in the first place. The failure of this particular example, however, does not invalidate Lakoff's general principle.
17. Both from McCawley 1971.
18. Cf. McCawley 1968, 138.
19. Zuber, 15.
20. Here we have a paradigm case of *correspondence* versus *coherence*. ESP is not accepted by scientists because, however good the evidence for it (though this is a dubious and controversial matter) it does not *cohere* with accepted theories of the world's nature. One might plausibly suggest that until a new theory arrives which incorporates psi phenomena together with physical phenomena in a new total picture of the world, ESP will continue to be dismissed. In short, we can hardly see how psi phenomena can *correspond* to anything 'real' until we see how they *cohere* with what we accept already.
21. See in particular Hebb 1964–5 and 1972, 197–216, for the basis of what follows (rather, that is, than the speculation I engage in).
22. Hebb thinks that the nasty prejudices we suffer from are natural to us. And indeed, we all know how alarming the average man finds the unfamiliar, under whatever guise it goes, a black skin, a red flag, long hair, the unfamiliar gestures of someone speaking a foreign language, a 'plummy' accent, or a 'proletarian' one, or simply the sound of the word 'intellectual'. And this cannot always be held to be the effect of prejudice learnt or taught, however unconsciously. When a new element intrudes into our environment, we notice it and are suspicious: the effects may be unfortunate when the new element is a man; but they are clearly beneficial and necessary to our own healthy survival, when it is a wet stain on the

ceiling or a snake in the grass.
23. Richards 1926, *passim.*

Chapter Seven.
Does Literature Refer?
1. Frege 1960, 63. (The text dates
from 1892.) Statements discounting
the truth of poetry are quite easy to
find. For instance H. H. Price writes:
'Shakespeare . . . was specially
good at inventing factually false but
aesthetically moving propositions.'
(1953, p. 246.) See also Isenberg
1965 and Elliott 1967.
2. Ogden & Richards, 149. It is
actually much *less* simple, since prior
experience of 'references' is an
essential part of it. Cf. also Kaplan
1954, for an excellent discussion of
reference in literature.
3. Ogden & Richards, 150.
4. Austin 1970, 116.
5. Richards 1926, 269.
6. It would hold up the argument to
expand on this: but let me emphatically repeat that both Richards'
conditions are necessary.
7. This at least is my guess about
their motives. The whole question of
Tel Quel's attitude to reference in
literature—or more particularly of
Julia Kristeva's views in this matter
—is discussed in my article, Martin
1971*b*. The view that literature does
not refer has wide currency in
France at the moment. Cf. M. Arrivé
1969, who, although he says
literature does not 'refer', rightly
asserts it has relevance to experience.
What form this relevance might
take, however, he does not discuss.
8. I am indebted to Paul van Buren
for this term, which he invented
while discussing the content of this
chapter with me.
9. Hepburn, 16.
10. Todorov 1969.

Chapter Eight.
Amputating the Referent
1. In addition to the other readers

mentioned in the preface, I am indebted to Professor Carl Barbier for
discussing this chapter with me.
Naturally, this does not necessarily
imply his assent to the point of view
advanced here.
2. Cf. Popper 1969, 304–11 for an
unconventional approach to self-
reference.
3. Sollers uses the term 'unreadable'
quite proudly, as a term of literary
praise. See Martin 1971*b*. Henri
Meschonnic sarcastically observes
that there is no interest in writers
who spend their days 'writing that
they are writing that they are
writing'.
4. This at least is what I seem to
dimly descry through the thickets of
Derrida's impenetrable jargon. See
Derrida 1970. I must add that I am
indebted to Professor A. J. Steele for
first convincing me that it is plausible
to interpret Mallarmé in this way.
5. On the other hand, a statement
such as 'le monde est fait pour
aboutir à un beau livre' (Mallarmé
1945, 872) could almost be taken to
invert the two arms of the semiotic
triangle, so that the world (the
system of referents) takes on the
function of the word (the system of
signs), and vice-versa: that is, the
world would then become word or
sign, thus:

Cf. Nabokov's short story 'Signs and
Symbols': its hero suffers from the
delusion that everything happening
around him is 'a veiled reference to
his personality and existence,' a
delusion called 'Referential Mania' in
Nabokov's witty little fiction.
6. Mallarmé 1945, 368, 857.
7. It is discussed by G. Stern. See my
own discussion of this on pp. 68–70.
8. Mallarmé 1945, 368. See also 857.

9. Ibid., 283–6.
10. I.e., by the rustling sound he has just heard, and interpreted as her arrival.
11. See *Le Roi des Aulnes*.
12. Mallarmé 1945, 67, 285, 69 respectively.
13. Ibid., 69, 67, 76, 54, 74, 54 and 68 respectively.
14. Ibid., 74.
15. Noulet, 164.
16. Mallarmé 1945, 368.
17. Ibid.
18. Richards 1936, 49.
19. Quoted in Davies 1955, 201. My italics.
20. J.-P. Richard, 554. Mallarmé is indeed singularly fond of the word 'nue', and one frequently hesitates about which sense of it he intends.
21. Mallarmé 1945, 53. The very next line contains one of the poet's characteristic uses of 'nue'.
22. Ibid., 67.
23. See J.-P. Richard, 555–6, and Mallarmé 1945, 1447.
24. 'Faîte' (crest) seems to be interpreted by Richard as at once the frontier between one facet and the next, and as 'altitude' (the impression of loftiness which this procedure is supposed to give it.).
25. J.-P. Richard, 553 and Mallarmé 1945, 382.
26. Mallarmé 1945, 386.
27. Mallarmé 1945, 855.
28. Ibid., 55.
29. J.-P. Richard, p. 443 and Mallarmé 1953, 181, 183, 198.
30. I have perhaps made out a fairly good case for this interpretation of Mallarmé's intentions. However, it must be admitted that elsewhere Mallarmé seems to assert a quite different view. In his remarks on poetry made to Jacques Huret (Mallarmé 1945, 866 ff.) for instance, he makes the famous recommendation: '*Nommer* un objet, c'est supprimer les trois quarts de la jouissance du poème qui est faite de deviner peu à peu: le *suggérer*, voilà le rêve. C'est le parfait usage de ce mystère qui constitue le symbole: évoquer petit à petit un objet pour montrer un état d'âme, ou, inversement, choisir un objet pour en dégager en état d'âme, par une série de déchiffrements.' (p. 869) [To *name* an object is to suppress three-quarters of the pleasure of a poem, which consists of gradually guessing: to *suggest* it, that's the dream. It is the perfect use of this mystery which constitutes the symbol: to evoke an object little by little so as to show a state of mind, or conversely, to choose an object so as to liberate a state of mind from it, by progressively decoding.] Here it seems as if 'objects' (i.e., referents) are not by any means totally rejected; though it is true that what he is mainly interested in is evoking a state of mind in the reader. His position here does not seem to be radically different from that of Eliot and his 'objective correlative'. The contradiction may perhaps be resolved by pointing out that Mallarmé seems to be talking here about the poetry of his young contemporaries in general. And then again, as we have already noted, it is only a '*quasi*-disappearance' of referents to which Mallarmé lays claim.

Chapter Nine.
Two Philosophical Fallacies
1. Cf. or rather contrast, a quite different attempt to apply linguistic principles to philosophical problems in Schnitzer 1971.
2. Linsky, 7.
3. Frege 1960, 56.
4. Linsky, 5–6.
5. Ibid., 128.
6. Ibid., 129.
7. It is of course Leibniz's Law that is being appealed to by the logician. It runs: 'Given a true statement of identity, one of its two terms may

be substituted for the other in any true statement and the result will be true.' But what *is* 'a true statement of identity'?

8. Linsky, 130–1.

9. See Quine 1953, and the discussion of his views in ch. VII, Linsky 1967. Linsky rightly makes the point that Quine's logician's approach falsifies the facts of language.

10. Russell 1956, 50–1. Cf. 1918, 223–9.

11. See the discussion of Frege's views in Dummett, 186–92.

12. I am of course simplifying: there may be breaks on the chain of referent-concept-word in the case of *Waverley* too: I may not know which book it is.

13. Cf. too Waismann, 'Analytic-Synthetic', and my remarks in ch. 12 on the relations between logic and science.

14. And many others. It would have been nice to have used such an analysis of meaning as Austin's fascinating exploration of 'per-formative verbs' (Austin 1962). Perhaps I am being obtuse, but it did not seem to have any bearing on my concerns here. And for a crystal clear recognition of the difference between the mental content of a statement and its referent, let me mention John Wisdom (1957, 98–9) arguing that two statements may (1) be used when we have two different things in mind, but (2) stand for the same verifiable facts.

Chapter Ten.
Mere Recognition

1. Bruner & Postman 1949.

2. Quoted from Kuhn 1970, 62–3.

3. Ibid., 64.

4. Kuhn 1970, 115.

5. Cf. also Kuhn's account (ibid., 69–72) of the slow collapse of the phlogiston theory. Priestley, though it was he who had shown the way to Lavoisier, refused to the end of his life to accept the latter's theories about combustion; for then his own 'paradigm' of reality would have had to alter. See also Kuhn 1959, for the Copernican Revolution, and scientific resistance to it. Cf. also Lord Kelvin's resistance to the ideas of Roentgen and Rutherford; or the fact that physiologists and psychologists for years disregarded the self-re-exciting paths discovered in the human cortex by S. Ramón y Cabral, simply because these did not fit the current orthodox theory of stimulus-response. (Hebb 1972, 277).

6. Saussure, 113.

7. Quoted in Cassirer, vol. I, 290.

8. Goldstein 1948, 115; cf. p. 66. By 'fixate' Goldstein evidently means 'fix' or 'stabilize'. Cf. Brain 1965, 14.

9. Conducted by Carmichael, Hogan and Walter, and described in Crafts 1938, chapter 22. See especially pp. 393–5.

10. Koestler 1964, 189–90.

11. Whorf 1956, 136.

12. Ibid., 261.

13. The episode is presumed to rest on the report of a Roman historian.

14. A caution is in order here: I use this view of Whorf's merely as an instance, since it seems that Whorf's analysis of Hopi grammar is some-what questionable. (Landar, p. 27 & ch. 27) However, this does not affect my point, which is not that our view of the world is *necessarily* affected by the language we speak, but simply that different unstated assumptions are present in different languages.

15. Austin 1970, 76.

16. Consider, for instance, the phlogiston theory.

17. Whorf, 269–70.

18. See for instance Margenau, 313 ff.

19. For a useful, and sceptical, dis-cussion of this, see Max Black, 1972, 94–100.

20. See Hoijer, 1954. There is occasional fascinating material here,

for instance on colour systems, and on the curious inability of the Bororo of Brazil to 'note the features common to all parrots' (p. 96); but no consistent picture seems to emerge.

21. R. Brown 1970, 235 ff. See also Carroll 1964, 110. Berlin and Kay (1969) adduce interesting evidence of there being eleven definable areas in the continuum of colour, (1) black, (2) white, (3) red, (4) green, (5) yellow, (6) blue, (7) brown, (8) purple, (9) pink, (10) orange, (11) grey, and that these are the focal areas for the vocabulary of colour in all languages. Although different languages contain a different assortment of these terms, there is a natural hierarchy in them, and all languages with only two basic colour terms have words whose focal point is the area of black and white; all languages with only three have words for black, white and red; and so on. The conclusion is that all human beings have a natural tendency to see colours in the same way. This, I would not dispute. But neither would Berlin and Kay dispute that there are interesting variations of detail within this general consistent picture. I am not, however, concerned to assert in this chapter that Whorf's view is right. If there is any tendency, however slight, however easily rectifiable, for us to take the classifications of our language for granted, then that is all that I am concerned to argue here.

22. Burgess, 167.

23. Robin Lakoff has argued (1972) that English uses forms of words that are equivalent to honorifics; and (1973) that there are different ways in which women speak and are spoken of (as opposed to men) in English. It is clear however that these usages do not correspond exactly to Japanese! The two languages thus embody different systems. But more importantly, Robin Lakoff's evidence seems mostly both true and surprising: she brings to our notice facts of usage that we had never observed before: and her observations are thus further evidence for my thesis here, namely that language embodies structures that we may be quite unconscious of, but which reflect our equally unconscious attitudes and prejudices.

24. Edmund S. Glenn, in Hayakawa, 1959, 13–14.

25. Actually, this is an over-simplification: for, since the inner connotations of a concept delimit the area which its denotation covers, absolute identity of denotation too is ruled out.

26. I write 'for normal purposes', for it is a commonplace that this is not true of poetry. For poetry depends upon the precise connotations attaching to the words of the language in which it is couched—and to correspondences between these connotations.

27. i.e. at a level where connotations have become important to him, as in Glenn's political work or in any literary study.

28. See note 21, p. 123 above.

29. Valéry vol. I, 1510; Martin 1971a, 83.

Chapter Eleven.
The Language of Science

1. Ogden & Richards, 238.

2. Waismann 1951, 121–2.

3. Cf. Harré 1970, 43.

4. Margenau, 50–1.

5. Ibid., 49 '. . . pure elements of sense perception, such as the blue of the sky as cursorily apprehended, or the fragrance of the flower, or the seen shape of this desk, can never figure by themselves in physical theories. They must be translated into wavelengths, chemical compounds, and geometrical figures: they must be "rationalized" before being scientifically treated.'

6. Margenau, 65.
7. Ibid., ch. v.
8. Eddington, 251–2. Quoted also by Pollock, 87–8.
9. See above, p. 127.
10. Thus, science may serve well enough as an instrument and safeguard for society as a whole. But it is no guarantee to *individuals.* People sometimes wonder why such superstitions as astrology are still, in an 'age of science', almost universally popular. Might this not be the reason? For only the astrologer dares predict one's *personal* future. The scientist can give us an account of the number of people likely to be run over by buses in the course of next year. But unlike the astrologer, he does not pretend to be sufficiently familiar with the behaviour of buses to predict where tomorrow's accidents will take place and who will suffer them.
11. Cf. above, p. 118.
12. Firsoff 1968, 21.
13. Clearly, a great deal more could be said about this incident. For instance, small asteroids sometimes approach the sun closer than Mercury does, and although one encyclopedia drily comments that professional astronomers never sighted 'Vulcan', it is possible that some of these sightings *were* of actual objects, possibly of yet unknown asteroids.
14. Firsoff 1968, 20.
15. Margenau, 75–6.
16. An interesting sidelight on the Cartesian attitude claimed by French intellectuals.
17. Margenau, 81.
18. Ibid., 96–9.

Chapter Twelve.
Ravens, Postage Stamps
1. That is, it is characterized by brevity and narrowness.
2. Wheelwright 1954 where, in a long and interesting discussion, he also lays down antithetical principles for poetic discourse.
3. Langer 1967, 66.
4. Ryle 1954, 116.
5. Ryle's account of all this (Ibid., ch. 8) is admirably clear and incisive.
6. Langer 1967, 333.
7. *Met,* $\lceil$, 4, 1006 a 3–4.
8. Ibid., 14.–15.
9. Sommers, 270.
10. J. L. Austin 1970, 76.
11. Hacking 1967, 160 ff.
12. Ibid., 162.
13. I am not of course suggesting that 'likely' and 'possible' are synonymous, but merely that in such very similar cases gradation is quite thinkable.
14. Hacking 1967, 160 ff.
15. Rosser & Turquette, 4.–6.
16. Margenau 1950, 83–4.
17. Reichenbach 1965.
18. In Reichenbach's systems it is a special case of many-valued logic.
19. Reichenbach 1932, 1935, and 1961.
20. Reichenbach 1966, 1.
21. Ibid.
22. Harré, 140–1.
23. Hempel 1965, 12 ff. Harré 1970, 119 ff.
24. Hempel 1965, 18.
25. A small selection of relevant books and articles: Alexander 1958–9 and 1959–60, Baumer 1964.–5, Brody 1968, Good 1960–2, Goodman 1954, Hempel 1958, Hosiasson-Lindenbaum 1940, Popper 1968 and 1969, Salmon 1969, Scheffler 1964, Watkins 1957, 1958 and 1959–60, P. R. Wilson 1964.–5. An account of some of the controversy can be found in Mackie 1963. The equivalence of the two propositions was attacked by Schoenberg 1964–5 and Smokler 1967. Similar points to Harré 1970 (whom I mainly rely upon below) had already been made by Rozeboom 1968, in a thought-provoking article.
26. The Popperian solution of the

paradox is one way of avoiding this particular difficulty. As Watkins (1958, 351) writes, 'On a Popperian theory of confirmation, ("All ravens are black") is confirmed by an observation-report of a black raven, not because this reports an instance of the hypothesis — a white swan is also an instance of it — but because it reports a satisfactory test of the hypothesis: a raven has been examined unsuccessfully for non-blackness.' Popper's principle of confirmation, as can be seen from this quotation, is a falsifiability principle: according to him, science seeks to disprove hypotheses, and the best hypothesis is that which (for the time being) survives the most rigorous efforts to disprove it.

27. This sort of argument is used for instance by Hosiasson-Lindenbaum, Alexander and Good.

28. As Hempel himself assumes, 1958, 345.

29. Harré 1970, 120–1.

30. Ibid., 121.

31. In support of this, it can certainly be said that the formula 'If a raven, then black', as in 'If it freezes tonight, then my car won't start in the morning,' is normal statement, frequently heard, and implies a causal connexion. Rozeboom 1968, points this out, and he is obviously right (despite those critics he mentions, 147, note, who demurred).

32. Rozeboom 1968, 143 and 154.

33. Cf. Halliday 1970*a*, 160 ff.

34. Margenau, 57.

Chapter Thirteen.
Scientific Discovery
1. Cohen & Nagel, 407.

2. A word of caution and two words of emphasis may be in order here. We must distinguish between Koestler's theory of bisociation and the evidence he adduces for it. As the reader will see, I personally find the theory highly attractive, but one is at perfect liberty to dissent from it if one wishes. The same is not perhaps so true of Koestler's evidence for it, for it is the kind of thing that has often been noted, and that by the most impressive authorities. Such major scientists as Einstein, Planck, Kekulé, Poincaré, Gauss, Von Helmholz, Darwin, Semmelweiss, Otto Loewi and many others have all personally borne witness to the importance, even the vital importance, of insight and intuition in scientific discovery. See Beveridge 1950, especially chapter 6; see also his strictures in the chapter entitled 'Reason' on the limitations of deductive reasoning in science, and on the sometimes disastrous role it has played in slowing down the acceptance of new and more accurate theories. If anyone doubts these facts, I would suggest they consult Beveridge's excellent book. But I should say that the importance of apparently irrational processes in scientific discovery is an established commonplace.

As a second word of emphasis, I would refer the reader to Einstein's own 'obituary', written by himself (Einstein 1951), where it is clear that he was led to abandon the study of pure mathematics and take up that of physics *because his intuitions were stronger* in the field of physics: 'I saw that mathematics was split up into numerous specialties . . . Consequently I saw myself in the position of Buridan's ass which was unable to decide upon any specific bundle of hay. This was obviously due to the fact that my intuition was not strong enough in the field of mathematics in order to differentiate clearly the fundamentally important, that which is really basic, from the rest of the more or less dispensable erudition . . . In [the field of physics], however, I soon learned to scent out that which was able to lead to fundamentals and to turn aside from everything else, from the multitude of things which clutter up the mind and divert it from the essential.' (Ibid., 15–17).

3. Koestler 1949, 24. I.e., 'the eagle's first flight/theft'.

4. Dunciad IV.

5. Koestler 1964, 33.

6. Koestler's theory disagrees with that of Bergson in *Le Rire*, where the latter claims that it is our seeing something human as machine-like that produces laughter. Thus Chaplin's puppet-like gyrations on the ice-rink would be what arouse our amusement. But on the well-established principle that if explanation A includes explanation B within it, A is preferable, we can assert that Bergson's theory of humour is simply a particular *case* of Koestler's: namely that of the overlapping of the *human* matrix with the *mechanical*. See Koestler's own discussion of Bergson 1964, 46 ff.

7. Ibid., 331.

8. Koestler 1949, ch. 23.

9. H. Sachs 1946, 98. Quoted in Koestler 1964.

10. Findlay, 36–8, 1948. Quoted in Koestler 1964, 117–18.

11. Koestler 1964, 212. See Platt & Baker 1931.

12. It may be worthwhile appending here a brief and more recent footnote to Koestler's own plethora of theory and evidence about 'bisociation'. E. C. Zeeman (1969) has suggested that a theory of very similar type can be formulated mathematically.

13. Hesse 1953, 199. The 'model' in question is a nineteenth century one, for to use a 20th century model here might have involved mathematics. Hesse seems to think, however, that even with mathematical models the scientific principles are the same. Cf. Hutten 1948–9, Schlanger 1970, and Hesse 1963, which includes an imaginary controversy on the neces-

sity or otherwise of models in science.

14. Hutten 1953, 299.

15. Hesse, passim. She is insistent that even nineteenth-century mechanistic science was often aware of the metaphoric nature of its models.

16. Heisenberg 1969, 113, on Bohr's principle of complementarity. For a clear and fairly detailed account, see Margenau, 313 ff., and for a more popular one Oppenheimer 1954, 75 ff.

17. Allers 1955.

18. Translated by Oliver Bernard (Penguin Poets collection).

19. Beveridge 1950, 82, quoting F. C. S. Schiller 1917.

20. That is, referents.

21. Margenau, 56–7.

22. Paraphrased from p. 36.

23. Bronowski, 48–9.

24. The Soviet literary critic B. Runin writes (in *Vechny poisk*): 'It may be that scientific knowledge and artistic knowledge cannot be brought together or deduced one from the other precisely because the relationship between them is a complementary one.' Quoted in *Gromova* 1970.

25. And indeed, no doubt Wittgenstein's intention was to validate art, to leave it untouched by the frosty breath of his 'logical space'. E.g., *Tractatus* 6.421, 6.522.

Chapter Fourteen.
Rĕcreation and Rēcreation

1. Bonnefoy, 95–6.

2. Ritchie, 56.

3. Ibid., 113.

4. Ibid., 35.

5. Ibid., 45–6.

6. Ibid., 29.

7. Interview on B.B.C. Radio Four, Summer 1971.

8. Ritchie, 128.

9. On inquiry, it transpired that 'rosy-fingered dawn' in the last few lines was responsible.

10. Pritchett, 69.
11. Ibid., 34.
12. Ramsey, 69.
13. Lyons 1968, 89. See above, p. 14
14. Shklovski 1923, 11.
15. In Todorov 1965, 94.
16. Jakobson 1933–4, quoted in Erlich, 154.
17. Kunjunni Raja, 283–4.
18. Ibid., 266.
19. Ibid., 298.
20. At Edinburgh University, 14th November 1972.
21. Jean Cohen 1966, 224.–5. A partial list of other writers who have seen some kind of deviation from the norm as the clue to poetic discourse or at least to 'style', would include: Charles Bruneau 1951–2, 6; P. Guiraud 1954; R. A. Sayce, 1953, 1, 88, 131; Leo Spitzer 1948, 11; Leech 1966; J. Mukařovský 1970; Iván Fónagy 1961; and all those modern Anglo-Saxon linguists who have discussed Chomsky's notion of 'ungrammaticalness', see *infra*.
22. Cohen, 223.
23. Ibid., 76.
24. Ibid., 51.
25. Ibid., 72.

Chapter Fifteen.
Apparency
1. Evidently, it is more like a network than a set of drawers—except in the respect mentioned here. It is however interesting that some mental systems used by human beings to memorize information apparently resemble this picture. And the language itself evidently acts as such a system. The user imagines a filing cabinet: he imagines such and such data as being present in such and such a drawer; he 'goes to the drawer', 'opens it' and 'looks at' the information.
2. Cf. Berkeley: 'It is not necessary (even in the strictest reasoning) significant names which stand for ideas should, every time they are used, excite in the understanding the ideas they are made to stand for; in reading and discoursing, names being for the most part used as letters are in algebra, in which though a particular quantity be marked by each letter, yet to proceed right it is not requisite that in every step each letter suggest to your thoughts that particular quantity it was appointed to stand for.' (*Principles of Human Knowledge*, Introduction, Section xix)
3. As has often been remarked on; different languages imitate the same sound according to different conventions. Thus French and English dogs ('oua, oua' / 'bow-wow') and cocks ('cocorico' / 'cockadoodledoo') appear to speak with different accents—if one were to believe the onomatopoeia of the languages in question.
4. Quoted in Tuve, p. 30, where a brief discussion of *Enargia* may be found. Chapman p. 49.
5. Quintilian VI, ii, 29 ff. and VIII, iii, 61 ff. (Translated by J. S. Watson). Quintilian goes on to say that obscure figures of speech should be avoided, but it must be remembered that he is advising orators, not poets. (ibid., 73)
6. Hulme 1924, 137.
7. Richards 1936, 128 ff.
8. Cf. Abercrombie, 29, where he sees the rhythms of prose as a constant hesitation between different rhythmic patterns.
9. Eliot 1965, 187.
10. This whole question is most complicated, and I have no intention of coping with it here, since I wish merely to illustrate rhythmic irregularity as one relevant variety of 'oddness'. The reader should consult Chatman 1965 and Epstein & Hawkes for two fine bird's-eye views of the complications. An *actual* performance of spoken verse is as

impossible to symbolize on paper as an *actual* performance of *Alligator Blues*: for that we need the gramophone.

11. Shapiro & Hentoff, 263.

12. Fraser 1970, 76–7.

13. My thanks to Mr Norman Macleod for reminding me of this tour-de-force.

14. 1971. I am indebted to Mr Norman Macleod for pointing this article out to me.

15. *Collected Earlier Poems*, p. 277.

16. And which has been made for instance by Winifred Nowottny (Tomlinson 1972, 304–5).

17. Nowottny, loc. cit., evidently agrees.

18. For patterns of cognate sound such as this, cf. Burke 1941, 369–78, on 'concealed alliteration'.

19. See Jespersen, 557–78. On the other hand, we must surely reject such wild aberrations as Fónagy 1971, where for instance the rolled 'r' is supposed to symbolize an erect penis!

20. Bloomfield 1935, 245.

21. Marchand, 154.

22. Ibid., 159

23. I refer to the very formalized and rigid *cynghanedd* systems. Even these however are not totally regular, in that they do not require the monotonously exact repetition of a totally rigid pattern.

24. Quoted from Graves & Riding, 64–5.

25. Ibid., 68–9.

26. Thorne 1970, 196. There is one deep structure violation, namely 'littlest', but even this is in fact a commonplace of children's speech.

27. I trust it will be evident what this is about.

28. See under that heading in Breton & Eluard's *Dictionnaire abrégé du surréalisme*: 'A game with folded paper in which a sentence or a drawing is composed by several people, without any of them know-

ing what has already been written down. The now classic example which gave its name to the game is the first sentence ever obtained in this manner: "The exquisite—corpse—will drink—the new—wine".' (Eluard vol. I, p. 730).

29. Cf. Barfield 1928, 189: 'On examination, the sole condition is found to be this, that the strangeness shall have an *interior* significance; it must be felt as arising from a different plane or mode of consciousness, and not merely as eccentricity of expression. It must be a strangeness of *meaning*.'

30. Bierwisch 1970*b*, 110–11.

31. Cf. p. 249, ch. 19, for a brief discussion of the application of the term 'ungrammaticalness' to semantic oddness.

32. Bierwisch 1970*b*, 110.

33. Thorne 1970, 196–7.

34. See ch. 19.

35. Macdonald, 218–19.

36. As I pointed out in ch. 4.

37. And this, it will be recalled, was precisely Bierwisch's criterion, p. 188 above.

38. Empson 1961, 26.

39. The above remarks are repeated almost verbatim from Martin 1974. I am indebted to Norman MacLeod for observing that just as we can succeed in emptying a word of all its apparent meaning simply by pronouncing it to ourselves over and over again, so a way of opening out the connotations of a word in poetry, of ridding that word of too precise an interpretation, is simple repetition. Thus, in this Eluard poem, the word 'feu' is repeated in each of the first four lines. And I was referred to Burckhardt p. 285: 'For an even more primitive way than punning to strip words of their meanings is repetition. Say "a rose is a rose is a rose" a few more times, and what you have is a meaningless sound, because you have torn the word out of its living linguistic matrix and so are left with nothing but a vile phonetic jelly.'

40. Garelli 1966*b*, 130–1.
41. Ibid.
42. Cf. Paris 1967, to name but one product of the *Finnegan's Wake* industry.
43. Eliot 1934, 145.
44. In my technical sense of 'psychological overtones', as in ch. 4.
45. See ch. 16.
46. Eisenstein 1943, 34.

Chapter Sixteen.
On Metaphor
1. Cf. Chapman & Chapman's views, briefly referred to by R. E. Johnson, 261. Oddly enough, cf. also Skinner 1957, 91 ff, who I perceived some time after reaching this conclusion, places these 2 forms of extension close to each other.
2. And above, ch. 4.
3. Any attempt to establish a positive definition of 'literal' on the basis of correspondence to fact is doubtless foredoomed to failure. As Urban points out, 'strictly speaking, there is no such thing as literal truth in any absolute sense, for there is no such thing as absolute correspondence between expression and that which is expressed. There can be no such thing as identity, or even complete similarity between expression and the state of affairs which it expresses, for they belong to wholly different categories.' (Urban, 382) Cf. Austin's remarks on 'roughness of correspondence' to reality, see p. 74. It is therefore best, I think, to concentrate on the differences between literal and metaphoric expressions. But as always, the solutions to these questions will be found to be a matter of degree: degree of correspondence to reality, degree of correspondence to normal usage, degree of intention to distinguish differences between two

protuberances by calling them 'mountain' and 'hill', etc.
4. Stern, 298, quoting Stählin, 14.
5. G. Stern, 298–9.
6. See also above, p. 63
7. The situation is complicated, as the use of 'tail' and 'nose' for an aeroplane may show. Is the 'tail' of an aeroplane literally a tail? Is its nose literally its 'nose'? Perhaps the latter is more metaphoric than the former. (For birds have tails, but not noses. And when one speaks of *Concorde's* 'beak', this is, at least at the moment, still a conscious descriptive metaphor.) Perhaps not. But in any case, the ground for the metaphor (if it *is* a metaphor, for what else would one say?) is clear. And a much more interesting matter than whether the metaphor is a metaphor or not, is why and on what grounds the attribution is made.
8. G. Stern, 301–2.
9. Ibid., 302.
10. 'The two motives converge on that element ("courage"), giving it a predominant position, and evoking it to the exclusion of the other, more or less irrelevant, elements.' Ibid., 305.
11. Cf. Konrad.
12. G. Stern, 305.
13. Ibid., 307.
14. Max Black 1959, 25–47. Note also Shibles' discussion of his views, Shibles 1971, 151–7.
15. Shibles 1971, 153–4. I have requoted his summary of Black's views here, as it is a lucid and handy account.
16. Erwin 1970, 114–25, attempts to operate a *reductio ad absurdum* on Max Black's argument, but succeeds only in reducing himself to absurdity. He claims that when Black says we see 'man' through a filter of 'wolfness', this is then supposed to remain true of all further uses of the terms 'wolf' and 'man', and that consequently the meaning of the

term 'man' should have changed since Black and others discussed the metaphor. This he stigmatizes as absurd, and goes on to dismiss Black's whole thesis. However, Black nowhere claims that the metaphor alters our entire future apprehension of the terms in question; although he does not say so explicitly, he quite evidently believes that our apprehension of men and wolves is altered *momentarily* and *in context*.

17. Black 1959, 41.

18. Stanford, 105. According to this exceedingly interesting book, only one ancient theorist, Hermogenes of Tarsus (170 a.d.), clearly perceived the dual nature of metaphor. This was because rhetoricians detested ambiguity, though poets practised it. A most remarkable example of it is Aeschylus'

αὐτότοκον πρὸ λόχου μογερὰν πτάκα θυομένοισι (*Agamemnon*, l. 136) which means both 'Sacrificing a hapless hare with her unborn brood before the birth' and 'Sacrificing a poor trembling victim, his own child (i.e., Iphigenia) on behalf of the host'. (Ibid., 148).

19. Ian T. Ramsey, 49.

20. Cf. above p. 66.

21. See above pp. 39–40, 51–4, 65–6.

22. 'He clasps the crag with crooked hands . . .'

23. Cf. Brooke-Rose 1958, 'Introduction', which gives a conveniently rapid sketch of thinking on metaphor from Aristotle onwards. Doubtless some reservations should be added to her remarks there. She does not mention such figures as Gracián, nor consider the scholastic tradition; and such a work as Henry Wells' *Poetic Imagery*, for all the strangeness of its terminology (images are classified as 'decorative, sunken, violent or fustian, radical, intensive, expansive, exuberant and humorous'), does nonetheless contain some

insights of a structural nature. (Wellek & Warren 1963 take him very seriously indeed). One might also mention Leakey 1954, who provides quite a useful classification from a literary point of view. However, I am broadly in agreement with her opinions, and in particular with the view that classification by domain of thought is a very limited critical tool.

24. Other exceptions are Gustaf Stern 1932, Brinkmann 1878, Clemen 1951, Konrad 1939.

25. There are, however, clear cases of covert comparison by juxtaposition, as we shall see.

26. Liu, 106–7.

27. Wellek & Warren 1963, 197.

28. Most authorities from Aristotle onwards have either actively asserted or reluctantly admitted that metaphor is based on analogy (which I do not mean in the sense of Aristotle's κατὰ τὸ ἀνάλογον, i.e. as an equality of ratios containing at least four terms (A is to B as C is to D), but simply as a perceived or intuited similarity. E.g. G. W. Allen, G. M. Graham, Middleton Murry (1950, 86; 1956, 12), O'Neill, Ransom 1950, Stanford, Urban, to name but a few. See Laurentano, however, for a flat denial of this point of view; Wheelwright 1962 for a distinction between metaphor that is analogical and metaphor that is radically other (cf. below, p. 216); and MacLeish (cf. below, p. 216) for the view that metaphor is analogical, and that this is why it is *not* the basis of the truest poetry.

29. Translation by Robert Payne, quoted in MacLeish 1965, 60.

30. For parallelism, cf. Liu 1962 and Scott & Martin 1972, 159 ff.

31. Quoted in MacLeish 1965, 63.

32. Ibid.

33. Eisenstein, 14.

34. Ibid., 45–6.

35. Liu, 106–7.
36. Liu writes 'exhale', but 'disgorge' is clearly more accurate by his own account.
37. Friedrich 1968.
38. 'Le Flacon'.
39. The addition of parallelism here is mine.
40. Eluard, I, 232.
41. See Gregory, 15–17. See above, p. 103.
42. Wheelwright 1962, 78. Cf. E. E. Cummings' well-known poem 'next to of course god america i/ love you land of the pilgrims and so forth oh . . . '
43. Ibid., 72.
44. MacLeish 1965, 74: 'But if the relation of the unrelated is the ultimate, or, in any case, the characteristic, meaning of poetry— poetry's truth, to borrow Day Lewis's umbrella word—why then is not the coupling of images, which is the relation of the unrelated in practice and in fact, the characteristic means to meaning? I should have to reply that I think it is. But in so saying I should find myself at once in a distinct, and not very distinguished minority of one with the great and dangerous weight of authoritative opinion leaning above me like a cliff: the opinion of the psychologists in letters and the literary men in psychology who have reserved that central place for the symbol, and the opinion of the critics of poetry, headed by the greatest of them all, who holds (I am referring, of course, to Ivor Richards) that '*metaphor* is the supreme agent by which disparate and hitherto unconnected things are brought together in poetry.' Mine is not a comfortable position to be in even in the relative privacy of a Harvard classroom. In cold public print it demands explanation.'
45. Wheelwright 1962, 72–3.
46. Ibid., 79.

47. Rather differently, George Whalley (1965) calls 'sphinx-woman' juxtaposition. But it is clearly not juxtaposition, because the two elements, 'sphinx' and 'woman', are not just placed side by side but placed in a certain relationship, just as when we say 'ape-man', or the French say 'porte-fenêtre', or the Germans in bad wartime thrillers say 'schwein-hund'. The relationship is that of the 'woman' taking over many of the features of the 'sphinx'. (In 'woman-sphinx' the converse would occur—except that since sphinxes are fabulous beasts, we should then feel a stronger sense of the metaphoric.)
48. 'Image' in this context is used simply as a handy portmanteau term to include all of the following: juxtaposition, parallelism, comparison, substitution (metaphor) and symbol.
49. Vela 1965, ch. 18, 'Metáfora y enigma', 101–19.
50. 'The First Anniversary', lines 409–12.
51. Cf. Wells 1924, 126.
52. *Matthew* X, 16. 'Behold, I send you forth as sheep in the midst of wolves: be ye therefore wise as serpents, and harmless as doves.'
53. See Bronowski's remarks, p. 157.
54. Empson, at the end of *Seven Types of Ambiguity*, admits that at any rate for some readers, dissection may destroy.
55. Empson 1961, 26–7.
56. Brooke-Rose 1958, 30, during her interesting account of the 'literal symbol'.
57. Jouve 1966, 139.

Chapter Seventeen.
Taxonomy and Feeling
1. John M. Wilson 1849, vol. I, 227.
2. Ponge 1961, vol. III, 201–2.
3. Stanford, 85.
4. Ponge 1961, vol. II, 278–9.
5. Yonge 1960, 16. His italics.

6. Ibid. My italics.
7. Burke 1941, 138–67.
8. There is, in fact, a Ponge text on the oyster, 1967, 43.
9. Ponge 1961, vol. II, 17–18. My italics.
10. *Dictionary of Gardening*, ed. F. J. Chittenden 1951, 2249.
11. Ponge 1961, vol. III, 65.
12. This and the following botanic definitions come from B. D. Jackson 1916.
13. Cf. my remarks above on p. 124.
14. Saussure 1966, 120: 'In language there are only differences *without positive terms.*'
15. This, broadly, is what certain French Structuralist efforts to explain and analyze literature amount to. To the extent that they assert literary language to be purely 'negative' and 'differential', and at the same time direct our attention towards the abstract structures that might be deduced from it, rather than towards its actual content, it is clear that they are focussing their attention in quite the wrong direction.
16. Ponge 1961, vol. II, 25–6. Ponge has been closely associated with the structuralists of *Tel Quel*. But it will be clear that this close association rests upon a fundamental misapprehension. Garelli's view of Ponge is no less mistaken, in my opinion. He devotes a whole chapter of his *Gravitation poétique* to Ponge (72–9) and, tempted as so many French writers are by impressive-sounding negatives, concludes: 'A un niveau plus profond de lecture, le poème de Ponge ne désigne plus: il est ouverture sur un monde qui se dévoile par la constitution même du langage poétique et qui ne renvoie en dernier ressort à l'objet de départ que par *l'entrelacs de ses sens niés*. .' (op. cit., 78. My italics) But why Ponge should be taken to be *denying* meanings is by no means apparent

. . . except that it is necessary for Garelli's thesis that he should!
17. That is, the *Dictionary*.
18. Ibid., 271.
19. Ibid., 277.
20. John M. Wilson vol. 3, 472.
21. Ponge 1961, vol. II, 281–3.
22. Proust vol. I, 849.
23. Ibid., 860–3.
24. Ibid., 75–9.
25. A proem is of course a prelude. Cf. the use of the latter in music. But the word also masquerades as a portmanteau combination of 'prose' and 'poem'.
26. Richards 1936, 117–18 (passage *re* 'leg').
27. Marckwardt, 111.

Chapter Eighteen.
Three or Four Languages
1. See above, p. 96.
2. Valéry, vol. I, pp. 1502, 1371; Martin 1971*a*, 84–5.
3. Richards 1926, 267.
4. Burke 1941.
5. Ransom 1941, 293.
6. Ibid., 1941, 290–1. An icon is a symbol which in some respect *resembles* what it stands for. The simplest linguistic icons are thus onomatopoeic words like 'splash' or 'bow-wow'.
7. Brooks 1947, 9.
8. Wheelwright 1960.
9. Wheelwright 1954 and 1962.
10. Wheelwright 1954. He gives a long and interesting list of the main characteristics of his two opposing types of discourse.
11. Ransom 1941, 279–80. (My italics)
12. Last chapter of Ransom 1941, passim.
13. Cf. also my remarks on 'Le gui la glu', p. 233.
14. Huxley 1963, 13–14.
15. C. S. Lewis 1961, 15–16.
16. Cf. Hungerland, 122ff. on the undoubted apparency of Robert Frost, despite his discursiveness.

17. This is merely a tendency, of course. But we have already seen Harré asserting the dangers of this tendency (ch. 12).
18. On the dangers of assuming such an absolute distinction, see Martin 1971*b*.
19. Hungerland, 43.

Chapter Nineteen.
Linguistics and Subjectivity
1. Cf. Todorov 1968, where general statements are specifically said to be the purpose of a structuralist approach.
2. Thorne 1970, 196.
3. Ibid., passim. Cf. Riffaterre 1959, 158.
4. Thorne 1970.
5. Chomsky 1965, 148–60.
6. Thorne 1970, 196.
7. Thorne 1965. So have others, e.g. Fowler 1971, 219–37. Much the same remarks apply here: again we have a distaste for talking about meanings.
8. See Hendricks 1969 and Thorne 1969.
9. Cohen 1966, 224–5. For an account of Cohen's book from the point of view of a brilliant practising poet, see Michel Deguy 1967. Deguy too notes Cohen's reluctance to deal with meaning.
10. Catford 1965.
11. Sinclair 1970, 140 and 142.
12. Sinclair 1968. A later article than 'Taking a Poem to Pieces', which first appeared in 1966. My italics.
13. Quoted in Ullmann 1964, 119.
14. Cf. for further 'paucity of lexical comment' the following: M. A. K. Halliday 1970; S. R. Levin 1970.
15. Hill 1956.
16. Ransom 1955, 395.
17. Hill 1956, 51.
18. Ibid., 53–4.
19. Ibid., 55–6.
20. Carroll, 98–9.
21. Hill 1956, 55.
22. Ibid.

23. Ibid.
24. Ibid., 56.
25. The reader might also find it interesting to consult Hill 1955, 1965, and Matchett 1955, for a discussion of A. Hill's approach to Hopkins' *Windhover*.
26. Jakobson & Lévi-Strauss 1962.
27. Riffaterre 1966, 200–1.
28. Ibid., 206.
29. For an account of how far parallelism was taken in traditional Chinese poetry, for instance, see Scott & Martin 1972, 157–65.
30. Translation from the Penguin Poets, 82, slightly altered.
31. Riffaterre notes that the poem has not been much admired by critics. As for its carrying a special charge for Baudelaire, it is best to refer the reader to Riffaterre's closing remarks about other Baudelaire poems in which cats appear.
32. All but one of these are noted by Riffaterre, 217–27, who can be consulted for still more.
33. Riffaterre 1966, 215.
34. Jakobson & Lévi-Strauss 1962, 21.
35. Riffaterre 1966, 235. I don't like the suggestion either. But it is perhaps possible to argue that it is an element in this particular poem.
36. Halliday 1970*b*. The same author's comments on Golding's *Inheritors*, however, contain some extremely valuable insights. (Halliday 1973, 103–40, reprinted from Chatman 1971, 330–68)
37. Lyons 1968, 267–8.
38. Proof in science depends on evidence, not on fact.
39. Leech 1969, 6.
40. Leech 1970.
41. E.g. Roger Fowler 1966, John Spencer & M. J. Gregory 1970, and Michael Riffaterre passim. Riffaterre's approach to literature is discussed by Hardy 1969 and Culler 1972. Culler points out, rightly, that the moment Riffaterre has to deal with the actual detailed interpre-

tation of a text, he adopts the methods of the ordinary literary critic. The point I am trying to make here is that this is not only inevitable, but actually desirable.

42. See above 251.

43. Reverdy 1969, 'Tête', 240.

44. Spitzer 1948, 27.

45. See in particular Chatman 1965, and Epstein & Hawkes, among sundry others.

46. An example given in Spencer & Gregory 1970, 80. My remarks here are perhaps misleading. It is precisely the point of 'collocation' that its users seek at all costs to *avoid* bringing in such subjective elements as meaning. It is therefore not accurate of me to *explain* this collocation by speaking of 'nouns of time', since the collocationist's intention is to indicate the mere statistical frequency of words *a, b* and *c* being associated with word *d*, and on no account to explain such an association. This makes my point even stronger, of course, as it is precisely the substitution of 'grief' for [month?], [year?], etc., which gives it its special meaning of *a long grief*; and unless the linguist goes on to mention this, his observations are—well, not exactly pointless— but he is not *making* a point.

47. I except the *Tel Quel* lunatic fringe. But consult for instance Morhange-Bégué or Jean-Claude Chevalier for detailed analysis of Apollinaire's poetry, though again one might level the charge of too chilly a formalism. I must also welcome Sinclair 1968, and Halliday on William Golding, both mentioned in notes above. Finally, for further controversy, see the disagreement between Fowler and Bateson in Fowler 1971.

Chapter Twenty.
Literary Critics and Objectivity
1. Marckwardt 1966, 111.

2. See ch. 15.

3. Riffaterre 1959, 172.

4. There are exceptions. Mallarmé and Valéry both made a virtue of the poet's conscious labour in seeking out the *mot juste*.

5. The discussion here refers, of course, to *Macbeth* Act III scene II: 'Light thickens; and the crow/ Makes wing to the rooky wood . . . '

6. Empson 1961, 81–2.

7. From Hopkins's 'The Windhover'. See Hill 1955 and 1965, 354.

8. Martin 1971a, 40.

9. It also of course suggests much more that I did not mention at the time, such as a destructiveness on the part of the divine itself.

10. Mind you, they still do so a great deal. However, if the principle of multiple interpretation is accepted, the problem is much reduced in scale.

11. A summary of the correspondence can be found in *Time* November 12th 1951, 31.

12. Beardsley 1958, 151, where a brief discussion of this controversy may be found.

13. Sitwell, 1957, 14–15.

14. Nokes & Amis 1952.

15. Sitwell 1957, xxxiv.

16. Nokes & Amis 1952.

17. Cf. Jouve, who says that poems are organisms (Jouve 1970, 11). And organisms develop. The ambiguity and mobility of surrealist poetry too might be taken as effecting this sort of operation.

18. Valéry, vol. I, 1507.

Chapter Twenty-one.
Real-ativity, or, The Use of Poetry
1. Gautier, 22. M. Carrel was a contemporary journalist, and was presumably instanced by Gautier as a man who wrote for a political and social purpose.

2. Ibid., 19.

3. As Beardsley says (ch. 13), the art for art's sake position has never been properly worked out.

4. Gautier, 20.
5. Ibid., 5.
6. Ibid., 20–1.
7. Ibid., 22. See also his remarks on Charles Fourier, p. 25 f.
8. G. Moore 1917, 144–5.
9. Beardsley, 574–6.
10. Frye 1957, 33–4. He notes a tendency of literature to concentrate its interest, as time passes, upon progressively less superhuman, less noble heroes.
11. Lehmann-Haupt, 243–4.
12. Among those described as 'decadent' are Breton, Camus, Gide, Giraudoux, Larbaud, Malraux, Proust, Montherlant and Sartre. Jean-Richard Bloch, Jean Cassou, Romain Rolland, Aragon and Eluard are approved of. Struve, 387.
13. See M. Adams 1968. The complete works of Gide, Sartre, Maeterlinck and Moravia, as also three works by Bergson, were prohibited by the Roman Catholic Index.
14. Ibid., 97.
15. C. P. Snow, a convinced opponent of modernism, has accused it of being fascistic. See Rabinovitz 1967, where, however, it rapidly becomes evident that Snow has got his facts quite wrong.
16. Republic 607.
17. Ibid., 401.
18. Republic 397.
19. Republic 396A, Laws VII 815B, 816E, XI 935B.
20. Lesser Hippias, 365D, 369E, Menon 95D, Lysis 214A–216B.
21. Republic 398.
22. Quoted in L. Richard 126.
23. Ibid., 132.
24. Struve, 343–4. My italics.
25. L. Richard, 132.
26. Quoted by L. Richard, 125.
27. Mosse, 157.
28. L. Richard, 133.
29. Claude Grander, 1941, quoted by L. Richard, 161.
30. L. Richard, 158–9.
31. Rauschning 1945, 288.

32. Struve, 272–5.
33. Zhdanov, 19–20. An amusingly close parallel is the words of Senator Sean Goulding in the 1942 debate on the Irish censorship: 'Apart from the moral censorship I think there should be a censorship of books that portray us Irish people in the way I have indicated (as a nation of drunkards, and as immoral)'. The Senator also asserted that 'the growth of crime in England is due to the unfettered reading in that country'. *Seanad Debates*, vol. 27, cols. 31–2.
34. Struve, 342. The episode he cites actually precedes Zhdanov's witch-hunt.
35. Mosse, 193.
36. See chapter 13.
37. Quoted, along with other entertaining examples, by Vickery, 31.
38. Cf. Plato again.
39. Yarmolinsky, 57–8.
40. Ibid., 58. It should however be added that in this respect the Nazi experience was slightly different. Though when they came to power their mood was prudish, and for instance Dreiser's *The Genius* and *An American Tragedy* were burned on the bonfires of 1933 because they 'deal with low love affairs' (Haight, 71), eroticism soon began to be thought of as a product of the racial life force.
41. Anon, *Esprit* 1959.
42. Ibid., 346.
43. Ibid., 354.
44. Ibid., 358 ff. At least one account I have seen of this penetrating article seems to have been unaware of its pervasive irony. To claim that classicism ought to be officially admitted as the style which Socialist Realism should logically result in, is after all a highly ironic statement.
45. Struve, 383.
46. Mikhalkov. Quoted in English in Vickery, 80–1.
47. It is of course no accident that there are few totalitarian critics of

any complexion worth reading. Lukács is practically the only exception. Hence, ironically, his fame.

48. See Lukács 1963, for this and the following list.

49. Ibid., Cf. L. Richard, 126.

50. Lukács 1963, p. 25.

51. Ibid., p. 30.

52. Ibid., p. 28–30.

53. Ibid., p. 36.

54. Ibid., p. 25.

55. Ibid.

56. Lukács 1963: 'Let me say here that, in any work of art, perspective is of overriding importance. It determines the course and content; it draws together the threads of the narration; it enables the artist to choose between the important and the superficial, the crucial and the episodic. The direction in which characters develop is determined by perspective, only those features being described which are material to their development. The more lucid the perspective—as in Molière or the Greeks—the more economical and striking the selection.'

57. Ibid., 60: 'A simple solution would appear to be available at this point. Is not the decisive distinction that between the presence of a socialist perspective in socialist realism, and its absence in decadent bourgeois literature? The conclusion is tempting, but false.'

Lukács' solution (ibid.): 'Not everyone who looks for a solution to the social and ideological crisis of bourgeois society . . . will be a professed socialist. It is enough that a writer takes socialism into account and does not reject it out of hand. But if he rejects socialism . . . he closes his eyes to the future, gives up any chance of assessing the present correctly, and loses the ability to create other than purely static works of art.'

58. Ibid., p. 49.

59. See above, note 56.

60. Similar remarks could be made about all points of view that insist upon an absolute truth of some kind, e.g. of the Christian world-view, cf. Fuller 1958 or Gardiner 1960. Both seem to regard a Christian world-view as a *sine-qua-non* of literary value.

61. Ibid., 66. Lukács' early *Theory of the Novel* (1915–16) expresses existentialist *angst*; and Zitta thinks it was perhaps to rescue himself from the insecurity of this system-less anguish that he called on time and history, in the shape of Marxism, to be his saviour. For the devotees of systems are often those whose personal insecurity is greatest. As Popper writes (1960, p. 161), 'May it not, after all, be the historicists who are afraid of change? And is it not, perhaps, this fear of change which makes them so utterly incapable of reacting rationally to criticism, and which makes others so responsive to their teaching? It almost looks as if historicists were trying to compensate themselves for the loss of an unchanging world by clinging to the faith that change can be foreseen because it is ruled by an unchanging law.'

62. Mosse, 160.

63. It is relevant to note that Jarrett-Kerr finds that the deficiencies of certain modern Catholic writers are due to their being 'incapable of full-blooded doubt'. (p. 172)

64. Also 'racialist' and 'fascist'. It is amusing to recall that institutes of genetics were closed down in Nazi Germany precisely because they were *not* racialist or fascist.

65. See Medvedev, whose incisive book points out just how self-perpetuating and self-destructive the application of dogma to scientific fact becomes: when Konstantinov produced evidence to show that Lysenko's 'vernalization' did not increase grain yields, he was accused

of sabotage. (Medvedev, 152–3)
Now there is nothing illogical in this.
If one's presuppositions are that
(1) Communism has been proved
scientifically correct for all time;
(2) Communism declares Lysenko's
theory to be correct; then it follows
as the night the day that: Anyone
who disproves Lysenko must either
be applying an unscientific system
or deliberately cheating. One disastrous consequence of this attitude
of mind is the difficulty of changing
received ideas, and hence of making
any scientific progress whatever.
66. Zhdanov, 109–10. 'In like
measure, the Kantian subterfuges
of contemporary bourgeois atomic
physicists lead them to deductions
of the "free will" of the electron and
to attempts to represent matter as
only some combination of waves and
other such nonsense.'
67. Some of Thüring's remarks are
quoted at length in Mosse, 208–15.
68. Not that art 'progresses', exactly.
But its picture of reality is never
definitive, and the corpus of literature continually expands (like the
modern astronomer's universe) to
admit new works, even new genres.
69. Popper 1968, 280–1.
70. Popper 1945, Vol. II, 209. Cf.
Mitroff 1973 on the value of
scientists' having conflicting viewpoints.
71. Cf. Eliot's remark on new classics
coming to supplement the old, thus
altering our sense of the whole.
72. E.g., Rothfels, 35–8.
73. E.g., Friedberg, 1962.
74. D. H. Lawrence 1968, 416–26.

Chapter Twenty-two.
Speculative Appendix
1. Hebb 1972, 185. W. Dement
seems to have been the first to point
this out, see Dement 1963.
2. Probably not. Yet in a very
general way, why not? Cf. Beardsley's Defence no. 1, ch. 20. Cf. also

Karpman p. 485. Cf. also Artaud,
whose theatre of cruelty was to
perform a similar cathartic effect:
'I defy that spectator to give himself
up, once outside the theatre, to ideas
of war, riot and blatant murder.'
3. *Le Temps retrouvé*, 264–5.
4. That it was totally unconscious
must be accounted doubtful, in the
case of a man so conscious of his own
inner processes as *A la recherche*
proves Proust to have been. Cf.
Painter's remarks on Proust's
deliberate avoidance of a cure for
his neurosis, Painter, vol. II, ch. 3.
5. Painter, vol. II, ch. 17.
6. Ibid., 307–9 and 361. As Painter
remarks, 'the real presence of death
in Proust was now crystallized in the
terrible figure known to psycho-
analysts as the Dread Mother,
whose monstrous image consum-
mates and punishes the child's sin of
love and hatred . . . ' (Ibid., 309)
And the identification is further supported by the episode in *A la
recherche* where the narrator dreams
he is talking to the dead Albertine,
while 'at the far end of the room my
grandmother moved to and fro,
with part of her chin crumbled away
like corroded marble.' (Ibid., and
see Proust, vol. III, p. 539.) For it
must be recalled that the grandmother in the novel is the alter ego
of the mother who survives: she is
the mother who dies.
7. See Jung 1967, 213–15.
8. See Jung 1960, para. 135.
9. Ibid., para. 136.
10. Ibid., para. 162.
11. Jung 1967, 359 ff.
12. Jung, 1960, vol. 8, para. 170.
13. Ibid., para. 172–4.
14. Ibid., para. 147. Jung gives an
instance of mere 'concretistic' as
opposed to purposeful interpretation
on p. 76 of that book.
15. Brief accounts of the deaths of
the first four of these may be found
in Alvarez 1972, 190 ff.

16. Whence probably the origin of this famous surrealist 'recommendation'. Breton 1969, 18.

17. Ibid., 20.

18. Recorded by André Breton, and quoted in Cowles 1959, 114. For his Hitlerian admirations, ibid., 158–68.

19. Alvarez 1972, 215.

20. Ibid., 214.

21. My translation. For the original, Eluard, vol. I, 148.

22. Alvarez, 215–6. In fact I should say that Plath's suicide points to a missing factor in her work: the factor of control, any intimations of an exit from the dark tunnel, any counterbalancing life impulse.

23. Ibid.

24. Since Alvarez wrote his book, John Berryman too has committed suicide.

25. Booth 1961, 391. The quotation within the quotation is from Burke 1931, 104.

26. This fallacy was discussed above on p. 323, note 16.

27. Karpman, 1954, 485, disagrees. His argument is that overt sexual offences may be reduced by a kind of Aristotelian catharsis. Violence however must not be confused with sex, nor children with adults. And Wertham's case is indeed a hard one to answer, so often does his evidence seem to link the literally pornographic sadism of the crime comic with the violent behaviour of the American child.

28. It would doubtless be fascinating to apply these principles to the other arts. The argument of difficulty, and of the necessity for the reader to have learnt the language of literature may perhaps not apply in some other art forms, notably the film. My first argument (that variety of artistic experience is a safeguard) can be used to defend 'extremism' in the cinema, certainly, but I suspect that to increase difficulty there would merely increase the already too naked, purely subconscious, effect of the pure visual image.

29. τὸ ἀντίξουν συμφέρον καὶ ἐκ τῶν διαφερόντων καλλίστην ἁρμονίαν . . .

Bibliography
(*Works referred to*)

ABBREVIATIONS
Am. phil. Q. = *American Philosophical Quarterly*
Brit. J. Aesth. = *British Journal of Aesthetics*
Brit. J. Phil. Sci. = *British Journal for the Philosophy of Science*
Fdns Lang. = *Foundations of Language*
J. Aesth. & Art Crit. = *Journal of Aesthetics and Art Criticism*
J. Chem. Educ. = *Journal of Chemical Education*
J. Ling. = *Journal of Linguistics*
J. Phil. = *Journal of Philosophy*
Lang. & Style = *Language and Style*
Lang. fr. = *Langue Française*
Lang. Soc. = *Language in Society*
NRF = *Nouvelle Revue Française*
New Sci. = *New Scientist*
Phil. Rev. = *Philosophical Review*
PMLA = *Publications of the Modern Languages Association of America*
Proc. Ari. Soc. = *Proceedings of the Aristotelian Society*
Romance Philol. = *Romance Philology*

Abercrombie, David (1965) *Studies in Phonetics and Linguistics*, London
Adams, Michael (1968) *Censorship: The Irish Experience*, Dublin
Alexander, H. G. (1958–9 and 1959–60) 'The Paradoxes of Confirmation'
    Brit. J. Phil. Sci. 9, 227–33 and 10, 229–34
Allen, Gay W. (1961) 'Metaphor' *Encyclopaedia Britannica* 15, 328
Allers, Rudolf von (1955) 'Vom Nutzen und den Gefahren der Metapher in
    der Psychologie' *Jahrbuch für Psychologie und Psychotherapie* 3, 3–15
Alston, William P. (1963*a*) 'The Quest for Meanings' *Mind* 72, 79–87
    (1963*b*) 'Meaning and Use' *Philosophical Quarterly* 13, 107–24
    (1964*a*) 'Linguistic Acts' *Am. phil. Q.* 1, 138–46
    (1964*b*) *Philosophy of Language*, Englewood Cliffs
Alvarez, Alfred (1972) *The Savage God*, London
Anonymous (1959) 'Le Réalisme socialiste' *Esprit* 27 no. 270 (Feb.) 335–67
Arrivé, Michel (1969) 'Postulats pour la Description linguistique des textes
    littéraires' *Lang.fr.* 3 (Sept.) 3–13
Austin, J. L. (1962) *How to Do Things with Words*, Oxford
    (1963) 'The Meaning of a Word' and 'Performative–Constative' in Caton
    1963
    (1970) *Philosophical Papers*, Oxford
Ayer, A. J. (1946) *Language, Truth and Logic*, 2nd ed., London
Bally, Charles (1940) 'L'arbitraire du signe' *Le Français Moderne* 8
Barfield, Owen (1928) *Poetic Diction*, London
Baruch, John (1973) 'A New Massive Nuclear Particle?' *New Sci.* 59 no. 861
    (30 Aug.) 488–95

Baumer, W. M. (1964–5) 'Confirmation without Paradoxes' *Brit. J. Phil. Sci.* 15, 177–95

Beardsley, Monroe C. (1958) *Aesthetics*, New York

Bendix, E. H. (1966) *Componential Analysis*, Bloomington

Berlin, B. & P. Kay (1969) *Basic Color Terms*, Berkeley

Beveridge, W. I. B. (1950) *The Art of Scientific Investigation*, London

Bickerton, Derek (1969) 'Prolegomena to a Linguistic Theory of Metaphor', *Fdns Lang.* 5, 34–52

Bierwisch, Manfred (1967) 'Some Semantic Universals of German Adjectivals' *Fdns Lang.* 3, 1–36
  (1970*a*) 'Semantics' in Lyons 1970*a*, 166–84
  (1970*b*) 'Poetics and Linguistics' in Freeman 1970, 96–115

Black, Max (1959) *Models and Metaphors*, Ithaca & New York
  (1972) *The Labyrinth of Language*, Penguin

Bloomfield, Leonard (1935) *Language*, London
  (1939) *Linguistic Aspects of Science*, Chicago (Vol. 1 no. 4 of Carnap, Morris & Neurath)

Bohm, David J. (1952) *Quantum Theory*, London
  (1963) *Problems in the Basic Concepts of Physics*, London

Bolinger, Dwight (1965), 'The Atomization of Meaning' *Language* 41, 555–73

Bondi, Hermann (1967) *Assumption and Myth in Physical Theory*, Cambridge

Bonnefoy, Yves (1967) *Un Rêve fait à Mantoue*, Paris

Booth, Wayne, C. (1961) *The Rhetoric of Fiction*, Chicago & London

Brady, Frank, J. Palmer & M. Price (1973) *Literary Theory and Structure*, New Haven & London

Brain, Sir Russell (1951) *Mind, Perception and Science*, Oxford
  (1959) *The Nature of Experience*, London
  (1965) *Speech Disorders: Aphasia, Apraxia and Agnosia*, 2nd ed., London

Braithwaite, R. B. (1955) *Scientific Explanation*, Cambridge

Breton, André (1969) *Les Pas perdus*, Paris

Brinkmann, Friedrich (1878) *Die Metaphern*, Bonn

Brody, B. A. (1968) 'Confirmation and Explanation' *J. Phil.* 10 (May) 282–99

Bronowski, J. (1967) *The Identity of Man*, Penguin

Brooke-Rose, Christine (1958) *A Grammar of Metaphor*, London

Brooks, Cleanth (1947) *The Well Wrought Urn*, New York

Brown, Roger (1958) *Words and Things*, New York
  (1970) *Psycholinguistics*, New York

Bruneau, Charles (1951–2) 'La Stylistique' *Romance Philol.* 5, 1–14

Bruner, J. S. & Leo Postman (1949) 'On the Perception of Incongruity: A Paradigm' *Journal of Personality* 18, 206–23

Burckhardt, Sigurd (1956) 'The Poet as Fool and Priest' *ELH* 23, 279–98

Burgess, Anthony (1964) *Language Made Plain*, London

Burke, Kenneth (1931) *Counter-Statement*, New York
  (1941) *The Philosophy of Literary Form*, Baton Rouge

Carnap, Rudolf, C. W. Morris & O. Neurath (1939) eds *International Encyclopaedia of Unified Science*, Chicago

Carroll, John B. (1964) *Language and Thought*, New York
Carroll, Lewis (1965) *The Annotated Alice* Martin Gardner (ed.), Penguin
Cassirer, Ernst (1953) *The Philosophy of Symbolic Forms* vol. I: *Language*, New York & London
Catford, J. C. (1965) *A Linguistic Theory of Translation*, London
Caton, Charles E. (1963) *Philosophy and Ordinary Language*, Urbana
Chapman, George (1941) *The Poems of George Chapman* Phyllis Bartlett (ed.), New York & Oxford
Chatman, Seymour (1965) *A Theory of Meter*, The Hague
   (1971) ed. *Literary Style: A Symposium*, Oxford
Chatman, Seymour & Samuel R. Levin. (1967) ed. *Essays on the Language of Literature*, Boston
Chevalier, Jean-Claude (1970) *Alcools d' Apollinaire*, Paris
Chisholm, A. R. (1962) *Mallarmé's Grand Oeuvre*, Manchester
Chittenden, F. J. (1951) *Dictionary of Gardening*, Oxford
Chomsky, Noam (1959) 'Review of B. F. Skinner's "Verbal Behaviour"', *Language* 35, 26–58, reprinted in Fodor & Katz 1964, 547–78
   (1965) *Aspects of the Theory of Syntax*, Cambridge, Mass.
   (1966) *Cartesian Linguistics*, New York
   (1972) *Language and Mind*, 2nd ed., New York
Clemen, Wolfgang (1951) *The Development of Shakespeare's Imagery*, London
Cohen, Jean (1966) *Structure du langage poétique*, Paris
Cohen, L. Jonathan & Avishai Margalit (1972) 'The Role of Inductive Reasoning in the Interpretation of Metaphor' in Davidson & Harman, 722–40
Cohen, Morris R. & Ernst Nagel (1934) *An Introduction to Logic and Scientific Method*, London
Cowles, Fleur (1959) *The Case of Salvador Dali*, London
Crafts, L. W., T. C. Schneirla, E. E. Robinson & R. W. Gilbert (1938) *Recent Experiments in Psychology*, New York
Culler, Jonathan (1972) Review of Riffaterre 1971, *J. Ling.* 8 no. 1 (Feb.) 177–83
Davidson, Donald & Gilbert Harman (1972) ed. *Semantics of Natural Language*, Dordrecht
Davies, Gardner (1955) 'The Demon of Analogy' *French Studies* 9, 195–211 and 326–47
Deguy, Michel (1967) 'A propos de la *Structure du langage poétique* de J. Cohen' *Promesse* 18, 3–8
   (1969) *Figurations*, Paris
Delgado, José M. R. (1971) *Physical Control of the Mind*, New York & London
Dement, William (1963) 'The Effect of Dream Deprivation' *Science* 131
Derrida, Jacques (1970) 'La Double Séance' *Tel Quel* 41–42
Diamond, A. S. (1959) *The History and Origin of Language*, London
Dubois-Charlier, Françoise (1972) 'La Sémantique générative: une nouvelle théorie linguistique?' *Langages* 27 (Sept.) 5–77
Dummett, Michael (1973) *Frege: Philosophy of Language*, London
Ebeling, Carl L. (1960) *Linguistic Units*, The Hague
Eddington, Sir Arthur S. (1928) *The Nature of the Physical World*, Cambridge

Einstein, Albert (1922) *Sidelights on Relativity*, London & New York
   (1951) 'Autobiographical Notes' in Paul A. Schilpp (ed.) *Albert Einstein:
   Philosopher-Scientist*, New York, 1–95
Eisenstein, Sergei M. (1943) *The Film Sense*, London
Eliot, T. S. (1934) *Selected Essays*, 2nd ed., London
   (1965) *To Criticize the Critic*, London
Elliott, R. K. (1967) 'Poetry and Truth' *Analysis* 27, 77–85
Eluard, Paul (1968) *Œuvres complètes*, Pléiade, Paris
Empson, William (1961) *Seven Types of Ambiguity*, Penguin
Epstein, Edmund L. & Terence Hawkes (1959) *Linguistics and English
   Prosody* (Studies in Linguistics: Occasional Papers 7) University of
   Buffalo
Erlich, Victor (1954) *Russian Formalism: History — Doctrine*, The Hague
Erwin, Edward (1970) *The Concept of Meaninglessness*, Baltimore &
   London
Fillmore, C. J. (1968) 'The Case for Case' in Emmon Bach & R. T. Harms
   (ed.) *Universals in Language*, New York, 1–88
Findlay, A. (1948) *A Hundred Years of Chemistry*, 2nd ed., London
Firsoff, V. Axel (1967) *Life, Mind and Galaxies*, Edinburgh & London
   (1968) *The Interior Planets*, Edinburgh & London
Flew, A. G. N. (1951 & 1953) ed. *Logic and Language*, Vols. I and II,
   Oxford
Fodor, Jerry A. & J. J. Katz (1963) 'The Structure of a Semantic Theory'
   Language 39, 170–210
   (1964) *The Structure of Language*, Englewood Cliffs
Fónagy, Iván (1961) 'Communication in Poetry' *Word* 17, 194–218
   (1971) 'The Function of Vocal Style' in Chatman 1971
Forster, E. M. (1962) *Aspects of the Novel*, Penguin
Fowler, Roger (1966) ed. *Essays on Style and Language*, London
   (1971) *The Languages of Literature*, London
Fowles, John (1969) *The French Lieutenant's Woman*, London
Fraser, G. S. (1970) *Metre, Rhythm and Free Verse*, London
Freeman, Donald C. (1970) ed. *Linguistics and Literary Style*, New York
Frege, Gottlob (1960) *Translations from the Philosophical Writings of
   G. Frege*, P. Geach & M. Black (eds.), Oxford
Friedberg, Maurice (1962) *Russian Classics in Soviet Jackets*, New York
Friedrich, Hugo (1968) 'Einblendungstechnik und Metaphern' *Die Struktur
   der modernen Lyrik*, Hamburg, 206–11
Fries, Charles C. (1954) 'Meaning and Linguistic Analysis' *Language* 30,
   57–68
   (1961) 'The Bloomfield "School"' *Trends in European and American
   Linguistics*, Christine Mohrmann et al. (eds.), Utrecht & Antwerp
Frye, Northrop (1957) *Anatomy of Criticism*, Princeton
Fuller, Edmund (1958) *Man in Modern Fiction*, 3rd ed., New York
Gardiner, Sir Alan H. (1940) *The Theory of Proper Names*, London
   (1951) *The Theory of Speech and Language*, Oxford
Gardiner, Harold C., S. J. (1960) *Norms for the Novel*, New York
Garelli, Jacques (1966a) *Brèche*, Paris
   (1966b) *La Gravitation poétique*, Paris
Gautier, Théophile (1895) 'Préface' *Mademoiselle de Maupin*, Paris
Geach, Peter (1957) *Mental Acts*, London

Genette, Gérard (1968) 'Langage poétique, poétique du langage' *Informa-tion sur les Sciences Sociales* 7

Goldstein, Kurt (1942) *Aftereffects of Brain Injuries in War*, London (1948) *Language and Language Disturbances*, New York

Good, I. J. (1960–1 & 1961–2) *Brit. J. Phil. Sci.* 11, 145–9 and 12, 63–4

Goodman, Nelson (1954) *Fact, Fiction and Forecast*, London

Gracián, Baltasar (1944) *Agudeza y arte de ingenio*, Buenos Aires

Graham, Gladys M. (1928) 'Analogy: A Study in Proof and Persuasion Values' *Quarterly Journal of Speech* 14 (Nov.) 534–42

Grander, Claude (1941) *Panorama de l' Allemagne actuelle* (July) Paris

Graves, Robert & Laura Riding (1927) *A Survey of Modernist Poetry*, London

Gregory, Richard L. (1970) *The Intelligent Eye*, London

Gromova, Ariadne (1970) 'Introduction' *Vortex: New Soviet Science Fiction*, C. G. Bearne (ed.), London

Guiraud, Pierre (1954) 'Stylistiques' *Neophilologus* 38, 1–12

Haas, William (1954) 'On Defining Linguistic Units' *Transactions of the Philological Society*, 54–84

(1973) 'Meanings and Rules' *Proc. Ari. Soc.* 73, 135–55

Hacker, Peter M. S. (1972) *Insight and Illusion*, Oxford

Hacking, Ian (1967) 'Possibility' *Phil. Rev.* 76, 143–68

Hagopian, John V. (1968) 'Symbol and Metaphor in the Transformation of Reality into Art' *Comparative Literature* 20 (Winter) 45–54

Haight, Anne L. (1970) *Banned Books*, New York

Halliday, Michael A. K. (1970a) 'Language Structure and Language Function' in Lyons 1970a, 140 ff.

(1970b) 'Descriptive Linguistics in Literary Studies' in Freeman 1970, 57–72

(1973) *Explorations in the Functions of Language*, London

Hardy, A. (1969) 'Théorie et méthode stylistique de M. Riffaterre' *Lang. fr.* 3, 90–6

Harré, Romano (1970) *The Principles of Scientific Thinking*, London

Hayakawa, S. I. (1959) *Our Language and Our World*, New York

Hebb, Donald O. (1964–5) 'The Evolution of Mind' *Proceedings of The Royal Society*, Series B 161, 376–83

(1972) *Textbook of Psychology*, 3rd ed., London & Toronto.

Heger, Klaus (1969) 'L'Analyse sémantique du signe linguistique' *Lang. fr.* 4 (Dec.) 44–66

Heisenberg, Werner (1969) *Der Teil und das Ganze*, Munich

Hempel, Carl G. (1958) 'Empirical Statements and Falsifiability' *Philosophy* 33, 342–8

(1965) *Aspects of Scientific Explanation*, New York

Hendricks, William O. (1969) 'Three Models for the Description of Poetry' *J. Ling.* 5, 1–22

Henle, Paul (1958) ed. *Language, Thought and Culture*, Ann Arbor

Hepburn, R. W. (1972) 'Poetry and "Concrete Imagination"' *Brit. J. Aesth.* 12 no. 1, 3–18

Hesse, Mary B. (1953) 'Models in Physics' *Brit. J. Phil. Sci.* 4, 198–214

(1963) *Models and Analogies in Science*, London & New York

Hill, Archibald A. (1955) 'An Analysis of "The Windhover"' *PMLA* 70, 968–78
  (1956) 'Pippa's Song' *Texas Studies in English* 35, 51–6, also in Harold B. Allen (ed.) 1958 *Readings in Applied Linguistics* I, New York
  (1965) '"The Windhover" Revisited' *Texas Studies in Literature and Language* 7, 349–59
Hintikka, Jaakko (1969) *Models for Modalities*, Dordrecht
Hoijer, Harry (1954) ed. *Language in Culture*, Chicago
Hollander, John (1973) '"Sense Variously Drawn Out": Some Observations on English Enjambement' in Brady 1973, 201–25
Hosiasson-Lindenbaum, Janina (1940) 'On Confirmation' *Journal of Symbolic Logic* 5, 130–48
Hughes, George E. & M. J. Cresswell (1968) *Introduction to Modal Logic*, London
Hulme, T. E. (1924) *Speculations*, London & New York
Hungerland, Isabel (1958) *Poetic Discourse*, Berkeley
Hutten, E. H. (1948–9) 'On Semantics and Physics' *Proc. Ari. Soc.* 49
  (1953) 'The Role of Models in Physics' *Brit. J. Phil. Sci.* 4, 284–301
Huxley, Aldous (1963) *Literature and Science*, London
Isenberg, Arnold (1965) 'The Problem of Belief' in Cyril Barrett (ed.) *Collected Papers on Aesthetics*, Oxford, 125–43
Jackson, Benjamin D. (1916) *A Glossary of Botanic Terms*, London & Philadelphia
Jacobs, Roderick A. & P. S. Rosenbaum (1970) *Readings in English Transformational Grammar*, Waltham (Mass.), Toronto & London
Jakobson, Roman (1933–4) 'Co je poesie' *Volné smery* 30, 229–39
  (1971) *Selected Writings* Vol. 2, The Hague
Jackobson, Roman & L. G. Jones (1970) *Shakespeare's Verbal Art in 'Th'Expense of Spirit'*, The Hague
Jakobson, Roman & Claude Lévi-Strauss (1962) '"Les Chats" de C. Baudelaire' *L'Homme* 2, 5–21
Jarrett-Kerr, Martin, C. R. (1954) *Studies in Literature and Belief*, London
Jespersen, Otto (1929) *The Philosophy of Grammar*, London & New York
  (no date) *Selected Writings*, London & Tokyo
Johnson, Richard E. (1964) 'Imaginative Sensitivity in Schizophrenia' *Review of Existential Psychology and Psychiatry* 4 no. 3, 255–64
Jouve, Pierre Jean (1966) *Les Noces, suivi de Sueur de sang*, Paris
  (1970) *En miroir*, Paris
Jung, Carl Gustav (1960) *Collected Works*, Vol. 8 *The Structure and Dynamics of the Psyche*, London
  (1967) *Memories, Dreams, Reflections*, London
Kaplan, A. (1954) 'Referential Meaning in the Arts' *J. Aesth. & Art Crit.* 12, 457–74
Karpman, Benjamin (1954) *The Sexual Offender and his Offences*, New York
Karttunen, Lauri (1973) 'La Logique des constructions anglaises à complément prédicatif' *Langages* 30 (June) 56–80
Katz, Jerrold J. (1966) *The Philosophy of Language*, New York
  (1972a) *Linguistic Philosophy*, London
  (1972b) *Semantic Theory*, New York

Katz, Jerrold J. & P. Postal (1964) *An Integrated Theory of Linguistic Descriptions*, Cambridge (Mass.)

Koestler, Arthur (1949) *Insight and Outlook*, London
  (1959) *The Sleepwalkers*, London
  (1964) *The Act of Creation*, London
  (1967) *The Ghost in the Machine*, London

Konrad, Hedwig (1939) *Etude sur la métaphore*, Paris

Kristeva, Julia (1969) *Recherches pour une sémanalyse*, Paris

Kuhn, Thomas S. (1959) *The Copernican Revolution*, Cambridge (Mass.)
  (1970) *The Structure of Scientific Revolutions*, 2nd ed., Chicago & London

Kunjunni Raja, K. (1963) *Indian Theories of Meaning*, Madras

Lakoff, George (1972) 'Linguistics and Natural Logic' in Davidson & Harman, 545–665

Lakoff, Robin (1972) 'Language in Context' *Language* 48, 907–27
  (1973) 'Language and Woman's Place' *Lang. Soc.* 2, 45–80

Landar, Herbert (1966) *Language and Culture*, Oxford

Landesman, Charles (1972) *Discourse and its Presuppositions*, New Haven & London

Langer, Suzanne (1967) *An Introduction to Symbolic Logic*, 3rd ed., New York.

Lauretano, Bruno (1964) *Ambiguità e metafora*, Naples

Lawrence, D. H. (1968) *The Phoenix* Vol. 2, London

Leakey, F. W. (1954) 'Intention in Metaphor' *Essays in Criticism* 4, 191–8

Leech, Geoffrey N. (1966) 'Linguistics and the Figures of Rhetoric' in Fowler 1966, 135–56
  (1969) *A Linguistic Guide to English Poetry*, London
  (1970) ' "This Bread I Break" ' in Freeman 1970, 119–28
  (1974) *Semantics*, Penguin

Leeper, Robert (1951) 'Cognitive Processes', 730–57, *Handbook of Experimental Psychology*, Stanley S. Stevens (ed.), New York & London

Lefebve, Maurice-Jean (1970) 'Discours poétique et discours du récit' *NRF* (1 Feb.) 269–78

Lehmann-Haupt, Hellmut (1954) *Art under a Dictatorship*, Oxford

Levin, Samuel R. (1970) 'Coupling in a Shakespearian Sonnet' in Freeman, 197–205

Lewis, C. S. (1961) *Experiment in Criticism*, Cambridge

Linsky, Leonard (1967) *Referring*, London

Liu, James (1962) *The Art of Chinese Poetry*, London

Lukács, György (1963) *The Meaning of Contemporary Realism*, London (republished as *Realism in Our Time*, New York 1964)

Lyons, John (1963) *Structural Semantics*, Oxford
  (1968) *Introduction to Theoretical Linguistics*, London & New York
  (1970a) ed. *New Horizons in Linguistics*, Penguin
  (1970b) *Chomsky*, London
  (1973) 'Structuralism and Linguistics' in David Robey (ed.) *Structuralism: An Introduction*, Oxford, 6–19

MacCaig, Norman (1966) *Surroundings*, London

McCawley, James D. (1968) 'The Role of Semantics in a Grammar' in Emmon Bach & R. T. Harms *Universals in Linguistic Theory*, New York & London, 125–70

(1971) 'Where do Noun Phrases come from?' in Danny D. Steinberg & Leon A. Jakobovits (eds.) *Semantics*, Cambridge, 217–31

Macdonald, Dwight (1960) ed. *Parodies*, London

McIntosh, Angus (1961) 'Patterns and Ranges' *Language* 37 no. 3

Mackie, J. L. (1963) 'The Paradox of Confirmation' *Brit. J. Phil. Sci.* 13, 265–77

MacLeish, Archibald (1965) *Poetry and Experience*, Penguin

Mallarmé, Stéphane (1945) *Oeuvres complètes*, Paris

(1953) *Propos sur la poésie*, ed. H. Mondor, 2nd ed., Monaco

Marchand, Hans (1959) 'Phonetic Symbolism in English Word-Formation' *Indogermanische Forschungen* 64, 146–68

Marckwardt, Albert H. (1966) *Linguistics and the Teaching of English*, Bloomington

Margenau, Henry (1950) *The Nature of Physical Reality*, New York

Martin, Graham Dunstan (1971a) ed. Paul Valéry *Cimetière marin*, Edinburgh

(1971b) 'Structures in Space: *Tel Quel*'s Attitude to Meaning' *New Blackfriars* (Dec.) 541–52

(1972) ed. and trans. *Anthology of Contemporary French Poetry*, Edinburgh

(1974) 'Yves Bonnefoy and the Temptation of Plato' *Forum for Modern Language Studies*

Matchett, William H. (1955) 'An Analysis of the "Windhover"' *PMLA* 70, 310–11

Medvedev, Jaurès (1969) *The Rise and Fall of T. D. Lysenko*, New York & London

Mikhalkov, S. (1956) 'Tri portreta' *Literaturnaya Moskva* 2, 528–9

Mill, John Stuart (1906) *A System of Logic*, London

Miller, Neal E. (1970) 'Psychological Aspects of Hypertension, Learned Modifications of Autonomic Functions' *Circulation Research* 27 no. 1, Supplement 1, I. 3–I. 11

Mitroff, Ian (1973) 'On Studying the Moon Scientists' *New Sci.* (27 Dec.) 900–1

Moore, George (1917) *Confessions of a Young Man*, New York

Moore, G. E. (1953) *Some Main Problems of Philosophy*, London

Morhange-Bégué, Claude (1970) *La Chanson du mal-aimé d'Apollinaire*, Paris

Morris, Charles W. (1939) 'Foundations of the Theory of Signs' in Carnap, Morris & Neurath, I, 1, 77–137

Mosse, George L. (1966) *Nazi Culture*, London

Mukařovský, Jan (1970) 'Standard Language and Poetic Language' in Freeman, 40–56

Murry, John Middleton (1950) 'Metaphor' *John Clare and Other Studies*, London & New York, 85–97

(1956) *The Problem of Style*, Oxford

Nokes, Geoffrey & Kingsley Amis (1952) in *Essays in Criticism* 2, 338–45

Noulet, E. (1967) *Vingt poèmes de S. Mallarmé*, Geneva

Ogden, C. K. & I. A. Richards (1949) *The Meaning of Meaning*, 10th ed., London

O'Neill, Joseph (1956) 'The Metaphorical Mode: Image, Metaphor, Symbol' *Thought* 31, 79–113

Oppenheimer, Robert (1954) *Science and the Common Understanding*, Oxford

Osgood, Charles E., G. J. Suci & P. H. Tannenbaum (1957) *The Measurement of Meaning*, Urbana

Painter, George D. (1961 & 1965) *Marcel Proust, A Biography*, London

Pap, A. (1958) *Semantics and Necessary Truth*, Glencoe, Ill.

(1963) *An Introduction to the Philosophy of Science*, Glencoe, Ill.

Parain, Brice (1969) *Petite métaphysique de la parole*, Paris

Paris, Jean (1967) 'Finnegans, Wake!' *Tel Quel* 30 (Eté) 58–66

Pears, David (1971) *Wittgenstein*, London

Peterfalvi, J.-M. (1970) *Introduction à la psycholinguistique*, Paris

Pitcher, George (1964) ed. *Truth*, New Jersey

Platt, W. & R. A. Baker (1931) 'The Relationship of the Scientific "Hunch" to Research' *J. Chem. Educ.* 8

Polanyi, Michael (1967) *The Tacit Dimension*, London

Pollock, Thomas Clark (1942) *The Nature of Literature*, Princeton

Ponge, Francis (1961) *Le Grand Recueil*, Paris

(1967) *Le Parti pris des choses*, Paris

Popper, Karl R. (1945) *The Open Society and its Enemies*, London

(1960) *The Poverty of Historicism*, London

(1968) *The Logic of Scientific Discovery* Revised ed., London

(1969) *Conjectures and Refutations*, 3rd ed., London

Price, H. H. (1953) *Thinking and Experience*, London

Pritchett, V. S. (1966) *The Saint and Other Stories*, Penguin

Proust, Marcel (1954) *A la recherche du temps perdu*, Pléiade, Paris

Quine, W. V. (1953) *From a Logical Point of View*, Harvard

(1961) 'The Problem of Meaning in Linguistics' in Saporta

(1969) *Ontological Relativity and Other Essays*, New York & London

Rabinovitz, Rubin (1967) *The Reaction against Experiment in the English Novel* 1950–60, New York

Ramsey, Ian T. (1964) *Models and Mystery*, New York & London

Ransom, John Crowe (1941) *The New Criticism*, Norfolk, Conn.

(1950) 'William Wordsworth: Notes Toward an Understanding of Poetry' *Kenyon Review* 12 (Summer) 498–519

(1955) 'The Concrete Universal' II *Kenyon Review* 17, 383–407

Rauschning, Hermann (1945) *Hitler m'a dit*, Paris

Reichenbach, Hans (1932) 'Wahrscheinlichkeitslogik' *Berichte der Berliner Akademie Wissenschaften (Phys. Math. Kl.)* Berlin

(1935) *Wahrscheinlichkeitslehre*, Leiden

(1961) *Experience and Prediction*, Chicago & London

(1965) *Philosophical Foundations of Quantum Mechanics*, Berkeley

(1966) *Elements of Symbolic Logic*, New York & London

Richard, Jean-Pierre (1961) *L'Univers imaginaire de Mallarmé*, Paris

Richard, Lionel (1971) *Nazisme et littérature*, Paris

Richards, Ivor A. (1926) *Principles of Literary Criticism*, 2nd ed., London

(1936) *Philosophy of Rhetoric*, Oxford

(1970) *Poetries and Sciences*, London

Riffaterre, Michael (1959) 'Criteria for Style Analysis' *Word* 15, 154 ff.
    (1966) 'Describing Poetic Structures: Two Approaches to Baudelaire's
    "Les Chats"' *Yale French Studies* 36/37, 200–42
Ritchie, Claire (1962) *Writing the Romantic Novel*, London
Robbe-Grillet, Alain (1953) *Les Gommes*, Paris
    (1957) *Pour un nouveau roman*, Paris
    (1957) *La Jalousie*, Paris
Rosser, J. B. & A. R. Turquette (1958) *Many-Valued Logics*, Amsterdam
Rothfels, Hans (1961) *German Opposition to Hitler*, London
Rozeboom, William W. (1968) 'New Dimensions of Confirmation Theory'
    Philosophy of Science 35, 134–55
Russell, Bertrand (1918) *Mysticism and Logic*, London
    (1937) *Principles of Mathematics*, 2nd ed., London
    (1956) *Logic and Knowledge*, London
Ryle, Gilbert (1954) *Dilemmas*, Cambridge
    (1963) *The Concept of Mind*, Penguin
    (1971) *Collected Papers Vol. 2: Collected Essays*, London
Sachs, H. (1946) *Master and Friend*, London
Salmon, W. C. (1969) *The Foundations of Scientific Inference*, Pittsburgh
Saporta, Sol (1961) ed. *Psycholinguistics*, New York & London
Saussure, Ferdinand de (1966) *Course in General Linguistics*, New York
Sayce, R. A. (1953) *Style in French Prose*, Oxford
Scheffler, Israel (1964) *The Anatomy of Inquiry*, London
Schiller, F. C. S. (1917) 'Scientific Discovery and Logical Proof' in *Studies
    in the History and Method of Science*, Charles Singer (ed.), Oxford
Schlanger, Judith (1970) 'Metaphor and Invention' *Diogenes* 69 (Spring)
    12–27
Schnitzer, Marc L. (1971) 'Linguistic Philosophy and the Chomskyan
    Syntactic Framework' *Semiotica* 4, 263–85
Schoenberg, Judith (1964–5) 'Confirmation by Observation and the
    Paradox of the Raven' *Brit. J. Phil. Sci.* 15, 200–12
Scott, John & Graham Dunstan Martin (1972) *Love and Protest (Chinese
    Poems)*, London
Sebeok, Thomas A. (1960) ed. *Style and Language*, New York & London
Shapiro, N. & N. Hentoff (1958) *The Jazz Makers*, London
Shibles, Warren A. (1971) *An Analysis of Metaphor in the Light of
    W. M. Urban's Theories*, Paris & The Hague
Shklovski, Viktor (1923) *Literatura i Kinematograf*, Berlin
Sinclair, John McH. (1968) 'A Technique of Stylistic Description' *Lang. &
    Style* 1, 215–242
    (1970) 'Taking a Poem to Pieces' in Freeman 1970, 129–42
Sitwell, Edith (1957) *Collected Poems*, London
Skinner, Burrhus F. (1957) *Verbal Behavior*, London & New York
    (1961) *Cumulative Record*, 2nd ed., London & New York
    (1972) *Beyond Freedom and Dignity*, London
Smart, J. J. C. (1953) 'Theory Construction' in Flew 1953
Smokler, H. (1967) 'The Equivalence Condition' *Am. Phil. Q.* 4, 300–7
Sommers, Fred (1965) 'Predicability' in *Philosophy in America*, Max
    Black (ed.), Ithaca
Spencer, John & Michael Gregory (1970) 'An Approach to the Study of
    Style' in Freeman, 73–95

Spitzer, Leo (1948) *Linguistics and Literary History*, Princeton
Stählin, W. (1913) *Zur Psychologie und Statistik der Metapher*, Würzburg
Stanford, William B. (1936) *Greek Metaphor*, Oxford
Stern, Gustaf (1931) *Meaning and Change of Meaning*, Göteborg
Strawson, P. F. (1963) 'On Referring' in Caton 1963, 162–93, also in *Mind*
    59 (1950) 320–44
Struve, Gleb (1971) *Russian Literature under Lenin and Stalin*, 1917–53,
    Norman, Oklahoma
Sturrock, John (1969) *The French New Novel*, Oxford
Thorne, James P. (1965) 'Stylistics and Generative Grammars' *J. Ling.* 1,
    49–59
    (1969) 'Poetry, Stylistics and Imaginary Grammars' *J. Ling.* 5, 147–50
    (1970) 'Generative Grammar and Stylistic Analysis' in Lyons 1970,
    185–97
Todorov, Tzvetan (1965) ed. *Théorie de la littérature: Textes des formalistes
    russes*, Paris
    (1968) 'Poétique' in Oswald Ducrot et al. *Qu'est-ce que le structuralisme*,
    Paris, 97–166
    (1969) 'Note sur le langage poétique' *Semiotica* 1, 322–8
Tolstoy, Leo (1898) *What is Art?* London
Tomlinson, Charles (1972) ed. *William Carlos Williams: A Critical An-
    thology*, Penguin
Tuve, Rosemond (1947) *Elizabethan and Metaphysical Imagery*, Chicago
Ullmann, Stephen (1962) *Semantics*, Oxford
    (1963) *The Principles of Semantics*, Oxford
    (1964) *Language and Style*, Oxford
Urban, Wilbur M. (1939) *Language and Reality*, London
Valentine, C. W. (1942) *The Psychology of Early Childhood*, London
Valéry, Paul (1957 & 1960) *Oeuvres*, 2 Vols., Pléiade, Paris
Vela, Arqueles (1965) *Análisis de la Expresión literaria*, Mexico City
Vendler, Zeno (1967) *Linguistics in Philosophy*, Ithaca
    (1972) *Res Cogitans*, Ithaca & London
Vickery, W. (1963) *The Cult of Optimism*, Bloomington
Waismann, Friedrich (1945) 'Verifiability' *Analysis and Metaphysics:
    Proceedings of the Aristotelian Society*, Supplementary Volume
    (1949–52) 'Analytic-Synthetic' *Analysis*
    (1951) 'Verifiability' in Flew 1951
Watkins, J. W. N. (1957) 'Between Analytic and Empirical' *Philosophy* 32,
    112–31
    (1958) 'A Rejoinder . . . ' ibid. 33, 349–55
    (1959–60) 'Confirmation Without Background Knowledge' *Brit. J.
    Phil. Sci.* 10, 318–20
Weinreich, Uriel (1966) 'Explorations in Semantic Theory' in Thomas A.
    Sebeok 1966 (ed.) *Current Trends in Linguistics*, Vol. 3, The Hague
Wellek, René & Austin Warren (1963) *Theory of Literature*, 3rd ed.,
    Penguin
Wells, Henry W. (1924) *Poetic Imagery*, New York
Wells, Rulon (1954) 'Meaning and Use' *Word* 10, 235–50. Also in
    Saporta
Werner, Heinz (1952) Review of Ullmann's *Principles of Semantics*,
    Language 28, 249–56

Wertham, Frederic (1954) *The Seduction of the Innocent*, New York
Whalley, George (1965) 'Metaphor' in *Encyclopaedia of Poetry and
      Poetics*, ed. Alex Preminger, F. J. Warnke & O. B. Hardison Jr.,
      Princeton
Wheelwright, Philip (1954) *The Burning Fountain*, Bloomington
   (1960) 'Semantics and Ontology' in L. C. Knights & Basil Cottle (eds.)
      Metaphor and Symbol, London
   (1962) *Metaphor and Reality*, Bloomington
Whorf, Benjamin Lee (1956) *Language, Thought and Reality*, Cambridge,
      Mass.
Whyte, L. L. (1962) *The Unconscious before Freud*, New York
Wilson, Rev. John M. (1849) *The Rural Cyclopedia*, Edinburgh.
Wilson, P. R. (1964–5) 'On the Confirmation Paradox' *Brit. J. Phil. Sci.*
      15, 196–9
Winograd, Terry (1972) *Understanding Natural Language*, New York &
      Edinburgh
Wisdom, John (1957) *Philosophy and Psychoanalysis*, Oxford
Wittgenstein, Ludwig (1961*a*) *Notebooks 1914–16*, Oxford
   (1961*b*) *Tractatus*, London
   (1968) *Philosophical Investigations*, 3rd ed., Oxford
Wulf, Joseph (1963) *Literatur und Dichtung im 3. Reich*, Gütersloh
Yarmolinsky, Avrahm (1957) *Literature under Communism*, Bloomington
Yonge, C. M. (1960) *Oysters*, London
Zeeman, E. C. (1969) 'A Mathematical Explanation of Creativity' in
      D. Paterson (ed.) *The Brain*, BBC, London, 74–7
Zhdanov, A. A. (1950) *On Literature, Music and Philosophy*, London
Zitta, Victor (1964) *Georg Lukács' Marxism: Alienation, Dialectics,
      Revolution*, The Hague
Zuber, Ryszard (1973) 'Quelques problèmes de logique et langage' *Langages*
      30 (June) 3–19

Indexes

Stählin, W., 203, 323
Stanford, W. B., 206, 324
Stein, G., 217
Stern, G., 21, 68-9, 113, 203-6, 309-10, 314, 323-4
Stevens, W., 164
Strawson, P. F., 15, 112, 308, 313
Struve, G., 329
Sturrock, J., 311
Suci, G. J., 13

Tannenbaum, P. H., 13
Tel Quel, 87, 89, 314
Tennyson, A., 177-8, 210
Thomas, D., 85-6, 92, 214, 237, 261, 262
Thomas Aquinas, St, 134
Thorne, J. P., 185, 189, 248-50
Thüring, B., 290, 294
Todorov, T., 91-2, 327
Tolstoy, L., 290-1
Turquette, A. R., 140-1
Tuve, R., 168

Ullmann, S., 25, 38, 113, 306, 309
Urban, W. M., 202, 323, 324

Valentine, C. W., 35-6, 310
Valéry, P., 46, 55, 239, 264, 267, 269, 328
van Buren, P., 62, 314
Vela, A., 218
Vendler, Z., 13, 248, 307, 309
Vickery, W., 329

Waismann, F., 128, 162, 312, 316
Warren, A., 211, 324
Watkins, J. W. N., 319
Waugh, E., 161, 243
Weinreich, U., 312
Wellek, R., 211, 324
Wells, H., 324, 325
Wells, R., 308
Wertham, F., 304, 332
Whalley, G., 325
Wheelwright, P., 136, 216-17, 240, 318, 324, 326
Whorf, B. L., 120-5, 133, 316-17
Whyte, L. L., 117
Williams, W. C., 174-6
Wilson, J. M., 325-6
Winograd, T., 53
Wisdom, J., 138, 316
Wittgenstein, L., 7, 15, 55, 56, 66, 71, 127, 131, 308, 313, 320
Wordsworth, W., 180

Yarmolinsky, A., 286
Yeats, W. B., 259
Yonge, C. M., 228-9

Zamyatin, Y., 273
Zeeman, E. C., 320
Zeno, 61
Zhdanov, A. A., 281, 284-5, 289-94, 331
Zitta, V., 330
Zoshchenko, M., 284-5
Zuber, R., 313

Subjects
absolutism, 44, 73, 279-94, 330-1
abstract attitude, 31, 310
abstraction, 128-31, 155
abstract language, 169
adequacy, 90-1, 162, 164, 187-8, 197
ambiguity, 7, 99-105, 182-5, 191-7, 221-3, 266-9, 279, 282, 324
  full and empty, 191-7
analogy, 47-8, 211-13, 324
aphasia, 31, 119
apparency, 167-201, 207-10, 218, 224-38, 239, 241-3, 326
  imposed, 197-201
Arabic vocabulary, 119

associative field, 42, 46, 54
astrology, 318

Behaviourism, 7, 9-15, 17-18, 60, 306-7, 309
bisociation, 150-5

card experiment, 117-18, 120
certainty, 1-2, 134-5, 156-7, 292, 294
classification, 27, 30-2, 117-26, 128-9, 158-9, 164, 167, 169, 201, 202-3, 209-10
  unconscious, 117-26, 309
coherence/correspondence theories of truth, 71-4, 81, 313

Acknowledgments

The Publisher is grateful to the following authors
or their representatives and/or publishers for per-
mission to reproduce from their works: Robert
Payne from *The White Pony* (Allen and Unwin);
Henry Reed 'Chard Whitlow' from *A map of Ver-
ona* (Jonathan Cape Ltd.); Robert Graves (A.P.
Watt & Son) 'The Cool Web' from *Collected Poems
1965*; Dylan Thomas [the Trustees for the copy-
rights of the late Dylan Thomas] 'After the Funeral'
from *Collected Poems* (J.M. Dent & Sons Ltd.) and
from *The Poems of Dylan Thomas* (New Directions
Publishing Corporation); T.S. Eliot 'Virginia' from
Collected Poems 1909–1962 also from 'Prelude IV',
Prufrock, The Waste Land, East Coker IV, and *4
Quartets* (Faber and Faber Ltd./Harcourt Brace
Jovanovich, Inc.); Ezra Pound from *Hugh Selwyn
Mauberley* and 'In a Station of the Metro' from *Collected Shorter Poems* (Faber and Faber Ltd.) and
from *Personae* (New Directions Publishing Corpora-
tion); Robert Lowell 'The Public Garden' from *For
the Union Dead*, and John Berryman from *Homage
to Mistress Bradstreet* (Faber and Faber Ltd./Far-
rar, Straus & Giroux Inc.); W.H. Auden 'On this
Island' ['Seascape'] from *Collected Shorter Poems
1927–1957* (Faber and Faber Ltd./Random House
Inc.); Ted Hughes 'Thrushes' from *Lupercal* (Faber
and Faber Ltd./Harper and Row, Publishers, Inc.);
Jacques Réda from *Amen*, Apollinaire from *Alcools*,
Paul Eluard from *Œuvres complètes*, Francis Ponge
from *Pièces*, Pierre Reverdy from *La Plupart du
temps*, Paul Valéry from *Le Cimetière marin*, Philippe Jaccottet from *Airs* (Editions Gallimard); Carl
Sandburg 'Splinter' from *Good Morning, America*
(Harcourt Brace Jovanovich, Inc.); Norman Mac-
Caig 'Questionnaire', 'Frogs' and 'To a Pragmatist'
from *Surroundings* (The Hogarth Press/Wesleyan

University Press); Jacques Garelli 'Combat' from *Brèche* (Mercure de France); William Carlos Williams 'The Red Wheelbarrow' from *Collected Earlier Poems* (New Directions Publishing Corporation); E. E. Cummings 'YgUDuh' [copyright 1944, by E.E. Cummings; 1972, by Nancy Andrews], 'anyone lived in a pretty how town' [copyright 1940, by E.E. Cummings; 1968, by Marion Morehouse Cummings], 'here's a little mouse' [copyright 1926, by Horace Liveright; 1954, by E.E. Cummings] and 'it may not always be so; and i say' from *Complete Poems 1913–1962* (Harcourt Brace Jovanovich, Inc.) and *The Complete Poems* (Hart-Davis, Mac-Gibbon); Gerard Manley Hopkins from 'No worst, there is none...' and Allen Tate from 'The Swimmers' (Oxford University Press); W. Vickery from *The Cult of Optimism* (Indiana University Press)